Empowering Family-Teacher Partnerships

I dedicate this textbook to the many student teachers whose creativity, energy, and ideas have contributed to my own professional growth.

Empowering Family-Teacher Partnerships

Building Connections Within Diverse Communities

Mick Coleman

University of Georgia

Los Angeles | London | New Delhi
Singapore | Washington DC

Los Angeles | London | New Delhi
Singapore | Washington DC

FOR INFORMATION:

SAGE Publications, Inc.
2455 Teller Road
Thousand Oaks, California 91320
E-mail: order@sagepub.com

SAGE Publications Ltd.
1 Oliver's Yard
55 City Road
London EC1Y 1SP
United Kingdom

SAGE Publications India Pvt. Ltd.
B 1/I 1 Mohan Cooperative Industrial Area
Mathura Road, New Delhi 110 044
India

SAGE Publications Asia-Pacific Pte. Ltd.
33 Pekin Street #02-01
Far East Square
Singapore 048763

Senior Executive Editor: Diane McDaniel
Assistant Editor: Rachael Leblond
Editorial Assistant: Megan Koraly
Production Editor: Libby Larson
Copy Editor: Rachel Keith
Typesetter: C&M Digitals (P) Ltd.
Proofreader: Wendy Jo Dymond
Indexer: Diggs Publications
Cover Designer: Candice Harman
Marketing Manager: Katie Winter
Permissions Editor: Adele Hutchinson

Copyright © 2013 by SAGE Publications, Inc.

Printed in the United States of America

Library of Congress Cataloging-in-Publication Data

Coleman, Mick.

Empowering family-teacher partnerships : building connections within diverse communities / Mick Coleman.

p. cm.
Includes bibliographical references and index.

ISBN 978-1-4129-9232-9 (pbk.)

1. Early childhood education—Parent participation. 2. Parent-teacher relationships—United States. I. Title.

LB1139.35.P37C65 2013
372.21—dc23   2011049053

This book is printed on acid-free paper.

12 13 14 15 16 10 9 8 7 6 5 4 3 2 1

BRIEF CONTENTS

DETAILED CONTENTS

PREFACE

Purpose

As with many things in life, the impetus for this textbook came from a challenge. A number of years ago, I was charged with the task of integrating two courses in our teacher training program into one stand-alone course. Previously, the first course had covered diverse family structures and the principles underlying family dynamics. The second course had covered the more pragmatic aspects of helping teachers to communicate and work with families and community professionals. Combining these two courses into one required an integration of professional knowledge from two fields of study: (a) Human Development and Family Studies and (b) Early and Middle Childhood Education. To meet this challenge, I began by developing a series of papers and supplemental materials, all of which were refined and expanded based on student feedback at the end of each semester. It is these papers and materials that over time evolved into this textbook.

The development of *Empowering Family-Teacher Partnerships* was guided by an early acknowledgment of the dramatic transformations in family-teacher partnerships. In short, families' involvement in their children's education has progressed from a well-intentioned but poorly implemented ideal into a federal mandate under No Child Left Behind. In addition, current educational trends indicate a growing view of public schools as community centers that are responsive to the interests and needs of children and their families. This trend is evident in a quote from U.S. Secretary of Education Arne Duncan (2010):

> The fact is that it takes more than a school to educate a student. It takes a city. It takes a community that can provide support from the parks department, health services, law enforcement, social services, after-school programs, nonprofits, businesses, and churches. We can only turn around the worst performing schools with an all-hands-on-deck approach in the local community.
>
> I'd like to see public schools open 12, 13, 14 hours a day, year-round, offering not just mentoring and tutoring programs but art, chess, family literacy nights, debate teams, and GED and ESL programs for parents.

Goals

Empowering Family-Teacher Partnerships is based on a core set of goals that reflect the above mandates and trends as well as professional teacher training standards concerning family involvement (Association for Childhood Education International, 2007; National Association for the Education of Young Children, 2009).

To prepare students to work with diverse family structures. Teachers today face the challenge of not only understanding but also appreciating the various contextual factors underlying the diverse family lives represented in their classrooms. To meet this challenge, students are provided with theoretical and research-based information from leading family journals and books concerning different family structures, lifestyles, and challenges (see, for example, Chapters 5, 6, 7, 10, and 15). Equally important, throughout the textbook students are presented with a range of practical strategies for reaching out to and engaging families in their children's education.

To prepare students to work with culturally diverse families. We all face the challenge of learning to live in a society that is culturally diverse. Teachers in particular need to understand how cultural differences can influence their interactions with children and families. This theme is first introduced in Chapter 1, supported by professional standards in Chapter 2, and highlighted in various ways throughout the remainder of the book. Special attention is given to cultural diversity in Section II, including a review of cultural worldviews, teaching practices, and parenting issues in Chapter 8, along with a review of the anti-bias education model and steps for becoming a culturally responsive teacher in Chapter 9.

To promote equity and empowerment within family-teacher partnerships. It is because of diverse family structures, lifestyles, and cultural backgrounds that expectations regarding family-teacher partnerships also vary. Thus, in this textbook students are warned against adopting a traditional teacher-centered approach in which the parameters of family involvement are set by teachers and school administrators. Instead, an emphasis is placed on helping students form equitable partnerships with families that are characterized by shared decision making and frequent and open communication.

The benefits of such a proactive approach to family involvement are reviewed in Chapters 3 and 4. In addition, attention is given to practical strategies for promoting family empowerment in Chapter 11, along with similar empowerment themes in Chapter 10 (addressing family involvement challenges), Chapter 12 (creating a welcoming environment for families), and Chapter 13 (communicating with families).

To facilitate students' sense of professional self-efficacy. Instructors throughout the country recognize the importance of going beyond textbook information to helping students develop the skills needed to monitor, assess, and plan for their professional growth. Likewise, a sense of self-efficacy is needed that facilitates students' creativity and motivation in reaching out to families. Subsequently, Albert Bandura's theory of self-efficacy is used in Chapter 4 to present steps that students can take to gain confidence in their ability to work with families. In addition, the ancillaries and pedagogy in the textbook provide hands-on and reflective experiences that reinforce students' sense of self-efficacy.

Writing Style

A personalized and student-centered writing style is used to engage students' interest. For example, key concepts and principles are printed in bold letters and clearly defined. Likewise, research and theoretical principles are linked to practical applications, thereby demonstrating the importance of professional knowledge in facilitating teachers' work with families.

Target Audiences

The primary target audience for *Empowering Family-Teacher Partnerships* is students who plan to work in educational settings with children in prekindergarten through fifth grade. Specific department designations in which these students may enroll vary among institutions, but some examples include Early and Middle Childhood Education, Elementary Education, and Human Development and Family Studies. Course names likewise vary, but typically include titles such as Family-School-Community Partnerships; Collaborating With Parents and Community Professionals; and Children, Families, and Communities.

   The textbook will also be of interest to teachers, administrators, counselors, family service coordinators, and social workers employed in schools and other educational settings. Likewise, educational training consultants will find the textbook and ancillaries useful in their work.

Organization of the Textbook

Empowering Parent-Teacher Partnerships includes four sections and one appendix.

Section I: Foundations of Family Involvement

Section I begins with coverage of basic family, school, and community concepts that establish a common language. Professional standards, reality checks, theories and models related to family-teacher partnerships, and research on the benefits of family involvement are also reviewed. Together, these items establish the need for pursuing positive family-teacher partnerships. Equally important, and as noted above, early in this section students are provided with the opportunity to begin formulating their own family involvement philosophies, a process that continues throughout the textbook.

Section II: Understanding Family Lives in Contemporary Society

Section II begins with a research- and theory-based review of diverse family structures and cultures, including single-parent families, stepfamilies, grandparent caregivers, gay and lesbian families, families living in poverty, families with children with disabilities, immigrant families, and families from nondominant cultures. Importantly, chapter reviews include not just the potential challenges faced by these families but also their potential strengths. In addition, strategies are presented for working with the different families. Section II ends with guides to help students become culturally responsive teachers.

Section III: Planning for and Facilitating Family Involvement

Having established a foundation for students' understanding of family involvement concepts and standards, along with contemporary family lives, Section III is devoted to practical steps for engaging families in their children's education. The section begins with a review of logistical and personal challenges to family involvement, along with strategies for addressing them. Also addressed are strategies for working with children of military families and children of incarcerated parents. Other chapters in Section III address strategies for empowering the family-teacher partnership and welcoming families and their children into the classroom. In addition, a separate chapter is devoted to practical strategies for communicating with parents, along with strategies for facilitating positive communication and carrying out meaningful parent-teacher conferences. Section III ends with planning models that students can use to organize their family involvement plans.

Section IV: Promoting the Well-Being of All Children

This final section addresses three important challenges to children's well-being: (a) infectious illnesses, (b) overweight and obesity, and (c) child maltreatment. As with the other sections, these topics are accompanied by strategies for teachers to use in their social exchanges with families and community professionals.

Appendix: Position Statement: NAEYC Code of Ethical Conduct and Statement of Commitment

The Appendix contains two sections from the NAEYC position statement on ethical conduct that are most relevant to the content of *Empowering Family-Teacher Partnerships*: (a) Section 2, Ethical Responsibilities to Families, and (b) Section 4, Ethical Responsibilities to Community and Society.

Special Features

A number of features make this textbook unique in preparing students to pursue meaningful family-teacher partnerships.

Professional standards. Professional standards that directly or indirectly relate to teachers' work with families are reviewed in Chapter 2. Selected standards are also highlighted in boxes at the beginning of each chapter. These boxes are designed to remind students that their work with families is not an option but a professional responsibility. Such reminders are important, as students especially do not always fully recognize the many ways by which families impact teachers' success in the classroom. Thus, the highlighted standards allow for discussions about their relevance to the content of each chapter.

A personal philosophy of family involvement. Students are often asked by potential employers to explain their philosophy of working with families. Guides are provided in

Chapter 2 to help students meet this expectation. In addition, at the end of each chapter students are invited to reflect on and refine their developing philosophies.

Family involvement portfolios. Students who are able to document their professional competencies hold a distinct advantage when entering the job market. As part of the ancillary package, students are given guidance in developing a family involvement portfolio. Students may choose to focus on one or more parts of the portfolio. Likewise, they may choose to selectively incorporate parts of their portfolio into their more general teaching portfolio. One example of a family involvement portfolio is also provided.

Planning models. Students sometimes feel overwhelmed when learning about the numerous family involvement strategies available to them. Planning models are thus presented in Chapter 14 to help students organize and manage a cohesive family involvement program.

Pedagogical Aids

The following pedagogical features extend students' knowledge, build their professional skills, and provide opportunities for application.

Community Learning Guides. Bulleted guides at the beginning of each chapter are used to focus students' attention on key concepts and principles. In addition, students are invited to use the guides to participate in a "community of learners," the purpose of which is to share and discuss their concerns, questions, and ideas.

Reflections. Reflections are widely recognized as important devices in facilitating students' self-awareness and self-examination. Subsequently, students are invited to reflect on their reactions to information presented in the textbook. They are also invited to share their reflections with each other.

Tip Boxes. Students need more than learning guides and reflections to gain confidence in their ability to work with families. For this reason, Tip Boxes are used to provide practical ideas for supporting family-teacher partnerships.

Case Studies. These allow students to examine and respond to specific types of family situations they may encounter upon entering the teaching field.

FYI (For Your Information). FYIs provide visual examples of family involvement strategies as well as summaries of family involvement issues, trends, and practices.

Field Assignments. These are found at the end of each chapter. Their purpose is to give students experience in relying on their collective insights and problem solving skills to address family involvement tasks.

Capstone Activities. These also are found at the end of each chapter and focus on students' application of family involvement principles, concepts, and strategies.

Internet Resources. With careful screening, websites are useful in extending the narrative of any textbook. The websites included at the end of each chapter have been chosen specifically to provide students with additional information about, and highlight examples of, family involvement resources, programs, and practices.

Ancillaries

Instructor Teaching Site

A password-protected site, available at **www.sagepub.com/coleman**, features resources that have been designed to help instructors plan and teach their course. These resources include

- **Test Bank.** True/false, multiple choice, and discussion items are provided for each chapter.
- **PowerPoints.** Instructors may choose to use the PowerPoints as they are presented or adapt them to the needs of their students.
- **Learning From SAGE Journal Articles.** Access is provided to recent, relevant full-text SAGE Journal Articles and accompanying article review questions.
- **Video Clips.** Video clips are useful in extending students' interest in and understanding of textbook material. The video clips for each chapter of this textbook were produced or researched by the author. In addition, pre- and post-viewing questions and/ or activities are presented that students can respond to on their own or as a class.
- **Web Resources.** The internet resources at the end of each chapter are also presented as online ancillaries for easy access to each site.

Student Study Site

A Web-based study site is available at **www.sagepub.com/coleman**. This site provides access to several study tools, including

- **eFlashcards**. Students will find this resource helpful prior to exams as they test their understanding of key concepts, theories, models, and principles.
- **Web Quizzes**. Web quizzes will allow students to test their knowledge of the content of each chapter.
- **Learning Objectives.** The Community Learning Guides presented at the beginning of each chapter are also presented as online ancillaries.
- **Learning From SAGE Journal Articles.** Access is provided to recent, relevant full-text SAGE journal articles and accompanying article review questions.
- **Video Clips.** Video clips are useful in extending students' interest in and understanding of textbook material. The video clips for each chapter of this textbook have been produced or researched by the author. In addition, pre- and post-viewing questions and/or activities are presented that students can respond to on their own or as a class.
- **Web Resources.** The Internet resources at the end of each chapter are also presented as online ancillaries for easy access to each site.
- **Family Involvement Portfolio.** These guides are included for students who wish to demonstrate their competencies in planning for and working with families.

ACKNOWLEDGMENTS

I would like to acknowledge several people for their contributions to *Empowering Family-Teacher Partnerships*. At SAGE, I was fortunate to have the expertise and guidance of executive editor Diane McDaniel, whose advice was invaluable in helping me problem-solve challenges and identify creative ways to deliver critical information. In addition, SAGE editorial assistant Megan Koraly, assistant editor Terri Accomazzo, and assistant editor Rachael Leblond provided prompt responses to my questions and useful information regarding the publishing process. All of these individuals were gracious in their praise and generous in their encouragement.

I am likewise grateful to the scholars who reviewed my proposal and provided excellent feedback on early drafts of my chapters. Their suggestions made the textbook much stronger. My reviewers included the following individuals:

Ann Barbour, California State University, Los Angeles

Vikki B. Boatman, Stephen F. Austin State University

Jane Broderick, East Tennessee State University

Deborah Farrar, California University of Pennsylvania

Rhonda Harrington, Henderson State University

Barbara E. Kurtz, Cleveland State University

Alice Moss, DePaul University

Debbie Stoll, Cameron University

Laura Wilhelm, University of Central Oklahoma

SECTION I

Foundations of Family Involvement

CHAPTER 1

Contemporary Family Lives and Early Childhood Learning Environments

n this textbook, we focus on the families of children enrolled in prekindergarten through fifth-grade classrooms. Working with families may seem like a simple task, since we all grew up in some type of family arrangement. Yet, as noted by two family scholars, "a variety of family forms are accepted and practiced widely today" (Smock & Greenland, 2010, p. 588).

Indeed, contemporary families and the communities in which they live are more complex and diverse than those even a generation ago (Cherlin, 2010).

It is because of such family diversity that, as a teacher, you will want to assess how the family and community lives represented in your classroom are similar to but also different from your personal experiences. The insights that result from this assessment will guide you in creating a classroom where all families feel respected, welcomed, and have multiple opportunities for supporting their children's education (Muscott et al., 2008).

In this chapter we explore basic concepts and dilemmas associated with contemporary family and community lives. We also examine concepts associated with childhood learning environments. We conclude with a review of how family systems theory can provide us with insight into the dynamics of family lives.

COMMUNITY LEARNING GUIDES

One of the most important challenges for any beginning teacher is to transition from the role of student to that of professional. While this transition does not happen overnight, it need not be a daunting task. You can begin the transitioning process now by participating in a "community of learners" where you share your concerns, questions, and ideas with your peers. As you read each chapter, write down your responses to the items that appear at the beginning of the chapter, such as those that follow. Then use your notes to address the Reflections, Discussion Questions, Field Assignments, and Capstone Activities found in each chapter.

(Continued)

(Continued)

- Describe the various definitions of "family."
- Describe the difference among traditional families, "normed" families, vulnerable families, and emerging families.
- Describe the difference between biological parents and sociological parents. Explain why this distinction is important.
- Describe the childhood outcomes associated with authoritarian, permissive, and authoritative parenting styles.
- Describe how teachers can use family systems theory to better understand the families in their classrooms.

Family Concepts

The American Family Versus American Families

Many scholars in the family studies field have replaced the traditional phrase "the American family" with "American families" to signify the diversity of family life experiences found in contemporary society. This change in terminology is also reflected in debates over what is and is not a family. Consider, for example, Reflection 1.1.

The information in this chapter supports the following family-school-community partnership standards. These standards are reviewed in Chapter 2.

NAEYC Standards and Associated Key Elements	1b, 1c, 2a, 2b, 2c, 3c, 4b, 6a, 6c, 6d, 6e
ACEI Standards	1.0, 3.2, 5.1, 5.
PTA Standards	1, 2, 3, 5, 6

REFLECTION 1.1   Defining Family

How do you define a family? Compare your definition with those of your peers.

Your **personal definition of family** is just that, your personal beliefs as to how families should be structured and how they should behave. Individuals who had positive family life experiences as children are likely to use those experiences when defining family. In contrast, individuals who had negative family life experiences while growing up are likely to avoid using those experiences when defining family. In addition, our personal definitions of family are influenced by social trends and events that shape our views of the world in general and interpersonal relationships in particular.

Our personal definitions of family stand in contrast to two other definitions. First, **professional definitions of family** are provided by organizations that set professional standards for their members. Two examples of professional definitions of family follow.

The family is a group of individuals with a continuing legal, genetic and/or emotional relationship. Society relies on the family group to provide for the economic and protective needs of individuals, especially children and the elderly. (American Academy of Family Physicians, 2009)[1]

A family consists of two or more people who share resources, responsibilities for daily decisions, share values and goals, and show a commitment to one another over time. (American Association of Family and Consumer Sciences, 1997, p. 8)

Second, a **legal definition of family** is provided by the U.S. Census Bureau (2010): "A family is a group of two people or more (one of whom is the householder) related by birth, marriage, or adoption and residing together." Unfortunately, this legal definition can at times be too narrow to capture the diversity of family arrangements found in classrooms. Consider, for example, Case Study 1.1.

CASE STUDY 1.1   Kim

Kim, a nine-year-old, has lived with her grandmother since she was three years of age, at which time her father had abandoned the family and her mother had been sent to prison for drug trafficking. Kim and her grandmother are very close. The grandmother is a loving person and clearly wants the best for Kim. She attends every parent-teacher conference prepared to discuss Kim's academic progress.

Kim's mother, who is preparing for release from prison, has failed to maintain contact with Kim. Nevertheless, you have recently received a letter from the mother asking about Kim's classroom work and requesting a parent-teacher conference. Kim's grandmother asks that you deny these requests, noting, "My daughter is manipulative and a troublemaker. Mark my words. She'll be back in prison within the year."

How might this situation be handled, depending on the definition of family used by Kim's teacher?

Kim's situation reflects only one of the many challenges we face in defining family. In fact, throughout our lives, some if not most of us will live in multiple types of families. Think about the types of families in which you have lived or might live at some point in the future as you read about traditional, normed, vulnerable, and emerging families.

Traditional Families

Traditional families are considered the norm in society. In truth, the traditional family is a relative concept since what is considered traditional today is different from what was considered traditional as recently as a generation ago. Likewise, we can expect that families will continue to change as society itself changes. Nevertheless, traditional family concepts like those that follow are useful in describing many contemporary family arrangements.

Nuclear families consist of a husband and wife and their children. In the United States today, approximately two thirds (67.3%) of children under age 18 live in nuclear families, a percentage that has steadily declined since 1970, when 85.2% of children lived in two-parent families (U.S. Census Bureau, 2007). **Extended families** consist of the nuclear family as well as immediate relatives such as grandparents, aunts, uncles, and cousins. Finally, **fictive** or **affiliated kin** are individuals who have no biological or legal relationship to family members but are nevertheless viewed as part of the family and are given family responsibilities. Fictive kin have always existed, as evidenced during the period of slavery when African American families were torn apart and the welfare of children depended on the care and support provided by multiple adults, not all of whom were biological family members.

Today, the concept of fictive kin has expanded. For example, neighbors who care for children after school while their parents are at work can be considered fictive kin, as can godparents and youth workers who help to socialize children and provide for their well-being (Crosbie-Burnett & Lewis, 1993). Even teachers can be considered fictive kin when they work closely with families to help children reach their full potential.

Normed Families

Normed families include those who a generation ago would have been considered atypical but are now increasingly considered part of "normal" life in American society. Single-parent families, stepfamilies, and grandparent caregivers are three examples of normed families that carry less negative stigma today when compared to the past. We examine these family structures in Chapter 5.

Vulnerable Families

Vulnerable families are families who, because of their life circumstances, experience financial, emotional, and physical stress that can impair their functioning and well-being. Two examples of vulnerable families include homeless families and working-poor families. **Homeless families** are those who lack permanent housing. **Working-poor families** are those who remain in poverty even though their family members work full time.

Working-poor families exist for a number of reasons. Family members who earn a minimum wage often have difficulty covering the cost of basic family needs like clothing, housing, and food. Medical expenses likewise can lead families into a financial crisis. Still other families lack access to the type of reliable and affordable transportation needed to reach better-paying jobs. We take a closer look at the potential challenges and strengths associated with families living in poverty or at the poverty threshold in Chapter 6.

Teachers can be considered fictive kin when they work closely with families to help children reach their full potential.

Emerging Families

Emerging families include family arrangements that are becoming more visible and gaining greater recognition within American society. For example, **network** or **friendship families**, also referred to as **families of choice** (Bigner, 2006, p. 21; Tasker, 2005), are formed when individuals who are not related join together to support one another. For example, a group of single mothers may join together to provide one another with emotional and financial support. A network family may also be formed among newly arrived immigrant families. In fact, some colleges and universities today use the phrase "friendship families" to characterize campus programs that help foreign students build social support networks.

Gay and lesbian families also are emerging families. They consist of same-sex partners with or without children. Only a few states currently give some type of legal standing to gay and lesbian families (Davey & Robbins, 2009; Goodnough & O'Connor, 2009, Gramlich, 2011). In states that sanction **same-sex marriages**, gay and lesbian couples receive the same rights given to heterosexual couples. Other states grant **civil unions** to same-sex couples. Unlike same-sex marriages, civil unions provide gay and lesbian couples with many, but not necessarily all, of the rights given to heterosexual couples (Gramlich, 2011).

Based on the U.S. Defense of Marriage Act (DOMA) of 1996, the federal government does not recognize same-sex marriages or civil unions. In addition, DOMA does not require same-sex marriages or civil unions to be recognized outside the states in which they take place. This is one of the forces behind current court challenges to DOMA, along with the fact that over 1,000 federal rights automatically granted to married heterosexual couples by the U.S. government are denied to married gay and lesbian couples (Human Rights Campaign, 2006). These rights include the right to social security payments upon the death or disability of a spouse, the right for the spouse of a deceased worker to receive survivor benefits, the right to inherit property from a spouse in the absence of a will, and the right to job protection while taking up to 12 weeks of unpaid leave from work to care for an ill spouse or a child (Human Rights Campaign, 2006). Perhaps in part because of these discrepancies, in 2011 President Barrack Obama announced that the U.S. Justice Department would no longer defend DOMA (Gramlich, 2011). This ruling reflects the fluid nature of same-sex marriages and civil unions in the United States.

We take a closer look at the potential challenges and strengths associated with gay and lesbian families in Chapter 6. For now, we continue with another concept associated with emerging families that can be applied to heterosexual and same-sex marriages. That is the concept of serial monogamy.

The phrase **serial monogamy** describes the series of monogamous relationships many individuals go through during their lifetime. As one marriage, or some other type of union, ends, another one takes its place. Serial monogamy can in turn lead to **multiple partner fertility**, meaning that adults have children with more than one partner (Cherlin, 2010; Smock & Greenland, 2010). Both serial monogamy and multiple partner fertility reflect just how much family living arrangements can shift even within a few decades.

Standing in contrast to serial monogamy is the concept of **covenant marriage**. Covenant marriages are designed to reinforce marriage by making it more difficult for individuals to divorce. Currently, only a few states offer couples the voluntary option of signing an oath honoring their commitment vows. These couples also agree to premarriage counseling. In addition, the covenant marriage oath specifies a limited number of conditions under which the state will grant a divorce. These situations usually involve family abuse, adultery, and abandonment. Postdivorce counseling and a waiting period before a divorce is granted may also be required.

Households

A **household** includes everyone who occupies a housing unit (U.S. Census Bureau, 2010). In a **family household**, at least one individual is related to the householder by birth, marriage, or adoption (U.S. Census Bureau, 2010). A **nonfamily household** includes a householder living alone or with nonrelatives only, for example, boarders, roommates, or live-in girlfriends or boyfriends (U.S. Census Bureau, 2010). Like many other family arrangements, family and nonfamily households have the potential to create interesting situations for teachers. Consider, for example, Case Study 1.2. Then complete Reflection 1.2.

CASE STUDY 1.2   Nolan

Nolan lives with his parents in a family household. His parents rent out their basement apartment to a young woman, Maria, who recently immigrated to the United States with her young son. According to the U.S. Census Bureau (2010), Maria and her son are defined as an *unrelated subfamily* living within Nolan and his parents' family household. Maria and Nolan's parents have an agreement that substantially reduces her monthly rent. Maria cares for Nolan and her son, who are the same age, in the afternoon and during the summer when school is not in session. Because both of Nolan's parents travel as part of their jobs, Maria also cares for Nolan when they are away.

Nolan's teacher has recently asked each student in her classroom to draw a picture of something they do at home with their parents. These are to be used to make a family mural. Nolan draws a picture of himself, Maria, and Maria's son baking cookies. The teacher's assistant asks Nolan to redraw his picture showing something that he does with his parents. Nolan's teacher takes the opposite view. She feels Nolan's drawing should be honored and that it should be included in the family mural. What would you do in this situation?

REFLECTION 1.2   Identifying Family Arrangements

Refer back to the family definitions presented in this section. Which definition or definitions apply to the following family arrangements?

- A husband and wife with an adopted child.
- Three female friends and their children, all of whom live in a house owned by one of the women. The women share living expenses.
- A man, his girlfriend, and her child, all of whom live in the man's house.
- Describe another family arrangement that you have encountered in your personal or professional life that reflects one or more of the above family definitions.

Parenting Concepts

Like the concept of family, our understanding of what it means to be a parent can be understood from different viewpoints. In this textbook, we will use the term **parent** as a generic term to refer to any family member or nonfamily member (e.g., legal guardian) who cares for a child. We can define at least three types of parents. **Biological parents** are genetically related to a child. The wishes of biological parents are usually given primary consideration in legal matters, unless they relinquish their parenting rights or are denied those rights by the state. **Extended parents** include the relatives of a nuclear family who, when required to do so, assume parenting responsibilities. For example, social workers often turn to grandparents, aunts and uncles, adult siblings, or cousins as caregivers when a child's biological parents are unable or unwilling to carry out their parenting responsibilities.

Finally, **sociological parents** assume the mother or father role even though they are not biologically related to a child. For example, *foster parents* are given temporary rights, and *adoptive parents* permanent rights, by the state to care for a child following the death of the biological parents or the child's removal from the biological parents' home. *Stepparents* also assume the parenting role when they marry a child's biological parent. However, they must adopt the child in order to make legal decisions about his or her welfare. Stepparents are a good example of how the rights of biological and sociological parents can conflict and create additional dilemmas for teachers. Consider, for example, Case Study 1.3.

CASE STUDY 1.3   Toni

Toni's father and mother, who divorced two years ago, hold joint custody rights. Toni's father recently married Melissa, who is now Toni's stepmother. While Toni's biological parents manage to get along for the sake of Toni's well-being, this is not true for Toni's biological mother and Melissa. In fact, they rarely speak to one another.

The negative relationship between Toni's mother and stepmother is now creating a dilemma for you, Toni's teacher. Toni's mother is insisting that Melissa be denied access to Toni's school records and that she not attend parent-teacher conferences.

As Toni's teacher, what is the first question you must answer to identify your legal responsibilities regarding the requests made by Toni's biological mother? How might you justify the importance of the involvement of both Toni's mother and stepmother in her education? What ideas might you present to achieve this compromise?

The above case study reflects the need for a **professional definition of parenthood** that acknowledges the parenting role played by any adult, regardless of his or her legal standing, who protects and provides for the needs of a child. While such a definition would no doubt prove difficult to defend from a legal perspective, it nevertheless reminds us that, as teachers, we have a professional obligation to at least consider the viewpoints of the various adults who support children's development and education.

Diane Baumrind's Model of Parenting Styles

The term **parenting** refers to the child guidance practices parents use to socialize their children. Most parenting practices fall under one of three styles that were first introduced by Diane Baumrind (1989, 1991a, 1991b) as she followed the development of children into adolescence: (a) authoritarian, (b) permissive, and (c) authoritative. Within this model, each parenting style is associated with two parenting dimensions: (a) parents' responsiveness to their children's need for attention and affection, and (b) parents' demands for children to follow adult-imposed rules of behavior. For example, **authoritarian parents** are autocrats in that they display a high level of demanding behavior but a low level of responsiveness to their children's ideas and expressions of independence. Put another way, these parents are obedience and status oriented, expecting their orders to be obeyed without explanation (Baumrind, 1991b, p. 750). This stern form of parenting may also be accompanied by few displays of affection and/or little encouragement.

Compared to other children, those with authoritarian parents are described as "discontented, withdrawn, and distrustful" (Baumrind, 1989, p. 351). In addition, girls are described as being overly dependent on their parents and submissive in interpersonal relationships (Baumrind,

1989, p. 352, Baumrind, 1991a, p. 127; Teti & Candelaria, 2002, p. 157), while boys are described as resistive and more hostile or shy with peers (Baumrind, 1989, p. 352; 1991a, p. 127; Teti & Candelaria, 2002, p. 157). As adolescents, children of authoritarian parents are obedient and conform to standards set by adults, do well in school, and are less likely than their peers to get into trouble (Lamborn, Mounts, Steinberg, & Dornbusch, 1991). However, such conformity comes at a price in that they also lack self-confidence. In short, these children appear to have been "overpowered into obedience" (Lamborn et al., 1991, p. 1062). Indeed, we can argue that the hostile and resistive behavior displayed by some boys of authoritarian parents may reflect their attempts at fighting back against their parents' demands for conformity.

Permissive parents are the opposite of authoritarian parents in that they make few demands of their children and instead allow them to make their own choices and to assert their independence (Baumrind, 1991b, p. 750). In short, permissive parents take a hands-off approach to parenting, setting few rules of behavior. When rules are set, they may not be consistently enforced.

Children of permissive parents are described as "the least self-reliant, explorative, and self-controlled" (Baumrind, 1989, p. 352). Girls in particular are less socially assertive, but both sexes are less achievement oriented (Baumrind, 1989, p. 355). By adolescence, these children score high on measures of social competence and self-confidence (Lamborn et al., 1991). On the other hand, they are more disengaged from school and show a higher frequency of school misconduct and drug and alcohol abuse (Lamborn et al., 1991).

Authoritative parents are responsive to their children's wishes but also demand that they follow clear standards of behavior (Baumrind, 1991a, p. 750). Likewise, these parents involve their children in setting rules, but also apply consequences when those rules are broken. One key objective behind authoritative parenting is to help children become assertive and independent but also socially responsible (Baumrind, 1991b, p. 750).

This combination of support and control seems to fall within a "Goldilocks zone" in that the children of authoritative parents exhibit the best adaptive behavior. Compared to other children, they are "the most self-reliant, self-controlled, explorative, and content" (Baumrind, 1989, p. 351). Based on multiple measures, children of authoritative parents are friendly with peers, independent and assertive, cooperative with their parents, and achievement oriented (Teti & Candelaria, 2002, p. 157). Girls of authoritative parents exhibit greater achievement-oriented behavior while boys exhibit friendly and cooperative behavior (Baumrind, 1991a, p. 128). Similarly, as adolescents these children are well adjusted, competent, confident about their abilities, and less likely than their peers to get into trouble (Lamborn et al., 1991).

A number of programs are available to help parents develop skills that promote these types of positive child outcomes. We review some of the programs in Chapter 4. In addition, we revisit Baumrind's parenting styles as they apply to race in Chapter 8. For now, however, we briefly examine the implications of parenting styles for teachers.

Implications of Parenting Styles for Teachers

One of the more difficult challenges teachers face is reconciling the child guidance practices carried out in the classroom and the parenting styles of parents. For example, teachers today are taught to follow an authoritative guidance approach in which children are provided with a nurturing environment that also involves rules of behavior. Children help to set classroom rules and are taught that consequences follow broken rules. Further, teachers are taught to actively involve children in discussions about their behavior as a way of teaching self-reflection, impulse control, and problem solving skills.

Some permissive and authoritarian parents may question these authoritative approaches to classroom behavior management. For example, permissive parents may feel the teacher is being "overly strict" in setting rules and delivering consequences for misbehavior. In contrast, authoritarian parents may feel the teacher is being "soft" and abdicating his or her disciplinary responsibility by inviting children to help set rules and engaging them in discussions about their behavior. Because of these types of concerns, teachers often take great care to explain their classroom behavior management practices. This may be done in multiple ways: (a) during registration, (b) in the family handbook (see Chapter 12), and (c) on a classroom website. You will find one example of a teacher's behavior management philosophy on the Family Involvement Portfolio section of the student study site. Before continuing to the next section, complete Reflection 1.3.

REFLECTION 1.3   Assessing Parenting Styles

Think about the parents you have observed in your family, in your neighborhood, or while travelling. Identify a situation where a parent demonstrated an authoritarian or permissive style of parenting. Describe this situation and the parent's child guidance practices. How might an authoritative parent have handled this situation?

Learning Environment Concepts

The **learning environment** encompasses a number of concepts related to the classroom and community at large. You will be introduced to key concepts in this section.

Classrooms and Other Learning Environments

In this textbook, the terms *classroom* and *learning environment* are used synonymously to describe any location in which children receive instruction and care. Most often, these locations include public and private elementary schools, nonprofit and private early learning centers, and Head Start programs. In addition, some libraries, gardens, museums, hospitals, and community centers set aside educational space for children, as do some homeless shelters for abused women. Likewise, there are numerous youth organizations that sponsor after-school, summer, and holiday learning environments (e.g., recreation centers, boys and girls clubs). Think about the role teachers can play in these different locations as you complete Reflection 1.4.

REFLECTION 1.4   Learning Environments Beyond the Classroom

Identify a learning environment in which you might like to work other than a school. As a teacher, how might your daily work in this alternative setting be similar to and different from a classroom setting? What might be the advantages and disadvantages of working in this setting?

Teachers, Educators, and Caregivers

For the purposes of this textbook, a **teacher** is anyone who receives a professional license from his or her state to teach and care for children. The phrase "teach and care for" is used to emphasize that one cannot be an effective teacher without also being a good caregiver, and vice versa. Put another way, teachers not only have instructional responsibilities, but they also have responsibilities for attending to children's emotions, health, and safety.

Education

The education of children can be divided into formal and informal categories. **Formal education** involves designing a learning environment to help children master state educational standards. **Informal education** involves families supporting their children's learning experiences in the classroom, at home, and in the community. One goal of this textbook is to help you link children's formal and informal education by using various family involvement activities. You will learn more about these activities in upcoming chapters. For now, continue to the next section to read more about how education extends beyond the classroom and into the community.

Bowen's Model of Community Social Capacity

A **community** is defined not only by its geographic location but also the quality of life it provides through its institutions (e.g., schools, libraries, museums, and religious institutions), services (e.g., police protection, sanitation, recreation, medical care, and transportation), cultural events (e.g., fairs and festivals), and cohesion of its neighborhoods. All of these characteristics help to highlight why the social capacity of communities is an important component of the learning environment.

The concept of **social capacity** refers to the efficiency of formal and informal community systems in providing for the physical, psychological, social, and material care of its members (Bowen, Richman, & Bowen, 2000). Put another way, a community's social capacity reflects how well individuals and families are able to manage their daily lives, life transitions, and responses to emergencies. We will use Bowen and his colleagues' model of social capacity to better understand this idea (Bowen et al., 2000). This model makes use of three concepts: (a) social capital, (b) collective efficacy, and (c) human capital. We end this section by considering the use of community scans as a strategy for assessing social capacity.

Social Capital

Social capital refers to the time and energy families and communities devote to supporting the development of children and youth (Coleman, 1994). When assessing the social capital of communities, it is helpful to ask three questions (Bowen et al., 2000; Coleman, 1988). First, what types of *informal obligations* are shared among families that reflect their willingness to help one another with daily tasks such as child care and house repairs? Second, are the *information channels* in a community sufficient to assist families in identifying the services and resources needed to meet their daily needs and accomplish their life goals? Good information flow is supported through community centers, public libraries, safe neighborhoods that encourage social exchanges, Web-based community bulletin boards, and school meetings where parents are invited to share their views and ask questions. Finally, what are the *social norms* of a community? Ideally, social norms discourage disruptive behavior and encourage behaviors that support families as well as community pride, safety, and development. Examples of programs that reflect these social norms include neighborhood watch programs, enforcement of traffic and noise ordinances, and mentoring programs for youth whose objectives include building self-pride, respect for others, and community citizenship.

Collective Efficacy

Collective efficacy is defined not only by the level of social capital in a community but also by the ability of its members to use that capital to improve the lives of others (Sampson, Raudenbush, & Earls, 1997). To assess a community's collective efficacy, ask the following question: Is the community able to mobilize its social capital to successfully address an identified challenge? An affirmative response to this question means that the community not only possesses a core set of social norms (Vega, Ang, Rodriguez, & Finch, 2011) but a willingness to act upon those norms (Sampson, Morenoff, & Earls, 1999; Sampson, Morenoff, & Gannon-Rowley, 2002).

While the concept of collective efficacy has proved useful in explaining how communities with high collective efficacy are able to help children from dysfunctional homes make adaptive adjustments (see Yonas et al., 2010), of greater interest to teachers is its application to the classroom. One such application can be found in a study of primary and secondary students where collective efficacy was defined by class cohesion and trust among class members. Such collective efficacy was associated with less frequent bullying victimization, most likely because students and teachers took action when they witnessed bullying (Sapouna, 2010).

Human Capital

While collective efficacy is concerned with group well-being, **human capital** is concerned with individual well-being. One way to appreciate the importance of human capital is to compare it to business capital. In short, while businesses raise economic capital in the form of money, families, schools, and communities raise human capital in the form of knowledge and skills (Scanzoni, 2000, p. 149), which ensure children will lead healthy and productive lives (Parcel, Dufur, & Zito, 2010). Human capital is "cashed in" when children reach adulthood and use their knowledge and skills to become productive workers and community citizens. In a sense, the social capital of a community can be used to support human capital.

It is important to note that societies have needed different types of human capital at different points in time. For example, knowledge and skills related to farming were needed during the *agricultural era* while engineering skills and knowledge of machinery were needed during the *industrial era* (Scanzoni, 2000). Today we live in an *information era* where technological, interpersonal, and problem solving skills are of prime importance. What role might you play as a teacher in raising human capital in contemporary society?

REFLECTION 1.5   Human Capital in the Information Era

List some examples of teaching strategies or classroom lessons you will pursue to prepare children for productive lives in the information era.

Think about this question as you complete Reflection 1.5. Then proceed to the next section, where you will learn how to use a community scan to assess the social capacity of your community.

The Community Scan

As a teacher, you may live and teach in different communities (Schutz, 2006). If so, your understanding of social capacity must involve not only your home community but also the community in which you teach. Conducting a community scan can help you achieve both objectives.

A **community scan** is an informal strategy for assessing a community's social capacity. Tips for conducting a community scan are presented in Tip Box 1.1. When conducting your own community scans, consider the agencies presented in FYI 1.1. They reflect some of the most common resources communities rely on to build and maintain their social capacities. You may also find FYI 1.1 helpful when completing assignments in upcoming chapters.

Teachers can use a community scan to assess a community's social capacity.

TIP BOX 1.1   Conducting a Community Scan

A number of strategies can be used to carry out a community scan. The larger the community, the more strategies you may need to use to gain a complete understanding of its resources and values.

- **Drive or walk around the community.** Take note of activities on the street and the number and types of businesses that surround your school. Also note the presence of public parks, libraries, religious institutions, and social service agencies.
- **Listen to local radio and television programs.** What types of programs are broadcast? Are different views expressed about controversial issues?
- **Read the local newspaper.** What topics are addressed on the editorial page? Are different values reflected in letters to the editor?
- **Take note of the informal conversations that take place between parents who visit the classroom.** These too can help you better appreciate community values.
- **Attend local civic and government meetings.** Pay attention to discussion topics that reflect the community's strengths and challenges.
- **Visit the local chamber or commerce.** Learn about the businesses and industries that form the economic base of the community.
- **Use United Way 2-1-1.** Admittedly, conducting a community scan within a metropolitan area can be challenging. In these cases, use United Way 2-1-1, an Internet-based social service registry, to carry out an electronic community scan. To find a United Way 2-1-1 registry for your metropolitan area, visit the following website: www.211us.org/status.htm

FYI 1.1 Community Agencies That Support Social Capacity	
Agency*	Examples of Services*
Health Department	Health information, screenings, and immunizations; nutritional programs; food safety inspections; pest control; air quality inspections
Family and Children Services	Child and elder abuse prevention; adoption and foster care; food assistance; refugee support; employment assistance; financial assistance with medical care
Fire and Rescue Department	Fire response and other emergency services; containment of hazardous material; canine search and rescue; emergency medical assistance
Police Department	Community protection; criminal background checks; volunteer programs to assist with crime prevention; neighborhood watch programs; 911 emergency dispatch centers; animal control services
Public Works Department	Coordination of the construction, installation, and maintenance of roads and drains, street lights, and traffic signs; garbage pickup and recycling services
Workforce Centers	Job training and search services; educational programs for youth and adults; youth summer employment programs
Parks and Recreation Departments	Child, adult, and family recreational activities; gardening programs; social clubs; movies and concerts
City and County Libraries	Reading and audiovisual materials; meeting rooms; reading and study areas; computers and Internet services; literacy and musical performances; children's programs; adult education and English as Second Language classes; literacy outreach programs at homeless shelters, health centers, and other community sites
Food Banks	Distribution of food and groceries to people in need through pantries, community kitchens, shelters, and senior centers
Youth Centers: Boys & Girls Clubs, YMCA, YWCA	After-school programs, enrichment activities. and clubs; leadership activities, life skills education, and gang prevention; games and sports activities (some centers may also provide programs on building family strengths or addressing family stress)
Thrift Stores	Inexpensive clothing, furniture, household items, toys, books, and magazines
Arts and Culture Centers	Community educational programs and cultural events
Court-Appointed Special Advocate (CASA) or Local Child Advocate Center	Trained volunteers represent the interests of abused and neglected children who are being served by social services agencies and the courts

*Agency names and services will vary among states and locales

Family Systems Theory: Understanding Family Life Dynamics

The **family systems theory** helps us move beyond definitions to an understanding of the dynamics of family lives. This theory begins with the principle that families interact with but are separate from other social systems such as schools, religious institutions, and youth groups. As children move among these social systems they are exposed to different experiences and points of view that contribute to their development and education.

Within the family system are individuals who belong to subsystems such as mother-child, father-child, mother-father, and siblings (Parke, 2004). These subsystems, as well as individual family members, are *interdependent*, meaning that the behavior associated with one subsystem or family member has the potential to impact the entire family. For example, all family members experience stress when a child is diagnosed with a serious illness. Such stress can in turn upset the **family equilibrium**, broadly defined as a state of normalcy where all know what is expected of them. Practice applying the interdependent principle by completing Reflection 1.6.

REFLECTION 1.6   The Interdependent Principle

Think back to your childhood. Describe how a medical condition, achievement, or another life experience of a family member led to a temporary or permanent change in your family system. How did your family regain its equilibrium?

Family Rules

Family rules are the standards of behavior that govern life within a family system. Rules are found not only in families but also within other social systems, such as schools. This means that family rules can at times conflict with classroom rules (Christian, 2006). Assume the role of teacher and reconcile the rules of behavior listed in Reflection 1.7.

REFLECTION 1.7   Family Rules

Describe the rules you would set in your classroom regarding the following behaviors. How might your classroom rules conflict with family rules? How would you handle these conflicts?

- When or how a child should interact with adults
- When or how a child should express anger
- When or how children should put away materials

Family Boundaries

Family boundaries function like gates in regulating the flow of information and social interactions between the family system and the outside world. There are three types of family boundaries: (a) open boundaries, (b) closed boundaries, and (c) permeable boundaries.

Some families have *open boundaries* in which there are few if any rules governing the flow of information or social interactions. For example, parents may fail to monitor their children's social friendships. Likewise, children may be allowed to come and go as they please or to bring home friends without first checking with their parents.

Other families have *closed boundaries* in which information and social interactions are tightly controlled. For example, parents may set rules that severely limit children's after-school activities. Such rules can prevent children from forming friendships, developing a sense of independence, and taking part in extracurricular activities that advance their social development.

Fortunately, most families achieve a healthy balance between extreme open and closed boundaries by establishing *permeable boundaries*. In these families, rules are used to maintain family equilibrium while individuals are also encouraged to pursue age-appropriate experiences and social interactions outside the family that allow them to develop their own interests and identities. See if you can distinguish among permeable, closed, and open family boundaries by completing Reflection 1.8.

REFLECTION 1.8   Family Boundaries

Do the following situations represent open, closed, or permeable family boundaries?

- Mr. Beach's son is allowed to sign Mr. Beach's name to permission forms that are sent home.
- You send a note home asking parents to share their child's favorite bedtime story with you. Ms. Lexington returns your note with the following written message: "This is none of your business."
- Ms. Benton explains to her daughter the purpose behind a 9 P.M. bedtime rule.

Family Climates

A **family climate** describes the emotional environment in which family members live. Family rituals, stories, and myths are three factors that contribute to a family climate (Parke, 2004).

Family rituals are patterns of behavior or daily routines that give meaning to family life and interactions (Parke, 2004). Examples of family rituals include bedtime and dinner routines, holiday events, and recreational activities. **Family stories** are used to transmit core family values and rules between generations (Parke, 2004). Examples of family stories include explanations as to why a family follows a particular ritual, why they enforce certain rules of behavior, and why they do or do not participate in classroom activities.

Family myths include beliefs about family life that typically are not open for debate (Parke, 2004). Examples of family myths include beliefs about what makes a good husband or wife, how children should behave, and the respective responsibilities of teachers and parents in educating and socializing children.

With a little practice, teachers usually find that the family systems theory helps them to better understand and work with families. Tips for how you can use this theory are presented in Tip Box 1.2.

While family systems theory is one of the most popular theories for understanding the dynamics of family lives, it is not the only theory. Other theories and models are introduced in upcoming chapters, a summary of which can be found in the following section.

TIP BOX 1.2	Tips for Using the Family Systems Theory

Family Rules

- Encourage children to talk about classroom rules and how they differ from those they follow at home. Help them understand why different rules are needed in different settings.

Family Equilibrium

- If a child's behavior shows a sudden change, consult with the family regarding anything unusual that might be taking place at home.
- Avoid making dramatic changes in your classroom environment if you know that a child's family life has been disrupted (Christian, 2006).

Family Boundaries

- Families with more open boundaries may take a relaxed approach to making decisions or responding to notes that are sent home. In some cases, they may ask aunts, grandparents, or even siblings to sign school forms. Be persistent but patient and diplomatic in explaining that it is important for parents to assume responsibility for reading and signing classroom forms.
- Avoid becoming defensive if a family rejects your attempts to get to know them on a personal level. Families with more closed boundaries may prefer a formal family-teacher relationship that protects their privacy. Likewise, these families may feel more comfortable engaging in a one-on-one exchange than participating in group events.

Family Climates

- Even though you may disagree, be respectful of statements such as "Spare the rod and spoil the child." Such statements often reflect family beliefs that are shared across generations. Challenging such beliefs can have negative consequences for the family-teacher partnership. Instead, be diplomatic by providing alternative child guidance information in your classroom newsletter. Write articles on topics such as "Tips for Communicating With Children" and "Setting and Enforcing Age-Appropriate Limits."

A Brief Overview of Theories and Models Used in This Textbook

We broadly define theories and models as frameworks for understanding and describing our world (Smith, Hamon, Ingoldsby, & Miller, 2009). In this chapter, you were introduced to family systems theory, Baumrind's model of parenting styles, and Bowen and his colleagues' model of social capacity. A summary of other theories and models presented in upcoming chapters are summarized in FYI 1.2.

As you review the theoretical concepts in FYI 1.2, keep in mind the important function theories and models play in our professional lives. This function is best summarized by a quote from a famous social psychologist: "There is nothing so practical as a good theory" (Lewin, 1951, p. 169). Indeed, theories and models function as practical professional guides (Thomas, 1996, pp. 3–4; White & Klein, 2002, pp. 16–18) in a number of ways. They allow us to communicate efficiently with others by using concepts we all understand. They help us to explain or predict the behavior of the children and families with whom we work. Finally, they help us to organize our thoughts about how best to plan activities that meet the interests and needs of children and families.

FYI 1.2   Theories and Models Used in This Textbook

Theory/Model—Chapter	Key Concepts/Principles	Relevance to Family-Teacher Partnerships
Baumrind's model of parenting styles – Chapter 1	– Authoritarian parenting – Permissive parenting – Authoritative parenting	It is important that teachers explain the reasoning behind their classroom behavior management practices, since they may at times conflict with one or more parenting styles.
Bowen's model of community social capacity – Chapter 1	– Social capital – Collective efficacy – Human capital – Community scan	This model is useful in assessing a community's level of functioning.
Family systems theory – Chapter 1	– Interdependent principle – Family equilibrium – Family rules – Family boundaries – Family climate	Teachers can use this theory to understand the dynamics of family life.
Epstein's family–school-community partnership model – Chapter 2	– Overlapping spheres of influence – Parenting – Communicating – Volunteering – Learning at home – Decision making – Collaborating with the community	This model represents a popular framework for planning a comprehensive family involvement program.
Bronfenbrenner's ecological theory – Chapter 3	– Human ecology – Microsystem – Mesosytem – Exosystem – Macrosystem – Chronosystem	This model provides teachers with a lens for understanding how children's development and education can be supported at all levels of society.
Bandura's theory of self-efficacy – Chapter 4	– Self-efficacy – Mastery experiences – Vicarious experiences – Social persuasion	This theory provides a basis for replacing teachers' self–doubts about working with families with a "can do" mind-set.
Vygotsky's sociocultural theory of cognitive development – Chapter 4	– Scaffolding – Zone of proximal distance	Teachers can use the concepts associated with this theory to guide parents as they help their children acquire new skills.
Symbolic interactionism – Chapter 5	– Role overload – Role strain – Role ambiguity – Role conflict	This theory is helpful in understanding the role taking challenges faced by single parents, stepparents, and grandparent caregivers when interacting with teachers and schools.
Social exchange theory – Chapter 6	– Rewards – Costs	Teachers can support family involvement among gay and lesbian families, as well as families living in poverty, by maximizing the rewards and minimizing the costs of their participation.

Facilitated IEP meeting model – Chapter 7	– Neutral facilitator – The agenda – IEP goals – Ground rules – Fostering collaboration – Eliminating power imbalances – The parking lot	The components of this model are designed to create a respectful environment when working with families with children who have disabilities.
Model of cultural adaption – Chapter 8	– Assimilation – Acculturation – Enculturation	Teachers can work more effectively with immigrant families by understanding the processes involved in adapting to a new culture.
Poston's model of biracial identity – Chapter 8	– Personal identity – Choice of group categorization – Enmeshment/denial – Appreciation – Integration	This theory assists teachers in working with biracial children as they establish a healthy racial identity.
The anti-bias education model – Chapter 9	– Goal 1: To nurture children's multiple identities – Goal 2: To encourage children's expression of and joy regarding human diversity – Goal 3: To recognize and understand the impact of unfair and discriminatory acts – Goal 4: To take action to address acts of unfairness and discrimination	This model provides teachers with guidance in helping children acquire the attitudes, knowledge, and skills needed for a diverse social world
Three approaches for addressing multicultural education – Chapter 9	– Intervention – Tour and detour – Transformative	This model provides teachers with guidance in becoming culturally responsive teachers.
Model 1: Webbing family involvement – Chapter 14	– Structure – Construction – Benefits	Webs provide a visual picture of how teachers plan to link classroom lessons to family involvement activities, all of which support a central learning theme.
Model 2: Family involvement roles – Chapter 14	– Support – Teacher – Student – Advocate – Protector – Ambassador	This model allows teachers to match the interests of individual parents to different family involvement roles that can be played out in the classroom, at home, and in the community.
James Comer's school development program (SDP) model – Chapter 14	– The whole child – The SDP structure – SDP processes – SDP operations	The SDP is a comprehensive school reform model. It provides both the structure and operational procedures needed for school administrators, families, teachers, school staff, and community professionals to optimize children's development and education.

CHAPTER SUMMARY

The concepts of "family" and "parenting" are complex. Fortunately, we can use family systems theory to move us beyond definitions to a consideration of family dynamics.

- Today, learning environments extend beyond the traditional classroom and include such locations as libraries, gardens, museums, hospitals, and other community sites.
- The quality of life for individuals and families is in part influenced by the social capacity of their communities. Teachers can conduct an informal assessment of a community's social capacity by using community scans.

NOTE

1. Reproduced with permission from definition of family from the 2009 issue of http://www.aafp/org/onlline/en/ home/policy/policies/f/familydefinitionof.html. Copyright © 2009 American Academy of Family Physicians. All Rights Reserved.

DISCUSSION QUESTIONS

1. Discuss whether the difficulty we face in defining family is a positive or negative reflection of family life in contemporary American society.

2. Discuss the practical implications of the following distinctions for teachers: (a) biological versus sociological parents and (b) authoritarian, permissive, and authoritative parenting styles.

3. Like teachers, parents teach children life skills and attend to their health and safety. Given these similarities, discuss whether parents should be required to hold a state "parenting license," just as teachers must hold a state "teaching license." If so, what might be the criteria for holding such a license?

COMMUNITY OF LEARNERS' FIELD ASSIGNMENT

Conduct a Community Scan

Working in small groups, use the guides presented in Tip Box 1.1 to conduct a community scan. Use a picture collage, slide (e.g., PowerPoint) presentation, or videotape to present your findings.

How would you summarize the social capacity of this community? How can the community improve its social capacity?

CAPSTONE ACTIVITIES

Activity 1: Document Contemporary Family Images

Look through magazines for images of different family arrangements. Cut these out and bring them to class. How many different family images did you find? How do the images portray similar and unique aspects of family life in contemporary American society? How might teachers accommodate the different aspects of family life represented in the family images?

Activity 2: Apply the Family Systems Theory

Identify a family that appears on a television program or in a movie. Analyze this family's dynamics using the family systems theory. What types of subsystems are represented? How well are family rules defined? Does the family display more open, closed, or permeable boundaries? Is the climate of the family healthy or unhealthy?

Activity 3: Identify a Children's Book on Community Life for Your Teacher Resource File

Visit your local library to select a book that you can use to introduce a lesson on some aspect of community life. Share your book with your peers. As a class, develop a bibliography of all the books that are presented. Make copies for everyone in your class. Make a teacher resource file in which to place your bibliography. You will want to keep your resource file for future reference.

INTERNET RESOURCES

You may find that some URLs have been altered by the webmaster. In these situations, try entering the name of the document or agency in a search engine. Alternatively, enter the domain name (e.g., http://www.xxxx.org). This should take you to the revised home page and associated links.

American Association of Family and Consumer Sciences (AAFCS)

http://www.aafcs.org/

AAFCS provides support for professionals who are concerned with families' relationships, nutritional well-being, housing, and economic resources. As with most other professional organizations, AAFC publishes journals and sponsors annual conferences to share information about the programs and research being carried out by its members.

American Educational Research Association (AERA)

http://www.aera.net/

AERA is a national research society that advances our knowledge about education. AERA sponsors an annual conference and publishes journals and books. AERA also sponsors a number of professional divisions and special interest groups for members with similar interests. Some of these include (a) Teaching and Teacher Education, (b) Early Education and Child Development, and (c) Family, School, Community Partnerships.

American Psychological Association (APA)

http://www.apa.org/

The mission of the APA is to advance the creation, communication, and application of psychological knowledge to benefit society and individuals. In addition to holding annual conferences, APA publishes journals, books, videos, software, and newsletters. The APA also sponsors a number of divisions for its members, five of which include (a) School Psychology, (b) Society for Child and Family Policy and Practice, (c) Society for Family Psychology, (d) Educational Psychology, and (e) Developmental Psychology.

American Sociological Association (ASA)

http://www.asanet.org/

ASA supports the generation and application of knowledge related to the field of sociology. Beyond its sponsorship of conferences and journals, ASA also sponsors several membership divisions. Three of these include (a) Children and Youth, (b) Education, and (c) Family.

National Council on Family Relations (NCFR)

http://www.ncfr.org/

NCFR is a multidisciplinary professional organization focused on family research, practice, and education. NCFR publishes journals, sponsors annual conferences, and coordinates a Certified Family Life Education program.

Society for Research on Child Development (SRCD)

http://www.srcd.org/

SRCD is a multidisciplinary professional association composed of researchers, practitioners, and human development professionals from around the world. The purpose of SRCD is to promote multidisciplinary research in the field of human development.

STUDENT STUDY SITE

Log on to the Web-based student study site at **www.sagepub.com/coleman** for additional study tools including

- eFlashcards
- Web Quizzes
- Links to SAGE Journal Articles
- Author-created Videos
- Learning Objectives
- Web Resources
- Family Involvement Portfolio Guides

CHAPTER 2

Developing a Guiding Philosophy of Family Involvement

Individuals applying for a teaching or family service position often are asked to explain their approach to working with families. Developing a philosophy of family involvement can help you respond to this request in a thoughtful manner. In addition, your philosophy will guide you in planning family involvement activities. In this chapter we examine concepts, reality checks, and standards that will assist you in writing your philosophy of family involvement.

As you read this chapter, take notes on the following items. Use your notes to address the Reflections, Discussion Questions, Field Assignment, and Capstone Activities as you encounter them.

- Describe the six types of family-school-community partnerships.
- Describe the reality checks teachers can follow when working with families.
- Summarize what you see as two or three key themes represented in the various professional standards that guide family-teacher-school partnerships.
- Describe the purpose of writing a personal philosophy of family involvement.

COMMUNITY LEARNING GUIDE

Epstein's Family-School-Community Partnership Model

Contemporary **family involvement** programs include but go beyond linking children's home and classroom learning experiences (Coleman & Tymes, 2004). They also address the total needs of children and their families (Keyser, 2006; Vaughn, White, Johnston, & Dunlap, 2005). Thus, the social capacity of communities must also be considered.

The information in this chapter supports the following family-school-community partnership standards. These standards are reviewed in Chapter 2.

NAEYC Standards and Associated Key Elements	1b, 1c, 2a, 2b, 2c, 3b, 3c, 4b, 6a, 6c, 6d, 6e
ACEI Standards	1.0, 3.2, 5.1, 5.2
PTA Standards	1, 2, 3, 4, 5, 6

This comprehensive approach to family involvement is best reflected in the *family-school-community partnership model* developed by Joyce Epstein (2011) and her colleagues (Epstein et al., 2002). As its title suggests, three "overlapping spheres of influence" (p. 43) form the core of Epstein's model (2011) and highlight how important it is for the family (one sphere), the school (a second sphere), and the community (the third sphere) to work together to support children's development and education (see FYI 2.1).

FYI 2.1   Overlapping Family, School, and Community Spheres

Families' structures and resources, schools' policies and curricula, and communities' social capacity and strength of neighborhood connections are just a few examples of how all three spheres can influence family involvement planning and outcomes.

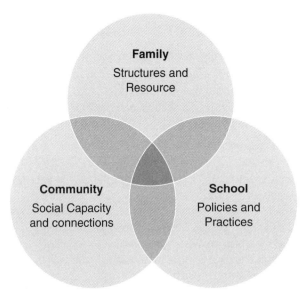

- Maximum overlap among the three spheres occurs when there is a true partnership that reflects frequent family-school-community communication and program planning that is responsive to the needs of all families and children (Epstein, 2011, p. 33). In contrast, the spheres minimally overlap when families, school, and communities operate with very little communication and mutual planning.
- The three spheres never completely overlap because families, schools, and communities each maintain their own unique functions and practices (Epstein, 2011, p. 33). At the same time, the boundaries among the three spheres remain permeable enough to facilitate communication and cooperation (Epstein, 2011, p. 69).

A comprehensive family-school-community plan includes six partnerships, each of which includes multiple activities that are responsive to the needs and interests of all families (see Epstein, 2011, pp. 33, 46, 577; Epstein et al., 2002, pp. 12–17). A review of these six partnerships follows.

Parenting

As a teacher, you can support the parenting partnership in numerous ways. To begin, make yourself available to listen to parents' concerns. We repeatedly return to this theme, especially in Chapter 10. After listening to parents' concerns, take action by providing them with information obtained from professional sources. Mechanisms for this communication include tip sheets (Chapter 3), parent education workshops and family support groups (Chapter 11), home visits (Chapter 12), and informal conversations (Chapter 13).

Another way to support the parenting partnership is to respect parents for who they are, not as you would like them to be. Typically, this means being patient and adapting to parents' personalities, which at times may seem aloof or demanding. Also make exceptions. Because each parent is unique, it is unrealistic to believe you can treat them all equally. Rather, it is more realistic to treat parents fairly. For example, you may be asked to accommodate the requests of a parent whose child has special needs. Flexibility in responding to such requests is vital in creating a classroom environment where parents trust you to have their best interest at heart. Practice implementing this suggestion by completing Reflection 2.1.

REFLECTION 2.1   Making Exceptions for Individual Differences

Describe a situation where you might need to alter a classroom rule, procedure, or activity to accommodate a family's unique needs.

Communicating

One hallmark of any family-teacher partnership is the exchange of honest and courteous communication. This explains the importance of three basic communication rules. First and most important, keep the information that families share with you confidential. Second, attend to families' verbal and written requests in a timely fashion. Finally, rely on multiple informal and formal communication strategies, such as those reviewed in Chapters 6, 10, and 13. Also attend to the communication needs of non-English-speaking families, such as those reviewed in Chapters 8, 9, and 10.

Volunteering

Volunteering is perhaps the most traditional of all family-school-community partnerships. In the past, parents volunteered primarily to help with bake sales and classroom celebrations. These activities are still important today, but the idea of volunteering has also expanded to include many other roles (Chapter 14). In Chapter 10, you will learn how to use a family survey to access family volunteer interests. We also briefly examine how parent volunteers can support a family resource center (Chapter 11) and classroom newsletter (Chapter 13).

Learning at Home

Traditionally, learning at home has been defined as parents helping children with their homework. Today, popular supports for learning at home include family backpacks, activity cards, and activity calendars. You will learn how to develop and manage these strategies in Chapter 3. In Chapter 4, you will learn how parents mediate children's learning. In addition, you will learn how to use activity folders in Chapter 11. For now, it is sufficient to note that all these examples have the dual purpose of keeping families informed about and actively involved in classroom learning objectives.

Decision Making

This is another partnership that, though dominated by schools in the past, today emphasizes parent-teacher collaboration. In some cases, this collaboration may include parents' serving on school advisory councils. It also includes teachers' helping parents from all backgrounds to advocate measures designed to meet their children's developmental and educational needs. For example, a central theme in Chapters 5 and 6 is the importance of showing respect for and seeking input from normed, emerging, and vulnerable families. In Chapter 7 you will learn how to work with families whose children have special needs. The information presented in Chapters 8 and 9 prepare you to engage families from nondominant cultures. Finally, as already noted, strategies for facilitating parents' active participation in parent-teacher conferences are reviewed in Chapter 13.

In all the above situations, joint parent-teacher decision making requires teachers to provide families with sufficient and appropriate information about a range of educational issues (Kaczmarek, Goldstein, Florey, Carter, & Cannon, 2004). To this end, some teachers develop a resource file like the one associated with at least one of the Capstone Activities at the end of each chapter of this textbook. Materials you place in your teacher resource file can in turn be shared with parents to support the decision-making process. Materials for your resource file can come from many different sources. Examples include articles from professional publications and websites as well as handouts from in-service workshops. Also remember to use your community scan to gather information about resources in your local area.

Collaborating With the Community

This final family-school-community partnership acknowledges that it is important for schools to join with other community agencies to meet the needs of children and their families. For example, most communities host one or more events where teachers can make themselves available to answer parents' questions about their children's development and education. You will have an opportunity to design a community event at the end of this chapter (see Community of Learners' Field Assignment). The Field Assignments and Capstone Activities in upcoming chapters are likewise designed to facilitate your engagement with different segments of the community.

Epstein also encourages teachers to assume a global perspective of collaboration that reflects the increasing economic and social ties among communities, states, and countries. For example, you might pursue a national collaborative partnership by tying classroom service learning projects to national emergency organizations that work with families impacted by natural disasters. For now, try your hand at applying the above six partnerships by completing Reflection 2.2.

REFLECTION 2.2   Redefining Traditional Family Involvement Strategies and Activities

Epstein (2011) and her colleagues (Epstein et al., 2002) encourage teachers to update traditional ideas about family involvement activities so they reflect contemporary family lives. Try your hand at updating the following activities.

Epstein's Family Involvement Partnerships	An Example of a Traditional Activity Associated With This Partnership	My Idea for an Alternative Activity That Would Be Meaningful to Families Today
Parenting: Assisting families with parenting and child rearing skills in support of children's development and education.	The teacher informs parents of the rules children are expected to follow in the classroom.	
Communicating: Promoting communication between families and teachers about children's educational progress.	The teacher sends home report cards.	
Volunteering: Recruiting families' assistance in support of children's education.	The teacher asks parents to make cupcakes for classroom birthday parties.	
Learning at Home: Engaging families in their children's learning experiences at home.	The teacher asks parents to help their children with their homework.	
Decision Making: Involving families in making decisions about school operations.	The teacher provides parents with membership forms for a parent-teacher organization.	
Collaborating With the Community: Coordinating families' access to community services that promote the total well-being of children.	The teacher sends parents a brochure about services provided by the community health department.	

Reality Checks: Developing a Positive Mind-Set

While disagreements between families and teachers can at times challenge the family-teacher partnership, they are not insurmountable. This reality check is useful in developing the philosophy that disagreements with families, rather than being something to avoid, can be resolved in a respectful manner. Other reality checks for guiding your development of a family involvement philosophy are reviewed in this section.

Teachers have the professional responsibility to reach out to all families.

Reality Check #1: Be proactive in reaching out to parents

There are at least three reasons why you should take a proactive approach in reaching out to parents rather than waiting for them to reach out to you. First, not all parents feel equally comfortable approaching teachers with questions or offers of assistance. Second, hectic work and family schedules may prevent families from reaching out to you. Finally, assuming a proactive stance in working with families is in keeping with professional standards (Copple & Bredekamp, 2009).

Reality Check #2: Teachers need not give up their own family values in order to respect the family values of others

There may be times when you disagree with a family's life priorities or behavior. For example, you may question why a husband and wife are having a second child when they are having financial difficulty raising just one child. You may also question why same-sex partners are allowed to adopt children. Adopting a philosophy that separates your personal values and beliefs from your professional responsibilities is essential if you are to work effectively with families whose lives differ from your own. One way to do this is to consult with colleagues about their approach to working with families from different backgrounds. Also make use of professional websites, books, and journals to seek objective information about the different family structures and behaviors represented in your classroom. In this textbook, we address different family living arrangements in Chapters 5 and 6. We address family cultural diversity in Chapters 8 and 9.

Reality Check #3: Look for family strengths rather than challenges

Teachers that make use of the family-school-partnership model look for opportunities to reinforce and make use of family strengths (Sheridan, Warnes, Cowan, Schemm, & Clarke,

2004). For example, teachers sometimes display drawings and posters in their classrooms to reinforce the cohesion that exists across diverse families. Another strategy is to develop activities that allow families themselves to celebrate their strengths (see Reflection 2.3). Focusing on family strengths has two practical implications (Sheridan et al., 2004). First, it helps you avoid the negative stereotypes sometimes associated with nontraditional families. Second, being alert to parents' hobbies, skills, and life experiences can help you plan classroom lessons that enrich children's lives. Consider, for example, Case Study 2.1.

REFLECTION 2.3   Celebrate Your Family's Strength

Design a banner or write a short song or poem that celebrates a strength associated with your own family. You may choose to use your childhood family or your current family for this activity. You may want to consider using this activity in your own classroom as a way to help families celebrate their strengths.

CASE STUDY 2.1   Juan

Juan, the father of Marc, owns his own lawn care business. Marc's teacher invites Juan to share his work with Marc's class as part of their unit on community workers. Juan is at first resistant but agrees to the teacher's request after she points out the usefulness of his work and the joy Marc will experience in seeing his father teach the class. The teacher helps Juan prepare a 10-minute presentation on planting a flower bed. His presentation is a big success, and he agrees to visit the classroom again to show the children how he cares for plants. What lessons about looking for family strengths are to be learned from this case study?

Reality Check #4: There is diversity within diversity

As you will discover later in this chapter, understanding and planning for family diversity is a central theme in the standards set by professional organizations. It is equally important to remember that there is diversity within diversity. This applies to both cultural and family structural diversity. For example, while most individuals believe that children living in traditional two-parent families have an advantage over children living in other family arrangements, this is not always true, as noted in the following quote: "Family structure in itself is not predictive of parenting quality" (Pryor, 2004, p. 124).

Before continuing, practice debunking stereotypes about family lives by completing Reflection 2.4.

REFLECTION 2.4   Debunking Stereotypes

- Describe a situation in which the family climate of a single-parent family might be better for a child than the family climate of a two-parent family.
- Describe a situation in which the family climate of a family living in poverty might be more supportive of a child than the family climate of a high-income family.

Reality Check #5: Family involvement requires planning

Because of the proactive stance taken toward family involvement today, it is important that teachers take time to reexamine traditional assumptions about how best to plan for family participation inside and outside the classroom. Some of the assumptions that distinguish traditional from contemporary family involvement planning are presented in FYI 2.2.

FYI 2.2 Traditional and Contemporary Planning Assumptions Associated With Family Involvement	
Traditional Planning Assumptions	**Contemporary Planning Assumptions**
All families will attend each activity that I plan.	Families will attend only those activities that are of interest to them.
Only families with a certain level of education have the skills to help me plan family involvement activities.	All families, regardless of their background, can help me plan family involvement activities.
Two family-teacher conferences per year are sufficient.	It is important that I communicate with families about their children's classroom performance on an ongoing basis.
I will plan a family involvement activity whenever I feel it is needed.	I will plan family involvement activities throughout the year.
Planning a family involvement activity takes very little time.	Planning a family activity requires me to answer a number of questions: Why am I offering this activity? Will it be interesting to all the families represented in my classroom? How will I explain the link between the activity and classroom learning objectives? Where and when will the activity be conducted? What resources do I need to carry out the activity?
I must lead all family involvement activities.	I can join with other teachers and community professionals to provide a range of family involvement activities.

Reality Check #6: Reinforce families' efforts, not their successes

Rewarding only those families who directly participate in classroom activities sends a message that only this type of contribution is noteworthy. Such a selective reinforcement of family involvement can create feelings of anger, resentment, and failure among families who are unable to meet such a narrowly defined criterion. A more useful approach is to reinforce the efforts of all families, no matter how small those efforts may be. Reinforcing family efforts rather than narrowly defined successes helps to empower families who, in turn, are more likely to communicate with teachers and remain involved in their children's learning experiences. You will be introduced to strategies for reinforcing family efforts in Chapter 11.

Reality Check #7: Families care

At times you may hear teachers complain that some families do not care about their children's education—otherwise they would keep in better contact, return assignments, and volunteer to help in the classroom. To avoid this cynical mind-set, it is important to remember how the school environment can influence families' motivation to work with teachers. For example, **school discourse** refers to the language, materials, norms, expectations, and practices used by teachers on a daily basis (Souto-Manning & Swick, 2006). Unfortunately, not all families are equally adept at understanding school discourse. For example, families with a limited education may feel unprepared to talk with teachers about their children's learning experiences or needs (Van Velsor & Orozco, 2007). In contrast, highly educated parents are more likely to understand school discourse and, as a result, obtain educational advantages for their children. Meanwhile, children of less savvy parents are left with relatively few advantages (Muscott et al., 2008).

As a teacher, it is important that you take a proactive stance in explaining school discourse to families. The family handbook represents one way to do this. A description of how to develop a family handbook can be found on the Family Involvement Portfolio page of the student study site that accompanies this textbook. Other opportunities for sharing school discourse with families include family orientation meetings at the beginning of the school year (Chapter 12), parent-teacher conferences (Chapter 13), and family workshops (Chapter 11).

Reality Check #8: Begin small when first planning a family involvement program

The importance of this reality check is based on the fact that teachers who plan too many or unrealistic family involvement activities ultimately feel overwhelmed or, even worse, experience disappointing results. One way to make immediate use of Reality Check #8 is to avoid the feeling that you must implement all the strategies presented in this textbook. Instead, follow two rules of thumb: First, match your selection of family involvement activities to your family involvement philosophy. Second, select family involvement activities that can be realistically supported by the resources available to you and that reflect the interests and needs of families represented in your particular classroom. These issues are addressed in Chapters 10 and 14.

An Overview of National Programs and Policies Influencing Family Involvement

In this section we review national programs, reports, and policies that have influenced family involvement philosophies and practices over the past century.

1912 – The Federal Children's Bureau

The **Federal Children's Bureau** was originally proposed during the first White House Conference on Children in 1909 (Child Welfare League of America, n.d.). It had one purpose: to collect and disseminate information that would in turn assist individuals and communities in taking action to address the needs of children (Perkins, 1937, pp. 1–2). Today, many different government-sponsored programs provide not only information but also direct services to children and their families.

1933 – The Works Progress Administration (WPA)

The **Works Progress Administration** was a government agency established during the great depression to provide jobs for the unemployed. One aspect of the WPA was the establishment of nursery schools and the employment of teachers (White & Coleman, 2000, p. 40). WPA nursery schools represented one of the first federally sponsored programs that focused on providing community-based services for families and children living under economic stress.

1941 – The Lanham Act

The **Lanham Act** provided funding for child care programs for mothers who entered the workforce during World War II to support the war (Garwood, Phillips, Hartman, & Zigler, 1989). Like the WPA nursery schools, the Lanham Act expanded the government's role in linking family needs to community needs.

1965 – The Head Start Program

The **Head Start** program was created as part of President Lyndon Johnson's war on poverty. The purpose of Head Start was and is to promote school readiness among low-income preschool children. Some of the other services coordinated by Head Start programs include parent education, nutrition, and medical care. Parents also are involved in the administration of local Head Start programs. Together, all these characteristics reflect an early endorsement of the family-school-community partnership model.

1975 – The Education for All Handicapped Children Act

Operating under the auspices of the U.S. Department of Education (2009), the **Education for All Handicapped Children Act** required teachers to join with parents and community professionals to design lessons and classroom environments accommodating the needs of children with disabilities. You will learn more about the contemporary version of this act in Chapter 7.

1983 – *A Nation at Risk*

The key theme in the report ***A Nation at Risk*** was that the public schools were failing to prepare children for productive lives in the new world economy (U.S. Department of Education, National Commission on Excellence in Education, 1983). A number of recommendations were made to strengthen education, primarily dealing with curriculum, administration, and teacher preparation issues. Only at the end of the report was "a word to parents" issued that asked them to support their children's education.

1994 – Goals 2000: Educate America Act

The **Goals 2000: Educate America Act** was a natural progression of the *Nation at Risk* report. As its title implies, Goals 2000 set eight national goals for schools to meet by the year 2000. With grants to states from the federal government, schools were to develop standards, assessments, and accountability systems that would reform the American educational system (Superfine, 2005). Significantly, Goals 2000 went beyond addressing the responsibilities of teachers and schools to also address parents. In particular, Standard 8: Parental Participation read, "By the year 2000, every school will promote partnerships that will increase parental involvement and participation in promoting the social, emotional, and academic growth of children" (U.S. Department of Education, National Goals Education Panel, 1997, p. xvii).

2002 – The No Child Left Behind Act (NCLB)

The **No Child Left Behind Act** (No Child Left Behind Act of 2001, 2002) replaced Goals 2000 and, having undergone some refinements since its passage (see Spellings, 2007), continues as the major federal policy guiding American public school education.

One significant aspect of NCLB is that it defines specific requirements for ensuring that families are involved in their children's education. Some examples follow (No Child Left Behind Act of 2001, 2002; U.S. Department of Education, 2003).

- School are to develop a written parent involvement policy.
- Schools are to provide parents with frequent reports about their children's academic progress, at least one of which must include a parent-teacher meeting.
- Schools are to involve parents in the planning, review, and improvement of family involvement programs.
- Schools are to provide parents and teachers with materials and training that will allow them to work together on behalf of children's education.

2010 – Schools as Community Centers

Under the Obama administration, there is a renewed focus on not just family involvement but also implementation of **schools as community centers**—what some refer to as *full-service schools* or *community schools*. Examples of specific services and programs provided by full-service schools will be discussed later in this chapter. For now, it is sufficient to note that the goal of these schools is to provide children and their families with a comprehensive set of educational, welfare, health, and recreational services throughout the school day, into the evening, and on weekends (Dryfoos & Maguire, 2002, pp. 10–13, 20–21; Parson, 2004, pp. 10–11).

One goal of full-service schools is to make it easier for children and families to have all their needs met in one setting. Another goal is to make it easier for community professionals to work closely together to address child and family needs and challenges, some of which can be complex. The justification behind expanding the presence of full-service schools is best explained in a speech delivered by Secretary of Education Arne Duncan (2010):

The fact is that it takes more than a school to educate a student. It takes a city. It takes a community that can provide support from the parks department, health services, law enforcement, social services, after-school programs, nonprofits, businesses, and churches. We can only turn around the worst performing schools with an all-hands-on-deck approach in the local community.

I'd like to see public schools open 12, 13, 14 hours a day, year-round, offering not just mentoring and tutoring programs but art, chess, family literacy nights, debate teams, and GED and ESL programs for parents.

No doubt, the family-school-community partnership emphasized in this speech will become increasingly important as states move forward in adopting President Obama's call for a national set of educational standards, collectively referred to as "Race to the Top." This "race" will also need to consider the professional standards that guide family involvement practices.

National Standards Guiding Family Involvement

The information in this textbook reflects the family-school-community partnership standards of three organizations: (a) the National Association for the Education of Young Children (NAEYC), (b) the Association for Childhood Education International (ACEI), and (c) the National Parent Teacher Association (PTA). The standards relevant to family-school-community partnerships are summarized in this section. Some of these standards also appear at the beginning of each chapter to summarize its professional content.

National Association for the Education of Young Children (NAEYC) Teacher Training Standards

NAEYC is a member of the National Council for Accreditation of Teacher Education (NCATE), the organization that accredits teacher training programs at institutions of higher education in the United States. NCATE uses NAEYC professional preparation standards as part of its accreditation process. Brief adaptations of NAEYC's six teacher training standards follow, along with the "key elements" that directly or indirectly support family-school-community partnerships (Lutton & Ahmed, 2009; NAEYC, 2009). The entire NAEYC position statement can be found online at the following website: www.naeyc.org/files/naeyc/file/positions/ ProfPrepStandards09.pdf. The standards are reprinted with permission from the National Association for the Education of Young Children (NAEYC). www.naeyc.org.

Standard 1: Promoting child development and learning. Teacher candidates are grounded in child development knowledge and the application of that knowledge to early childhood learning environments. This includes understanding how development and learning are influenced by things such as cultural context, the economic conditions of families, and family characteristics (Key Element 1b). Candidates use their knowledge of the whole child to design age-appropriate learning environments that promote children's health and safety and are respectful of children's cultures, abilities and disabilities, families, and communities (Key Element 1c).

Standard 2: Building family and community relationships. Teacher candidates are provided with a knowledge of family theory and research that allows them to understand family structures and relationships (Key Element 2a). They know how to build positive relationships and communicate with families, including those whose children have disabilities or special characteristics. They also assist families in identifying and using community resources (Key Element 2b). Finally, candidates know how to employ family involvement strategies that go beyond parent-teacher conferences. They modify those strategies to engage all families (Key Element 2c).

Standard 3: Observing, documenting, and assessing to support young children and families. Teacher candidates involve family members and community professionals in assessing children's development, strengths, and needs. They know how to communicate with families and colleagues from other disciplines about their observations and assessments (Key Element 3b). Candidates use their observations of children in the classroom, at home, and in the community to develop a broad sense of children as individuals and family members (Key Element 3c).

Standard 4: Using developmentally effective approaches to connect with children and families. Teacher candidates develop the cultural competence needed to develop respectful relationships with children and families whose cultures and languages are different from their own, as well as with children who have developmental delays, disabilities, or other learning challenges. They know the cultural practices and context of the children they teach and maintain continuity between children's home and classroom lives (Key Element 4b). For example, they link children's language and culture to the early childhood program (Key Element 4c).

Standard 5: Using content knowledge to build meaningful curriculum. Teacher candidates use their knowledge of academic disciplines, appropriate learning standards, and other resources to design, implement, and evaluate meaningful and challenging curricula for each child. They recognize that every child constructs knowledge in personally and culturally familiar ways. Subsequently, their curricula address developmental delays or disabilities as well as cultural and linguistic diversities (Key Element 5c).

Standard 6: Becoming a professional. Teacher candidates know about the connections between the early childhood field and other related disciplines and professionals with whom they may collaborate as teachers (Key Element 6a). They learn about relevant laws related to child abuse and disabilities (Key Element 6b). They learn how to collaborate with colleagues and other community professionals to exchange ideas and address challenges (Key Element 6c). Candidates show evidence of reflective approaches that allow them to modify or improve their work; they also demonstrate a tolerance for respectful questioning and dialogue concerning professional issues (Key Element 6d). Finally, candidates are able to advocate on behalf of children, families, and the teaching profession (Key Element 6e).

Additional NAEYC Publications Addressing Family Involvement

Three additional NAEYC publications also address family-school-community partnership issues. Because of space constraints, brief summaries follow, accompanied by links or reference citations for these publications. You will have an opportunity to examine one of them in greater detail at the end of this chapter (see Capstone Activity 1).

NAEYC code of ethical conduct and statement of commitment. This position statement highlights teachers' ethical responsibilities to children, families, colleagues, and communities (NAEYC, 2005) and is endorsed by the Association for the Education of Children International. Nine "ideals" and 15 "principles" address teachers' ethical partnerships with families, which, as NAEYC notes, may include adults other than parents who are involved in educating, nurturing, and advocating on behalf of children. Eight ideals and 13 principles address teachers' responsibilities to communities and society. These two sections are presented in Appendix A. The entire position statement can be found at the following website: http://faculty.weber.edu/tlday/2610/code05.pdf.

Developmentally appropriate practices. This well-known book sets criteria for the delivery of quality care and education for children, and includes examples of appropriate versus inappropriate parent-teacher relationship practices (see Copple & Bredekamp, 2009).

NAEYC early childhood program standards and accreditation criteria. This publication consists of 10 standards for early childhood programs (infancy through kindergarten) seeking accreditation through NAEYC (NAEYC, 2007). Two standards are specifically relevant to teachers' work with families and communities (Standards 7 and 8, respectively). The publication can be found at the following website: https://oldweb.naeyc.org/accreditation/Standardscriteria/default.asp.

Association for Childhood Education International (ACEI)

Like NAEYC, ACEI is a member of NCATE. NCATE also uses ACEI standards as part of its accreditation of elementary teacher education programs located at institutions of higher education. ACEI standards are divided into five sections: (a) development, learning, and motivation, (b) curriculum, (c) instruction, (d) assessment, and (e) professionalism. Below, you will find summaries of the standards related to the family-school-community partnerships issues addressed in this textbook (ACEI, 2007). A complete listing of all ACEI standards can be found at the following website: www.acei.org/images/stories/documents/ACEI ElementaryStandardsSupportingExplanation.5.07.pdf.

Development, Learning, and Motivation: Standard 1.0—Development, learning, and motivation. "Candidates know, understand, and use the major concepts, principles, theories, and research related to development of children and young adolescents to construct learning opportunities that support individual students' development, acquisition of knowledge, and motivation." They understand the ways in which cultures differ, consider diversity an asset, and respond positively to it. Candidates also recognize individual differences and collaborate with specialists to plan appropriate learning experiences that address individual needs.

Curriculum: Standard 2.6—Health education. "Candidates know, understand, and use the major concepts in the subject matter of health education to create opportunities for student development and practice of skills that contribute to good health." They keep up to date on major health issues concerning children.

Curriculum: Standard 2.7—Physical education. "Candidates know, understand, and use—as appropriate to their own understanding and skills—human movement and physical activity as central elements to foster active, healthy life styles and enhanced quality of life for elementary students." They recognize physical inactivity as a major health risk and help students maintain a health-enhancing level of physical fitness.

Instruction: Standard 3.2—Adaptation to diverse students. "Candidates understand how elementary students differ in their development and approaches to learning, and create instructional opportunities that are adapted to diverse students." Teacher candidates understand different learning styles. They also know that learning is influenced by individual experiences, talents, disabilities, and cultural, family, and community values. Candidates understand the importance of collaborating with school and community specialists, as well as with families, to address students' exceptional learning needs.

Assessment: Standard 4.0—Assessment for instruction. "Candidates know, understand, and use formal and informal assessment strategies to plan, evaluate and strengthen instruction that will promote continuous intellectual, social, emotional, and physical development of each elementary student." They use a variety of formal and informal assessment techniques (e.g., observations, portfolios, teacher-made tests, projects, and standardized tests). They modify their teaching and learning strategies and collaborate with specialists on accommodating the needs of students with exceptionalities.

Professionalism: Standard 5.1—Professional growth, reflection, and evaluation. "Candidates are aware of and reflect on their practice in light of research on teaching, professional ethics, and resources available for professional learning; they continually evaluate the effects of their professional decisions and actions on students, families and other professionals in the learning community and actively seek out opportunities to grow professionally."

Professionalism: Standard 5.2—Collaboration with families, colleagues, and community agencies. "Candidates know the importance of establishing and maintaining a positive collaborative relationship with families, school colleagues, and agencies in the larger community to promote the intellectual, social, emotional, physical growth and well-being of children." They understand different cultural beliefs, traditions, values, and practices. They involve families as partners inside and outside the classroom. They also understand that schools operate within a larger community.

National Parent Teacher Association (PTA)

The National PTA serves as a voice for parents and families. To this end, the PTA has developed the following six national standards for family-school-community partnerships (National PTA, 2009). A resource page devoted to these standards can be found at the following website: Adaptation of National Standards for Family-School Partnerships. http://www.pta.org/national_standards.asp.

Standard one: Welcoming all families into the school community. "Families are active participants in the life of the school, and feel welcomed, valued, and connected to each other, to school staff, and to what students are learning and doing in class."

Standard two: Communicating effectively. "Families and school staff engage in regular, two-way, meaningful communication about student learning."

Standard three: Supporting student success. "Families and school staff continuously collaborate to support students' learning and healthy development both at home and at school, and have regular opportunities to strengthen their knowledge and skills to do so effectively."

Standard four: Speaking up for every child. "Families are empowered to be advocates for their own and other children, to ensure that students are treated fairly and have access to learning opportunities that will support their success."

Standard five: Sharing power. "Families and school staff are equal partners in decisions that affect children and families and together inform, influence, and create policies, practices, and programs."

Standard six: Collaborating with community: "Families and school staff collaborate with community members to connect students, families, and staff to expanded learning opportunities, community services, and civic participation."

The standards reviewed in this section provide another source of support in writing your family involvement philosophy. The following section represents a final source of support.

Goals of Family Involvement

The following goals and objectives provide a framework for addressing family involvement at any grade level. As a teacher, your task will be to decide which goal or goals are most helpful in guiding the development of your own family involvement philosophy. You will be guided through this process in the last section of this chapter.

Goal #1: Supporting Children's Education

Most individuals who pursue a teaching career do so because they want to help children acquire the knowledge and skills needed to lead productive and happy lives. One way to achieve this goal is to adopt one or more of the following family involvement objectives.

Objective: To share information. Parents and teachers support children's development and education when they share information about children's learning experiences, social interactions, daily routines, and changes in health status. Likewise, it is important that parents inform teachers about their children's accomplishments, strengths, and challenges that are observed at home (Moseman, 2003).

Objective: To link children's classroom and home learning experiences. Such links make it easier for children to not only master new skills but to transfer those skills to different parts of their world. As noted earlier in this chapter, you will be introduced to a number of strategies for achieving this objective later in this textbook.

Objective: To keep families informed about current childhood issues. As also noted earlier, you can support parents in their role as teachers by summarizing the professional information you receive through professional publications, in-service trainings, and conferences.

Goal #2: Linking Children and Families to Community Resources

You no doubt remember that the family-school-community model requires teachers to address not only the needs of children but also their families. Fortunately, urban and rural communities alike contain a number of professionals who are available to support families. Some objectives associated with this goal include the following.

Objective: To use community workers to promote child and family well-being. Some examples of how you can use community professionals to address family concerns, conduct family workshops, and develop informational materials are presented in FYI 2.3.

FYI 2.3   Using Community Workers to Address Family Concerns

Community Workers	Things They Can Do for Families
Doctors	− Explain why childhood physicals are important − Explain why certain screenings are performed at different ages − Answer questions about childhood illnesses
Nurses	− Explain how children's bodies work − Explain how to carry out CPR and first aid techniques − Explain how to prevent common childhood illnesses
Dentists	− Explain how children's teeth develop − Answer questions about common childhood dental problems
Dental Hygienists	− Show children how to properly brush their teeth − Explain how to select toothpaste − Explain how to handle a toothache
Ophthalmologists	− Answer questions about common childhood eye problems − Explain what steps to take to protect children's eyes − Explain common terms used during an eye exam
Nutritionists	− Explain the food pyramid for children − Give examples of healthy snacks children enjoy − Explain pitfalls to avoid when eating out with children
Housing Specialists	− Explain how to weatherproof one's home − Explain how to ensure home safety − Explain how to conduct simple, cheap home repairs

Physical Therapists	– Answer questions about common childhood injuries – Explain how to treat sore muscles – Help children appropriately interact with someone with a physical disability
Emergency Paramedics	– Teach children when and how to make 911 calls – Explain how to develop a home emergency medical kit – Teach children about car safety
Garbage Collectors	– Explain recycling techniques – Teach children about where their garbage goes
Safety Inspectors	– Explain how to check the safety of home playground equipment – Explain proper mulching under swings and slides – Explain how to weatherproof outdoor equipment
Pharmacists	– Answer questions about common childhood medications – Provide information on common side effects of popular childhood medications – Explain how to prevent or respond to childhood poisoning
Librarians	– Suggest books on different topics of interest to children – Explain how to help children get the most out of their reading experiences – Help children make their own books
Police Officers	– Teach children about pedestrian safety – Help children understand that police officers are their friends – Teach children how to respond to strangers
Counselors	– Explain how to help children deal with their emotions – Provide understanding regarding how children display their thoughts and feelings verbally, behaviorally, and in their artwork – Give positive child guidance strategies
Family Life Educators	– Explain how to build strong families – Explain how to communicate effectively with other family members – Explain how to plan successful family events and vacations
Firefighters	– Explain how to prevent a home fire – Explain how to develop and practice a home fire escape plan – Explain when and how to put out small home fires

SOURCE: Adapted from Wallinga, C., Coleman, M., & Bales, D. (2007).

Objective: To introduce children to community life. Inviting community workers to class is one popular strategy for helping children learn about being good community citizens. To make these visits a success, invite each community worker to eat lunch with children or informally participate in some other activity before making their presentation. Children are more likely to listen to and focus on the message a community worker delivers when they have a relationship with that person (Kourofsky & Cole, 2010).

Objective: To provide advocacy. As reflected in Epstein's model, teachers also serve as community resources. In particular, you are in a position to advocate for children and families who are unable to advocate for themselves. Advocacy is not as complicated as it sounds. The most basic requirements include (a) having a genuine desire to help push for positive change in the lives of children, families, and communities, (b) keeping oneself informed about issues of importance to children, families, and communities, (c) building relationships with others to bring about change, and (d) taking action through letter writing, emails, telephone calls, and other communication strategies to deliver your message (Royea & Appl, 2009). A few simple strategies follow that many teachers use to meet these requirements:

- Keep families up to date about changes in school policies and practices.
- Participate in annual Week of the Young Child events.
- Join your local or state early childhood professional organization.

Goal #3: Building Human Capital

The purpose of this family involvement goal is to promote children's full potential (see Chapter 1). The goal of building human capital is perhaps best reflected in the emergence of full-service schools, which we reviewed earlier in this chapter. The logistics and services associated with full-service schools vary depending on the types of links that exist between community agencies, the availability of space and trained community workers, and the ease of scheduling service delivery.

Objective: Addressing children's needs. Examples of full-service programs that address children's needs include school-based after-school programs, health clinics, individual and group counseling, developmental assessments, and enrichment programs that focus on the arts, foreign languages, or other subjects that may receive little attention during the typical classroom day.

Objective: Addressing parents' needs. Examples of full-service programs that address parents' needs include literacy classes, job skills training, job fairs, computer and math classes, immigration information, mental health counseling, nutritional counseling, and medical services.

Sometimes the needs of children and their families can be combined. Consider, for example, one truancy intervention project that sponsored of a free "Back to School Day" at a city zoo (Markiewicz, 2008). This event served multiple purposes, including providing children with backpacks filled with school supplies, encouraging parents to send their children to school and to get them to school on time, and helping parents address health, legal, and other challenges that might interfere with children's school attendance.

Now that you have finished reading this section, think about which of the preceding family involvement goals and objectives are most appealing to you. You may find such reflection helpful as you learn how to write a draft of your family involvement philosophy.

Steps for Writing a First Draft of Your Family Involvement Philosophy

As noted at the beginning of this chapter, your philosophy statement will serve multiple purposes. To elaborate, it will (a) demonstrate your commitment to and understanding of families, (b) serve as a guide as you develop your family involvement program, and (c) serve to justify the actions you take on behalf of children and their families. *Remember, this is only a draft.* You will want to keep revising your draft as your read upcoming chapters and gain additional insight into family lives and family-teacher partnerships. Likewise, you will want to keep revising your philosophy statement throughout your career as you gain direct experience in working with families. Here are a few steps to follow in writing your first draft.

Your family involvement philosophy statement will serve multiple purposes.

Step 1. Reflect on your definition of family. How did you define family in Chapter 1 (Reflection 1.1)? Is your definition broad enough to meet the reality checks we examined in this chapter?

Step 2. Reflect on the family-school-partnership model. Identify the partnerships of most interest to you. What types of family involvement activities might you tie to these partnerships?

Step 3. Reflect on your understanding of family involvement standards. Identify the professional standards that are most important to you.

Step 4. Reflect on your choice of family involvement goals. Identify the goal(s) and objectives of most interest to you. Do these fit with your previous selection of partnerships (Step 2) and standards (Step 3)?

Step 5. Review examples. Talk to one or more teachers about their philosophies of family involvement (see Capstone Activity 2). You may also which to review the philosophy statement found in Ms. Adams Family Involvement Portfolio on the student study site.

Step 6. Write a family involvement goal statement. Use your notes from the previous steps to write a draft of your family involvement goal. Keep your goal statement brief so you can easily share it with others.

Step 7. Identify the objectives you will use to implement your goal. You may choose to skip this section for now and return to it as you read about specific family involvement strategies in upcoming chapters. In fact, one of the Capstone Activities at the end of each chapter will invite you to revisit your philosophy statement.

CHAPTER SUMMARY

- Writing a philosophy of family involvement can be guided not only by the family-school-community partnership model but also by reality checks, professional standards, and goals for engaging families in their children's education.

DISCUSSION QUESTIONS

1. Identify one family-school-community partnership that you are likely to pursue. Discuss your choice with your peers.

2. Discuss how you and your peers plan to use the reality checks reviewed in this chapter to work with families from different backgrounds.

3. Discuss whether there is one central goal or standard that should be reflected in all family involvement philosophies.

COMMUNITY OF LEARNERS' FIELD ASSIGNMENT

Develop a Plan for Collaborating with the Community

In this assignment, you will pursue the last component of Epstein's model of family-school-community partnerships: collaborating with the community.

Your task. As a class, brainstorm an educational event that you might pursue in collaboration with one or more community agencies. Develop a plan for "collaborating with the community" by addressing the following questions. Share your plan with the other workgroups in your class.

- What will be the title of your event?
- What will be the goal of your event?
- What age group(s) will you serve?
- What activities will you provide that support children's development and education?
- Where will your event be held?
- Describe the roles and responsibilities that teachers and agency personnel will assume in planning and carrying out the event.
- How will you involve families in your event?

CAPSTONE ACTIVITIES

Activity 1: Develop a Personal Code of Ethics Statement

As a class, identify two ethical dilemmas that teachers might face when working with children and families. Discuss how you would handle these dilemmas using the nine NAEYC ideals and 15 principles related to teachers' ethical partnerships with families.

Activity 2: Gather Information About Family Involvement Philosophies

Interview a teacher about her or his family involvement philosophy. Possible questions to ask include the following:

- How would you describe your approach to working with families?
- Has this always been your approach, or have you made changes over the years?
- What do you hope to accomplish through your family involvement activities?

Activity 3: Apply Epstein's Model to a Classroom Service Learning Project

Expand Epstein's "collaborating with the community" by identifying a state, national, or international organization that works on behalf of children and families. Write a brief summary of how you would tie a classroom service learning project involving children and their families to the work being done by this organization. Share your ideas in class. Compile the summaries into a handout. Place your handout in your teacher resource file for future reference.

INTERNET RESOURCES

You may find that some URLs have been altered by the webmaster. In these situations, try entering the name of the document or agency in a search engine. Alternatively, enter the domain name (e.g., http://www.xxxx.org). This should take you to the revised home page and associated links.

National Association for the Education of Young Children (NAEYC)

http://www.naeyc.org/

NAEYC is the world's largest organization working on behalf of the education and development of children from birth to age eight. NAEYC facilitates the professional practices of teachers of young children through conferences, journals, books, and advocacy. The NAEYC website includes a "Families" link. Clicking on this link leads to books, brochures, and other resources families can use to promote their children's development and education.

Association for Childhood Education International (ACEI)

http://www.acei.org/

The global mission of ACEI is to promote and support the education and development of children from birth through early adolescence. This is done through ACEI publications, conferences, grants, and awards.

National Parent Teacher Association (PTA)

http://www.pta.org/

The National PTA is an advocacy agency that works to promote children's education. The national office supports local affiliates through sponsored programs, events, trainings, and publications that advance family involvement policies, practices, and activities.

Johns Hopkins University, National Network of Partnership Schools, Center on School, Family, and Community Partnerships

http://www.csos.jhu.edu/P2000/center.htm

The mission of this center is to conduct and disseminate research and programs to help parents, schools, and communities work together to improve schools, strengthen families, and enhance student learning and development. The Epstein partnership model reviewed in this chapter can be accessed by clicking on the "NNPS" (National Network of Partnership Schools) link and then the "School Model" link. Also click on the Success Stories link to read about family involvement programs based on the Epstein model.

National Parent Information and Resource Center (PICR)

http://nationalpirc.org/

The PIRC, funded by the U.S. Department of Education, is a technical assistance project whose goal is to support policies and programs that increase parent-school collaboration and student achievement. The website provides a link for locating the PIRC contact person in each state.

Head Start

http://www.acf.hhs.gov/programs/ohs/

Visit this site to learn about the mission and purpose of the federal Head Start office as well as the programs it offers.

No Child Left Behind

http://ed.gov/parents/academic/involve/nclbguide/parentsguide.html

The U.S. Department of Education developed this site to provide parents with general information about NCLB and to respond to commonly asked questions.

Child Welfare Information Gateway

http://www.childwelfare.gov/index.cfm

This website is a service of the Children's Bureau, Administration for Children and Families, U.S. Department of Health and Human Services. It promotes the safety and well-being of children and families by connecting community professionals and citizens to timely information about child welfare issues. Click on the link "Family-Centered Practices" to learn about the tasks performed by community child welfare professionals.

National Education Association (NEA)

http://www.nea.org/index.html

The mission of the NEA is to "advocate for education professionals and to unite our members and the nation to fulfill the promise of public education to prepare every student to succeed in a diverse and interdependent world." Visit the NEA website to learn about contemporary topics of interest to teachers.

National Social Work Association (NSWA)

http://www.socialworkers.org/

Click on the link "Children, Youth and Families" to learn about initiatives associated with child welfare and family support. Click on the specialty practice section "School Social Work" to learn about the networking activities of NSWA members who work in educational settings.

Hawaii Department of Education, Parent Community Network Centers (PCNC)

http://familysupport.k12.hi.us/PCNC/PCNC.html

Visit this site to see how the State of Hawaii has incorporated Epstein's partnership model into its family support programming. Click on the "Standards for Parents" link to read about the types of educational support parents themselves helped to develop.

STUDENT STUDY SITE

Log on to the Web-based student study site at **www.sagepub.com/coleman** for additional study tools including

- eFlashcards
- Web Quizzes
- Links to SAGE Journal Articles
- Author-created Videos

- Learning Objectives
- Web Resources
- Family Involvement Portfolio Guides

CHAPTER 3

Benefits of Family Involvement for Children

W hy does family involvement matter? This question has taken on greater importance over the past few decades as more attention has been devoted to involving families in their children's education. In this chapter we review the benefits of family involvement for children.

As you read this chapter, take notes on the following items. Use your notes to address the Reflections, Discussion Questions, Field Assignment, and Capstone Activities that you find in the chapter.

- Explain why it is important for teachers to have an ecological perspective of their work with children and families.
- Explain how family involvement contributes to children's academic achievement.
- Explain the purpose of family backpacks, tip sheets, activity calendars, and activity cards. Summarize the guides for their development.

COMMUNITY LEARNING GUIDE

Bronfenbrenner's Ecological Theory and Family Involvement

Appreciating the benefits associated with family involvement requires us to first take a broad perspective of children's development and education. Indeed, as reflected in Chapters 1 and 2, children's well-being is the responsibility of not just families or schools but also the entire community. Bronfenbrenner's (1979, 2005) ecological model of human development provides us with a lens for appreciating these multiple sources of influence and their interconnections.

The information in this chapter supports the following family-school-community partnership standards. These standards are reviewed in Chapter 2.

NAEYC Standards and Associated Key Elements	1b, 1c, 2a, 2b, 2c, 3b, 3c, 5c, 6a, 6c, 6d, 6e
ACEI Standards	1.0, 3.2, 4.0, 5.1, 5.2
PTA Standards	1, 2, 3, 5, 6

Let's begin with the term *ecology*. When we hear this term, most of us think about the interconnections between plant and animal life that form physical ecosystems such as rivers, mountains, and deserts. Bronfenbrenner (2005) built on this idea to describe a **human ecology** of interacting social systems:

> Over the life course, human development takes place through processes of progressively more complex reciprocal interaction between an active, evolving biopsychological human organism and the persons, objects, and symbols in its immediate external environment. (p. 6)

Reflected in this quote is Bronfenbrenner's belief that children are active players in their development. In short, children both adapt to and influence the interactions that take place around them. For example, children learn to distinguish between the different expectations associated with their home and classroom environments. At the same time, teachers and parents learn how to interact with different children, based on their unique personalities and needs. An abbreviated summary of other ecological principles governing children's development include the following (Bronfenbrenner, 1990, pp. 27–38):

- **Mutual attachment.** In order to develop, a child requires progressive interactions on a regular basis over an extended period of time with one or more persons with whom the child develops a strong, mutual, and emotional attachment.
- **Responsiveness to the environment.** The establishment of progressive interpersonal interactions under conditions of strong mutual attachment promotes a child's responsiveness to other aspects of the physical and social environment. This in turn invites exploration, manipulation, and imagination, all of which accelerate the child's psychological growth.
- **Admiration from a third adult.** Progressively more complex interactions and emotional attachment between a caregiver and child depend on the involvement of another adult who assists, encourages, and gives status to the caregiver engaging in joint activities with the child.
- **Socially supportive exchanges.** Effective child rearing in the family and other settings requires an exchange of information, two-way communication, mutual accommodation, and mutual trust among the settings in which children and their parents participate (home, school, parent's place of work, etc.).
- **Supportive child rearing policies and practices.** Effective child rearing in the family and other settings requires public policies and practices that support child rearing activities not only on the part of parents but also on the part of relatives, neighbors, communities, and economic, social, and political institutions within society.

These principles are reflected in the structure of our human ecology, a summary of which follows.

The Structure of the Human Ecology

Bronfenbrenner (2005) described the structure of the human ecology as taking place within "a series of nested and interconnected structures" (p. 45). These structures include five social systems: the microsystem, the mesosystem, the exosystem, the macrosystem, and the chronosystem. In this section, we briefly review each of these systems and how they support children's development and education (see FYI 3.1). In some cases, educational influences are *proximal*, meaning they have a direct impact on children. Other educational influences are *distal*, meaning their influence on children is more indirect. For example, a parent-teacher conference includes both proximal and distal influences. Proximal influences include the teacher's and parent's conversations with the child about the conference and their following up with assistance in the classroom and at home. Distal influences include the teacher and parent's adherence to a conference schedule set by the school principal and discussion of academic standards set by the state board of education.

FYI 3.1   Supports for Children's Development and Education in the Human Ecology

Microsystem Supports

- Children learn how expectations and rules of behavior change across different microsystems (e.g., home, classroom, youth group).
- Children learn the language and routines associated with different microsystems.
- Children learn new life skills by participating in different microsystems.
- Children observe how individuals interact and treat each other across different microsystems.
- Children learn to apply basic human values, such as honesty and respect, across different microsystems.
- Children learn how to get along with their peers by participating in group activities across different microsystems.

Mesosystem Supports

- Parents and teachers collaborate in sending children consistent messages about their behavior.
- Parents and teachers collaborate in reinforcing similar learning experiences in the classroom and at home.
- Parents, teachers, and other school personnel collaborate in assessing the physical, cognitive, and emotional needs of children.
- Schools collaborate with community agencies to provide children's physical, cognitive, and social-emotional needs.
- Teachers enrich children's education and provide cultural learning experiences by using interactive technologies to cooperate with other teachers within and outside the United States.

Exosystem Supports

- School administrators, as well as teacher and parent groups, work together to plan and implement policies that ensure all children receive a quality education.
- School boards develop educational budgets and policies that take into account the lives of diverse families.
- Communities support the well-being of children and families' through social, health, sanitation, recreational, and protective services. They also offer ongoing cultural and artistic events that enrich human lives and reinforce a sense of community identity.
- Local, state, and federal governments pass legislation that takes into account the diversity of community life.

Macrosystem Supports

- Children receive consistent and positive messages about "American values" and customs through the media, community events, and classroom lessons.
- Children learn to respect the values and customs of all cultures within and outside the classroom and home.
- Children are taught democratic principles through the social studies curriculum, use of respectful behavior management practices, and daily routines such as the morning pledge of allegiance.
- Children are taught about the value of healthy self-expression through literature, dance, art, and music.

The microsystem. The microsystem refers to the social systems closest to children's daily lives. The classroom and home are the most common examples of childhood microsystems. Within these immediate social systems, children are socialized and educated as they interact with and learn from adults and peers. Other microsystems important to children include after-school programs, youth organizations, and religious institutions.

The mesosystem. The mesosystem refers to the number and quality of linkages between children's microsystems. Children's development and education are supported best when there are frequent and strong linkages among their microsystems. For example, our focus on family-school-community partnerships is, primarily, a mesosystem issue. Indeed, the upcoming chapters in this textbook deal with information and practical strategies you can use to strengthen the continuity among children's home, classroom, and community lives. In addition, many of the Community of Learners' Field Assignments and Capstone Activities at the end of each chapter are designed to strengthen various aspects of the family-school-community mesosystem.

The exosystem. So far, we have talked about ecological systems in which children directly participate. In contrast, the exosystem refers to social systems in which children do not participate but that nevertheless influence children's actions. For example, every school sets policies that guide children's daily behavior, schedule, and dress. Yet children themselves have little or no role in establishing these policies.

Other exosystems in which decisions and policies are set without input from children include community agencies, businesses, and the federal government. Community agencies decide what types of services children will receive, when they will be available, and how they will be accessed. The work schedule, pay, and benefits businesses set for parents impact children's quality of life. For example, some businesses are more flexible than others in allowing parents time off to attend parent-teacher conferences. Finally, the federal government establishes policies and programs that, depending on your particular view, benefit or harm children.

The macrosystem. Bronfenbrenner (2005) describes the macrosystem as a "societal blueprint for a particular culture or subculture" (p. 81). Put another way, each culture establishes values and beliefs that govern the priorities of all the previously noted ecological systems. In the United States, we have two predominant macrosystem blueprints. We live under a democratic style of government and we operate as a capitalist society. Thus, rather than being ruled by a monarch, we elect individuals to represent our views in Congress. Likewise, rather than allowing our government total control over our economy, we rely on businesses to produce goods and compete for customers in a free market.

Before leaving the macrosystem, it is important to touch on one additional issue. Although all Americans share the values of democracy and capitalism, we also come from different geographic, religious, and cultural backgrounds. Subsequently, one can argue that nested within our American macrosystem are subculture macrosystems.

The chronosystem. Bronfenbrenner added this social system to his original model to acknowledge that, like physical ecologies, human ecologies change over time. More precisely, in every generation there are events and people that alter the course of history. Likewise, new technology influences the way we behave and work, and new educational research reshapes the way children are taught in the classroom.

Try your hand at assessing our human ecology in relationship to educational issues you may face as a teacher. Complete Case Study 3.1.

CASE STUDY 3.1   Assessing the Human Ecology From a Teacher's Perspective

- In response to the recent recession, some schools have cut art and music programs as a way to save money. What does this exosystem policy say about our American macrosystem?
- As a teacher, how might you compensate for these cuts in the classroom microsystem?
- As a teacher, how might you join with others in your community to create a school-community collaborative project (i.e., school-community mesosystem) to ensure all children have access to art and music during or after school hours?
- How have chronosystem trends addressed in Chapter 1 and Chapter 2 altered the way families and teachers interact today?

Teachers often find the ecological model helpful in thinking about how contemporary educational issues are influenced by school, family, and community links. For example, one group of researchers noted the limitations of current educational policies in relying too heavily on school professionals to ensure children's educational achievement (Whipple, Evans, Barry, & Maxwell, 2010). Taking an ecological perspective, these researchers measured two different types of proximal risks that they believed were associated with student academic performance. The first measure involved elementary school risk factors such as student mobility, teachers' years of experience, and school building conditions. The second measure involved neighborhood risk factors such as proportion of households living in poverty, proportion of single mothers as heads of households, proportion of crowded households, and proportion of vacant buildings. As the researchers predicted, the percentage of students meeting state English and math standards decreased significantly as the number of neighborhood and school risk factors increased. The researchers pointed to this finding as evidence of the range of proximal ecological factors, many outside the control of school professionals, that can impact students' educational performance.

With this brief introduction to ecological theory, we next turn to a review of key research reviews and studies that confirm the power of the home–school mesosystem in promoting children's learning skills and their motivation to do well in the classroom.

Research on the Benefits of Family Involvement

As you will discover in this section, there is ample evidence to reinforce the importance of teachers' working collaboratively with parents on behalf of children's development and education.

Longitudinal Studies: Answers to Four Common Questions

Researchers conducting **longitudinal studies** focus on changes in behavior over time. Findings from a number of longitudinal studies provide answers to the following frequently asked questions about the importance of family involvement.

Does family involvement have a lasting impact on children's academic achievement? A number of studies have explored this question. Perhaps the best known study, the Perry preschool project (PPP), provided preschool educational services to children as well as family support services to parents (Schweinhart, 2005; Schweinhart & Weikart, 1993, 1997). Family services included group meetings and home visits to work with parents on supporting their children's learning skills.

Researchers using the PPP database found that teacher ratings of high maternal involvement during kindergarten were related to more academically motivated children who also displayed more socially appropriate behavior (Luster & McAdoo, 1996). Children's academic motivation in kindergarten was in turn positively related to high academic achievement in the eighth grade, which in turn was associated with higher educational attainment at age 27. Finally, higher educational attainment was associated with higher income at age 27.

A second well-known longitudinal study, the Chicago Child-Parent Center program (CCPC), provided educational services to three- to nine-year-old children, as well as family involvement support to their parents. Children's social adjustment and academic achievement were measured through high school. Family involvement support again was significantly related to short- and long-term positive school achievement (Barnard, 2004; Reynolds, Temple, Robertson, & Mann, 2002), including lower school dropout rates and increased on-time high school completion (Barnard, 2004). In addition, both the frequency and number of CCPC family involvement activities used during preschool and kindergarten were significantly associated with higher reading achievement, lower rates of grade retention, and fewer years in special education up to age 14 (Miedel & Reynolds, 1999).

In another study that spanned kindergarten to fifth grade, children with less educated but highly involved mothers displayed more positive feelings about reading activities over time when compared to children with less involved mothers, regardless of their level of education (Dearing, McCartney, Weiss, Kreider, & Simpkins, 2004). In addition, while there was an achievement gap in the literacy performance of children of more and less educated mothers, in favor of children of mothers with higher levels of education, this gap disappeared between kindergarten and fifth grade if family involvement levels among mothers with lower levels of education were high (Dearing, Kreider, Simpkins, & Weiss, 2006).

Taken together, the above longitudinal studies indicate that early family involvement has the potential to influence children's academic achievement across grades. This finding is important, since administrators are more likely to support family involvement activities if they are given evidence of their beneficial impact on children's academic achievement. With this in mind, the preceding results suggest three reasons why schools should support family involvement programming.

First, the results reinforce the need to support and proactively reach out to all families, regardless of their economic and educational backgrounds (Reality Check #1). Second, the results reflect how parents' commitment to education can be transmitted to their children, perhaps contributing to both their skill development and motivation to do well in the classroom (Reality Check #7). This is a topic we address in further detail in Chapter 4.

Finally, family involvement should be given greater recognition as a mediator in reducing the achievement gap between lower- and higher-income children (Dearing et al., 2006; Haskins & Rouse, 2005). Put another way, rather than viewing family involvement as an extra chore or secondary goal, we should view it as a primary protective factor in counteracting living conditions that have the potential to detract from classroom achievement (Miedel & Reynolds, 1999).

To be effective, must family involvement activities always occur in the classroom? In a study that began with first grade and ended when children reached age 16, family involvement in children's education during the first three years of school was associated with higher math achievement in the sixth grade (Jimerson, Egeland, & Teo, 1999). In addition, a positive association was found between families' creation of a supportive home learning environment and children's improved reading scores in the sixth grade and at age 16 (Jimerson et al., 1999).

Two other researchers looked at the association between home-based family involvement activities and the reading skills of children between kindergarten and third grade (Senechal & LeFevre, 2002). Results of this study showed that children's exposure to storybooks at home while in kindergarten was related to the development of language skills (vocabulary and listening comprehension) in the first grade, which in turn were associated with positive reading skills in the third grade. Likewise, parents' involvement in teaching children about reading and writing during kindergarten was associated with emergent literacy skills in the first grade (knowledge of alphabet, word reading), which in turn were associated with positive reading skills in the third grade.

These findings support the conclusion of other longitudinal studies that home-based educational materials and activities are associated with improvements in children's math scores (Izzo, Weissberg, Kasprow, & Fendrich, 1999; Sheldon & Epstein, 2005) and reading scores (Izzo et al., 1999). Considered collectively, all these studies support the importance of home-based family involvement activities in promoting children's emerging academic skills. Examples of three home-based family involvement strategies that you can use in your work with families are presented later in this chapter.

Can family involvement impact children's classroom behavior? Using survey data collected over the course of a school year, researchers found that schools that offered more opportunities for family involvement reported a lower incidence of student referrals to the principal's office for disciplinary problems, along with a lower incidence of in-school suspensions (Sheldon & Epstein, 2002). The researchers used these findings to reinforce the importance of parent-teacher communication regarding school goals and student behavior.

Interestingly, another study found that indicators of parent involvement as reported by teachers (e.g., parents' attendance at back-to-school meetings or school events, parents' volunteering to help in the classroom, parents' initiation of contact with the teacher to discuss their child's progress) helped to reduce the negative influence of the arrest or incarceration of household members on children's aggressive, hyperactive, and withdrawn behaviors (Ziv, Alva, & Zill, 2010). Although the researchers called for more research on this topic, they nevertheless advocated parental involvement as a strategy for reducing negative socialization risks pertaining to children's home environments.

Can family involvement improve school attendance? Because academic achievement is associated with classroom attendance, a pair of researchers investigated how various school-home communication practices promoted attendance over the course of a school year (Epstein & Sheldon, 2002). They found that communicating with families about school attendance policies and the importance of attendance in advancing a child's learning skills was associated with an improvement in student attendance. In addition, the use of a school contact person to discuss school attendance and to make home visits was linked to a reduction in chronic absenteeism. Indeed, some schools already employ family resource coordinators to facilitate parent-teacher communication, help parents support their children's education at home, and assist families in accessing community resources that address children's developmental and educational needs.

Reviews of Research: Answers to Six Common Questions

Researchers periodically undertake a review of studies to provide a summary of themes associated with a particular body of work. Recent reviews of family involvement research point to a number of positive themes for children, some of which complement those from the longitudinal studies summarized earlier.

A positive association between family involvement and academic achievement holds across race and gender (Jeynes, 2005.) Furthermore, this significant association holds when measured by grades, teacher ratings, and standardized tests (Jeynes, 2005). One conclusion reached by the scholar conducting this review is that family involvement represents an untapped resource for equalizing the academic achievement of children from all racial and ethnic groups.

Family involvement has a stronger association with classroom grades than standardized test scores (Desimone, 1999; Jeynes, 2005). This finding should not be too surprising, since families are more likely to focus their energy on helping children with class assignments and exams personally prepared and explained by teachers than on helping them with standardized tests designed by unknown specialists outside the classroom. In addition, because grades are more dependent on teachers' personal assessments than are standardized tests, greater family involvement is likely to give teachers a more complete picture of children's true skills (Desimone, 1999). This in turn is likely to influence the grades children receive. For example, teachers may add an extra point to a final grade based on a child's completion of homework assignments or other indicators of achievement. Such an extra point would not be possible on a standardized test.

One final point is in order regarding the preceding research findings. In short, avoid making general statements that suggest all indicators of student achievement benefit equally from family involvement. Instead, focus on the positive link between family involvement and classroom grades (versus standardized tests).

Family involvement matters, regardless of family income. Two researchers reviewed a number of studies in which families were trained to work at home with their children on academic skills. Results indicated that these programs had a positive effect on children's grades and teacher ratings, regardless of family income (Henderson & Mapp, 2002). Furthermore, the more families were involved in the home training programs, the greater their children's achievement scores. In some cases, children showing the greatest gains were those having the most difficulty in school. These findings support Reality Check #7: All families, regardless of their educational or economic background, want to be involved in their children's education. Indeed, most families recognize that it is through education that we achieve healthy and happy lives.

Family involvement promotes children's interest in and responsibility for learning. A group of researchers who reviewed studies related to the motivational aspects of family involvement found that children reported more effort and greater personal responsibility for learning when their families were active participants in their education (Gonzalez-DeHass, Willems, & Holbein, 2005). One explanation given for this finding is that families who are actively involved in their children's education model effective strategies for dealing with the classroom environment. For example, an involved parent might model how to handle a disagreement with a teacher or how to check a class assignment before turning it in.

Children benefit academically when their parents are actively engaged in their homework. A group of researchers found a positive association between parental assistance with homework and children's academic achievement (Hoover-Dempsey et al., 2001). The researchers concluded that this association was mediated by several factors, including families' modeling of appropriate study behavior, reinforcement of children's study habits, and provision of in-home instruction. Another group of researchers found that setting rules as to when and where homework was to be conducted had a strong and positive relationship with academic achievement (Patall, Cooper, & Robinson, 2008).

In-home family involvement activities can be as effective as those based in the classroom. A review of studies related to children's reading scores found pronounced gains when families received training on exercises designed to support in-home reading activities (Darling & Westberg, 2004). In another publication, a group of researchers reviewed 19 studies to determine if parents' support of their children's schoolwork outside of school (e.g., reading activities or completing supplemental math problems with their child) would impact their children's academic performance. The researchers found that parental support had a positive and significant effect on children's overall academic performance and an especially strong effect on children's reading performance (Nye, Turner, & Schwartz, 2006a). Indeed, a summary of the researchers' review by the Harvard Family Research Project revealed that parents' engagement in academic enrichment activities with their children for an average of less than 12 weeks resulted in children's demonstrating an equivalent of four to five months' improvement in their reading or math performance (Nye, Turner, & Schwartz, 2006b).

These findings reinforce our earlier review of longitudinal studies (Izzo et al., 1999; Jimerson et al., 1999; Sheldon & Epstein, 2005), as well as other research reviews (see Gonzalez-DeHass et al., 2005; Henderson & Mapp, 2002; Hoover-Dempsey et al., 2001), indicating that in-home family involvement activities can be as effective in promoting children's academic success as those conducted in the classroom. Nevertheless, supporting families in their implementation of in-home family involvement activities is essential in yielding the most positive outcomes (see Patall et al., 2008; Senechal & Young, 2008). Thus, four strategies to assist you in this endeavor are presented in the following section. Before continuing, however, put the information presented in this section to practical use by completing Reflection 3.1.

Home-Based Family Involvement Strategies

Given the support for in-home family involvement found in the professional literature, it is important that we next examine a few practical strategies for linking children's classroom and home learning experiences. Descriptions of four popular in-home family involvement strategies follow: (a) family backpacks, (b) tip sheets, (c) activity calendars, and (d) activity cards.

Family Backpacks

Family backpacks contain all the materials and directions parents need to complete an educational activity at home with their children. As such, they represent a popular strategy for helping parents reinforce their children's mastery of new concepts and skills. Likewise, family backpacks facilitate children's ability to transfer new knowledge and skills learned in one environment (the classroom) to another environment (the home). One example of a family backpack is presented in FYI 3.2. (The backpack was developed by Meredith Galligan, a graduate student in the Department of Child and Family Development, University of Georgia, Athens, under the direction of the author and Dr. Charlotte Wallinga.) You will have an opportunity to develop your own backpack at the end of this chapter (see Capstone Activity 2).

Family backpacks can be used in a number of ways. Most often they are sent home during the week to reinforce classroom learning objectives. However, they also can be used during school holidays and summer breaks to help children review and practice skills that will be incorporated into lessons when classes resume.

FYI 3.2   Family Backpack: Imogene's Antlers—Directions for Families

Imogene's Antlers

Dear Families,

This week we have been practicing our sorting and counting skills. In this backpack you will find a storybook called *Imogene's Antlers* by David Small (1985). In the storybook, Imogene wakes up with antlers on her head.

You will find a set of your very own antlers in the backpack. Just like Imogene's antlers, these antlers are useful for holding (and counting) different things.

- The antlers can hold **DOUGHNUTS**.
- The antlers can hold **CANDLES**.
- The antlers can hold **RED, YELLOW, AND BLUE BIRDS**.

Use the cards in the backpack to determine how many of each object the antlers can hold at one time.

Directions

1. After reading *Imogene's Antlers* with your child, invite him or her to select a card.

2. Ask your child to read the *type* and *number* of objects on the card.

3. Take those objects out of the bag.

4. Invite your child to count each object as she or he places them on the antlers. Your child may place the objects on the antlers while they are lying on a table or while wearing them (or while you wear them). Choose whichever is more fun.

5. When you are done, ask your child to take the objects off the antlers one by one. After each object is removed, ask your child to count the number of objects that remain.

6. Repeat the above steps until you have gone through at least two sets of cards.

7. Give your child the sheet of paper and crayons found in the backpack. Ask him or her to draw a picture of himself or herself wearing antlers. Encourage your child to decorate his or her antlers.

8. Ask your child to write a short sentence about her or his antlers at the bottom of the paper. Then, ask your child to sign her or his name.

9. Return your child's drawing with the backpack. We will share everyone's drawings in class.

Family Backpack:
Imogene's Antlers.

Contents of Family
Backpack: Imogene's
Antlers.

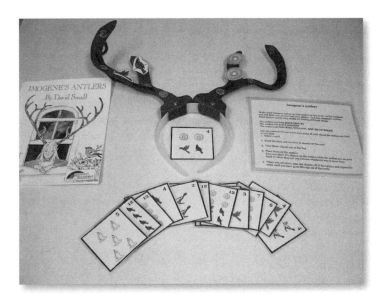

Developing a Family Backpack

Tie the backpack to a classroom learning objective. This will ensure that the backpack activity reinforces key concepts and skills taught in the classroom. Remember to be selective in choosing which classroom lessons to use as a foundation for developing family backpacks. Choose only lessons that lend themselves to an affordable and age-appropriate backpack that will also be fun for families and children to work on at home.

Tell families about the learning skills on which the backpack is based. Families who understand the skills associated with a backpack are more likely to reinforce and talk with their children about those skills while carrying out the activity.

Keep the activity focused. Include no more than one or two activities in a backpack so families will take time to complete it. Including a number of activities can be overwhelming and lead some families to ignore the backpack altogether.

Keep backpacks safe. Make sure the materials you include in a backpack are safe. Also, if needed, provide instructions regarding adult supervision. This tip is especially important if the children in your classroom have younger siblings at home whom parents may include in the backpack activity.

Review new backpacks in the classroom before sending them home. This will help ensure that children understand the activity and its relationship to their classroom work (Kokoski & Patton, 1997). It will also allow them to work cooperatively with their parents in completing the backpack activity.

Use an integrated approach when designing a family backpack. This means you will want to address two or more curriculum areas (e.g., math, science, reading, art, social studies) in each backpack (Kokoski & Patton, 1997). One approach for achieving an integrated backpack is to use a children's book to introduce the activity. Consider, for example, the backpack activity in FYI 3.2. Parents and children begin their exploration of this backpack by reading the book *Imogene's Antlers.* They then count different objects that are placed on and removed from their own antlers. The backpack activity ends as the children draw themselves wearing antlers and write about their drawings. Upon completing this backpack activity, parents will have involved their children in exercising reading, math, art, and writing skills.

Ask for feedback. Ask families to evaluate each backpack activity and to provide suggestions for improvement. Possible questions to ask include the following:

- Were the directions easy to understand?
- Was the activity easy to complete?
- Did your child demonstrate mastery of new skills or knowledge while carrying out the backpack activity?

Try your hand at introducing a family backpack by completing Reflection 3.2.

REFLECTION 3.2   Introducing a Family Backpack

While books represent one way to introduce a backpack, other strategies also can be used. What materials other than *Imogene's Antlers* might you use to introduce the family backpack in FYI 3.2?

Managing Family Backpacks

Consider material costs. The cost of developing a family backpack includes not only the materials needed for initial development but also the cost of replacing torn and lost materials. Likewise, it is important to consider the cost of replacing consumable materials such as art and craft supplies, glue, and crayons. Other issues to consider when estimating the cost of creating a backpack include the following:

- Are the backpack materials durable enough to be transported to and from children's homes without being damaged?
- Will you make a backpack for each child to take home or rotate a few copies of a backpack among children?
- Are costly and specialized materials required, or can alternative and less expensive materials be used?
- What is the cost of the backpack itself?

Consider the time needed to develop and distribute backpacks. It is not uncommon for teachers to have creative backpack ideas that, unfortunately, are never properly executed because of time constraints. Think carefully about how long it will take to put together a back-pack. In some cases, you may need to revise or scale back your idea to save time. Time becomes even more important if you decide to make multiple copies of a backpack. One way to address this concern is to use parent or community volunteers to help make multiple backpacks.

Consider packaging. Child-sized backpacks can be purchased from early-childhood supply catalogs. In some cases these backpacks are made of clear plastic, which makes it easier to see their contents. However, it is important to compare the durability of plastic backpacks to canvas backpacks. In particular, canvas backpacks may be easier to clean and prove more durable over the long term. Of course, other types of packaging are also possible. For example, you may choose to use large storage bags, cloth bags, pizza boxes, shoeboxes, and so on. You may even choose to use different types of packaging for different types of backpacks. Think through the types of backpack packaging that might work for you by completing Reflection 3.3.

REFLECTION 3.3 Advantages and Disadvantages of Different Packaging

Sketch out a backpack activity idea. Then identify the advantages and disadvantages of using the following options for packaging that backpack activity: (a) a shoebox, (b) a pizza box, (c) a plastic storage bag, and (d) a large paper envelope.

Consider storage. Storing backpacks is yet another practical consideration. Is there suffi-cient space in your classroom to store backpacks, or will they need to be stored elsewhere?

Develop a tracking plan. As noted earlier, backpacks are sent home for varying amounts of time. Regardless of how you choose to distribute backpacks, you will want to keep track of when they are sent home and when they are returned. For example, you may choose to develop a master calendar so each family knows when they will receive a backpack and when it should be returned (Kokoski & Patton, 1997). On the other hand, you may prefer establishing a checkout system to track when and by whom a backpack is taken home and the date the backpack is returned.

Because the tracking of backpacks takes time, consider assigning this task to a parent or com-munity volunteer. For quality control purposes, the parent or volunteer who tracks backpacks should also check them upon their return to make sure all materials are present and in good con-dition. Developing a checklist of materials found in each backpack can facilitate this process.

Tip Sheets

Tip sheets provide families with practical information about children's education and gen-eral well-being. One example of a tip sheet is presented in the photo on page 61.

Developing Tip Sheets

Identify topics that interest families. Tip sheet ideas can be identified using a number of strategies. Talk informally with families about topics that interest them. Take note of the topics families ask you about during the year. Review the family surveys completed at the beginning of the year (see Chapter 10). Pay attention to childhood topics covered in the media and posted on the Internet.

Keep tip sheets simple. Provide families with basic information that can be read quickly. Use simple language. Also use bullets to highlight key points as in the photo. The tip sheet in the photo was developed by the author. Ideas for the tip sheet were adapted from the American Red Cross website (www .redcross.org/). Additional information can be found by typing "Halloween safety tips" into the search box on this website.

Make tip sheets visually interesting. Place a logo at the top of each tip sheet. Use clip art, photographs, drawings, and/or colored print to provide additional visual appeal.

Include a resource list. If appropriate and space permits, list a few Internet sites, articles, or book references at the end of the tip sheet for families who would like more information.

Revise annually. Once you have developed a tip sheet, file it away for future use. Remember to review each tip sheet on an annual basis to determine if revisions are needed.

Halloween Tip Sheet.

Managing Tip Sheets

Begin each year with a transition tip sheet. Parents always appreciate receiving tips on helping children make a smooth transition into the classroom at the beginning of the school year. Potential topics for transition tip sheets include helping children get up in the morning, making healthy classroom snacks, classroom supplies the children need, strategies for encouraging children's interest in learning, and where parents can find coupons for or discounts on clothes and classroom supplies.

Identify a storage space. Place your tip sheets in clearly labeled folders for easy access.

Decide on a distribution schedule. Will you develop a monthly or a quarterly tip sheet? Will you use tip sheets selectively—for example, to address childhood health and safety issues that arise during the year? Alternatively, will you use tip sheets to reinforce classroom events, holiday themes (see the photo on this page), or selected classroom lessons?

Decide on a distribution plan. There are multiple ways for getting tip sheets to families. You might place them in daily folders (see Chapter 13), mail them, or incorporate them into family workshops (see Chapter 11) or parent-teacher conferences (see Chapter 13). You might also upload them onto your classroom or school Internet site (see Chapter 13).

Activity Calendars

Activity calendars serve two objectives. First, they include reminders about upcoming family involvement activities, workshops, events, and parent-teacher conferences. Second, they contain simple and brief educational activities for the home that are linked to lessons carried out in the classroom. One example of an activity calendar is presented in FYI 3.3.

FYI 3.3   November Activity Calendar

Dear Families:

This month we will be reading Dr. Seuss books. These will serve as the basis for some of our math, science, and writing activities. We also will look at harvesting fall foods. Finally, we will study American symbols and their importance to our country. Don't forget about the ANNUAL SCHOOL HARVEST. We are planning a number of fun activities. Have fun with the calendar activities!

Ms. Adams

November 2008					
Theme	**Mon**	**Tue**	**Wed**	**Thu**	**Fri**
Dr. Seuss	Read **The Foot Book** with your child. Then work with your child to make your own foot books by using your feet to paint with washable colors.	Read **Green Eggs and Ham** with your child. Make green eggs and ham with your child by adding a small amount of green vegetable food color to eggs.	Read **If I Ran the Zoo** with your child. Work with your child to design a new animal for a zoo. How does the new animal move? What does it eat? What sounds does it make?	Read **Hop on Pop** with your child and then practice rhyming together. Give your child a word and ask him or her to identify another word that rhymes with it. Provide help, as needed.	**Your Turn!** Work with your child to write a rhyming sentence (for example, "The cat played with the mat"). What other sentences can you and your child write using words that rhythm?
Harvesting Food	Visit a pumpkin patch or a grocery store. Talk with your child about the different shapes and colors of pumpkins you see.	Help your child string peppers and hang them in your window to dry. Discuss how early settlers preserved food using this drying process.	Work with your child to design a jack-o'-lantern on a piece of paper. Bring your design to the **School Harvest Festival** where you can participate in a pumpkin carving.	**Your Turn!** Talk with your child about any topic related to fall or fall foods.	SCHOOL HARVEST FESTIVAL! 5 to 8 P.M. • Games • Snacks • Pumpkin carvings • Meet with your child's teacher
Fall Break	Have a	Great	Fall	Break!	

November 2008					
Theme	Mon	Tue	Wed	Thu	Fri
American Symbols	Use crayons, strips of paper, glue, and glitter to make an American flag. Or, use other items.	Bake cookies with your child in the shape of the Liberty Bell. Have fun! The shapes do not have to be perfect. Closely supervise your child while baking.	Show your child pictures of eagles. Then, invite him or her to make an American eagle out or modeling clay. Talk with your child about the importance of this American symbol.	**Your Turn!** Work with your child to draw pictures of your favorite American symbols.	Look at pictures of the Statue of Liberty with your child. Take turns posing like the statue.

SOURCE: The calendar was developed by Lauren Shinn, a graduate student in the Department of Child and Family Development, University of Georgia, Athens, under the direction of the author.

Developing Activity Calendars

Decide on the scope of activity calendars. Like backpacks, not all classroom lessons lend themselves equally well to an activity calendar. Be selective. For example, during any given month you may have from one to four weeks of calendar activities, depending on the nature of the classroom lessons you will be covering.

Keep the activities simple. Activity calendars, like backpacks and tip sheets, should be simple. As shown in FYI 3.3, make sure your descriptions fit into small calendar boxes. This will help ensure families take the time to carry out the activities.

Encourage creativity. Encourage families to be creative by letting them decide how they will carry out at least one idea each week (see FYI 3.3 for examples).

Incorporate community outings into the calendar. Use your community scan to suggest a few family outings. This will help expand families' understanding of how they can contribute to their children's early learning experiences by taking advantage of community resources.

Highlight special dates and announcements. As noted in FYI 3.3, use activity calendars to remind families of special dates and events. Make the dates and events stand out by typing them in a different font or color.

Seek feedback. Ask families about the clarity and usefulness of your activity calendars.

Managing Activity Calendars

Suggest a placement location for the home. Suggest that families post their activity calendars where they can be easily seen. One popular location is the refrigerator door. What other locations might you suggest?

Decide on a distribution plan. The distribution options listed for tip sheets also are applicable for activity calendars.

Try your hand at developing an activity calendar by completing Reflection 3.4.

REFLECTION 3.4   Your Turn! Developing an Activity Calendar

Work alone or in pairs to develop an activity calendar. Similar to FYI 3.3, begin by identifying a weeklong theme on which to base your activities. Then develop five activities in support of that theme. Share your results with your peers.

FYI 3.4   Activity Card
Getting the Scoop: Researching and Writing an Informational Article

Grade: 3

State Learning Standard: ELA3W2 – The student produces informational writing.

By completing this activity, your child will gain practice in writing a brief informational article using multiple sources of printed information. We have been practicing this skill in class.

What You Need:

1. Internet*
2. Encyclopedia*
3. Magazines*
4. Books*
5. Paper, notepad, or index cards
6. Pencil or pen

*These can be found at home, in the family resource center at school, and at the public library.

What To Do:
1. Ask your child to use three of the above sources to gather information on any topic.

   Give your child paper, a notepad, or index cards for taking notes.
2. Your child is now ready to write a short informational article about a topic of interest.
3. Invite your child to read her or his article to you.
4. Verbally reinforce your child's skills in researching and writing the article.

Follow-Up: Ask you child to bring her or his article to class to share with others.
Extension: Place a copy of your child's article in a notebook. Allow your child to decorate the cover. Invite your child to place other writing projects in the notebook. You and your child will enjoy reviewing these projects in the years to come.

Activity Cards

Activity cards represent yet another strategy for delivering brief home-based educational activities that support classroom learning objectives. One advantage of activity cards is that families do not need to return them to the classroom. Thus, while activity cards fulfill many of the same objectives as family backpacks, they are often simpler to construct and implement. One example of an activity card is presented in FYI 3.4. You will have an opportunity to develop your own activity card at the end of this chapter (see Capstone Activity 3).

Developing Activity Cards

Decide how to access activity cards. Activity cards can be purchased through commercial companies. In addition, some can be downloaded for free from the Internet by typing the phrase *activity cards* into a search engine of your choice. Finally, you can develop your own activity cards following the directions given below. The last approach is encouraged, since it allows you to more closely match home activities with classroom learning objectives. In addition, while making activity cards takes time, purchasing them can be cost prohibitive.

Decide on the content. The content of activity cards can be tied to almost any classroom learning theme, or it can be tied to an educational skill such as reading or math. For example, you may choose to follow the example shown in FYI 3.4 by developing activity cards that are coded according to state learning standards.

Use sturdy and attractive cards. Use large index cards or sturdy cardstock to print the activities. Don't forget to add visual appeal by using graphics. Also, you may choose to use colored cards instead of white cards.

Keep it brief and simple. Because you are using a card, it is important that the activity be brief and simple. In contrast to family backpacks, activity cards do not include materials. Thus, they can be sent home in children's daily folders (see Chapter 13).

Managing Activity Cards

Share the work. Team up with other teachers to develop activity cards. Decide who will be responsible for developing activity cards for different educational themes or learning standards. After all the cards are developed, swap and review them. Make suggestions for revisions.

Explain their purpose. Just as you would introduce other educational materials, explain the purpose of activity cards to families. Since the activities will be easy to implement, you do not necessarily need to include an introductory letter. Instead, provide an explanation of their purpose during registration, family workshops, or in your classroom newsletter.

Filing the cards. As noted above, you can tie activity cards to classroom learning themes of your choosing or code them according to state learning standards. Whichever approach you choose to follow, set up an Internet filing system to keep the cards organized. Alternatively, you may choose to use filing boxes or folders.

Encourage families to keep their cards. Encourage families to file away the activity cards they receive for future reference or for use with siblings, nieces, nephews, or grandchildren.

Review and update. Remember to review each card on an annual basis to determine if it needs to be updated based on changes in classroom activities or revisions in state learning standards.

CHAPTER SUMMARY

- The ecological model is useful for understanding how different levels of society influence children's development and education.
- Research findings provide evidence of the many positive influences of family involvement on children's development and education.
- Family backpacks, activity calendars, and activity cards can be used to link children's classroom and home learning experiences.
- Tip sheets can be used to provide families with practical information about various aspects of children's development and education.

DISCUSSION QUESTIONS

1. Why is it important that we take an ecological perspective of teaching?
2. Discuss the relative advantages and disadvantages of backpacks, tip sheets, activity calendars, and activity cards.
3. **Your family involvement philosophy**. Return to the draft of your family involvement philosophy. Based on your reading of this chapter, what if any changes will you make to your philosophy statement? Discuss your answer to this question with your peers.

COMMUNITY OF LEARNERS' FIELD ASSIGNMENT

In this chapter, you learned about using tip sheets to provide families with a range of information. The purpose of this assignment is to give you practice in developing a tip sheet.

Your task. It is not unusual for parents to ask teachers, "How can I help my child with math [or writing, reading, science, etc.]?" Use your knowledge of child development, teaching strategies, and information found in this chapter as well as from other sources to develop a tip sheet that addresses this question for a particular age group (choose from prekindergarten through fifth grade) and a particular subject area. Don't forget to add visual appeal to your tip sheet. Share your tip sheet with your peers.

CAPSTONE ACTIVITIES

Activity 1: Interview a Parent About the Benefits of Family Involvement

Do the benefits shared by the parent reflect the research findings reviewed in this chapter? Does the parent mention benefits not addressed in this chapter? Share the results of your interview with your peers.

Activity 2: Your Turn! Develop a Family Backpack

Identify an age group (choose from prekindergarten through fifth grade). Check out a children's book from your local library that is appropriate for this age group. Use the book as the foundation for developing a family backpack. Remember to include all the directions and materials needed to carry out the activity. Also remember to explain the educational objective(s) of the backpack. Share your backpack with your peers.

Activity 3: Your Turn! Develop an Activity Card

Identify an age group (choose from prekindergarten through fifth grade). Develop an activity card that reinforces a lesson on math, science, reading, art, physical education, music, writing, or social science. Share the resulting activity cards in class. Then make copies of all the cards. Place your copies in your teacher resource file for future reference.

INTERNET RESOURCES

You may find that some URLs have been altered by the webmaster. In these situations, try entering the name of the document or agency in a search engine. Alternatively, enter the domain name (e.g., http://www.xxxx.org). This should take you to the revised home page and associated links.

Family Backpacks

Teacher's Net: #489. Take Home Backpack Ideas—from chatboard and mailring

http://teachers.net/lessons/posts/489.html

Visit this website to read about the personal experiences and recommendations of teachers who have used backpacks.

Rocburn's Math Backpack Program

http://res.hcpss.org

Visit this Maryland elementary school's webpage to learn about its kindergarten through Grade 5 math backpacks. Backpack descriptions are given in English and Spanish.

Activity Calendars

Reading Is Fundamental: Activity Calendars

http://www.rif.org/us/literacy-resources/activities/monthly-activity-calendars.htm

Visit this website to view activity calendars devoted to reading for age groups birth through 5 years and 6 through 15 years. Calendars are printed in English and Spanish.

Tip Sheets

Reading Rockets

http://www.readingrockets.org/article/7833

Visit this website to view tips sheets that families can use to build their children's reading interests and skills at home and in the community. Different tips sheets are available for different ages and grade levels. The tips sheets also are available in a number of languages.

American Academy of Pediatrics: Summer Safety—Part 1

http://www.aap.org/advocacy/releases/summertips.cfm

Families will appreciate these tips on keeping their children safe during summer.

Illinois Early Learning Project

http://illinoisearlylearning.org/

The tips sheets found at this website address a variety of educational, developmental, and parenting topics.

Parents Boost Learning: Literacy and Numeracy Tip Sheets for Parents

http://www.peelschools.org/parents/tips/num-index.htm

Both numeracy and literacy tip sheets can be found on this website sponsored by a school district in Ontario, Canada. Note that families can subscribe to this website to receive a monthly email package of parent-child activities.

Reading Is Fundamental: Literacy Resources

http://www.rif.org/us/literacy-resources.htm

This website includes a number of activities, articles, booklists, brochures, and multicultural resources related to reading. All of these can be used to develop reading tip sheets.

Homework Assistance

U.S. Department of Education: Helping Your Child With Homework

www.ed.gov/parents/academic/help/homework/index.html

U.S. Department of Education: Homework Tips for Parents

www.ed.gov/parents/academic/involve/homework/part.html

Maine Education Association: Help Your Child Get the Most out of Homework

http://www.maine.nea.org/assets/document/ME/Help_Your_Child_Get_the_Most_Out_of_Homework.pdf

Student Study Site

Log on to the Web-based student study site at **www.sagepub.com/coleman** for additional study tools including

- eFlashcards
- Web Quizzes
- Links to SAGE Journal Articles
- Author-created Videos

- Learning Objectives
- Web Resources
- Family Involvement Portfolio Guides

CHAPTER 4

Benefits of Family Involvement for Families and Teachers

The benefits of family involvement for families and teachers have received limited study, especially when compared to the benefits for children. Nevertheless, it is still possible to address the potential benefits of family involvement for these two groups of individuals. In this chapter we begin with an examination of two issues that, if not understood, can make it difficult for families and teachers to reap the benefits of family involvement: family-teacher expectations and shared family functions. We then review the benefits that families and teachers can expect from a collaborative parent-teacher partnership. We end by reviewing the ways by which families and teachers mediate the benefits of family involvement.

COMMUNITY LEARNING GUIDE

As you read this chapter, take notes on the following items. Use your notes to address the Reflections, Discussion Questions, Field Assignment, and Capstone Activities that you find in the chapter.

- Summarize some of the expectations that families and teachers have of each other.
- What are the potential benefits of family involvement for families?
- What are the potential benefits of family involvement for teachers?
- How do families mediate the benefits of family involvement?
- How do teachers mediate the benefits of family involvement?

Family-Teacher Expectations

To fully appreciate the benefits of family involvement, we must begin with an assessment of the expectations families and teachers have of other. Understanding these expectations can help prevent the types of misunderstanding and miscommunication that negatively impact family-teacher partnerships. Here are three factors that can at times create different family-teacher expectations:

> The information in this chapter supports the following family-school-community partnership standards. These standards are reviewed in Chapter 2.
>
> | NAEYC Standards and Associated Key Elements | 1b, 1c, 2a, 2b, 2c, 3b, 3c, 5c, 6a, 6c, 6d, 6e |
> |---|---|
> | ACEI Standards | 1.0, 3.2, 5.1, 5.2 |
> | PTA Standards | 1, 2, 3, 4, 5, 6 |

- **Meeting individual needs.** The limited number of people found in a home environment allows families to focus on the strengths and needs of each child and adult. In contrast, the number of children found in a classroom far outnumbers those found in families. In addition, each child comes to the classroom with different life experiences, strengths, and needs. As a result, teachers must balance the needs of each child against the needs of the group.

- **Environments.** Families are free to arrange their home environments to fit their personal tastes. Teachers, on the other hand, must arrange their classrooms to meet state and professional standards that govern group learning. Likewise, teachers must select classroom materials and implement instructional practices that reflect a particular curriculum.

- **Rules.** Family rules and child guidance practices in the home environment are based on personal values and beliefs about child rearing. In contrast, teachers must abide by school policies in setting classroom rules that ensure a safe learning environment and protect school property. These considerations can limit the types of activities that children are allowed to pursue in the classroom.

Teachers who are aware of these differences in the home and classroom microsystems are in a better position to develop a strong home–school partnership or, in ecological terms, mesosystem. Some examples of common expectations that families and teachers have of each other are presented in FYI 4.1. After reading FYI 4.1, continue on to the next section.

FYI 4.1   Expectations of Families and Teachers

It is reasonable to assume that most families want teachers to . . .

- clearly communicate classroom policies and practices.
- talk to them about their children's development and education.
- give them concrete evidence of their children's classroom performance.
- ask for their assessments of their children's development and academic skills.
- involve them in helping to set goals for their children's education.
- make them feel welcomed in the classroom.
- alert them in a timely fashion when concerns arise about their children's behavior or classroom performance.
- ask them for help in addressing their children's behavior or learning challenges.

(Continued)

(Continued)

- give them plenty of options for supporting their children's education inside and outside the classroom.
- show love and concern for children.
- create an interesting and supportive learning environment for children.
- implement classroom lessons that reflect the real world.
- support children's curiosity and creativity.
- be flexible when scheduling parent-teacher conferences.

It is reasonable to assume that most teachers want families to . . .

- monitor their children's educational progress.
- encourage their children to talk with them about their classroom activities.
- read to their children and encourage their children to read to them.
- provide children with in-home learning experiences that support their knowledge of math, science, art, and other subject areas.
- recognize and respect each child's unique strengths and challenges.
- provide children with opportunities to pursue their strengths and interests.
- encourage children to express their thoughts and feelings in age-appropriate ways.
- update them when there are changes in children's personal and family lives that can influence their classroom behavior or performance.
- help with classroom celebrations, activities, and projects.
- understand classroom routines, rules, and educational goals.
- speak up when they need more or different types of information.
- complete forms and respond to notes that are sent home.
- participate in parent-teacher conferences.

We next turn to another source of potential conflict that can stand in the way of teachers' and families' reaping the benefits of family involvement: the sharing of family functions.

Social Functions Schools Share With Families

Traditionally, families have fulfilled a number of social functions that help to maintain a stable society. A summary of these functions follow, along with an examination of how families today share them with other social institutions such as schools.

Education

Historically, families have always played a role in educating children. Today, families serve as teachers not only by reinforcing children's classroom learning experiences but also by using their own ideas to teach reading, writing, and other skills. In addition, families introduce new learning opportunities as they guide children in completing home chores, engage them in family projects, and take them on family outings or vacations. These activities allow families to make informal but important assessments of their children's physical, cognitive, and social skills. As a teacher, you will want to respect and make use of families' contributions to and assessment of their children's development and education during parent-teacher conferences and when planning classroom lessons.

Socialization of Children

Families are sometimes described as launching pads from which children learn the values needed to become responsible, independent, and productive adults. Put another way, families teach children basic social skills such as cooperating with others and saying "thank you" and "please." In addition, families help children understand the consequences that result when they engage in socially inappropriate behavior. Thus, it is important that teachers, along with youth leaders, understand and respect the values taught by families when responding to their concerns about group child guidance practices.

Economic Support

Families have primary responsibility for meeting the economic needs of their members. As noted in Chapter 1, homeless and working-poor families often find this family function difficult to fulfill on their own. This is why teachers sometimes work with school social workers to assist families with their economics needs.

Protection and Care

Families are responsible for the physical protection and care of their members. This means keeping the home environment safe and teaching children about potential community dangers. It also includes providing children with appropriate levels of adult supervision throughout the day. Single-parent families and dual-career families in particular may depend on extended family members or paid caregivers to provide adult supervision while they are at work. Alternatively, they may take advantage of before- and after-school programs operated by schools and recreation departments. In addition, law enforcement officers, fire departments, and neighborhood watch programs share responsibility for keeping children and their families safe.

Emotional Support

Families nurture and confide in each other, play with each other, and accept each other unconditionally. They provide the emotional support needed to face what can be a harsh world. Emotional support within the family system is especially important for children who have a difficult time making friends or adjusting to a new learning environment, or who experience developmental challenges. Today, peer groups, teachers, youth clubs, and counselors play a role in augmenting the emotional support children receive from their families.

As demonstrated earlier, few if any families today assume full responsibility for the social functions traditionally ascribed to them. Indeed, contemporary American society is too complex to place so many functions entirely within one social institution. Instead, families form a number of linkages (or mesosystems) with other community institutions who help them carry out their social functions. For example, the professional standards related to family-teacher collaboration that we reviewed in Chapter 2 are based on the assumption that teachers must join with families to help educate, socialize, and protect children.

Unfortunately, the sharing of social functions can at times lead to parent-teacher conflict—as, for example, when parents and teacher disagree on how best to educate, protect, or socialize children. This is why you will be introduced to various strategies in upcoming chapters for forming a positive parent-teacher partnership. Once formed, this partnership can help ensure that the preceding social functions are carried out without disruption, thereby allowing the benefits of family involvement to unfold.

Benefits of Family Involvement for Families

As noted at the beginning of this chapter, there is a limited amount of research on the benefits of family involvement for families themselves. Nevertheless, we can reasonably hypothesize at least five benefits that should result when teachers and families collaborate to honor each others' expectations and share responsibility for educating, socializing, and protecting children.

Benefit #1: Parents' Knowledge of Child Development

Schools sometimes publish flyers to educate families about the physical, mental, and social "readiness skills" children are expected to display at different ages, along with activities for helping children acquire those skills. This is an example of how one family involvement practice can increase parents' knowledge of child development and, in turn, provide them with greater insight into their children's classroom performance. Other activities that can increase parents' knowledge of child development are presented below.

- **Game cards.** Develop a series of game cards for parents to use in quizzing themselves about child development terms and principles. Different sets of cards can be developed for different age groups. Place a question on one side of each card and the correct response on the flip side of the card.
- **Game show.** After presenting a workshop on child development, divide parents into teams for a game show. Ask questions of the teams based on information presented in your workshop. Give each team a few seconds to decide on an answer. Tally points at the end of the game show.
- **Toy assessment.** Develop a booklet with pictures of toys for different age groups. Ask parents to (a) identify the age group for which they think the toy is designed and (b) list the physical, cognitive, and social skills the toy is designed to reinforce. Place answers at the end of the booklet. As an alternative, plan a workshop where you give the actual toys to parents and ask that they play with them before responding to the directions in the booklet.

Benefit #2: Parenting Skills

Teachers support children's development and education not only in the classroom but also by responding to parents' questions and concerns about their children's behavior. For example, parents sometimes ask for help in addressing what they perceive to be unusual childhood behavior or a behavior that is out of character for their child. Parents may also ask for help in improving their parenting skills or strengthening the parent-child relationship. Responding to such requests benefits children and families in the short and long term (Knopf & Swick, 2008). A few examples for addressing parenting skills follow.

Publish a child guidance column. Your classroom newsletter represents a perfect venue for sharing your classroom child guidance practices and addressing common guidance issues raised by parents. When writing your newsletter column, remember to consult with parent educators as well as professional journals, books, and Internet sources. In addition, remind parents that no guidance tip can magically transform a child's behavior. Each tip will need to be adapted to each home environment and parent-child relationship.

Conduct parent education workshops. A number of parent education curricula are available, some of the more popular of which are summarized in the Community of Learners' Field Assignment at the end of this chapter. As a teacher, you may choose to lead your own workshops or collaborate with a parent educator. You will have an opportunity to learn more about working with parent educators in your Community of Learners' Field Assignment. In the meantime, consider the following tips for planning and facilitating parent education workshops where participants feel respected and comfortable sharing their views and feelings.

- Select a curriculum that has a clear theoretical base and lasts long enough to give parents an opportunity to practice and discuss new parenting skills (Small, Cooney, & O'Connor, 2009).
- Make sure the information you present is relevant to the backgrounds of the parents in attendance (Small et al., 2009).
- Seek training in teaching the curriculum you deliver or, as noted above, team-teach with a community parent educator who has experience with the curriculum (Small et al., 2009). Also make sure you incorporate social activities and/or refreshments into each workshop to build rapport among everyone in attendance.
- Make plans to evaluate the success of the parent education program (Small et al., 2009).
- Establish an emotionally safe environment for group discussion by reviewing a few ground rules at the beginning of each workshop. Writing the following ground rules on a large sheet of poster paper will serve as a visual reminder.

  o **Everyone has a right to be heard.** Use this rule when you need to gently remind a parent of the need to let others share their views.
  o **One speaker at a time.** Use this rule to remind parents of the need to maintain an orderly workshop.
  o **We have the right to remain silent.** This rule is helpful is letting reserved parents know they will not be pressured to share their views.
  o **We agree to disagree.** This rule comes in handy when you need to mediate a heated argument and move the discussion to a more respectful level.
  o **What is shared in this room stays in this room.** This rule is important in reminding parents that information shared during workshops is confidential and should not be shared outside the group setting.
  o **The more ideas the better. There are no bad ideas.** These rules accomplish two things: They encourage reserved parents to speak up while reminding everyone that all views are to be respected, even those with which we strongly disagree.

○ **We are here to learn from each other.** This is a helpful way to explain that your role is not to solve problems but to share information and facilitate discussion. It is important that parents assume responsibility for making final decisions about how they will guide their children's behavior.

- End on a positive note. Take the time each week to review the positive accomplishments parents are making. Post a large sheet of paper on a wall. After parents sign in, ask them to write down something positive that happened during the week related to their parent-child relationship. Add other positive things that come up during group discussions. Use the comments to bring a positive closure to each workshop.

Benefit #3: Parents' Self-Confidence as Advocates for Their Children

To form a truly collaborative family-teacher partnership, parents need the self-confidence to advocate for their children's education and general welfare (Hoover-Dempsey, Bassler, & Brissie, 1992; Hoover-Dempsey & Sandler, 1995, 1997). As a teacher, you can strengthen parents' self-confidence by acknowledging the importance of the issues they raise concerning their children's development and education. Also remind parents of how they contribute to their children's well-being by listening to their concerns and answering their questions. Finally, make use of empowering strategies such as those reviewed in Chapter 11.

Parents' self-confidence as advocates for their children is strengthened through a supportive family-teacher partnership.

Benefit #4: Parents' Creativity

The family involvement strategies presented in previous and upcoming chapters do more than provide opportunities to keep parents engaged in their children's learning experiences. They also stimulate parents' creativity in promoting their children's emerging skills at home and in the community. A few examples of ways that you, as a teacher, can encourage parents' creativity are presented below.

- **Activity idea books.** Provide activity idea books and magazines in the family resource center (see Chapter 11) to stimulate parents' creativity.
- **Make-and-take.** During a family workshop, review examples of inexpensive ways to make educational games at home. Ask parents to share their ideas for other educational activities and games.
- **Show-and-tell.** Invite parents to share with you the learning activities they carry out at home with their children.

Benefit #5: Higher Educational Aspirations

With support, children are able to live up to their parents' academic expectations (Fan & Chen, 2001). Family involvement can contribute to this positive outcome by increasing parents' self-confidence (Benefit #3) and creativity (Benefit #4) in helping children develop the skills and motivation needed to perform well in the classroom. A few examples of activities for helping parents develop high educational aspirations for their children are presented below.

- **Parent-teacher conferences.** Incorporate discussions of children's strengths into parent-teacher conferences. Use these discussions to encourage parents to reflect on the educational aspirations they hold for their children. Discuss ways for parents to act on their aspirations.
- **Link family involvement to children's academic achievements.** Let parents know how a family involvement activity contributed to children's learning something new or developing a new skill. Take this opportunity to educate families about how children live up to developmentally appropriate expectations when provided with proper encouragement and support.
- **Exploring a child's future.** During a family workshop, ask each parent to describe their child's biggest strength. Lead the group in identifying one or more occupations associated with the strengths parents describe. Brainstorm home and community activities parents can pursue to support those strengths.

Before moving on, use your own creativity to think of family involvement activities that can benefit families. Complete Reflection 4.1.

REFLECTION 4.1   Your Turn! Creating an Activity for Families

Select one of the family involvement benefits reviewed in this section. Create an activity that you might use to help families achieve this benefit.

Benefits of Family Involvement for Teachers

As with families, relatively little attention has been devoted to studying the benefits of family involvement for teachers. Nevertheless, we can identify at least five potential benefits.

Benefit #1: Understanding the "Ecological Child"

Because of their training, teachers naturally tend to focus on the "classroom child." Yet, your reading of the past three chapters should alert you to the limits of this focus. Only by considering the "ecological child" can we truly understand how children's classroom performance is grounded in family and community life. Subsequently, teachers who routinely communicate with families are better able to understand the human ecologies that define children's lives.

Consider, for example, cultural macrosystems. One hallmark of socially competent children in **high-context cultures** (e.g., Asian, Hispanic, and Native American cultures) is their mastery of subtle contextual communication signals (e.g., nonverbal facial and hand gestures) rather than explicit verbalizations (Han & Thomas, 2010). Children from **low-context cultures** (e.g., United States, Western Europe, Australia) are taught to value just the opposite. They are encouraged to be direct in their verbal communication rather than rely on subtle forms of nonverbal communication. Understanding these cultural differences, as well as others presented in Chapters 8 and 9, can help you avoid miscommunication and misunderstanding when interacting with children and their families.

Benefit #2: Professional Self-Efficacy: Bandura's Self-Efficacy Theory

You might remember Barack Obama's motto during the presidential race of 2008: "Yes we can." To understand self-efficacy, we can revise this motto to read "Yes I can." In short, our level of **self-efficacy** is defined both by our beliefs and actions. Thus, individuals with high self-efficacy believe they can successfully exercise influence over events that impact their lives (Bandura, 1998). As a result, they approach new tasks as challenges to be mastered rather than threats to be avoided. Likewise, they set challenging goals for themselves and persevere even when they encounter setbacks. In contrast, individuals with low self-efficacy question their ability to succeed. Subsequently, they avoid setting challenging goals and, likewise, quickly lose faith in themselves when they encounter setbacks.

When applied to family-teacher partnerships, self-efficacy can be defined as the core belief that we possess the skills and knowledge needed to work collaboratively with families in advancing children's education. Indeed, the development of a positive parent-teacher partnership is a strong predictor of teachers' sense of self-efficacy in general (Skaalvik & Skaalvik, 2010). Likewise, teachers who perceive themselves as more efficacious in their ability to work with families make more attempts to involve families in their children's education (Garcia, 2004; Vartuli, 2005). Three strategies associated with self-efficacy theory that you may find helpful—**mastery experiences**, **vicarious experiences**, and **social persuasion**—are presented below (see Bandura, 1977, 1998).

Mastery experiences: Remember Reality Check #8. The best way to summarize this source of self-efficacy is through the often-heard quote "Success builds success." This is one reason why Reality Check #8 (begin small) is so important. Dividing your involvement with families into small tasks that are within your comfort zone is one of the best ways to experience mastery and, subsequently, self-efficacy.

Vicarious experiences: Find a mentor teacher. Our sense of self-efficacy is reinforced when we have mentors who give us constructive criticism as we try out new skills. Role-playing a parent-teacher conference, discussing the professional experiences of our mentor teacher, and keeping a journal in which we document what we learn from our mentor teacher are three examples of how to structure vicarious experiences that build our sense of self-efficacy.

Social persuasion: Seek positive feedback. The importance of mentors is extended to this third source of self-efficacy. To summarize, our sense of self-efficacy improves when others take steps to persuade us that we have the capability to succeed. This requires mentor teachers to be honest but supportive in their feedback. As a supervisor, I follow this advice when asking student teachers to assess their lessons. I begin with the request, "Tell me what you liked best about your lesson." I follow up by reinforcing the positive statements I hear and then ask students to share something they might do differently. When discussing revisions, I invite student teachers to brainstorm new ideas and help them put those ideas into action. I take care to end our discussion by repeating the positive skills I observed, as well as by voicing my belief that the new ideas we discussed will lead to an even higher level of success.

Benefit #3: Parent-Teacher Trust

Ask anyone who works in the counseling field and she or he will tell you that very little can be achieved to advance a client's concerns until a mutual sense of counselor-client trust is established. The same is true of any other partnership, including parent-teacher partnerships. Indeed, as noted earlier in this chapter, a mismatch in expectations can negatively influence the degree to which parents embrace their role as a collaborator in the parent-teacher partnership and their feelings of acceptance by school staff (Barbarin, Downer, Odom, & Head, 2010). This is one reason why it is important to reinforce families' sense of empowerment (see Chapter 11) by creating a welcoming classroom environment (see Chapter 12) and facilitating positive parent-teacher communication (see Chapter 13).

Benefit #4: Families' Commitment to Classroom Learning Objectives

Teachers' sense of self-efficacy increases and their jobs become easier when families commit to supporting classroom learning objectives, events, and activities. Likewise, teachers benefit when families commit to encouraging their children to follow teachers' directions, behave appropriately in school, and do their very best when completing lessons and homework assignments. Achieving such commitment requires teachers to follow Reality Check #1 by proactively reaching out to and communicating with families, as well as Reality Check #5 by planning family involvement activities that meet families' needs and interests. This is not always easy, as reflected in three questions that teachers should ask themselves when assessing the effectiveness of their family involvement program (Knopf & Swick, 2008):

- Can parents easily participate in activities, or is the process too cumbersome or restrictive?
- Are there adequate supports that allow parents to take advantage of family involvement offers?
- Are there several family involvement options from which families can choose?

Upcoming chapters related to family diversity, family involvement challenges, family empowerment, and family involvement planning will help you in addressing these questions and ensuring families' commitment to the family-teacher partnership.

Benefit #5: Improved Student-Teacher Relationships

Increases in family involvement have been found to predict improved student-teacher relationships

Increases in family involvement have been found to predict improved student-teacher relationships, which in turn predict children's positive attitudes toward school (Dearing, Kreider, & Weiss, 2008). These findings suggest that children who see their parent and teacher working as a team are more likely to join that team and take responsibility for their schoolwork than they are to avoid ownership of classroom difficulties by pitting parent and teacher against each other.

The benefits of family involvement reviewed in this chapter and the previous one do not come about on their own. Instead, they are mediated by a number of factors. In the following section, we examine a few examples of how families and teachers mediate positive family involvement outcomes.

Mediators of Family Involvement Benefits

As you read this section, think about how you have seen the following factors mediate your own development and education, or the development and education of other children.

Parents as Mediators

In this section, we review three ways that parents mediate the benefits of family involvement. We begin with parents serving as a type of human "scaffold."

Supportive scaffolding. Parents provide **supportive scaffolding** for their children when they help them acquire new knowledge and skills at comfortable but increasingly challenging levels (Bempechat, 1990, p. 3). The concept of scaffolding is well known in the field of education and is associated with Russian psychologist Lev Vygotsky's **zone of proximal distance**. Vygotsky (1978) defined the zone of proximal distance in the following way:

It is the distance between the actual developmental level as determined by independent problem solving and the level of potential development as determined through problem solving under adult guidance or in collaboration with more capable peers. (p. 86)[1]

In practical terms, we see supportive scaffolding operating within the zone of proximal distance when parents provide children with prompts as they learn new skills (Pentimonti & Justice, 2010). For example, when helping children learn about the plot of a book that deals with anger, parents may ask the following scaffolding questions: "Who in this story is angry?" "How do you know these people are angry?" "Are all the characters showing their anger in the same way?" and "Tell me about a time when you were angry." Parents may also provide supportive scaffolding for their children's understanding of prediction by asking the following questions: "What do you think will happen next in this story?" and "How do you think this story will end?" Think of other examples of supportive scaffolding as you complete Reflection 4.2.

REFLECTION 4.2   How Did Supportive Scaffolding Contribute to Your Education and Development?

Consider your own childhood. Describe how your family, teachers, or youth leaders provided you with supportive scaffolding to help you learn new skills or information.

Moseman (2003, p. 146) provides another example of supportive scaffolding when she distinguishes between **family knowledge**, which is based on the life experiences and hobbies of individual family members, and the research- and theory-based **professional knowledge** that teachers acquire through teacher training programs. At times, you may hear the phrase *funds of knowledge* instead of *family knowledge*. That is because the two phrases are closely related. In fact, *funds of knowledge* refers to the historically accumulated and culturally developed knowledge and skills that define an individual's real level of functioning (Moll, Amanti, Neff, & Gonzalez, 1992). Like *family knowledge*, *funds of knowledge* is used to distinguish between children's total knowledge base and skill level, as exhibited in their home and neighborhood, versus the more limited knowledge base and skill level they demonstrate in an isolated classroom (Moll et al., 1992).

As a teacher, you will want to looks for ways to integrate family knowledge and professional knowledge in order to maximize children's learning potential. To help you meet this objective, some examples of how family knowledge can contribute to children's learning and development are presented in FYI 4.2. After reading FYI 4.2, complete Reflection 4.3.

Skills development resources. **Skills development resources** describes the skills children need to succeed in the classroom (Pomerantz, Moorman, & Litwack, 2007). Examples include cognitive skills such as reasoning and problem solving, language skills, academic skills such as spelling and arithmetic, impulse control and attention skills, and the ability to plan ahead and monitor one's progress while working on assignments. These skills not only help children accomplish classroom learning objectives, but they also influence their ability to respect and follow classroom rules and routines.

FYI 4.2   Examples of Family Knowledge as an Instructional Tool

- Families use their own words and ideas to tutor children in their homework assignments and class projects.
- Families help children develop specialized skills as they teach them about their hobbies and the work they do.
- Families provide children with words to express themselves.
- Families structure their children's learning opportunities through the toys and games they provide in the home.
- Families expose children to new learning environments in the community and while on family trips.
- Families assess their children's skills in deciding how and when to introduce new home responsibilities, personal choices, and community learning experiences.
- Families support their children's curiosity while enforcing limits that keep them safe.
- Families teach children personal responsibility by enforcing age-appropriate consequences for misbehavior, reinforcing age-appropriate social behavior, and assigning age-appropriate chores.
- Families model social skills that children can use to negotiate successful relationships with their classmates and teachers.
- Parents share personal life experiences with children as a way of teaching life lessons about morality, responsibility, and cooperation.

REFLECTION 4.3   Using Family Knowledge in the Classroom

One hallmark of Moll and his colleagues' work (Moll et al., 1992) was their use of the family knowledge of children's homes and communities to inform classroom instruction. Follow Moll's lead by identifying one example of family knowledge presented in FYI 4.2. How would you incorporate this example of family-based knowledge in your classroom?

Teachers promote children's skill development resources when they provide parents with information about how to reinforce academic skills at home. For example, children display greater homework completion and fewer homework problems when parents receive training on how to support them in completing their homework assignments (Patall, Cooper, & Robinson, 2008). Likewise, training parents to teach specific literacy skills such as letter sound recognition and correcting reading errors has a positive effect on children's reading performance (Senechal & Young, 2008).

Motivational development resources. The degree to which parents are motivated to support their children's education is mediated by three **motivational development resources**: (a) their role construct, that is, their belief that they need to be involved in their children's education; (b) their sense of self-efficacy, that is, their belief that they have the knowledge and skills to support their children's education, and (c) invitations from teachers for family involvement (Hoover-Dempsey & Sandler, 1995, 1997). These three factors have been shown to be useful in designing family involvement programs (see Chrispeels & Gonz, 2004; Chrispeels & Rivero, 2001). For example, two researchers reported on a program for immigrant Latino parents who attended classes to learn about the U.S. educational system, how to interact with American-trained teachers, and how to help their children at home (Chrispeels & Rivero, 2001). Upon completion of the program, parents demonstrated more parent-initiated teacher contacts, more positive parent-child

---

FYI 4.3   An Invitational Bookmark for Parents

Welcome

Back to School!

I look forward to working with you.

Ms. Adams

Why is parent support important?

Children do better in school when their parents reinforce their learning at home. I will send home fun activities throughout the year. Use these to reinforce the skills your child is learning in the classroom.

Three things you can do to support your child's education:

1. Let me hear from you. Share your thoughts and concerns with me.

2. Ask your child the same question each day: **"What did you learn about today?"**

3. Reinforce and encourage your child's learning. Show excitement about his new math skill. Tell her how much you enjoy reading her poem.

Your child and I invite your participation!

- This is your classroom too! Please visit anytime.
- Here are a few upcoming family activities you will want to put on your calendar. Look for details soon.

√ <u>Sept. 9</u> Family Fun Night
√ <u>Oct. 30</u> Family Fall Festival
√ <u>Nov. 29</u> Family Morning Breakfast Stop

---

interactions, greater involvement in reading and homework support, and greater advocacy efforts on behalf of their children.

As a teacher, you can motivate parents in equally important but more subtle ways. Consider, for example, the invitational bookmark in FYI 4.3 that you might give to parents at the beginning of the school year.

Motivational development resources also can be addressed from another perspective. In particular, parents' approach to motivating their children's academic pursuits include (a) process- versus person-focused attitudes toward their children's educational efforts and (b) positive versus negative beliefs about their children's academic potential (Pomerantz et al., 2007; see FYI 4.4).

FYI 4.4	Parental Attitudes and Beliefs That Mediate Children's Classroom Performance
Attitudes and Beliefs	**Examples of Behaviors and Statements Displayed by Parents**
Helpful: Process-focused family involvement	Parents focus on children's efforts rather than their outcomes. They talk about the importance of learning and education. They encourage their children's curiosity. They make statements such as "I can see you worked very hard on this project."
versus	
Not Helpful: Person-focused family involvement	Parents tie the worth of their children's efforts to high test scores. Success is valued over effort. They make statements such as "Make us proud. Show us how smart you are."
Helpful: Positive beliefs about children's potential	Parents believe in their children's skills and set reasonable academic expectations. They make statements such as "I know this is difficult, but I have faith in you. Let me know if you would like me to give you feedback as you work on your project."
versus	
Not Helpful: Negative beliefs about children's potential	Parents fail to appreciate their children's skills, instead focusing on their difficulties. They make statements such as "I don't think you'll be able to do this assignment by yourself. We'll have to get you help."

Parents who assume a **process-focused attitude** emphasize the pleasure of educational pursuits and reinforce the effort children put into accomplishing classroom assignments. These messages are intrinsically motivating for children, thereby helping them to develop the self-confidence needed to master new skills and view learning as not just a necessary task but a worthwhile and lifelong pursuit (Pomerantz et al., 2007). In contrast, parents who assume a **person-focused attitude** emphasize the importance of specific outcomes, such as receiving a certain grade or recognition. This type of attitude interferes with children's pursuit of educational goals when they are not accompanied by external rewards.

Parents display **positive beliefs** about children's academic potential when they express confidence in their ability to overcome learning challenges (Pomerantz et al., 2007). For example, these parents are more likely to attribute their children's classroom difficulties to a lack of effort rather than a lack of skill. Furthermore, they are more likely to act on this positive belief by helping children master new concepts. This combination of positive beliefs and helpful behaviors promotes the additional effort needed for children to persevere and successfully accomplish challenging learning tasks.

In contrast, parents display **negative beliefs** about children's academic potential when they focus on their learning challenges while at the same time ignoring or even downplaying their ability to meet those challenges. Pomerantz and her colleagues (2007) suggest that these parents are likely to provide limited if any assistance in promoting children's skill development. As a result, children are robbed of the encouragement they need to fully apply themselves when confronted with new learning challenges. For example, they may fail to carry through on a task they find uninteresting or frustrating.

You will want to diplomatically guide parents in using process-focused forms of support that send positive messages about their child's potential. Two examples are provided in Reflection 4.4. Complete this reflection by adding your own ideas.

REFLECTION 4.4   Reinforcing Positive Parental Attitudes and Beliefs

Complete this tip sheet on "Helping Your Child Succeed."

- **Example of a process-focused tip that supports children's efforts:** Pay equal attention to all the assignments your child brings home this year. Ask her to discuss the steps she took to complete each assignment. Also ask her to describe what she learned as a result of completing each assignment. This will help your child develop the reflective skills she needs to think through other assignments both in school and eventually in the workplace.
- **Add another tip to reinforce process-focused support of children's efforts.**
- **Example of a tip supporting positive beliefs about children's potential:** Children sometimes have difficulty understanding the benefits of a new learning assignment, especially if it is challenging. Encourage your child by telling him about a learning assignment you received as a child, the steps you took to master that assignment, and the benefits that resulted in the short and long term. For example, how did your mastery of multiplication help you as a child, adolescent, and adult? Reinforce the idea that your child too can master his new learning assignments. Offer to answer his questions and give suggestions, but avoid doing the work for him.
- **Add another tip to reinforce positive beliefs about children's potential.**

Teachers as Mediators

The bulk of information in this textbook directly or indirectly addresses five ways that teachers mediate the benefits of family involvement. These themes can be summarized as the five "Cs" of caring, commitment, cultural sensitivity, creativity, and communication.

Caring. As a teacher, you have a professional responsibility not only to care for the minds of children but also to protect their lively spirits and general well-being. Caring also reflects a family-school-community partnership philosophy, since caring for the whole child typically involves working collaboratively with families and community professionals.

Commitment. Demonstrating a commitment to the family-teacher relationship is one of the professional standards you will be expected to demonstrate as a teacher (Copple & Bredekamp, 2009, p. 22–23). In fact, your commitment to children will in part be judged by your commitment to their families.

Cultural sensitivity. Teachers are expected to create a welcoming and inclusive classroom environment for children and families from all walks of life. Likewise, teachers play a unique role in preparing children for a culturally diverse social environment. You will read more about these issues in Chapters 8 and 9.

Creativity. The diversity of family backgrounds in any classroom requires a flexible and creative mind-set in working through various family involvement challenges. This is why you are asked to think creatively when completing many of the reflective activities and assignments in this textbook.

Communication. Teachers learn early in their careers that communicating with families on a frequent basis is essential to ensuring family support and involvement. We examine the importance of various communication strategies in building and maintaining strong family-teacher relationships in Chapter 13. For now, complete Reflection 4.5.

REFLECTION 4.5   How Will You Mediate the Benefits of Family Involvement?

- Which "C" will you emphasize as a means of promoting the benefits of family involvement for children and families?
- Which "C" is your biggest challenge? How might you address this challenge?

CHAPTER SUMMARY

- Understanding the expectations that families and teachers have of each other can help us avoid the misunderstandings that stand in the way of family involvement benefits.
- Families mediate the benefits of family involvement through supportive scaffolding, skills development resources, and motivational development resources.
- Teachers mediate the benefits of family involvement in many ways, including through their caring, commitment, cultural sensitivity, creativity, and communication.

NOTE

1. Reprinted by permission of the publisher from MIND IN SOCIETY: DEVELOPMENT OF HIGHER PSYCHOLOGICAL PROCESSES by L. S. Vygotsky, edited by Michael Cole, Vera John-Steiner, Sylvia Scribner, and Ellen Souberman, p. 86, Cambridge, Mass: Harvard University Press, Copyright © 1978 by the President and Fellows of Harvard College.

DISCUSSION QUESTIONS

1. Review FYI 4.1. Then discuss the following questions:
   - Which family expectation presents the biggest challenge for teachers? How can this expectation be met?
   - Which teacher expectation should be given the most importance? How can this expectation be communicated to families?

2. Identify and discuss a potential family involvement benefit for families not addressed in this chapter. Do the same for teachers.

3. **Your family involvement philosophy.** Return to the draft of your family involvement philosophy. Based on your reading of this chapter, what if any changes will you make to your philosophy statement? Discuss your answer to this question with your peers.

COMMUNITY OF LEARNERS' FIELD ASSIGNMENT

As noted earlier in this chapter, there are a number of parent education curricula to choose from when responding to parents' request for assistance with child guidance. A few examples follow.

- **Parent Effectiveness Training (P.E.T.).** P.E.T. provides parents with communication and conflict resolution skills for maintaining a healthy parent-child relationship (Gordon, 2000). Certified P.E.T. instructors lead workshops that include brief lectures, demonstrations, workshop exercises, role playing, homework assignments, and group discussion. Family Effectiveness Training (F.E.T.) is a home study program for families who do not have access to a certified P.E.T. instructor. To learn more about P.E.T., visit the following website: http://www.gordontraining.com/parentingclass.html.

- **Systematic Training for Effective Parenting (STEP).** The STEP curriculum promotes healthy family relationships and responsible childhood behavior (Dinkmeyer, McKay, & Dinkmeyer, 1997). Examples of topics addressed in STEP include parent-child communication, cooperation, and child guidance strategies based on an authoritative parenting style. To learn more about STEP, visit the following website: www .steppublishers.com/.

- **Active Parenting.** Active parenting involves a series of video-based parent education lessons for parents of children ages 1 through 4, 5 through 12, and preteen and teen. A parent involvement curriculum is also available for helping parents support their children's education in Grades K through 7. Additional curricula include, among others, parenting after divorce and parenting in stepfamilies. To learn more about Active Parenting, visit the following website: http://www.activeparenting.com/.

- **SOS Help for Parents.** The SOS curriculum includes a book, DVD, and audio CDs that address over 20 parenting practices representing different theoretical perspectives (Clark, 2005). Over 46 childhood behavior challenges are addressed. The curriculum is available in nine languages. To learn more about SOS Help for Parents, visit the following website: http://www.sosprograms.com/parents_home.html.

There also are a number of national organizations that you, as a teacher, can collaborate with to conduct parent education workshops. Following are two organizations that support a network of parent educators.

- The **National Parenting Education Network (NPEN)** fosters linkages among practitioners and organizations involved in parenting education, promotes the education of parent educators through online articles and conferences, and shares successful programs and materials developed by parent educators from across the country. Visit the following website to learn more about this organization: www.npen.org/index .html. Click on the "State Networks and Connections" tab for contact information regarding parenting initiatives in your home state.

- The mission of **Parents as Teachers (PAT)** is to provide parenting education and family support programs for families that begin during a mother's pregnancy and last until her child enters kindergarten. While the focus of PAT is birth to age five, it is important to note that some school districts sponsor PAT programs. Such sponsorship is another reflection of full-service schools' adoption of an ecological perspective. In short, school administrators realize the importance of forming a strong mesosystem with families of very young children as a means of promoting parenting skills and preparing children for successful entry into school. Find organizations and school districts that sponsor PAT programs in your home state at the following website: www.parentsasteachers.org

Your task. As a class, divide into small groups. Each group should identify a parent educator in your local community. You may do this by visiting one of the above websites. Alternatively, visit a local school, health department, church, synagogue, or temple to determine if it sponsors parent education workshops. Volunteer to help with one of the workshops. Focus on the following observations.

- Did the parent educator use a particular curriculum?
- What topics did the parent educator cover?
- What strategies did the parent educator use to engage parents?
- What concerns and questions did parents present?
- How well did the parent educator respond to those concerns and questions?
- What tips did you learn about planning and facilitating a parent education workshop?

Make plans to meet briefly with the parent educator following the workshop. Ask the following questions:

- What was the most satisfying part of this workshop for you?
- Is there anything about the workshop that you would change?
- Did anything occur during the workshop that would be a good lesson for me to learn about planning and facilitating a parent education workshop?

Share the results of your observations and interviews in class. Compare and contrast the different materials, curricula, and strategies used by the parent educators.

CAPSTONE ACTIVITIES

Activity 1: Interview a Teacher About Her or His Expectations

Interview a teacher about the expectations she or he has of families. How does the teacher communicate these expectations to families?

Activity 2: Interview a Parent About Family Involvement Benefits

Use the information presented in this chapter to develop a list of ways that family involvement benefits families. Present the list to a parent. Which benefits ring true for the parent? Can the parent identify other benefits not addressed in this chapter? Share your results with your peers.

Activity 3: Develop a Bookmark

Identify an age group from prekindergarten through fifth grade. Develop a bookmark that will motivate parents to support any aspect of their child's academic life. Share your bookmark with your peers. Make a copy of everyone's bookmark. Place your copies in your teacher resource file.

INTERNET RESOURCES

You may find that some URLs have been altered by the webmaster. In these situations, try entering the name of the document or agency in a search engine. Alternatively, enter the domain name (e.g., http://www.xxxx.org). This should take you to the revised home page and associated links.

Johns Hopkins University, National Network of Partnership Schools, Center on School, Family, and Community Partnerships

http://www.csos.jhu.edu/P2000/center.htm

The mission of this center is to conduct and disseminate research, programs, and policy analyses to help families, teachers, and communities work together to strengthen family-school relations and enhance student learning and development.

Harvard Family Research Project, Harvard Graduate School of Education

http://www.hfrp.org/family-involvement

Personnel at the Harvard Family Research Project provide information on effective ways to support family involvement in children's education. The center publishes a newsletter, maintains a family involvement network of educators, and sponsors various family involvement projects.

National Coalition for Parent Involvement in Education (NCPIE)

http://ncpie.org/AboutNCPIE/

The mission of NCPIE is to advocate family involvement and promote family-teacher relationships. Click on the "Resources" link to gain access to family involvement resources for teachers, families, and administrators. You can also search for family involvement information by subject (e.g., assessment, communication, diversity).

STUDENT STUDY SITE

Log on to the Web-based student study site at **www.sagepub.com/coleman** for additional study tools including

- eFlashcards
- Web Quizzes
- Links to SAGE Journal Articles
- Author-created Videos
- Learning Objectives
- Web Resources
- Family Involvement Portfolio Guides

SECTION II

Understanding Family Lives in Contemporary Society

Normed Families

CHAPTER 5

Single-Parent Families, Stepfamilies, and Grandparents as Caregivers

I n this chapter we examine the strengths and challenges associated with three recently "normed" families whose numbers have increased over the past few decades: single-parent families, stepfamilies, and grandparent caregivers.

COMMUNITY LEARNING GUIDE

As you read this chapter, take notes on the following items. Use your notes to address the Discussion Questions, Field Assignment, and Capstone Activities that you find in the chapter.

- Describe the strengths and challenges associated with single-parent families, especially single-mother families.
- Describe the strengths and challenges associated with stepfamilies.
- Describe the strengths and challenges associated with grandparents who serve as caregivers for their grandchildren.
- Describe the role challenge that is faced by all normed families. Describe how each normed family may exhibit that challenge.

Single-Parent Families

Today, approximately 23% of children under age 18 live only with their mother in a single-parent arrangement (Federal Interagency Forum on Child and Family Statistics, 2009). Another 4% live only with their single father. Still other children live with single parents who are cohabitating with an unmarried partner (Cherlin, 2010). Recent demographic trends suggest that cohabitation is increasing and, as a result, more children will experience multiple family life transitions (Cherlin, 2010; Kennedy & Bumpass, 2008). Whether such transitions may lead to childhood behavior and relationship problems (Cherlin, 2010; Crosnoe & Cavanagh, 2010) or health problems (Schmeer, 2011) will require additional research. For now, we will examine the challenges and strengths associated with single-parent families in general and single-mother families in particular, since the majority of research on single parenthood has focused on single-mother households.

The information in this chapter supports the following family-school-community partnership standards. These standards are reviewed in Chapter 2.

NAEYC Standards and Associated Key Elements	1b, 1c, 2a, 2b, 2c, 6a, 6c, 6d, 6e
ACEI Standards	3.2, 5.1, 5.2
PTA Standards	1, 2, 3, 4, 5, 6

Challenges Associated With Single-Parent Families

Although single parenthood is no longer considered taboo (Goldscheider & Kaufman, 2006; Smock & Greenland, 2010; Waldfogel, Craigie, & Brooks-Gunn, 2010), these parents still face certain challenges when attempting to fulfill the family functions reviewed in Chapter 4. In this section, we review some of the more important challenges.

Insufficient income. Single mothers are especially likely to experience income challenges (Waldfogel et al., 2010). At least three factors account for this difference. First, women are paid less than their male counterparts. The median weekly pay of women is 80% of that paid to their male counterparts (U.S. Department of Labor, 2009). Second, as a general rule, women who retain custody of their children have income levels below that of their former husbands (Bianchi, Subaiya, & Kahn, 1999). Finally, less than half (47.1%) of custodial mothers receive full child support payments (Grall, 2009), which is especially important for mothers attempting to leave social welfare programs (U.S. Department of Health and Human Services, 2004).

The consequence of these three factors is that many single mothers have difficulty providing for the basic needs of their families. In fact, the overall standard of living for single mothers is only about half that of single fathers (Amato, 2000), and children who live with their unmarried mother are twice as likely to live in poverty as children who live with their unmarried father (Kreider, 2008).

Inadequate housing. Because of their lower incomes, single mothers in particular are likely to experience housing challenges. This perhaps explains why they also are more likely to make multiple moves (Amato, 2000). Unfortunately, frequent moves can set off a chain of events that are detrimental to children. For example, a change in residence may require a longer commute to work and school. If so, the subsequent change in the bedtime and morning departure schedule can negatively impact children's ability to pay attention to and actively participate in classroom lessons.

Normless norm. Single parents also face the challenge of a "normless norm," meaning they must define their own family norms, since society has not yet done so. This can create stress as single parents struggle to satisfy the multiple roles associated with household tasks,

Because single parents must assume multiple roles, they can experience role overload and role strain.

family finances, and their children's education and general well-being (Richards & Schmiege, 1993; Umberson, Pudrovska, & Reczek, 2010). The stress experienced in fulfilling multiple roles, and the associated feeling of being overwhelmed, is defined as **role overload** (White & Klein, 2002, p. 78). Role overload in turn is often associated with **role strain**, meaning that parents lack the resources needed to successfully carry out their roles (White & Klein, 2002, p. 67). For example, many single parents lack sufficient time to manage their work and home schedules.

Single parents may cope with their role overload and role strain in multiple ways. For example, social trends such as ready-to-eat meals, flexible work hours, and after-school programs are helpful in "norming" the lives of single-parent families. Single parents may also develop the multitasking skills needed to fulfill their multiple roles and thereby maintain their family equilibrium.

Finally, single parents may reduce the role strain that results from being a breadwinner, homemaker, caregiver, educator, and so forth by setting priorities. For example, some single parents may focus on their home management and breadwinning roles while assuming a more passive role in their children's education. In a way, this line of reasoning makes perfect sense. After all, teachers cannot clean a single parent's house, nor can they pay a parent's bill. On the other hand, teachers are trained to educate children, and, as noted in Chapter 4, parents expect teachers to let them know when additional educational support is needed at home.

Children's academic performance. Research findings suggest that, on average, children from single-parent families do not fare as well academically as their peers from two-parent families. Consider, for example, the following findings:

- Results from two international studies indicated that students living in single-parent families scored lower on math and science achievement than did their peers living in two-parent families. These findings were particularly pronounced in the United States (Heuveline, Yang, & Timberlake, 2010; Pong, Dronkers, & Hampden-Thompson, 2003).
- A United States government study found that fifth-grade children who had resided in single-parent families since kindergarten displayed lower average scores on reading, math, and science than did children from two-parent families (Tab, 2006). In a separate study, change scores in reading and math between kindergarten and fifth grade were significantly lower for children from single-parent families than for children from two-parent biological and married stepparent families (Shriner, Mullis, & Shriner, 2010).

- Results from another study indicated that fewer kindergarten children living with single mothers scored high in reading, math, and general knowledge than did their peers living in two-parent families (West, Denton, & Germino-Hausken, 2000).
- Finally, a smaller percentage of children in Grades 1 through 12 living with their single mothers received mostly As in school when compared to children from two-parent families (Nord & West, 2001). Yet they were more likely to have repeated a grade and (during Grades 6 through 12) to have been suspended or expelled from school.

Despite these findings, it is important to remember Reality Check #4: There is diversity within diversity. For example, the involvement of single mothers in their children's education, as well as educational outcomes for their children, were found to be similar to those of two-parent families when parents in both family structures had comparable levels of income and education (Entwisle & Alexander, 2000; Ginther & Pollak, 2004). In addition, there is some evidence that children's cognitive performance is less at risk when they are raised in stable single-parent families as opposed to unstable single-parent families (Waldfogel et al., 2010). Given these mixed findings, the most important lesson for us to remember is this: Just as in two-parent families, the more single parents are involved in their children's education, the better the school outcomes for their children (Nord & West, 2001). It is thus important that teachers do more than simply encourage single parents to hold high expectations for their children. They should also follow Realty Check #1 and be proactive in providing support for these high expectations. For example, in Chapter 3 you were introduced to a few home-based strategies that all parents can use to support their children's education. Other home- and classroom-based family involvement strategies are examined in upcoming chapters.

Strengths Associated With Single-Parent Families

Despite the above challenges, most single-parent families lead happy and healthy lives. In the following, we take a closer look at three specific strengths associated with single-parents families in general and single-mother families in particular.

Close parent-child relationships. Single mothers form close relationships with their children (Amato, 2000), especially their daughters (Hetherington & Stanley-Hagan, 2000). For example, one national study found that single mothers talked with, praised, and hugged their children more frequently than did single fathers (Amato, 2000). They also felt closer to their children and spent more time with them.

An interesting addition to the love and warmth shown by single mothers is the supervision they provide concerning homework completion and television viewing habits (Amato, 2000). You will remember from Chapter 1 that this combination of warmth and supervision is characteristic of an authoritative style of parenting, which has been shown to promote responsible childhood behavior. Thus, while single mothers may not have the income of many single fathers or two-parent families, their social parenting skills represent an important resource in advancing their children's development and education (Amato, 2000). Indeed, researchers have found that practical and emotional supports are especially important in facilitating adaptation and functioning among low-income single-mother families (Greeff & Fillis, 2009).

Behavioral expectations. Many single mothers hold mature expectations of their children (Amato, 2000). For example, assigning children home chores and involving them in decision making not only reinforces a sense of family cohesion and ensures an efficient management of household operations but also builds a sense of self-responsibility. While more research is needed to understand how involvement in decision making and household tasks influences children's classroom behavior, one reasonable hypothesis is that such activities may facilitate cooperative behavior, listening, problem solving, and carry-through skills.

Friend and kin support. Single parents look to friends and extended family members for various forms of support, including practical help and social camaraderie (Greeff & Fillis, 2009). In fact, single parents who live with kin report greater happiness, less depression, and better physical health (Amato, 2000). These outcomes are no doubt in part tied to the emotional support, companionship, and child care assistance that extended kin provide.

Strategies for Working With Single-Parent Families

As a teacher, you can take a number of steps to support single parents' involvement in their children's education. Some examples follow.

Arranging family-teacher conferences. Reality Check #1 reminds us to be proactive in reaching out to families. This reality check is especially relevant when working with single parents who, because of work and other constraints, find it difficult to attend parent-teacher conferences. One way to address this challenge is to arrange flexible meeting times before, during, and after school (see Chapter 10). In some situations it may also be necessary to conduct conferences by telephone or email (see Chapter 13). While such long-distance conferences are not as beneficial as face-to-face meetings, they are better than no conference at all.

Financial assistance. Single mothers in particular may not have the funds to help financially support a classroom project or to pay for their children's class pictures or field trips. Help single mothers as well as other families with limited income cover these expenses by joining with other teachers to set up a family involvement support fund. Seek donations for the fund from large businesses and corporations. Also work with civic groups and high school and college clubs to sponsor fundraising events.

Educational supports. Support of children's education was one of the family involvement goals we reviewed in Chapter 2. As already noted, consideration must be given to the schedules and financial resources of single parents when addressing this goal. Think simple and inexpensive. For example, explain that it is important for parents to set aside time each day to talk with their children about their classroom activities. Also send home inexpensive educational activities such as activity cards or family backpacks that can be carried out over the weekend. Finally, all parents will appreciate receiving information about inexpensive community events that they can attend with their children.

Support for the family emotional climate. School-based family recreation represents one approach to supporting the emotional climate of single-parent families, especially as leisure activities have been found to significantly predict a sense of family cohesion, adaptability, and overall functioning among single parents (Hornberger, Zabriskie, & Freeman, 2010). In addition, a community-based recreational program targeted specifically at single parents was found to increase their social connectedness (Azar, Naughton, & Joseph, 2009). In keeping with the idea of full-service schools from Chapter 2, school gyms and playgrounds represent ideal locations for early-morning, after-school, and weekend family recreation. An added benefit of such programming is the potential for greater parent-teacher contact and conferencing.

We next turn to another "normed" family: stepfamilies. These families became "normed" during the same period single-parent families did, in large part because a greater number of single parents led to a greater number of remarriages and, in turn, a greater number of stepfamilies.

Stepfamilies/Blended Families

According to the U.S. Census Bureau (Kreider, 2008), **stepfamilies**, also called **blended families**, contain stepchildren and their stepparents, half siblings, or stepsiblings. Based on this definition, approximately 17% of all children in the United States live in stepfamilies. These children may live exclusively within one blended family household or divide their time between the households of their divorced biological parents. In the latter situation, stepchildren are said to be living in a **binuclear family** arrangement (Crosbie-Burnett & Lewis, 1993). Put another way, binuclear arrangements can be described as "living apart together" (Cherlin, 2010). Managing family relationships across two households is one of many potential challenges faced by stepfamilies.

Challenges Associated With Stepfamilies

Researchers estimate that it may take from five to seven years for the stress level of remarried couples to match that of couples in a first marriage (Hetherington & Kelly, 2002, p. 263). Among children from divorced and remarried families, the "vast majority" are functioning well six years after divorce (Hetherington & Kelly, 2002, pp. 157–159). The need for this period of adjustment becomes clear when we consider the following challenges.

Multiple sets of relationships. One of the most obvious challenges facing stepfamilies is their management of relationships. Stepchildren can have multiple sets of residential and nonresidential parents, grandparents, and siblings that extend across their **families of origin** (i.e., the families into which they were born) and their new stepfamilies. In addition, if stepchildren live in binuclear families or have moved to a new neighborhood, they may also have multiple sets of friends.

As we will review later in this section, both time and permeable boundaries are needed to help stepchildren manage their multiple relationships (Hetherington & Stanley-Hagan, 2000). This is one reason why stepparents are warned against expecting instant love from their stepchildren (Hetherington & Stanley-Hagan, 2000). Instead, it is more realistic to expect warm relationships to develop slowly as stepchildren and stepparents establish rapport with each other.

Role ambiguity. Like single parents, stepfamilies are faced with the challenge of a "normless norm" (Lemanna & Riedmann, 2000, p. 506; Sweeney, 2010) in which there are no clearly defined or agreed-on societal rules or norms to follow. This can lead to **role ambiguity** in which family members are unsure of their particular roles or what is expected of them. Worse yet, they may rely on unrealistic and stereotyped roles such as those depicted in the 1970s television series *The Brady Bunch* (Leon & Angst, 2005).

Role ambiguity can spill over into the classroom. For example, a stepchild may complain that she is having problems with her homework because her biological father and new stepmother cannot agree on who should help her. In this situation, the teacher might choose to diplomatically explain how the parents' role ambiguity is interfering with the child's homework. One follow-up suggestion might be that the parents decide who will assume the role of "homework helper" relative to their particular academic strengths.

Although stepfamilies can face the challenge of role ambiguity, the majority make good adjustments over time.

Stepfather versus stepmother attempts to bond with stepchildren. Perhaps because of the role ambiguity they experience, stepfathers often assume more of a friendship than a disciplinarian role with their stepchildren, preferring to do things that are fun for the child, share new skills or activities, and work together on chores or projects (Ganong, Coleman, Fine, & Marin, 1999; Pryor, 2004). This approach appears to be advantageous in that stepfathers who establish warm and supportive friendships have better overall relationships with their stepchildren than do stepfathers who try to provide direct discipline (Coleman, Ganong, & Fine, 2001; Ganong et al., 1999; Hetherington & Stanley-Hagan, 2000; Pryor, 2004). The importance of the friendship role for stepfathers is reflected in the following quotes from stepchildren (Ganong et al., 1999):

> He takes me hunting, and he's teaching me to play golf. He takes me a lot of places he goes. The more I've lived with him, the more I've learned to trust him. He's a pretty all right guy in my mind. (p. 316)

> He's always treated me like one of his real kids. He always asked me what I wanted to do and if I didn't want to do something he didn't want to make me mad or anything so [we] didn't do it. (p. 317)

Stepmothers, like stepfathers, also gradually form positive relationships with their stepchildren. However, there are at least two reasons why their transition into the parenting role is more difficult than it is for stepfathers. First, because nonresidential biological mothers usually remain more involved in their children's lives, stepmothers can find it difficult to assert their parenting role or to receive respect for that role from their stepchildren (Pryor, 2004). Second, when stepmothers are pressured to assume a disciplinarian role, the time they have to gradually engage with their stepchildren can be short (Hetherington & Stanley-Hagan, 2000). This often is the case, as stepmothers are typically given responsibility for negotiating the various relationships that exist within stepfamilies. For example, stepmothers typically are given responsibility for arranging the details of visits between various kin, facilitating family gatherings, remembering birthdays, and discussing personal life issues (Schmeeckle, 2007). The more active parenting role assumed by stepmothers is reflected in the following quotes from adult stepchildren who acquired stepmothers during childhood:

> We moved into her home and then she became sort of responsible for every aspect of our lives . . . we were basically her responsibility along with her own two children. (Schmeeckle, 2007, p. 178)

> My father is more than willing to let Jessica [stepmother] run things. And it's never occurred to him that he is half at fault in everything. He's just basically a spectator in his relationship. (Schmeeckle, 2007, p. 179)

The following quotes from stepmothers themselves reflect the role ambiguity they can face in defining their stepparent role and fulfilling the types of "kinkeeping" responsibilities noted above (Whiting, Smith, Barnett, & Grafsky, 2007):[1]

> You don't know how . . . authoritative you can be. You don't want to step on their mom's foot. (p. 101)

> At first it was hard because I was always nervous about disciplining the kids. You know, would this make their [biological] mother mad or would it make my husband angry. (p. 101)

> I wish there was a reference manual. (p. 100)

Despite the role ambiguity that accompanies the stepparent role, family scholars agree that, over time, a parenting model usually emerges that promotes family stability and positive stepparent-stepchild relationships (Coleman et al., 2001; Hetherington & Stanley-Hagan, 2000). This model includes stepparents being warm and supportive as well as administering discipline in partnership with the residential biological parent. Reflections of this model can be found in the following quotes from stepmothers (Whiting et al., 2007):[1]

> In the beginning you should just be a friend to the kids and see where that takes you. (p. 101)

> I knew that there were no real standards and that you just have to feel it through at the time. (p. 100)

Nonresidential biological parents. Nonresidential biological parents also experience role ambiguity when deciding how much to assert their parenting rights. Perhaps it is thus not too surprising that, in a recent study, more than a third of the children had not seen their nonresidential mothers and fathers the previous year (Stewart, 2010). Nevertheless, the researcher also found gender differences that reflected traditional ideas about motherhood (i.e., mothers focused more on visitation) and fatherhood (i.e., fathers focused more on child support). A review of earlier research likewise found that children preferred their nonresidential mothers' focus on remaining in close contact to their nonresidential fathers' focus on recreation and avoiding confrontations (Hetherington & Stanley-Hagan, 2000).

Lack of family history and traditions. Stepfamilies lack a family history and a set of traditions (Fuller & Marxen, 2003). Both of these are important since, as noted in Chapter 1, families use traditions and rituals to gain a sense of who they are and to celebrate their common experiences. Establishing this type of perspective can be especially difficult for children whose need for consistency has been disrupted by changes in family membership and perhaps housing and schools arrangements.

Divided loyalties and jealously. Stepchildren sometimes feel conflicted about being loyal to their biological parents and their stepparent (Fuller & Marxen, 2003). This can result in feelings of guilt and anxiety over how much time and attention to devote to each parent, especially if conflict between the former spouses makes children feel they are caught in the middle (Amato, 2010a; Amato, 2010b). Likewise, jealousy can arise among siblings in a stepfamily who vie for the attention of their biological parent and stepparent. Both divided loyalties and jealously are especially relevant to young children who have not yet developed the type of peer network older children rely on to augment their need for attention and companionship.

Unfulfilled dreams. While it is not uncommon for children living in stepfamilies to harbor dreams of their biological parents' getting back together, the opposite is also possible. Children who leave dysfunctional families may welcome forming new relationships with stepparents who are supportive and nurturing (Hetherington & Stanley-Hagan, 2000). Indeed, studies over the past two decades lend support to the idea that children fair well when divorce ends a high-conflict marriage (Amato, 2010b).

Family involvement and childhood outcomes among stepfamilies. There is both disturbing and good news regarding the academic performance of children who experience their parents' divorce and remarriage. On one hand, divorce itself has the potential to reduce children's psychosocial well-being, which may in turn explain their poorer performance on math and reading scores (Potter, 2010). In addition, children of divorced parents continue to face academic challenges once a new stepfamily is formed. For example, the authors of one government study reported that stepparents were less involved than biological parents in attending school events and volunteering in their stepchildren's schools (Nord & West, 2001). Such findings may in part help to explain why youth living with a stepparent tend not to fare as well as those living with two biological parents along a range of educational, cognitive, emotional, and behavioral outcomes (Sweeney, 2010).

On the other hand, the Nord and West study also found that even moderate levels of school involvement by stepfathers increased the odds that their stepchildren would receive good grades, while the involvement of stepmothers reduced the odds that their stepchildren would be suspended or expelled from school (Nord & West, 2001). These findings reinforce the importance of teachers' communicating and working closely with stepparents to make sure they feel empowered to make decisions about their stepchildren's education and that they feel welcomed in the classroom. We examine these topics in Chapters 11, 12, and 13.

Legal rights. As noted in Chapter 1, family disputes can erupt over the right of a stepparent versus a nonresidential biological parent to make decisions about a child's medical care and education. Currently, stepparents can acquire legal parental status through adoption, but only if the rights of the noncustodial biological parent have been legally terminated (Mahoney, 2006). Some have suggested that this dilemma might be resolved with a **residence order**, the purpose of which would be to grant stepparents certain decision making rights related to the best interests of their stepchildren while not taking away rights from nonresidential biological parents (Coleman et al., 2001; Hetherington & Stanley-Hagan, 2000). Whether or not such an order would work in all situations is unclear, but it is an example of an issue teachers are likely to encounter in the years to come as society attempts to resolve the ethical and legal dilemmas created by changing family structures and lifestyles.

Strengths Associated With Stepfamilies

As noted earlier, almost all stepfamilies make good adjustments over time (Fuller & Marxen, 2003; Hetherington & Stanley-Hagan, 2000), no doubt in large part because they are able to make use of three strengths identified in a study that followed stepfamilies during the first four years of their formation (Braithwaite, Olson, Golish, Soukup, & Turman, 2001).

Boundary management. Stepfamilies are most successful when they are willing and able to negotiate boundaries that allow for a smooth transition into new households and movement between households. Such permeable household boundaries are especially beneficial for children, who in turn are exposed to multiple role models. As you will recall from Chapter 3, the presence of multiple child-adult attachments is a core principle in Bronfenbrenner's ecological theory. Thus, in the case of stepfamilies, the life experiences and skills of multiple role models can broaden children's view of the world (Knox & Schacht, 2002, p. 411) and thereby facilitate their formal and informal education.

Family solidarity. Successful stepfamilies are able to create a sense of solidarity within their family system by confronting and dealing with the constant changes that accompany the formation of a new family. No doubt open and honest communication is one key to achieving this end result. Indeed, establishing the rules, roles, and traditions needed to create a healthy stepfamily climate requires negotiation in which adults and children must be able to express their needs in appropriate ways and offer verbal reinforcement to others for their help and support. Consider, for example, the following quotes from stepmothers (Whiting et al., 2007):[1]

> Listening and ... not criticizing, but reflecting back on what they have said and how it seems to be making them feel and maybe commenting on it is reinforcing, not judging. (p. 102)

> I let [my husband] know that I needed some expectations. I wasn't sure ... what I was supposed to do. Was I supposed to be a mom or not a mom? (p. 103)

An additional potential benefit of open and honest communication is that stepchildren may acquire more mature communication skills. These skills can in turn help them negotiate disagreements, avoid misunderstandings, and successfully complete class assignments.

Adaptability. Rather than trying to create an "instant family," successful stepfamilies take their time in adapting to a new mix of family personalities and new living situations. This willingness to adapt to new life demands allows them to avoid the trap of trying to replicate family roles and norms from their original families. In short, they focus on "becoming a family" rather than instantly "being a family." This process often requires stepchildren and their stepparents to learn the art of compromise (Fuller & Marxen, 2003). From deciding who sleeps where to who performs which home chores, stepfamilies must learn to problem-solve as they establish their new household. These home experiences translate well to the classroom, where conflicts frequently arise over taking turns, sitting arrangements, and sharing materials.

Strategies for Working With Stepfamilies

While there are as yet no established norms to guide stepfamilies, research findings and program models are available that teachers can use to help divorcing spouses, their children, and stepfamilies adjust to their new lives. Some examples follow.

Recognizing the diversity in child-stepparent relationships. Researchers recently identified a number of stepchild-stepparent relationship patterns (Ganong, Coleman, & Jamison, 2011), each of which is useful in appreciating the interactions that teachers might observe between children and stepparents. We will review three of these patterns.

In the *accepting as a parent* pattern, children typically were raised by their stepparent from infancy or early childhood. Except for periods of conflict during adolescent, parent-child relationships were emotionally close. In the *liking from the start* pattern, children generally were in middle childhood or early adolescence when they met their stepparents. "Liking from the start" relationships developed quickly, usually around mutual interests, common values, and shared pastimes. Stepparents focused on building the relationship rather than assuming parental responsibilities. Finally, in the *changing trajectories* pattern, children were school age to adolescent when their relationship began. Typically, these children initially disliked their stepparents until something changed and they made a conscious decision to build a closer relationship. No single event led to the change in trajectories; rather, it was a gradual process in which children began to recognize that the stepparent was a positive influence in his or her family life. Likewise, the stepparents were persistent in their efforts to build a bond with their stepchildren.

Divorce education and mediation programs. Legal, family, and mental health professionals across the country are collaborating to provide education programming for divorcing parents. The purpose of these programs is to minimize the potential negative impact of divorce on children (Blaisure & Geasler, 2006). Thus, for example, parents learn about the destructive impact of ex-spouse conflict on children. They also explore ways to maintain healthy relationships with their children by following such key principles as being physically present in children's lives and attentive to their needs, telling children what to expect and answering their questions related to changes in their relationships and daily routine, and helping them manage their feelings (Ricci, 2010).

Another option is for divorcing parents to participate in a mediation program with the objective of resolving specific marital and/or parenting disagreements (Amato, 2010b). Both parent education and mediation programs have proven helpful in reducing conflict, avoiding costly litigation, promoting more positive family functioning, facilitating greater satisfaction with divorce outcomes, and reducing psychological distress (Amato, 2010b). For example, one group of researchers found that mediation resulted in more contact between nonresident fathers and children, more communication between divorced parents, and less conflict between divorced parents (Emery, Sbarra, & Grover, 2005). Two examples of divorce education and mediation programs can be found under the Internet Resources section of this chapter.

Social support. As with most life disruptions, social support is essential in helping children cope with divorce and adapt to new life demands. This is why some schools offer school-based programs for children with divorced parents (Amato, 2010a). These programs allow children to develop a support system among peers who also are dealing with divorce. Such a support system is important in allowing children to vent their feelings, share positive coping strategies, and explore alternatives to handling personal and interpersonal dilemmas. Similar types of programs could be offered for children living in stepfamilies, using school or community counselors as group mediators.

Books and photographs. Consult with your local librarian to identify age-appropriate books that depict positive stories about children who experience divorce and live in stepfamilies. Share these books with divorcing parents and stepparents. Also make them available in your classroom reading center. As with other family arrangements, make sure any photographs or posters depicting family life include positive images of stepfamilies.

In the following section, we examine the lives of one more "normed" family: grandparent caregivers. As you read this section, consider how their potential challenges and strengths compare to those of single parents and stepparents. This comparison will help you with the discussion questions at the end of the chapter.

Grandparents as Primary Caregivers

The U.S. Census Bureau estimates that approximately 9% of all children live in a household with at least one grandparent present (Kreider, 2008). The phrase **grandparent caregiver** refers to grandparents who serve as their grandchildren's primary or co-caregiver. This definition requires a distinction between two types of grandparent caregiver households. **Multigenerational households** consist of three generations (child, parent, and grandparent) in which grandparents co-parent with parents (Tutwiler, 2005, p. 43). **Intergenerational** or **skipped households** involve grandparents who serve as sole caregivers for their grandchildren (Park, 2006).

Grandparents enter the above households for a variety of reasons. In some situations children are removed from their parents' homes following abuse, neglect, or abandonment. In other situations parents are unable to fulfill their parenting responsibilities because of their age (teenage pregnancy), drug or alcohol addiction, incarceration, illness, or death (Cherlin, 2010; Park, 2006; Tutwiler, 2005, p. 44).

Challenges Associated With Grandparent Caregivers

Regardless of the reason for grandparents' assuming the caregiver role, it can be a life-changing event. In this section, we examine some potential challenges faced by grandparent caregivers.

Disruption of the life cycle. The typical expectations, experiences, resources, and responsibilities associated with later adulthood can be disrupted when grandparents assume responsibility for their grandchildren's well-being. Social and recreational activities may have to be cut back or abandoned. New financial obligations arise. Grandparents who thought their parenting duties had ended suddenly find they must recycle that role (Landry-Meyer & Newman, 2004). Grandparents who experience these disruptions are said to be **offtime** in their life cycle (Dolbin-MacNab, 2006; Tutwiler, 2005, p. 44). This in turn can create emotional stress for grandparents, especially grandmothers (Hughes & Waite, 2002), who are unprepared to deal with their new responsibilities.

Behavior management. Being offtime is perhaps most evident in regard to grandparents' child guidance practices. For example, grandparents may object to their grandchildren's use of language as well as their dress, music, and choice of friends. Unfortunately, having reared their own children in a different social ecology, grandparents may lack the skills needed to effectively relate to their grandchildren and negotiate areas of disagreement (Dolbin-MacNab, 2006). For example, because of parenting norms when they were parents, grandparents may assume a more authoritarian approach to child guidance even though their grandchildren are accustomed to dealing with teachers and youth leaders who use an authoritative approach.

Physical health. A review of the literature (Hayslip & Kaminski, 2005b) and results from independent studies (Bachman & Chase-Lansdale, 2005) suggest that the health of grandparent caregivers is negatively affected over time. Indeed, grandparents cite lack of energy as one of the most challenging aspects of their caregiving role (Dolbin-MacNab, 2006). This is not surprising, since even young parents have problems maintaining their physical stamina when caring for active children.

Legal standing and access to community services. Many grandparent caregivers have informal custodial arrangements and not legal custody of their grandchildren. This can create problems when they attempt to access community services for their grandchildren, especially when legal consent is required for the delivery of such services. **Consent laws** are designed to give grandparents these rights (Smith & Beltran, 2000). The affidavits associated with consent laws, which do not require the signatures of biological parents, are especially important for children who need special educational and medical services after being removed from their parents' neglectful or abusive homes.

Financial strain. Some of the financial strain faced by grandparent caregivers includes the need to provide for their grandchildren's clothing, food, school supplies, transportation, and recreation. The cost of health care is an additional strain. In fact, researchers have found that a disproportionately high rate of children who live in intergenerational households are enrolled in public insurance programs or lack health insurance altogether (Baker & Mutchler, 2010). Both situations put children at risk for delayed health care.

Some grandparents postpone or give up their retirement plans to meet their financial obligations. Others, however, are forced to reduce their work hours to provide direct care for their grandchildren (Tutwiler, 2005, p. 44). Fortunately, the financial obligations faced by grandparents can be somewhat offset in states that allow them to receive foster care or kinship care payments (Kreider, 2008).

Role conflict. **Role conflict** results when we experience stress because of an inability to reconcile the different expectations that accompany our assumed or assigned roles. Grandparent caregivers experience role conflict when the expectations associated with the grandparent role conflict with those associated with the parent role. For example, grandparents typically are expected to indulge—even spoil—their grandchildren. In contrast, grandparents who assume the caregiver role are expected to assume a firm stance as the parenting figure in their grandchildren's lives (Landry-Meyer & Newman, 2004). Grandparent caregivers also can experience role conflict when they lack the legal authority to carry out their parenting duties or when they fail to receive the same degree of respect from teachers and other community professionals that is shown to biological parents (Landry-Meyer & Newman, 2004).

Social isolation and support systems. Social isolation and a lack of family and community support represent additional challenges for many grandparent caregivers (Hayslip & Kaminski, 2005a, 2005b; Sands & Goldberg-Glen, 2000). The demands of parenting can isolate grandparents from their peers who do not have this responsibility and are thus free to pursue adult-only activities.

Grandparent caregivers need two types of support: the **formal support** provided through community services and the **informal support** provided by friends and family (Landry-Meyer, Gerard, & Guzell, 2005). To be effective, both forms of support should match grandparents' specific needs (Landry-Meyer et al., 2005). Thus general offers to help or listen, while based on good intentions, are not enough. Instead, specific action is needed, such as provision of child care, transportation, or help in resolving grandparent-grandchild conflicts. Keep this tip in mind as you complete Case Study 5.1.

Grandparent caregivers can face the challenge of role conflict as they attempt to reconcile expectations of grandparents with those of parents.

CASE STUDY 5.1   Mr. and Mrs. Smith

Mr. and Mrs. Smith assumed parenting responsibilities for their grandson a little over a year ago when their daughter suddenly died and her ex-husband moved out of state. This child is now a student in your classroom. Although the Smiths are excellent caregivers, they appear depressed. They never smile and are hesitant to join in with other parents during classroom events. When you express your concerns to Mrs. Smith, she begins to cry and runs out of the building. Later, she and Mr. Smith call for an appointment. They explain that they love their grandson, but their caregiving responsibilities are beginning to take a toll on their emotional and physical health. These were to be their "golden years," when they were to relax and have fun. Those plans have now changed. Their friends do not call, and they do not have the free time to enjoy the types of social activities that were a part of their lives before the death of their daughter. They have talked about making other living arrangements for their grandson but feel that would mean abandoning him. They do not know what to do but feel their situation has to change. How would you handle this situation?

Strengths Associated With Grandparent Caregivers

The following strengths help to counteract many of the previously mentioned challenges.

Safety net. Perhaps the most obvious strength associated with grandparent caregivers is their provision of a safety net that ensures that their grandchildren receive the protection, love, and security needed to lead happy and healthy lives (Hayslip & Kaminski, 2005b). Without this safety net, social workers must turn to foster care placement using individuals who, although caring and competent, lack the history and sense of continuity that grandparents provide for their grandchildren.

Grandmothers' support of grandchildren's development and education. Children residing with their single mothers and their grandmothers in multigenerational households display better reading scores and work habits upon entering first grade than children in other single-mother living arrangements (Entwisle & Alexander, 2000). Grandmothers also serve as important socialization agents when residing in multigenerational households (Entwisle & Alexander, 2000). Both of these benefits no doubt reflect the additional parenting support provided by grandmothers.

Generational wisdom. One of the most important strengths associated with grandparent caregivers is their ability to build human capital by passing along a body of knowledge, skills, and experiences to a new generation (Dolbin-MacNab, 2006). As a teacher, you can help facilitate this transfer of human capital by using the strategies that are presented in the following section.

Strategies for Working With Grandparents

Use the following strategies to learn more about grandparents who serve as caregivers and to advance your skills in forming a positive parent-teacher partnership with them.

In-service training. Ask your administrator to arrange in-service training on working with grandparent caregivers. Such training might include, for example, representatives from various community agencies helping you and your colleagues learn how to assist grandparent caregivers in negotiating and understanding the social services delivery system, its paperwork, and its technical terminology.

Paying attention to grandparents' emotional state. Look for changes in their demeanor, energy level, and health. Gently inquire about their well-being, if you think they are experiencing stress. Make counseling referrals when appropriate and be sure to check back with grandparents to ensure they are getting the help needed to maintain their emotional well-being. Also take care to acknowledge grandparents. For example, an annual grandparents' day can be used to recognize grandparents for the contributions they make to their grandchildren's lives.

Information. Provide information to grandparent caregivers about contemporary parenting skills such as setting limits, logical consequences, and communication skills (Dolbin-MacNab, 2006; Hayslip & Kaminski, 2005a, 2005b). However, remember that parenting is a sensitive topic. Some grandparents may become defensive if they believe their parenting skills are being questioned. To avoid this situation, put everyone on the same stage. For example, introduce a child guidance workshop by asking for examples of how changes in society require everyone, including young parents and teachers, to take a fresh look at our expectations of children and our child guidance practices (Hayslip & Kaminski, 2005a, 2005b).

Support groups. The stressors placed on grandparents can be offset using networks that link them to the types of formal and informal supports noted earlier in this chapter (Silverstein & Giarrusso, 2010). As a teacher, you can apply this principle by working with school and community social workers and counselors to establish grandparent support groups. Use the groups to provide grandparents with opportunities to share stories about how they became caregivers, discuss their frustrations in fulfilling this role, explore solutions to caregiving challenges, and reinforce themes of hope and success (Dolbin-MacNab, 2006; Hayslip & Kaminski, 2005a, 2005b). Also remember to emphasize the many positive contributions that grandparents make to their grandchildren's well-being (Landry-Meyer et al., 2005). A recent review of research suggests that creating such a positive emotional environment can boost the satisfaction intrinsic to caring for grandchildren (Silverstein & Giarrusso, 2010).

Protection tips. Provide grandparent caregivers with tips for protecting their grandchildren from contemporary threats with which they may be unfamiliar. For example, sexual predators, drugs, gangs, bullying, and media violence represent threats that, while present in previous decades, are even more prevalent today and take on different dimensions than they did in the past (Dolbin-MacNab, 2006; Hayslip & Kaminski, 2005a, 2005b).

Empowerment. Almost all children enjoy learning about the lives of children from previous generations. Empower grandparent caregivers by encouraging them to share their life experiences. For example, grandparents might choose to talk about their home and school experiences when they were children, share songs they sang as children, or play games that were popular during their childhood. These activities need not be accompanied by a great deal of structure. Instead, keep them flexible and informal (Davidson & Boals-Gilbert, 2010). This will allow the resulting intergenerational exchanges to develop in a more natural manner (Larkin & Kaplan, 2010). Visit the following website, sponsored by Intergenerational Programs and Aging at Pennsylvania State University, to learn about other intergenerational activities and resources: http://intergenerational.cas.psu.edu/earlychildhood.html.

Printed materials prepared with grandparents in mind. Grandparents may not be able to see small print as well as younger parents. To facilitate their reading of classroom newsletters and other printed materials, use black print on white paper and a large font (at least 12-point type) (Birkmayer, Cohen, Jensen, & Variano, 2005).

Awareness of sensitive topics. For example, nursery rhymes such as "The Old Lady Who Lived in the Shoe" can be embarrassing for children who live with their grandparents (Birkmayer et al., 2005). In addition, children may ask why a peer's grandparent attends classroom events instead of the child's mother or father. Ask the grandparent how he or she would like you to respond (Birkmayer et al., 2005). Consider, for example, Case Study 5.2.

CASE STUDY 5.2   Kyle

Kyle's single mother is in jail, but his grandmother prefers that you tell others that she is away on a trip. As Kyle's teacher, you can honestly explain to his peers, "Kyle's grandmother says his mom is away, so she's taking care of Kyle right now."

Now that you have been introduced to the potential challenges and strengths associated with single-parent families, stepfamilies, and grandparent caregivers, proceed to the final section of this chapter to read about the one challenge they all face.

Symbolic Interactionism: Normed Families Facing a Normless Norm

Single parents, stepparents, and grandparent caregivers all face a similar contradiction. In short, all three "normed" families face the "normless norm" challenge of defining their family roles. This challenge is best reflected in the concepts of role overload, role strain, role ambiguity, and role conflict, all of which come from a theoretical perspective called **symbolic interactionism**. Simply put, this theory is concerned with how we use symbols (e.g., language and roles) to guide our social interactions (see White & Klein, 2002). As you will recall, single parents assume sole responsibility for most family tasks because of the absence of a spouse. This can result in both role overload and role stain. Because they are without family history and family rituals to guide their interactions, stepfamilies can experience role ambiguity. Finally, because of their roles as both parent and grandparent, grandparent caregivers can experience role conflict.

Each of these role challenges has practical implications for teachers. For example, you can decrease the role overload and role strain experienced by single parents by providing supports that make it easier for them to fulfill their educational role. Some examples of such supports were examined in Chapter 3 (backpacks, tip sheets, activity calendars, and activity cards). Additional parent-teacher communication supports are examined in Chapter 13.

You can help clarify the role ambiguity experienced by stepfamilies by asking them to make key role decisions associated with school. For example, during registration, engage biological parents and stepparents in a discussion about who will be on a child's pickup list. Also ask them to discuss who will receive academic reports, classroom notes, and invitations to attend parent-teacher conferences. Finally, ask them who will be notified in case of an emergency.

You can reduce the role conflict experienced by grandparents by making an extra effort to reinforce the important role they play in their grandchildren's lives. For example, you might join your colleagues to plan an annual grandparents' day or intergenerational classroom activities.

CHAPTER SUMMARY

- Before making assumptions about any normed family, first follow Reality Check #3 and look for family strengths, not just challenges.
- The "normed" families reviewed in this chapter also face the contradiction of adapting to a "normless norm."

NOTE

1. Whiting, J. B., Smith, D. R., Barnett, T., & Grafsky, E.L. (2007). Overcoming the cinderella myth: A mixed methods study of successful stepmothers. *Journal of Divorce and Remarriage, 47* (1/2), 95–109. Reprinted by permission of the publisher (Taylor & Francis Group, http://www.informaworld.com).

DISCUSSION QUESTIONS

1. Which of the strengths reviewed in this chapter do you believe are of greatest benefit to children's development and education? Which challenges are most detrimental to children's development and education?

2. Which normed family do you believe needs the most teacher support?

3. **Your family involvement philosophy.** Return to the draft of your family involvement philosophy. Based on your reading of this chapter, what if any changes will you make to your philosophy statement? Discuss your answer to this question with your peers.

COMMUNITY OF LEARNERS' FIELD ASSIGNMENT

Learn More About Working With Grandparents

Earlier in this chapter, we reviewed the possibility of teachers' arranging in-service workshops on working with grandparent caregivers. This assignment will allow you to gain firsthand knowledge of how professionals in your local community work with grandparents.

Your task. Interview a community professional who works with grandparents. These professionals may be found at recreation centers, councils on aging, retirement communities, and senior citizen centers. Ask the following questions during your interview. Share the results of your interview with your peers.

- What is your role in working with grandparents?
- Do you offer activities that involve both grandparents and their grandchildren? If so, what are those activities? How do grandparents and their grandchildren benefit from these activities?
- What topics come up when grandparents talk about their grandchildren?
- Do some of the grandparents in your program also care for their grandchildren? If so, what concerns do they express about carrying out their caregiving role? What do they enjoy about this role?
- What advice do you have for teachers with children in their classroom who are being cared for by their grandparents?

Capstone Activities

Activity 1: Interview a Parent

Interview a single parent, a stepparent, or a grandparent caregiver. How does this person define his or her family's biggest challenge and biggest strength? How does this person's responses compare to the information in this chapter? Share the results of your interview with your peers.

Activity 2: Celebrate Families Through Children's Books

Identify a children's book that celebrates single-parent families, stepfamilies, or grandparent caregiver families. Summarize the theme(s) in the book. Share your book with your peers.

Activity 3: "10 Tips for Working With [Family Type]"

Use the Internet, books, journals, and magazines to develop an educational brochure for your peers. Give your brochure the following title: "10 Tips for Working With [Family Type]." Share the resulting brochures in class. Make copies for everyone. Place your copy in your teacher resource file for future reference.

Internet Resources

You may find that some URLs have been altered by the webmaster. In these situations, try entering the name of the document or agency in a search engine. Alternatively, enter the domain name (e.g., http://www.xxxx.org). This should take you to the revised home page and associated links.

Parents Without Partners

www.parentswithoutpartners.org/

Parents Without Partners provides information, educational activities, family activities, and adult social and recreational activities in support of single parents and their children. Affiliates of Parents Without Partners can be found throughout the United State and Canada.

Kids in the Middle

http://www.kidsinthemiddle.org/

This organization, located in St. Louis, Missouri, provides counseling, education, and support to assist children and parents in coping with the divorce process. For example, children's fears and feelings are addressed through group and individual counseling. Parents also receive guidance in helping their children cope with the challenges brought about by divorce.

Kids' Turn San Diego

http://www.kidsturnsd.org/

This program assists families and children cope with separation, divorce, legal actions, and changes in custody arrangements. Staff members also assist with communication problems and issues surrounding children's exposure to domestic violence.

National Stepfamily Resource Center (NSRC)

http://www.stepfamilies.info/

The NSRC is a division of Auburn University's Center for Children, Youth and Families. Its mission is to serve as a clearinghouse for family science research and information on stepfamilies.

American Association of Retired Persons (AARP)

http://www.aarp.org/

AARP is a national organization that helps people 50 and over improve the quality of their lives. Click on the various links to learn more about grandparents in general as well as grandparents who serve as caregivers for their grandchildren.

Grand Magazine

http://www.grandmagazine.com/

This online magazine is published for "grandparents and the grandkids who love them." The magazine publishes a range of information related to grandparents and grandparent-grandchild relationships.

STUDENT STUDY SITE

Log on to the Web-based student study site at **www.sagepub.com/coleman** for additional study tools including

- eFlashcards
- Web Quizzes
- Links to SAGE Journal Articles
- Author-created Videos

- Learning Objectives
- Web Resources
- Family Involvement Portfolio Guides

CHAPTER 6

Emerging and Vulnerable Families

Gay and Lesbian Families and Families Living in Poverty

W e continue our discussion of family diversity in this chapter by examining two additional family arrangements that were first introduced in Chapter 1 and are topics of much discussion in contemporary society. Gay and lesbian families are perhaps the best example of an emerging family whose legality is recognized in only a few states. Families living in or at poverty are examples of vulnerable families. Like normed families, both of these family forms face potential challenges and possess potential strengths.

Gay and Lesbian Families

As with other family arrangements, "To study same-sex parenting . . . is to study not one phenomenon but many" (Meezan & Rauch, 2005, p. 100). Indeed, gays and lesbians reach parenthood through different routes (Meezan & Rauch, 2005; Patterson & Sutfin, 2004). Some have children from previous marriages that involved opposite-sex partners. Others adopt children or serve as foster parents. Some gay couples recruit a surrogate mother so that one of the males can donate his sperm. Regardless of their particular route to parenthood, most gay and lesbian families are likely to face at least some of the following challenges.

> The information in this chapter supports the following family-school-community partnership standards. These standards are reviewed in Chapter 2.
>
> | NAEYC Standards and Associated Key Elements | 1b, 1c, 2a, 2b, 2c, 6a, 6c, 6d, 6e |
> |---|---|
> | ACEI Standards | 3.2, 5.1, 5.2 |
> | PTA Standards | 1, 2, 3, 4, 5, 6 |

Challenges Associated With Gay and Lesbian Families

As you read this section, remember that not all gay and lesbian families face the following challenges to an equal degree. Likewise, no two families are likely to respond to any given challenge in the same way.

Acceptance. One understandable concern among gay and lesbian families is the treatment their children receive from teachers (Peplau & Beals, 2004; Tutwiler, 2005) and peers. Reviews of the literature indicate that while some children of gay and lesbian families do experience taunts from their peers, or fear taunts should they disclose the nature of their family arrangement (Biblarz & Savci, 2010), there is no indication that such encounters negatively impact their adjustment (Patterson, 2006; Tasker, 2005). Nevertheless, the difficulty in dismissing such concerns is reflected in the following quotes from lesbian parents:

> [My son] gets ribbed about his parent being a lesbian. He has to deal with that. It wasn't easy for him. It hasn't been as bad this year [because adults at the school have intervened]. (Mercier & Harold, 2003, p. 43)

> I've already asked him questions, like "[My partner] would like to watch you play [on a school sports team]. Would that be okay? Would you feel comfortable if [my partner] came with me?" (Mercier & Harold, 2003, p. 43)

Stereotypes. Like other minority family arrangements, gay and lesbian families must learn to deal with stereotypes. Perhaps the most insulting stereotype is reflected in the phrase "the gay and lesbian lifestyle," which implies that there is only one lifestyle available to gay and lesbian families. This line of thinking is frequently endorsed by critics who use the phrase to promote negative stereotypes and justify discriminatory behavior toward gay and lesbian families. In fact, gay and lesbian families are as diverse as those headed by heterosexual couples.

Concerns regarding parenting and children's adjustment. Based on years of research, there is overwhelming evidence that gay and lesbian parents demonstrate patterns of behavior that resemble those of heterosexual parents (Biblarz & Savci, 2010; Herek, 2006; Meezan & Rauch, 2005; Patterson, 2000, 2001, 2006; Perrin, 2002; Peterson, Bodman, Bush, & Madden-Derdich, 2000; Tasker, 2005). Similarly, there is no evidence that children or adolescents of gay or lesbian families differ from their peers raised by heterosexual parents in terms of behavioral problems, self-concept, depression, anxiety, feelings of social acceptance, gender roles, intelligence, moral judgment, personality characteristics, peer relations, delinquent behavior, or the likelihood of being sexually abused (Herek, 2006; Meezan & Rauch, 2005; Patterson, 2000, 2001; Peplau & Beals, 2004; Perrin, 2002; Peterson et al., 2000; Savin-Williams & Esterberg, 2000; Tasker, 2005). To date, no one has tracked a large sample of children raised by gay and lesbian parents into adulthood, making it difficult to assess their sexual identities (Biblarz & Savci, 2010).

In summary, and as noted in the most recent comprehensive review of gay and lesbian families, "Researchers have documented what most social scientists already know . . . that sexual orientations . . . per se have almost nothing to do with fitness for family roles and relationships, including parenting" (Biblarz & Savci, 2010, p. 480). Indeed, this statement is supported by the observation that, like children who are parented in any other family, children of gay and lesbian parents do best in families that are characterized by supportive relationships and low levels of conflict (Patterson, 2006; Perrin, 2002).

Legal standing. As briefly noted in Chapter 1, the tenuous legal standing of most gay and lesbian families can threaten their stability. For example, adoption laws related to gay and lesbian families, as well as their interpretations by local courts, vary considerably (Meezan & Rauch, 2005). Currently, only a few states allow **second-parent adoption** (also called **co-parent adoption**), in which a second same-sex partner is allowed to adopt the first partner's biological or previously adopted child (Human Rights Campaign, 2006; Meezan & Rauch, 2005). Without a second-parent adoption, the second partner is prohibited from making legal decisions about a child's welfare. The emotional stress this creates is reflected in the following quotes from lesbian parents:

> I feel like I have less legal rights . . . because we haven't been able to do the [second-parent] adoption, I have no real rights. And so I feel like people want to deal with [my partner], not with me. (p. 42)

> [Our daughter] has asked me before, "Why don't you go to my parent-teacher conferences?" . . . I think that [my daughter] would like it [if I were more involved]. But I don't feel it's my place. (Mercier & Harold, 2003, p. 42)

Similar to other family situations we have reviewed so far in this textbook, the legal challenges faced by gay and lesbian parents can create dilemmas for teachers. Consider, for example, Case Study 6.1.

Strengths Associated With Gay and Lesbian Families

Children from gay and lesbian families are exposed to a number of positive life experiences that have implications for their development and education. Some of these experiences are presented below.

CASE STUDY 6.1   Jorge

Jorge, a child in your classroom, has been diagnosed with attention deficit disorder. Jorge lives with his biological father Jacob and Jacob's partner Pete. Even though Pete is not an adoptive father, he attends classroom events and works closely with you to support Jorge's academic work and social development.

Because of his work in supporting classroom activities, another parent nominates Pete to head the classroom family advisory committee. The purpose of this committee is to assist you in thinking through your family involvement plans. One parent expresses her concern over this "illegal" move and asks that you not accept Pete's nomination. How do you respond?

Lessons in diversity and tolerance. Children who grow up in lesbian and gay families learn lessons about tolerance for individual differences and living arrangements that do not reflect societal norms. Such lessons facilitate children's ability to succeed in a society that is becoming increasingly diverse. As a teacher, you can support themes of diversity and tolerance by using gender-neutral terms such as *parent* or *guardian*, as well as by including the portrayal of gay and lesbian families in classroom posters and lessons (Burt, Gelnaw, & Lesser, 2010). The importance given to *parent* and *family* labels by gay and lesbian families is reflected in the following quote from a lesbian couple:

> and they were working on the wording of some of the things, and we wanted to know if they would change [the language] from "mother" and "father" to "parents" or something else. (Mercier & Harold, 2003, p. 40)

Social support networks. Gay and lesbian communities provide their members with strong social support networks (Tasker, 2005), which can be larger than those of heterosexual couples (Julien, Chartrand, & Begin, 1999). Such networks are especially important in preventing feelings of isolation for gay and lesbian families living in intolerant communities. Think about your own community as you complete Reflection 6.1.

REFLECTION 6.1   Working With Gay and Lesbian Families

What concerns might gay and lesbian families have regarding their treatment at schools in your community? As a teacher, how will you address these concerns?

Community support services. Gay and lesbian families living in most urban areas have access to community centers that coordinate a range of services, including parent education

Gay and lesbian families typically have strong social networks.

classes, family-oriented outings, social activities, and legal advice. Unfortunately, these services typically are lacking in rural and suburban areas.

Strategies for Working With Gay and Lesbian Families

Strategies that you (as a teacher) can use when working with gay and lesbian families are presented in this section.

Examination of your own feelings. The first step in working with gay and lesbian families is to examine your feelings toward them. Are you able to follow Reality Check #2 in respecting different family values? If not, you may find it helpful to talk about your concerns with gay or lesbian colleagues or consult community professionals who work with gay and lesbian families (Tasker, 2005).

A nonjudgmental approach. Some gay and lesbian parents may choose to share their sexual orientation with you. If so, adopt a low-key approach. Thank the parents for sharing their information with you, and note your willingness to listen to any ideas or concerns they have concerning their children's education. The importance of this type of nonjudgmental approach is reflected in the following quote from a lesbian parent.

In terms of dealing with us as a family and respecting each of us as parents . . . I don't think any of the classrooms did anything special to incorporate [his] family, but I didn't really push for that. (Mercier & Harold, 2003, p. 39)

Helping parents share sensitive information with their children. Some gay and lesbian parents turn to teachers for advice on explaining the nature of their relationship to their children. In these situations, it is best to avoid making decisions for parents. Instead, provide a listening ear and help parents think through their options. A few tips for facilitating this process are presented in Tip Box 6.1.

Protecting children of gay and lesbian families. Establishing a classroom rule that "We treat each other with respect" is vital to ensuring that all children are protected from taunts. It is also important that teachers follow the lead of gay and lesbian parents in explaining the nature of their relationship to others. Some parents may be very open about their family arrangement, while others may prefer a more subtle approach (Tasker, 2005). Consider, for example, the following quote:

Kids, starting in the first grade knew that [our son] had two moms. That was just the way it was, and . . . I'm really, really glad we did that. I think that was really important,

TIP BOX 6.1	Tips for Dealing With Children's Questions About Gay and Lesbian Relationships

- Use age-appropriate language when answering children's questions about gay and lesbian relationships (Tasker, 2005). The younger the child, the less need there is to share explicit information concerning sexual preferences. For all children, focus on themes of love and caring that characterize all families.
- If needed, help parents write out a short script to follow when responding to their child's questions. Emphasize that the script should be used as a general guide, not read verbatim.
- Respond to children's questions about family relationships by showing them pictures and reading them books about different family arrangements. Avoid talking about "typical" or "unique" family arrangements. Instead, treat each family as a legitimate collection of individuals who support and love one another.
- Allow children to share stories about how their families were formed (Tasker, 2005). Such sharing can be especially empowering for children who were adopted or conceived through a surrogate parent. If the children's stories are to be shared in class, perhaps as part of a lesson on "Me and My Family," work with each child and her or his parents to develop an age-appropriate storyline.

and not only for our satisfaction, but also for [our son] to know that it wasn't anything that he had to hide or worry about. (Mercier & Harold, 2003, p. 40)

Using language provided by families. Building on the previous tip, respect the language used by gay and lesbian families when describing their relationship to others (Burt et al., 2010; Tasker, 2005). For example, the partner of a gay biological father might be introduced as a "life partner." Another child might call his biological mother "Mamma" and her partner "Mom." It is also possible that the nonbiological parent will be called by her given name or a nickname.

Gay and lesbian couples are not the only families who must cope with stereotypes. In the following section, we address the stereotypes and other challenges faced by families living in poverty.

Families Living in Poverty

The U.S. government estimates that 20.1% of children under age 18 live in families with incomes below the poverty threshold (DeNavas-Walt, Proctor, & Smith, 2010, p. 15). However, this estimate presents an incomplete picture of the cost of living in different regions of the country (DeNavas-Walt et al., 2010, p. 20; Fass, 2009) and reflects only what families need to marginally exist (Fuller, 2003). Thus, families whose income is at or just above the poverty threshold, while not represented in poverty figures, nevertheless still may not earn enough to meet their daily living expenses.

As all these points demonstrate, there are in reality many different poverty experiences (Rank, 2000; Seccombe, 2001). For example, in Chapter 1 we noted the unique situation represented by working-poor families, whose incomes remain below the poverty threshold despite their family members' full-time employment. Other families experience short-term **poverty spells** because of a temporary change in their employment, a medical crisis, or some other life crisis (Rank, 2000; Tutwiler, 2005, p. 59). Still other families experience **chronic poverty** because of factors such as ongoing physical or mental disability, discrimination, and a lack of education or work skills that severely limit their employment options or place them in low-wage jobs (Rank, 2000; Tutwiler, 2005, p. 59). In the most severe cases, families experience **generational poverty**, where two or more generations of families survive on limited financial resources (Cuthrell, Stapleton, & Ledford, 2010).

Of course, the homeless represent the most extreme type of family poverty. Some families are **literally homeless**, meaning they live in their cars, tents, emergency shelters, or other temporary locations (U.S. Department of Housing and Urban Development, 2007). In contrast, the **precariously housed** avoid being homeless only by staying with friends or family members, or by paying a high proportion of their income on rent.

These various dimensions of poverty create a range of daily challenges. As you read about these challenges, keep in mind the different ways in which poverty is associated not only with material costs but also physical, cognitive, and emotional costs.

Challenges Associated With Families Living in Poverty

Different phrases are used to describe families living in poverty or at the poverty threshold, including *families with limited incomes, families with limited financial resources*, and *low-income families*. Regardless of which phrase you choose to use, one fact remains true: Family poverty affects one's total existence and almost every domain of development (Huston & Bentley, 2010). Indeed, the impact of poverty on children can be linked to multiple pathways and outcomes (Seccombe, 2007), some of which are reviewed in this section.

Balancing work-family demands. Perhaps the most obvious challenge facing families living in poverty is the time and energy they must devote to acquiring basic resources such as shelter, clothing, food, child care, transportation, and health care (Roy, Tubbs, & Burton, 2004) while maintaining a sense of family cohesion. The importance of this struggle is supported by a recent study in which parents who worked longer hours were found to spent less time with their children (Roeters, van der Lippe, & Kluwer, 2010). Furthermore, a decrease in parent-child time was associated with a decrease in the quality of the parent-child relationship.

Although the dilemma of balancing work-family demands is faced by many families, it is particularly stressful for families with limited incomes, since family members may have to work two or three jobs in order to pay their bills. The frustration that results from such a situation is reflected in the following quote.

> Of course my whole thing is time. There is no [time], you know, but in my life, in all that I do, there is only one place I want to be and that's at home with my family. (McBride, Sherraden, & Pritzker, 2006, p. 158)

Food insecurity. **Food insecurity** is defined as the lack of the economic resources needed to access enough food to lead an active and healthy life (Nord, Andrews, & Carlson, 2008). Not surprisingly, family households with incomes below the poverty threshold have a rate of food insecurity that is much higher than the national average (Nord et al., 2008). The consequences for children are dramatic. To summarize, children from food-insecure homes have been found to experience more colds, headaches, stomachaches, ear infections, and other health problems than children from food-secure homes (Children's Defense Fund, 2005; Murphy, de Cuba, Cook, Cooper, & Weill, 2008). Unfortunately, these physical symptoms are often difficult to address, since the probability that children will lack health insurance increases as family income decreases (DeNavas-Walt et al., 2010, p. 28; Valladares & Moore, 2009).

The consequences of food insecurity also impact children's emotional state and classroom performance. For example, hunger and a poor diet can create emotional distress that is displayed as impulsivity, hyperactivity, loss of self-control, sadness, and oppositional behavior (Children's Defense Fund, 2005; Murphy et al., 2008). Likewise, over time a lack of food and an unhealthy diet can have a negative impact on children's learning potential. Two examples are particularly noteworthy: first, when hungry children have difficulty concentrating and, second, when children from food-insecure homes have difficulty attending school on a regular basis (Children's Defense Fund, 2005; Murphy et al., 2008).

Lack of access to educational programs. A family's ability to access quality child care, after-school programs, and summer enrichment programs is directly tied to its level of income. This link between income and early care and education reflects a repeating principle that, although money may not bring happiness to families, it does provide greater life options and access to resources that contribute to children's well-being and academic success.

Lack of access to affordable and safe housing. Over half of *cost-burdened* households have low incomes (Joint Center for Housing Studies of Harvard University, 2009), meaning they spend more than 30% of their income on housing (U.S. Department of Housing and Urban Development, 2010). As a result, low-income families often are forced to cut back on other life essentials such as food, clothing, educational expenses, transportation, and utilities.

Setting life priorities. One consequence of all the challenges reviewed so far is that families with limited incomes are forced to prioritize their lives in ways that differ from those of higher-income families. For example, middle- and high-income families have the educational experiences, economic resources, and schedule flexibility to follow a **schoolcentric perspective of family involvement**. This perspective is evident in school policies and activities that are defined by and primarily conducted for the benefit of teachers and school administrators (Lawson, 2003). Examples of schoolcentric family involvement activities include parents' participating in fund-raising projects and taking time from their work to help with field trips or volunteer in the classroom. These examples help to explain the higher frequency of family involvement found among middle-class families relative to families with limited incomes (J. S. Lee & Bowen, 2006).

In contrast, families with limited incomes are more likely to assume a family-centered perspective in which their first priority is to take care of basic needs such as food, clothing, and housing. For example, parents with limited incomes may take on a second job, thereby making attendance at school events a secondary concern. In other cases parents may use their free time to seek out volunteer work that has tangible benefits for their family, as reflected in the following quote (McBride et al., 2006):

> And I thought Habitat [for Humanity] would be good because it teaches me how to work on my house. They're getting something out of me and I'm getting something out of them. So, I can learn at the same time, how to do some repairs on my house. (p. 156)

Before proceeding, read Case Study 6.2 to see if you can identify how the teachers switched from a schoolcentric to a family-centered perspective.

CASE STUDY 6.2 Switching From a Schoolcentric to Family-Centered Classroom

- Before Thanksgiving, the principal at Ms. Darity's school announces a schoolwide food drive. Donations of canned food will be given to a local church that sponsors an annual Thanksgiving dinner for families with limited incomes. Realizing that many of the children in her own classroom live in families with limited incomes, Ms. Darity suggests that, instead of asking families to donate food, they receive an invitation to help serve and participate in the Thanksgiving meal. Teachers can still donate food as well as help serve and participate in the Thanksgiving meal.
- Mr. Doug's fourth-grade class is studying about fire safety. He thinks about asking his students to draw maps of possible escape routes in their homes. After thinking about the different living arrangements represented in his classroom, including one child whose family is precariously housed, he instead asks the children to draw escape routes in their school.

The indirect impact of poverty. The negative impact of poverty on children can at times be indirect. For example, when studying families with limited incomes, researchers have found links between the depression and stress experienced by parents and the academic and behavioral problems experienced by their children (Conger, Conger, & Martin, 2010; National Institute of Child Health and Human Development, Early Child Care Research Network, 2005; Yeung, Linver, & Brooks-Gunn, 2002).

Another indirect influence of poverty involves the stability of family income. While it is generally agreed that chronic poverty is more disadvantageous for children than transitory poverty (Huston & Bentley, 2010), there are exceptions. For example, a fluctuating family income also can negatively impact children's behavior and classroom performance (Edin & Kissane, 2010). This is especially true for children living just at the poverty level, who may go through repeated cycles of seeing their hopes for a better life improve only to have their family return to public assistance (Moore, Glei, Driscoll, Zaslow, & Redd, 2002).

Taken together, the above findings reinforce the importance of low-income parents' having a strong support system to bolster their sense of family cohesion. Indeed, low-income parents with such a support system report better parent-child communication, more involve-ment with their children, and a greater confidence in their parenting skills (C. Y. S. Lee, Anderson, Horowitz, & August, 2009). This positive link is reflected in the following quote:

> Supportive relationships appear to serve a stress-reducing function by introducing knowledge of effective coping strategies, providing useful information, and supporting perceptions of self-efficacy. It is these coping skills and resources that can help to foster positive parenting. (C. Y. S. Lee et al., 2009, p. 425)

The direct impact of poverty. The direct impact of poverty on family lives is more straightforward. For example, it is not surprising that higher family incomes are associ-ated with more stimulating home environments, as reflected in a greater number of edu-cational games, toys, and electronic devices (Conger et al., 2010; Rank, 2000; Seccombe, 2001; Yeung et al., 2002). The result is that children from middle- and higher-income families experience less discrepancy between their home and classroom lives than do their peers from lower-income families. This requires teachers especially to keep in mind the unique ways in which children from homeless families may view their classroom envi-ronment (see FYI 6.1).

FYI 6.1   Understanding the Behavior of Children From Families Living in Poverty

- It is important that children experience the emotional safety associated with a consistent classroom schedule. On the other hand, homeless children may find such a routine confusing when compared to their more fluid family schedules. Be patient with these children. Explain how a consistent routine helps everyone in the classroom work together to learn new things. For example, two authors suggest using the routine feeding of a classroom pet to help young children understand the importance of following a consistent classroom routine (Meadan & Jegatheesan, 2010).
- Children who do not have access to books, computers, and educational materials at home need time to explore and understand these materials before using them to work on class assignments. For example, children from families with limited financial resources are less likely than their peers from higher-income families to be exposed to reading experiences at home (Dye & Johnson, 2007; Valladares & Moore, 2009). This may negatively influence their interest in classroom reading activities as well as their reading performance.
- Children who go hungry at home may have difficulty sharing their food with others when in the classroom. Some children may hoard food.

Stereotypes. In the past, families living in poverty were described as representing a **culture of poverty** characterized by defeatist attitudes (e.g., "We will always live in poverty"), dys-functional behaviors (e.g., lack of initiative), and a lack of intelligence (e.g., inability to learn new skills), all of which kept them from improving their economic situation (Tutwiler, 2005, p. 57). In short, the poor were to blame for their poverty. Today, we know that these stereo-types ignore the many economic and social factors that work against families attempting to leave poverty (Seccombe, 2001). For example, the federal government currently sets one nationwide **minimum wage** ($7.25 per hour [U.S. Department of Labor, 2011]), which in many communities is inadequate to meet the needs of working-poor families. In contrast, if implemented nationwide, a **living wage** would tie a standard wage to the cost of living in each community. Visit the Internet Resources at the end of this chapter to compare the living wages of different towns and cities in the United States (see the "Living Wage Calculator").

Children's academic achievement. Both research reviews and individual research studies indicate that children living in poverty face a number of academic challenges.

- They exhibit learning disabilities and developmental delays, receive lower grades and lower scores on standardized tests, and are less likely to complete as many years of schooling when compared to their peers living in higher-income families (Brooks-Gunn & Duncan, 1997; Seccombe, 2001).
- They also score lower on language development and school readiness skills (National Institute of Child Health and Human Development, Early Child Care Research Network, 2005). For example, results from one longitudinal study indicated that children from families with limited incomes display smaller vocabularies than their more affluent peers at age three (Hart & Risley, 2003). In addition, vocabulary usage at age three was predictive of language skills and reading comprehension at ages 9 to 10.
- Although children living in poverty are less likely to be found in gifted classes, they are more likely to repeat a grade (Lugaila, 2003).
- The greater the number of risk factors contributing to poverty, the greater the likelihood for developmental and educational problems (Zill & West, 2001).
- Poverty during early childhood appears to be especially damaging to children's educational achievement trajectories (Huston & Bentley, 2010). On the other hand, even a small increase in family income is accompanied by improvements in children's school achievement and social-emotional development.

Unfortunately, many low-income families do not have the resources or supports to address these academic challenges. For example, results from one national study found that low-income parents were significantly more likely than higher-income parents to lack the paid-leave and job flexibility needed to attend parent-teacher conferences (Heymann & Earle, 2000). Some strategies for addressing this challenge are presented later in this chapter (see heading "Maintaining Contact") and in Chapter 10 (see heading "Family Attendance Challenges").

Children's neighborhood environment. In many cases, the housing available to poor families is located in disorganized neighborhoods with high crime rates, environmental hazards, and limited positive contact between neighbors (Moore, Redd, Burkhauser, Mbwana, & Collins, 2009; Valladares & Moore, 2009). In addition, the schools in poor neighborhoods are likely to lack the resources and rigor of schools in more prosperous neighborhoods (Moore et al., 2009). Finally, children in poor neighborhoods are less likely to have access to parks, playgrounds, health care facilities, after-school programs, and summer enrichment programs that promote their development and education (Alexander, Entwisle, & Olson, 2001; Brooks-Gunn & Duncan, 1997).

Given this lack of community social capacity, it is not surprising that disadvantaged communities magnify the effects of family poverty (Huston & Bentley, 2010). For example, school-age children who live in poverty are less likely to participate in extracurricular and community-based activities (Dye & Johnson, 2007). They also are less likely to be taken on community outings (Lugaila, 2003), and they are less likely to visit a library, bookstore, museum, park, zoo, or historical site during the summer (Alexander et al., 2001; Meyer, Princiotta, & Lanahan, 2005; Valladares & Moore, 2009).

Parents' personal experiences with educational systems. Because poverty can extend across generations, it is important to consider the educational experiences of parents who themselves grew up in poverty. For example, some of these parents may fail to fully understand the importance of family involvement, or they may be distrustful of teachers because of their own negative experiences while in school (Fuller, 2003). As a teacher, you will want to follow Reality Check #1 and make an extra effort to diplomatically reach out to parents who are hesitant to interact with you or participate in family involvement activities.

Likewise, parents with limited income and education may hold lower educational expectations of their children in general (Child Trends, 2010; Dye & Johnson, 2007) and of their children's reading and math achievement in particular (Entwisle & Alexander, 2000). In addition, parents without a high school diploma may be less likely than parents with higher levels of education to attend school meetings, parent-teacher conferences, and classroom events (Vaden-Kiernan & McManus, 2005). Likewise, they may be less likely to serve as volunteers on school committees or participate in school fundraising events.

Strengths Associated With Families Living in Poverty

Although researchers have largely focused on the problems of families living in poverty, it is important that we also keep their potential strengths in mind. For example, one national survey found that families with limited income ate more meals together than families with moderate and high income (Valladares & Moore, 2009). This may seem to be an inconsequential finding. However, as it turns out, family meals have significant implications for children's long-term behavioral adjustment, as reflected in the following quote (Franko, Thompson, Affenito, Barton, & Striegel-Moore, 2008):

> These data suggest that families should be encouraged to eat together from an early age, as such activity may have multiple benefits in later years when adolescent health issues become paramount. (p. S116)[1]

Put another way, family meals serve as a positive socialization agent that, if established early in children's lives, can lessen the impact of negative socialization influences over time. This line of reasoning is supported by other studies that associated family meals with lower probability that adolescents would participate in a range of risky behaviors, such as drugs, drinking, smoking, running away, property destruction, stealing, and school suspension (Eisenberg, Neumark-Sztainer, Fulkerson, & Story, 2008; Moore, Chalk, Scarpa, & Vandivere, 2002; National Center on Addiction and Substance Abuse at Columbia University, 2009; Sen, 2010).

The simple act of eating meals together reminds us that the strengths exhibited by families may not always be readily observable. Other strengths associated with families living in poverty are summarized next.

Resiliency. For children to build resiliency, they must also encounter adversity, and poverty certainly represents an extreme example of adversity. Nevertheless, when accompanied by protective and nurturing parents and teachers, children who experience poverty have unique opportunities to observe and acquire the self-confidence, perseverance, and self-sufficiency needed to overcome life challenges. Such support sometimes requires creativity. As a teacher, how would you use your creativity and skills in collaborating with others in your school and community to handle the situation presented in Case Study 6.3?

CASE STUDY 6.3   Tamara, Xavier, and Nate

Tamara and her mother live in a battered-women's shelter. Tamara's mother would like to enroll Tamara in an after-school program, but she cannot afford the after-school enrollment fee. In addition, her job training class prevents her from accompanying Tamara on the two buses that provide transportation between Tamara's school, the after-school program, and the shelter.

The challenges faced by children living in poverty can be offset by protective and nurturing parents and teachers.

Resourcefulness. Families who live in poverty learn to develop a resourceful approach to dealing with daily life challenges. For example, lower-income families take greater advantage of "thrift economies" than do higher-income families (Brown, Goodsell, Stovall, & Flaherty, 2010). **Thrift economies** include thrift outlets, consignment and secondhand stores, and yard sales that offer below-market pricing. Participation in thrift economies allows families with limited financial resources to stretch their income by shopping for clothing and furniture at a discounted price. As a result, they are better able to meet other needs such as rent, transportation, and food.

It is reasonable to expect that children who experience such resourcefulness in their family lives will develop a resourceful mind-set. As a teacher, you can reinforce resourcefulness by cheerfully working around unexpected events or changes in the daily schedule as well as by helping children look for alternative approaches to completing classroom assignments and resolving interpersonal disputes.

Cooperation. Individuals who live in families with limited income typically learn to sacrifice and cooperate for the good of the family unit. For example, one study found that families with limited income were able to display a sense of family cohesion and to pull together to solve problems (Orthner, Jones-Sanpei, & Williamson, 2004).

This finding reminds us that being poor does not necessarily equal dysfunction. All families, including those with limited financial resources, have the potential to call on internal resources such as cooperation and problem solving skills. You will read about other internal resources that characterize "strong families" in Chapter 11.

Empathy and social justice. Young children who experience poverty learn firsthand the importance of having empathy for others. As these children grow older, many begin to understand how a lack of responsive social policies contributes to deteriorating neighborhoods, crime, and unequal access to education, parks, and other community services. It is reasonable to assume that some of these children will, upon reaching adulthood, rely on their personal experiences with poverty to advocate social justice within their respective communities.

Strategies for Working With Families Living in Poverty

Some strategies to consider when working with children and families living in poverty or at the poverty threshold are summarized in this section. After reading this section, complete Reflection 6.2.

Being helpful and empathetic. Look for signs of stress in parents and children, such as extreme irritability, aggression, or withdrawal. If these are present, helping the family gain access to appropriate counseling services will prevent stress-related physical and emotional problems. Also, listen patiently as parents and older children vent their feelings. This strategy (see Chapter 2) represents an important source of support, especially in cases where they may feel others misunderstand or dismiss their life experiences. In contrast, younger children are more likely to vent their feelings through drawings rather than words. Invite them to share their drawings with you, but do not force them.

Maintaining contact. Maintain contact with families to show your support and to keep abreast of changes in family living circumstances that might impact children's well-being. This does not mean you need to ask a lot of questions or overload families with information. Instead use brief and focused communication strategies, such as those presented in Chapter 13, to keep the contact informal and nonintrusive. Likewise, be flexible in where and how you meet with families. For example, you may need to conduct a parent-teacher conference during a parent's coffee break. This in no way lessens the importance of the conference, as noted in the following quote:

> For example, a parent conference held at McDonald's is equally as valid as a parent conference held at school. (Cuthrell et al., 2010, p. 107)[2]

Seeking parents' input. Parents from all socioeconomic backgrounds are able to provide teachers with valuable information about their children's knowledge base and learning styles, friendships, community networks, and life experiences (Van Velsor & Orozco, 2007). Indeed, it is always dangerous to make assumptions about any given parent's level of income and her or his commitment to working with teachers.

Understanding children's neighborhoods. Use a community scan (see Chapter 1) to better understand the lives of children who reside in disorganized neighborhoods. Pay particular attention to quality-of-life indicators, such as the number and types of food stores, the condition of housing facilities, the presence of mass transit, the condition of recreational facilities, and the presence or absence of police officers.

Before drawing conclusions about your community scan, remember that parents often are able to compensate for the dangers represented in their neighborhoods (Crosnoe & Cavanagh, 2010; Huston & Bentley, 2010). For some, this may mean expending more time and effort in protecting children who are most vulnerable to threats, such as boys who are impulsive or short in stature (Romich, 2009). For others, it may involve the use of *buffering* and *enhancing strategies* such as those presented in FYI 6.2.

FYI 6.2 Strategies Used by Mothers to Protect Children in Disorganized Neighborhoods

Buffering Strategies

- **Monitoring:** "You have to watch your kids ... There's a lot going on in the neighborhood ... drive bys, folks grabbing people's kids, stuff of that nature" (p. 30).
- **Cautionary warnings:** "[I tell them,] 'No meals, no candy from strangers, especially from a person you never know. Even if that person says "'hi'" two weeks in a row'" (p. 30).
- **Danger management:** "Like if anybody than myself picks them up from downstairs, from down the street, if they don't know the code word, then you don't go with that person" (p. 31).
- **Chaperoning:** "I don't let them go outside by themselves. If they want to go outside and I'm not taking them outside, they not going outside" (p. 31).
- **Confinement:** "Being in this house, keeping them together, I be in here and keep a close knit with them" (p. 32).

Enhancing Strategies

- **Resource brokering:** "I take David ... to the YMCA ... [I] try and teach him how to swim. I'll take him to the museum, the zoo ... I try to take him somewhere away from the neighborhood" (p. 34).
- **In-home learning:** "I know Donita can count to 20, but should be to 50. Some 4-year-olds can go further than that. ... We constantly be pushing, pushing. But, it'll come" (p. 35).

SOURCE: Adapted from Jarrett, R. L., & Jefferson, S. R. (2003). "A good mother got to fight for her kids": Maternal management strategies in a high-risk, African-American neighborhood. *Journal of Children and Poverty, 9*(1), 21–39. Reprinted by permission of the publisher (Taylor & Francis Group, http://www.informaworld.com).

Provision of home- and community-based supports. As noted in Chapter 3, home-based learning activities serve multiple objectives, including building families' self-confidence as teachers. In addition, they help children from low-income families remain interested in learning while reinforcing their academic skills (Fantuzzo, McWayne, Perry, & Childs, 2004). Another strategy for achieving these objectives is to work with community youth groups to plan and carry out neighborhood-based summer enrichment programs. Such programs can serve as substitutions for the extracurricular activities in which children from middle- and high-income families routinely participate.

Serving as a backup. As mentioned in Chapter 1, teachers sometimes serve as fictive kin in helping to address children's basic needs. Certainly, this is true for children living in families with limited incomes. For example, it is not unusual for teachers to set aside nutritious snacks (raisins and other dried fruit) and supplies (crayons and paper) for children from low-income families.

Updating your community scan. Remember to update your community scan every year in order to remain current on community services that might interest families with limited incomes. Begin by adding new resources to your family handbook. Also make contact with resources already in your handbook to inquire about revisions to their services.

> **REFLECTION 6.2   *Working With Families Living in Poverty***
>
> Describe how you would rely on one or more family strengths and your community scan to address a challenge faced by families living in poverty.

Social Exchanges: The Rewards and Costs of Family Involvement

When deciding whether to accept an invitation to a family involvement activity, all families make an informal assessment as to whether the rewards of their participation will exceed the costs of giving up their family, recreation, or work time. This comparison of rewards to costs is especially important for emerging and vulnerable families who also must consider the additional cost that their participation might bring regarding the negative stereotypes we reviewed in the chapter. **Social exchange theory** can help us to better understand this concern and ways to address it.

At the heart of social exchange theory is a businesslike view of relationships in which we strive to maximize our rewards and minimize our costs (Smith, Hamon, Ingoldsby, & Miller, 2009, p. 203). The various sources of our rewards and costs are personal. **Rewards**, for example, can include any material, physical, social, or psychological experiences that we find pleasurable. **Costs** can include anything that is not rewarding and therefore prevents us from interacting with others.

Now let's consider how these concepts apply to the two types of families we reviewed in this chapter. In the case of gay and lesbian families, there is the question of how their child's teacher will receive them. This question represents an emotional cost to interacting with the teacher except in the most superficial way. Fortunately, the classroom rule that "We treat each other with respect," reviewed earlier in this chapter, offsets this cost and encourages greater family-teacher social exchanges.

In the case of families with limited income, there are multiple time and financial costs to participating in schoolcentric family involvement activities. These costs can be overcome by using the equally valuable but more family-centered strategies presented in the previous section.

CHAPTER SUMMARY

- Like "normed" families, emerging and vulnerable families have both potential challenges and potential strengths.
- The parenting behavior of gay and lesbian parents resembles that of heterosexual parents. Likewise, there is no evidence that children of gay and lesbian families differ from their peers who are raised by heterosexual parents.
- The poverty threshold presents an incomplete picture of the cost of living in different regions of the country. Likewise, there are different types of poverty experiences.

NOTES

1. Franko, D. L., Thompson, D., Affenito, S. G., & Barton, B. A. (2008). What mediates the relationship between family meals and adolescent health issues? *Health Psychology, 27*(2), S109–S117 (American Psychological Association, Publisher). Reprinted with permission.

2. Cuthrell, K., Stapleton, J., & Ledford, C. (2010). Examining the culture of poverty: promising practices. *Preventing School Failure, 54*(2), 104–110. Reprinted by permission of the publisher (Taylor & Francis Group, http://www.informaworld.com)

DISCUSSION QUESTIONS

1. Which of the strengths associated with gay and lesbian families do you believe is most important for supporting children's classroom performance? Which challenge do you believe is most detrimental?

2. Review the buffering and enhancing strategies presented in FYI 6.2. How might parents generalize their use of these strategies in their neighborhood to their children's classroom or school?

3. **Your family involvement philosophy.** Return to the draft of your family involvement philosophy. Based on your reading of this chapter, what if any changes will you make to your philosophy statement? Discuss your answer to this question with your peers.

COMMUNITY OF LEARNERS' FIELD ASSIGNMENT

Homeless Shelters and Community Services

In a series of articles, Swick (2008a, 2008b, 2009) and his colleague (Swick & Williams, 2010) summarized the physically and emotionally damaging ecology of homeless families. This ecology includes (a) negative assessments from others about a family's economic condition, (b) questions about parenting skills, (c) a loss of control over daily decision making that is reinforced by a dependency upon others for daily needs, (d) witnessing and at times experiencing acts of violence at the hands of others living on the street or in homeless shelters, and (e) isolation from consistent and meaningful social supports and contacts.

It is difficult for most children to escape totally unharmed physically, emotionally, and academically from such an environment. For example, Swick (2008b) notes the "symbols" that prevent homeless children from being fully valued at school. These symbols include inadequate or ill-fitting clothing, poor hygiene, an inability to attend class on a consistent basis because of frequent moves and family disruptions, an accompanying inability to take part in school functions, and poor homework completion. Given these challenges, it is easy to see how children who live in poverty can develop a low self-esteem and, subsequently, give up on school (Cuthrell et al., 2010).

Your task. Swick (2008b) and his colleague (Swick & Williams, 2010) suggest that teachers participate in service-learning activities at homeless shelters to gain a deeper appreciation and understanding of the families they serve. Volunteer your time to work at a homeless shelter in your community. The shelter may already have programs in place in which you can participate. If not, you can make suggestions such as providing tutoring for children, working with case workers to help address the needs of individual parents and children, or developing a series of family "fun" nights where you arrange games and other activities for parents and children. Alternatively, volunteer to help at a local food bank or thrift store. This too will give you valuable experience in learning about and serving homeless children and their families.

Report on your experiences. What most surprised you about the strengths and challenges of homeless families? What lessons will you take away about how best to work with homeless children and families?

CAPSTONE ACTIVITIES

Activity 1: CenterLink

Use the following link to visit the office or website of a community center serving gays and lesbians: http://resources.lgbtcenters.org/Directory/Find-A-Center.aspx. Make a list of the programs and services provided by the center. Share your list with your peers.

Activity 2: Learn About the National School Lunch Program

The National School Lunch Program provides low-cost or free school-based meals to children from families with limited income. Use the following link to learn more about this program: www.fns.usda.gov/cnd/Lunch/. Then arrange an interview with a school administrator or nutritionist to talk about her or his participation in the program. Ask the following questions:

- What behaviors alert teachers to children's hunger?
- How many children in the school take part in the program?
- What rules must the school follow in order to participate in the program?
- What challenges does the school encounter in enrolling children in the program?
- What benefits have resulted from children's participation in the program?

Activity 3: "10 Tips for Working With [Family Type]"

To complement the brochure you developed in Chapter 5, develop another brochure for one of the families examined in this chapter. Give your brochure the following title: "10 Tips for Working With [Family Type]." Share your brochures in class and make copies for everyone to place in their teacher resource file.

INTERNET RESOURCES

You may find that some URLs have been altered by the webmaster. In these situations, try entering the name of the document or agency in a search engine. Alternatively, enter the domain name (e.g., http://www.xxxx.org). This should take you to the revised home page and associated links.

Gay and Lesbian Families

Parents, Families and Friends of Lesbians and Gays (PFLAG)

http://www.pflag.org/

PFLAG promotes the well-being of gay, lesbian, bisexual, and transgendered persons as well as their families and friends through its educational and advocacy work. The PFLAG website provides summaries of its initiatives and programs as well as updates on news from around the country related to gay, lesbian, bisexual, and transgender issues.

Human Rights Campaign (HRC)

http://www.hrc.org/

The HRC advocates and provides educational programs in support of equal rights and benefits in the workplace, as well as equal treatment of gay and lesbian parents and families. One outreach program conducted by HRC is Welcoming Schools. This program provides support for teachers, principals, and parents in promoting a respectful learning environment for children from all families.

Families Living in Poverty

Living Wage Calculator

http://www.livingwage.geog.psu.edu/

This site provides a breakdown of the costs associated with a living wage for different family arrangements in towns and cities across the United States.

Basic Needs Budget Calculator (National Center for Children in Poverty)

http://www.nccp.org/tools/frs/budget.php

This is another site that compares the incomes families living in selected cities need to meet minimum daily necessities.

United States Department of Labor, Wage and Hour Division

http://www.dol.gov/whd/minwage/america.htm#Georgia

Visit this site to compare each state's minimum wage to that of the federal government's minimum wage.

Feeding America

http://feedingamerica.org/

Use the Food Bank Locator at this site to find a food bank in your area.

Center for Law and Social Policy (CLASP)

www.clasp.org/

Clasp is a national organization that works to improve the economic security, educational advancement and family stability of low-income families. Click on the various tabs to access the latest news related to poverty, families, and children.

National Center for Children in Poverty (NCCP)

http://www.nccp.org/about.html

The NCCP uses research to inform policies and programs that promote the economic security, health, and well-being of low-income families. A sampling of projects sponsored by NCCP that are relevant to teachers include Pathways to Early School Success, Unclaimed Children Revisited, and Improving the Odds for Young Children.

STUDENT STUDY SITE

Log on to the Web-based student study site at **www.sagepub.com/coleman** for additional study tools including

- eFlashcards
- Web Quizzes
- Links to SAGE Journal Articles
- Author-created Videos
- Learning Objectives
- Web Resources
- Family Involvement Portfolio Guides

CHAPTER 7

Families of Children With Disabilities

N owhere is the family-teacher partnership more important than when addressing the strengths and needs of children with disabilities. In fact, federal law requires that partnerships in these situations extend beyond the family and teacher to include a team of individuals: paraprofessionals, other school staff, and/or community professionals. The responsibilities and work of this team are reviewed in this chapter, along with practical strategies for engaging and empowering families of children with disabilities.

COMMUNITY LEARNING GUIDE

As you read this chapter, take notes on the following items. Use your notes to address the Reflections, Discussion Questions, Field Assignment, and Capstone Activities that you find in the chapter.

- Describe the general work performed by professionals who assist children with disabilities.
- Define the acronyms IDEA, IEP, and IFSP.
- Describe the challenges faced by families of children with disabilities. Also describe some home-based strategies for helping families address their children's development and education.
- Define the purpose of a facilitated IEP model. Then describe the components of this model.

General Meaning of *Disability*

Three points are in order regarding use of the term *disability*. First, while *disability* is used by the U.S. Department of Education (Individuals With Disabilities Education Improvement Act, 2004) to encompass a range of exceptionalities (some examples include mental retardation, hearing impairments, speech and language impairments, visual impairments, emotional disturbances, orthopedic impairments, and autism [p. 2652]), others prefer different terms, such as "exceptional children," "differently abled," special needs," "developmentally delayed," and "at risk." You will want to consult your administrator about the particular language used in your school when communicating about disabilities.

A second point is that "disability," like "normal," is a relative concept (Gargiulo, 2009, p. 5) and will hold different meanings in different social, professional, and cultural settings. Finally, to the maximum extent possible, children with disabilities are to be educated and socialized within regular classrooms. This idea is referred to as the **least restrictive environment**, and its exact arrangement will differ with each child, depending on his or her educational needs (Gargiulo, 2009, p. 76). A related term is **mainstreaming**, which refers to integrating children with disabilities into classrooms with their typically developing peers (p. 75).

The information in this chapter supports the following family-school-community partnership standards. These standards are reviewed in Chapter 2.

NAEYC Standards and Associated Key Elements	1b, 1c, 2a, 2b, 2c, 3b, 3c, 4b, 5c, 6a, 6b, 6c, 6d, 6e
ACEI Standards	1.0, 3.2, 4.0, 5.1, 5.2
PTA Standards	1, 2, 3, 4, 5, 6

Professionals Who Work With Individuals With Disabilities

Begin this section by reading Case Study 7.1. This will allow you to develop a better appreciation for the professionals who work with children with disabilities.

CASE STUDY 7.1   Louisa

Louisa is in the fourth grade. When angry or frustrated, she displays aggressive behavior that includes biting, hitting, and throwing objects.

Louisa's parents, her teacher, and a school counselor meet to discuss Louisa's behavior and devise a plan of action. They decide that Louisa will begin meeting with the counselor on a weekly basis. In addition, the counselor will teach Louisa's teacher and parents how to help Louisa manage her anger and frustration at home and in the classroom.

After a few weeks, Louisa's parents and teacher report an improvement in her ability to talk about her feelings and to signal for help when she feels frustrated or angry. The parents express their gratitude to the team of professionals who worked with them to address Louisa's behavior.

As in Case Study 7.1, the well-being of children with disabilities often requires the expertise of specially trained professionals. Brief descriptions of the tasks carried out by some of these professionals are presented in FYI 7.1. All professionals assume three basic responsibilities: First, they use their individual expertise to address the needs of children with disabilities. Second, they work as part of a team to assist classroom teachers in making appropriate adaptations to their classroom lessons and materials. Finally, they work with families to provide home-based activities and exercises that are designed to advance children's daily life skills.

FYI 7.1	**Professionals Who Work With Children With Disabilities**
Occupational therapists . . .	help children with various mental, physical, developmental, or emotional disabilities perform daily life tasks. For example, they may assist children with dressing, eating, and using a computer. Physical exercises may be used to increase strength and dexterity.
School counselors . . .	advocate for students while helping them understand and deal with social, behavioral, and personal problems.
Audiologists . . .	assess children who have hearing, balance, and related ear problems.
Speech-language pathologists . . .	diagnose and treat disorders such as stuttering, pronunciation problems, inappropriate pitch, and swallowing difficulties.
School social workers . . .	coordinate the delivery of medical, safety-related, educational, nutritional, and other social services to improve children's well-being.
Teachers of special education . . .	modify the educational curriculum to meet children's individual needs and provide remedial instruction. Some special education teachers work with individual or small groups of children for a block of time each day. Others team-teach with regular classroom teachers.
Recreation therapists . . .	use arts and crafts, animals, sports, games, dance and movement, drama, music, and community outings to support children's physical, mental, and emotional well-being.

SOURCE: Adapted from U.S. Department of Labor, Bureau of Labor Statistics. (2010). *Occupational outlook handbook, 2010–11 edition/ Teachers–Special education.* Retrieved October 15, 2010, from http://www.bls.gov/oco/ocos070.htm.

The services provided by the professionals in FYI 7.1 are in part governed by federal law. Continue to the next section to read about one such law.

IDEA

The Individuals With Disabilities Education Act (**IDEA**) is the federal law that specifies the rights of children with disabilities and the responsibilities of schools to ensure those rights. Some of the objectives associated with the most recent reauthorization of IDEA (first enacted in 1975; see U.S. Department of Education, 2009), include the following (Individuals With Disabilities Education Improvement Act, 2004):

- "To ensure that all children with disabilities have available to them a free and appropriate public education that emphasizes special education and related services designed to meet their unique needs and prepare them for further education, employment, and independent living."

- "To ensure that the rights of children with disabilities and parents of such children are protected."
- "To assist states, localities, educational service agencies, and federal agencies to provide for the education of all children with disabilities" (p. 2651)

A team of individuals is responsible for planning, implementing, documenting, and assessing the delivery of educational services. A few examples of professionals who may serve on the team were presented in FYI 7.1. Parents also are important members of the team. Each team includes someone who is responsible for coordinating and overseeing service delivery (Keilty, 2010, p. 80). Finally, the team uses one of two forms to document its work: the individualized education program (IEP) or the individualized family service plan (IFSP).

The IEP

The **IEP** is the educational plan for children with disabilities who are three years of age and older. The IEP has two objectives: (a) setting educational goals and (b) arranging service delivery to meet those goals. Key components of the IEP are presented in FYI 7.2 (Individuals With Disabilities Education Improvement Act, 2004). An example of an IEP can be found at the student study site for Richard M. Gargiulo's *Special Education in Contemporary Society* (3rd ed.): www.sagepub.com/gargiulo3estudy

---

FYI 7.2   Components of the IEP (paraphrased from Individuals With Disabilities Education Improvement Act, 2004, pp. 2707–2709)

- **The child's present level of academic functioning.** This includes descriptions of the child's classroom performance and the ways in which the child's disability affects his or her involvement and progress in making academic gains.
- **Goals.** Goals for the child are based on what the parents and other IEP team members think he or she can reasonably accomplish during a one-year period.
- **Measurements and progress reports.** The IEP includes information about how annual goals will be measured and when periodic progress reports will be issued.
- **Services.** A summary of special education and supplementary services is provided. These services can include, among others, the use of educational aids, changes in the educational curriculum, modifications to the classroom environment, physical therapy and other intervention services, and supports for teachers and other professionals responsible for carrying out the IEP.
- **Removal from the regular classroom.** The IEP team reports on the extent to which the child will not participate with nondisabled children in regular classroom activities and nonacademic activities such as recess and lunch.
- **Assessment accommodations.** The IEP includes information about what, if any, accommodations will be made to measure the child's academic achievement and functional performance on statewide and districtwide assessments.
- **Logistics of service delivery.** The IEP includes the beginning date of service delivery; the anticipated frequency, location, and duration of services; and modifications made to service delivery.

The IFSP

The **IFSP** summarizes the planning of early intervention services for infants and toddlers (under age three) who have developmental delays or are at risk for developmental delays (Individuals With Disabilities Education Improvement Act, 2004). The IEP team may choose to use the IFSP as the IEP for children older than three years of age until they enter elementary school. Key components of the IFSP are presented in FYI 7.3 (Individuals With Disabilities Education Improvement Act, 2004). An example of an IEP can be found at the student study site for Richard M. Gargiulo's *Special Education in Contemporary Society* (3rd ed.): www.sagepub.com/gargiulo3estudy.

FYI 7.3 Components of the IFSP (paraphrased from Individuals With Disabilities Education Improvement Act, 2004, pp. 2751–2752)

- **Child's level of functioning.** The child's level of functioning is defined by his or her communication, physical, cognitive, social-emotional, and adaptive skills.
- **Family resources, priorities, and concerns.** A statement is given about the family's resources, priorities, and concerns in relationship to enhancing the development of the infant or toddler.
- **Measurable results or outcomes.** Information is provided regarding the measurable results or outcomes expected for the child and the family. This includes the criteria, procedures, and timelines that will be followed to determine the degree of progress being made and whether modifications to the IFSP are needed.
- **Intervention services.** A statement is given regarding specific intervention services that will be provided to meet the needs of the child and family, including the frequency, intensity, and method of service delivery.
- **Natural environments.** The IFSP includes a statement about the natural environments (e.g., classroom, home, child care center) in which early intervention services will be provided. An explanation of the extent to which the services will not be provided in a natural environment is also given.
- **Length and duration of services.** The projected dates for initiation of services are given along with their anticipated length and duration.
- **Service coordinator.** The name of the service coordinator is given. This person is responsible for coordinating implementation of the IFSP in collaboration with other IFSP team members.
- **Transition steps.** The IFSP includes the steps that will be taken to support young children's transition between child care facilities, classrooms, and other service programs.

The importance of IEPs and IFSPs becomes clearer when we consider not only a child's disability but also the family challenges that result from that disability. As you will discover in the following section, these challenges include financial, emotional, and interpersonal challenges.

Family Challenges and Strategies for Addressing Them

The hopes and dreams parents have for their children can be undone upon their learning of a childhood disability. Many, if not most, parents respond to such news by going through a period of adjustment before they begin to create new dreams and expectations (Ray, Pewitt-Kinder, & George, 2009; Taub, 2006). This process can be exacerbated by a number of family challenges, many of which are reviewed in this section (see FYI 7.4 for a summary). Also reviewed are strategies you can use as a teacher and member of the IEP team to help families address their challenges. Collectively, all of the strategies examined in this section achieve two goals: (a) They build positive and supportive partnerships among families, teachers, and other IEP members, and (b) they assist families in developing their existing skills while acquiring new skills that promote the well-being of children and the family system itself (Dempsey & Dunst, 2004).

Financial Hardship

Families of children with disabilities face financial burdens that go beyond those involved in raising children without disabilities. These include costs associated with therapy, specialized medical care, and making adaptations to the home environment (Parish, Rose, Grinstein-Weiss, Richman, & Andrews, 2008). For example, one study found that parents of children with disabilities fared worse on eight of 11 measures

IEP and IFSP meetings can include parents, teachers, other school staff, and community professionals.

FYI 7.4   Strategies for Addressing Family Challenges

Challenges and Concerns	Helping Strategies
Financial hardship	• Advertise job fairs that put employer and job training representatives in the same room as families in need of employment assistance. • Include a comprehensive community resource guide in the family handbook.
Behavior problems exhibited by children	• Assist families in recognizing their parenting skills and developing new skills. • Conduct trainings to build families' coping, problem solving, and assertiveness skills.
Role overload	• Fully engage families in the IEP process. • Make sure IEP goals are clear and easy to understand. • Inform families of their rights, under IDEA, to help direct their children's education.
Parental stress and community support	• Connect families to support groups. • Help families access respite care. • Provide families with educational and inspirational reading materials. • Encourage families to keep their hopes and dreams alive.
Safety concerns	• Be proactive in educating families about safety procedures used by teachers and other school staff. • Inform families of the steps teachers and other school staff take when reporting safety violations.

(Continued)

(Continued)

Challenges and Concerns	Helping Strategies
Concerns about children's acceptance and inclusion	• Invite families to co-lead training sessions for teachers. • Take advantage of "family knowledge" to plan IEP goals, adapt home tasks to classroom tasks, and gain children's trust and cooperation.
Concerns about peers	• Invite families to help educate their children's peers about disabilities. • When appropriate, help children themselves educate their peers about disabilities. • Turn the classroom into a "friendship group."
Concerns about transitions	• Invite teachers and staff who soon will be working with a child to attend his or her IEP meetings. • Arrange meeting dates for the family and new teacher to meet and discuss the child's interests, strengths, and needs. • Provide opportunities for the child and new teacher to interact and for the child to explore his or her new classroom. • Help families see the importance of not overprotecting their children.
Family functioning	• Encourage participation in family counseling. • Encourage participation in sibling support programs.

of material hardship associated with food security, phone service, rent, and timely receipt of health care when compared to families of children without disabilities (Parish et al., 2008). Childhood disability can also negatively impact family finances by requiring parents to reduce the number of hours they work so that they can attend to the needs of their children, or to take lower-paying jobs that allow more-flexible work hours.

One strategy for addressing the challenge of material hardship is for IEP teams to help advertise job fairs that put employer and job training representatives in the same room with families in need of employment assistance. Another strategy is to include contact information for these agencies, schools, and businesses in your family handbook. Also include contact information for financial counseling organizations.

Children's Behaviors

Parents of children with disabilities report significantly more **internalized behavior problems** in which frustrations and stress are internalized rather than expressed outwardly (e.g., withdrawal, somatic complaints, anxiety), **externalized behavior problems** in which frustrations and stress are outwardly expressed (e.g., destructive behavior, aggression, acting-out behavior), and other problems (e.g., poor social skills and attention spans) than do parents of children without disabilities (Dunlap & Fox, 2007; Nachshen & Minnes, 2005). Such behavior problems can impact parents' emotional state and stress-related physical symptoms (Umberson, Pudrovska, & Reczek, 2010). For example, in some cases parents may be embarrassed by their children's behavior, especially if they worry that others view such behavior as the result of poor parenting (Dunlap & Fox, 2007). In other cases children's problematic behaviors may be associated with parental depression (Gallagher, Phillips, Oliver, & Carroll, 2008).

Address parents' concerns about their children's behavior by assisting them in recognizing and using their existing parenting skills. Help them develop new skills by arranging child guidance classes that focus on challenging childhood behaviors. Also arrange for classes that emphasize coping skills, problem solving strategies, assertiveness training, and advocacy skills (Soresi, Nota, & Ferrari, 2007).

Role Overload

The concept of role overload that we applied to single parents in Chapter 5 also applies to the parents of children with disabilities. Consider three examples. First, parents assume not only the role of teacher for their children but also the role of public educator as they instruct teachers, social workers, physical therapists, counselors, and others about their children's strengths and needs. Second, parents assume the role of public advocate as they work with elected officials to push for the passage and enforcement of laws that ensure the delivery of timely and quality disability services. Finally, parents may need to serve as spokespeople for children whose speech, language, or behavioral challenges prevent them from speaking for themselves.

Support parents' efforts in dealing with these multiple roles by making sure they have an equal voice in planning, implementing, and evaluating IEP goals. Also make sure IEP goals are clear and easy to understand. A model for achieving these tasks is reviewed later in the chapter.

Parental Stress and Community Support

Parents of children who have disabilities report significantly more stress and less well-being (Nachshen & Minnes, 2005), along with greater depression and anxiety (Gallagher et al., 2008), than do parents of children without disabilities (Gallagher et al., 2008; Nachshen & Minnes, 2005). In addition, families of children with disabilities report significantly less community support than do parents of children without disabilities (Nachshen & Minnes, 2005).

It is important that the IEP team pay attention to these issues for at least three reasons. First, emotional stress, depression, and anxiety can compromise parents' ability to process diagnostic information, participate in the IEP process, seek out and make use of resources, and support their children's development and education (Head & Abbeduto, 2007). Second, parental stress has the potential to negatively impact parenting behavior, which in turn can negatively impact intervention outcomes (Hastings & Beck, 2004). Finally, parent support can help reduce parental stress (Hastings & Beck, 2004) and promote a sense of empowerment (Nachshen & Minnes, 2005).

As a teacher, help parents manage their stress by connecting them with support networks where their parenting experiences can be shared, solutions to challenges can be discussed, and play dates and other social events can be arranged (Dunlap & Fox, 2007; Nachshen & Minnes, 2005; Taub, 2006). Also put married parents in touch with respite care services (Summers et al., 2007) so they can plan for weekly "couple dates" and other outings that will help them maintain a healthy marriage. A few other community supports that you might suggest are presented in FYI 7.5.

FYI 7.5 Community Support Resources

Types of Family Support	Examples of Community Resources
• **Recreational supports** allow families to release pent-up stress.	• Parks and recreations departments • YMCA/YWCA • Employer-sponsored recreational programs • Hospital-sponsored recreational programs
• **Social supports** provide families with opportunities to share their feelings with others who face similar challenges.	• Behavioral healthcare and other community organizations that sponsor support groups for families whose children share similar disabilities
• **Psychological supports** provide counseling services to help families develop or maintain positive coping strategies.	• Psychologists • Psychiatrists • Clinical social workers • Religious leaders with training in counseling
• **Material supports** help families meet basic daily needs such as food, clothing, employment, and housing.	• Food banks. When visiting the following website, type in your local zip code to locate a food bank in or close to your town or city: **http://feedingamerica.org/foodbank-results.aspx** • Social service agencies • Community thrift stores • State labor departments • Training programs associated with technical schools • U.S. Department of Housing and Urban Development. When visiting the following website, type the name of your state into the search box to learn about services in your home state: **http://www.hud.gov/**
• **Instrumental supports** provide families with practical assistance such as medical care, transportation, and respite care.	• Local physicians and other health professionals. Check to determine which offices accept Medicaid and other health care assistance subsidies or provide a sliding scale fee for indigent clients. • Hospitals, health departments, and clinics • Local transportation authorities • Civic groups and religious institutions • National Respite Network's Respite Locator. When visiting the following webpage, type in the name of your state and the age and disability of the child in question to identify respite services in your area: **www.archrespite.org/search-for-respite**

If community supports like the one noted in FYI 7.5 are not available, develop a reading list that includes educational and inspirational materials (Taub, 2006). Invite parents to discuss their readings with you or other IEP members. This type of sharing can help keep families' hopes and dreams alive, thereby supporting their well-being (Nachshen & Minnes, 2005) and easing the frustrations they may feel when comparing their children's educational progress to that of children without disabilities.

Finally, help parents avoid destructive coping strategies, such as escape-avoidance and distancing, that contribute to depression, isolation, and marital problems (Dunn, Burbine, Bowers, & Tantleff-Dunn, 2001; Pottie & Ingram, 2008). **Escape-avoidance behaviors** include hoping for miracles, using drugs, and avoiding other people. **Distancing behaviors** include denying or trying to forget about the presence of stress as well as making light of stressful situations. To replace these behaviors, encourage families to use problem-focused coping strategies (Head & Abbeduto, 2007; Pottie & Ingram, 2008), such as positive reappraisal and confrontive coping, that contribute to emotional well-being (Dunn et al., 2001). **Positive reappraisal** involves seeking out personal growth opportunities (e.g., meditation, swimming), rediscovering the important things in life, and engaging in activities that are inspirational and creative. **Confrontive coping** involves asserting one's needs and expectations, expressing one's feelings, and taking chances in order to explore new life experiences.

Safety Concerns

Families of children with disabilities sometimes worry about injuries to their children while they are under the care of teachers and other school staff. For example, they may worry about falls, inappropriate use of specialized equipment, lack of adult supervision, or lack of appropriate assistance during recess and field trips (Taub, 2006). Likewise, they may express concerns about whether teachers and other staff have sufficient training to protect their children from bullies.

Address these concerns by informing families of the safety training conducted at your school. Demonstrate the safety measures teachers, paraprofessionals, and other staff take when working with children with disabilities (Taub, 2006). Explain the policies that staff follow when monitoring children's behavior during group activities. Finally, inform families about the steps that you and other staff take when reporting safety violations.

Concerns About Children's Acceptance and Inclusion

In addition to their concerns about safety, families worry about how teachers will respond to their children's disabilities (Taub, 2006). Will their children be allowed to fully participate in classroom activities and extracurricular activities? Will the services delivered by teachers and other staff meet the needs of their children (Summers et al., 2007)? Will their children be treated fairly, or will they be singled out for pity or ridicule? Will their children have a difficult time forming friendships because of frequent class absences to attend therapy sessions or communication challenges that necessitate adult translations?

To address these concerns, invite families to collaborate with you in preparing and/or co-leading in-service training to educate school staff about children with disabilities (Taub, 2006). Topics might include information about the disabilities represented in your classroom, the legal responsibilities of school staff to address children's disabilities, examples of educational programs and services related to different disabilities, resources for learning more about disabilities, and strategies for communicating and working with children with disabilities.

Also ask for families' assistance in adapting for the classroom chores and other tasks that children have mastered at home. Equally important, ask families to provide tips on recognizing and responding to their children's moods.

Concerns About Peers

Yet another worry noted by families is how information about their children's disabilities will be shared with classmates (Taub, 2006). For example, some worry about whether the focus will be on what their children cannot do versus what they can do. Others worry about the accuracy of information that will be shared.

One strategy for addressing these concerns is to involve families in sharing information about their children's disabilities. In addition, children with disabilities can themselves be invited to share information about their strengths and dreams. Hearing directly from a classmate with a disability can have a greater impact on peers than can hearing from a teacher or another adult. However, this option should be pursued only after you have consulted with the child and his or her family. As you may already have guessed, not all children will be equally comfortable assuming this role.

Another strategy is to transform the classroom into a friendship group (Taub, 2006) by engaging children in discussions about the meaning of empathy. Also invite them to examine the importance of individual differences and brainstorm ways to help each other. Recruit professionals from community youth organizations to engage the friendship group in exercises that build social and communication skills.

Concerns About Transitions

Each transition into a new classroom and therapeutic environment brings a new round of concerns for families. For example, families may worry about how best to educate new teachers, peers, and professionals about their children's disabilities and strengths. They may worry about whether educational and therapeutic services will be delivered in a timely and appropriate manner. Families also may worry about their children's responsiveness to new learning and therapeutic environments and how to help them adjust to those environments.

To address these concerns, invite teachers and other staff who work with a child with a disability to attend his or her IEP meeting to help plan for a smooth transition. Also arrange a date for the family and new teacher to meet and discuss the child's interests, strengths, and needs. Equally important, provide opportunities for the child to visit his or her new teacher and explore his or her new classroom.

Perhaps because of their concerns about safety issues, some families of children with disabilities may be overprotective (Taub, 2006), especially during periods of transition. Help families to see the advantages of allowing their children to develop appropriate levels of independence during these times. Some home-based strategies that can facilitate this process are presented later in the chapter.

Family Functioning

Childhood disabilities can negatively impact family relationships and the quality of life for individual family members (Dunlap & Fox, 2007). For example, families may worry about dividing their time between the needs of a child with a disability and the needs of that child's siblings. They also may worry about the quality of the sibling relationship. In addition, marital strains can appear if parents expend all their energy and time caring for a child with a disability while ignoring their own relationship. Finally, parents may feel a need to give up much of their social life in order to properly care for their child. Yet, as noted above, a social support network is critical to preventing parental stress, depression, and anxiety.

Addressing these challenges is essential if families are to maintain a healthy level of functioning (Bennett & Hay, 2007). To this end, a family systems approach is sometimes used to support the well-being of individual family members, subsystems within the family, and the collective family environment (Head & Abbeduto, 2007; Keen, 2007). For example, support programs designed specifically for typically developing siblings can promote healthy relationships within the sibling subsystem (Summers et al., 2007; Xu & Filler, 2008). Likewise, defining the "client" as the family unit, rather than as an individual child, creates a mind-set for addressing the needs of all family members (Keen, 2007).

To facilitate the strategies reviewed in this section, teachers must be able to relate to families of children with disabilities. In the following section, we briefly address some of the actions you can take to achieve this type of positive partnership.

It is important that children with disabilities be allowed to assume appropriate levels of independence.

Helpful Teacher Actions

Much has been written about the importance of respect, trust, communication, collaboration, and power sharing when planning for successful service delivery and IEP partnerships (Beckman, 2002; Dunst & Dempsey, 2007; Keen, 2007; Mueller, 2009; Prezant & Marshak, 2006; Xu & Filler, 2008). Of all the school and community professionals who make up the IEP team, parents view teachers as the most helpful in supporting their children's education and development (Prezant & Marshak, 2006). This observation is important, since families who perceive themselves as having a good partnership with their child's teacher also have elevated feelings of empowerment (Dunst & Dempsey, 2007).

Examples of helpful actions displayed by teachers that parents find particularly useful are presented in FYI 7.6. You may want to return to FYI 7.6 at the end of this chapter, where you will be invited to consider how families of children with disabilities fit into your philosophy of family involvement (see Discussion Questions). For now (after you read FYI 7.6), complete Reflection 7.1.

REFLECTION 7.1 Brainstorming Comments Parents Might Make

- With your peers, come up with other comments you are likely to hear from parents that reflect the helpful actions presented in FYI 7.6.
- Now identify examples of comments from parents that would indicate you were being unhelpful.

FYI 7.6 Helpful Actions Taken by Teachers Working With Families of Children With Disabilities

Helpful Actions	Comments From Parents
• Teachers who focus on attending to the needs of families and their children. – Example: "Here is John's plan for his science project. He has given a lot of thought to this project."	"She was a creative teacher. . . . The child became the focus—not the child learning to compensate for his own deficits to satisfy the expectations of others." (p. 37)

• Teachers who provide support to the family and child.
 	
  – Example: "I value your input."
 	
  – Example: "I really admire how you and your husband communicate with each other."
 	
  – Example: "I hope you are taking some time for yourself."
	"The school guidance counselor . . . was very helpful in crisis situations. She never blamed my son, was respectful of him and very supportive of me." (p. 37)

• Teachers who encourage inclusion. – Example: "I understand your concern about our field trip. I would like to explore how we can make sure John is safely and actively involved in field trip activities."	"The special education teacher supported our desire to mainstream and later included Matt in as much regular education as possible." (p. 37)
• Teachers who promote the self-esteem of children and their families. – Example: "John is like every other child. It will take him a little while to figure out who he wants as friends."	"[The teacher was] the first professional who made me feel my child is . . . normal." (p. 37)
• Teachers who hold high expectations of children. – Example: "John has made good progress, but I believe he is capable of showing even more progress. I would like to hear your thoughts about my plan for helping John improve his writing skills."	"The special teacher accepted only her best work." (p. 37)

SOURCE: Adapted from Prezant, F. P., & Marshak, L. (2006). Helpful actions seen through the eyes of parents of children with disabilities. *Disability and Society, 21*(1), 31–45. Reprinted by permission of the publisher (Taylor & Francis Group, http://www.informaworld.com).

An additional benefit associated with the actions in FYI 7.6 is that they can help ensure the successful implementation of home-based strategies suggested by the IEP team. In the following section, we review some of these strategies.

Support Strategies for Use at Home

All IEP teams recognize the pervasive and enduring influence of family environments on the lives of children with disabilities (Dunlap & Fox, 2007). Subsequently, they strive to identify strategies that support children's development and education in the home as well as the classroom. A few home-based strategies are reviewed in this section.

Positive Reinforcement

Positive reinforcement can be anything valued by an individual (see Reflection 7.2). It is delivered following the display of a target behavior, thereby resulting in more frequent displays of that behavior. For example, after Sally is given verbal reinforcement for putting away her toys, she increases this behavior without having to be reminded.

REFLECTION 7.2   Positive Reinforcements

As a teacher, it is important that you identify a range of positive reinforcements, since what will be reinforcing for one child may not be reinforcing for another. List all the positive reinforcements you might use to increase appropriate behavior in your classroom. Consider all the possibilities: social (child decides which workgroup to join), edible (raisins), activity (extra recess time), material (a happy face sticker), and verbal ("Thank you").

Videotaped Modeling

Videotaped modeling involves videotaping another child as he or she performs a target behavior (Carothers & Taylor, 2004). The videotape is then used to teach a child with a disability the skills involved in carrying out that behavior. For example, a videotape may be made of a child checking out a library book, bouncing a basketball, or making change at a local store. Videotaped modeling has a number of advantages. It can be used in multiple settings, allows the IEP team to bring the community to the child, is fairly inexpensive, and allows the child to repeatedly view a behavior or skill in small segments or in its entirety. In addition, the results a child achieves as a result of viewing a videotape can be incorporated into parent-teacher conferences and the IEP review process.

Prompting

Prompting is used to provide visual, gestural, verbal, and other cues that assist children in completing a task on their own. Prompting can be helpful in maintaining a behavior that has been modeled or gradually shaped through a series of positive reinforcements. For example, teachers use catchy statements such as "Eyes on me" every day to prompt children's attention.

Pictorial Activity Schedules

This strategy begins with a task analysis of a behavior or task, such as the one presented in FYI 7.7. A **task analysis** involves breaking down a complex behavior or task into its discrete parts, allowing each part to be reviewed and practiced. In the case of a *pictorial activity schedule*, photographs are taken of each component identified by the task analysis (Carothers & Taylor, 2004). The photographs are then combined to show the sequence of steps a child is to take in carrying out a behavior or task. Ultimately, the goal is for the child to complete the entire sequence of skills without relying on the pictorial activity schedule. After reading the example in FYI 7.7, try your hand at completing a task analysis by completing Reflection 7.3.

FYI 7.7   Task Analysis for Making an After-School Snack

Photographs are taken of the following steps to create a pictorial activity schedule.

1. The following items are laid out on a counter: two pieces of bread, peanut butter, jelly, butter knife, and bottled water.
2. The child uses the butter knife to spread peanut butter on one piece of bread and jelly on the second piece of bread.
3. The child puts the two pieces of bread together.
4. The child eats the sandwich and drinks the water.
5. The child puts the butter knife in the sink.
6. The child puts the empty water bottle in the recycling bin.

REFLECTION 7.3   Carrying Out a Task Analysis

Identify a behavior or task with which a family might request help during an IEP meeting. Conduct a task analysis of this behavior as a foundation for developing a pictorial activity schedule.

Putting It Together: Planning Charts

All the above strategies can be combined into a planning chart to show their coordination across classroom and home settings. One example of a planning chart that addresses a child's poor impulse control is presented in FYI 7.8.

FYI 7.8 A Planning Chart for Addressing a Child's Poor Impulse Control		
	Classroom	Home
Positive Reinforcement Target = General impulse control	The child receives a "high-five" sign after sitting quietly while the teacher gives directions for a lesson.	The child receives a verbal "Thank you" after waiting patiently until her mother gives her the okay to begin walking her dog.
Videotaped Modeling Target = Sharing	The child watches and discusses a videotape of his peers sharing materials during a science activity.	The child watches and discusses a videotape of his siblings sharing their toys.
Prompting Target = Getting ready for a transition or activity	The child's teacher uses visual, verbal, and gestural cues to get her ready for a lesson by pointing to, naming, and moving materials into certain positions. The child follows the teacher's prompts by naming and putting her own materials into the same positions.	The child's parents use verbal and visual cues to help her check her backpack before leaving for school: "Book, check. Pencil, check. Paper, check. Daily folder, check."
Pictorial Activity Schedule: Target = Self-help tasks	Putting on a jacket: A series of pictures show the jacket hanging on a hook, the child putting on the jacket one sleeve at a time, the child zipping up the jacket, and the child going outside to play.	Putting on a shirt: A series of pictures show a shirt, the child unbuttoning the shirt, the child putting on the shirt one sleeve at a time, the child buttoning up the shirt, and the child's mom helping to tuck in the shirttails.

The Facilitated IEP Meeting Model

Development of an IEP can at times create an adversarial environment in which family and school priorities conflict. The facilitated IEP meeting is used to avoid such conflict by creating an environment where ideas are exchanged and disagreements are resolved in a respectful manner. Components of the facilitated IEP meeting are reviewed in this section, as summarized by the Consortium for Appropriate Dispute Resolution in Special Education (2009) and Mueller (2009).

A Neutral Facilitator

The role of an unbiased and objective facilitator is pivotal to ensuring all IEP team members feel empowered. The facilitator may be a counselor, a religious leader, a youth leader, a social service worker, a lawyer, or someone else who has received specialized training in facilitating group work. Some of the communication and problem solving tasks associated with the facilitator's role include making sure everyone is heard, keeping the team on task by focusing its attention on one topic at a time, summarizing what others have said, suggesting strategies for looking at an issue from a unique perspective, facilitating brainstorming sessions, and keeping the meeting environment comfortable and safe.

The Agenda

Like the agenda used in a parent-teacher conference, the IEP agenda serves as a guide. It is the role of the facilitator to make sure every team member participates in identifying agenda topics and deciding how much time should be devoted to each topic.

IEP Goals

The facilitator asks each team member to identify his or her goals for the target child prior to the IEP meeting. These are in turn posted for the entire team to see. This technique validates each team member's priorities and helps to structure IEP discussions.

Ground Rules

The facilitator uses ground rules to remind all participants how they are to behave during the IEP meeting. Often, the facilitator engages team members in brainstorming the types of behavior they think are important for ensuring a successful IEP meeting. Alternatively, the facilitator may suggest a few ground rules for the team to consider.

Fostering Collaboration

Families are usually outnumbered by school staff and community professionals at IEP meetings. This can lead some families to feel intimidated and others to become defensive. Creating an environment that fosters collaboration is thus important. Some of the strategies used by the facilitator to create collaboration are similar to those used during parent-teacher conferences (see Chapter 13): (a) using round or U-shaped tables, (b) providing everyone with copies of handouts, and (c) reviewing the agenda. Other techniques resemble strategies used during family workshops or support groups (see Chapter 11): (a) posting and reviewing ground rules, (b) arranging for pleasant lighting and a comfortable temperature, (c) supplying paper and pens, (d) providing light refreshments, and (e) arranging for a quiet meeting space.

An additional strategy involves placing a photograph of the child for whom the meeting is being conducted in the center of the table. Although a seemingly simple gesture, the photograph serves as a reminder of the reason for the meeting and the need for collaboration. Use your creativity to build on this idea as you complete Reflection 7.4.

REFLECTION 7.4 Creating a Comfortable IEP Environment

Placing a photograph of the child in the center of the table is a creative way to facilitate a collaborative IEP meeting. What other strategies might you use to create a respectful environment that focuses everyone's attention on the best interests of the child?

Communication Strategies to Eliminate Power Imbalances

The facilitator models and if necessary teaches basic communication skills, such as those we review in Chapter 13. Some examples of practical communication strategies that may be introduced include (a) allotting each team member the same amount of time to discuss an agenda item, (b) making sure there are no unanswered questions or concerns before moving on to the next agenda item, (c) asking open-ended questions ("What are the advantages of this approach?") versus closed-ended questions ("Is this a good approach?"), (d) facilitating role playing, and (e) asking team members to paraphrase one another's comments.

The Parking Lot

The facilitator uses a large sheet of paper on which to write off-topic comments for future consideration. This sheet of paper is called the "parking lot" and reflects the facilitator's role in acknowledging the importance of each team member's views while making sure the group stays focused on the agenda at hand.

CHAPTER SUMMARY

- The term *disability* includes a number of exceptionalities, all of which require children to be educated within the "least restrictive environment."
- The Individuals With Disabilities Education Improvement Act guarantees children with disabilities access to a quality education.
- Families of children with disabilities face not only financial concerns but also emotional challenges and the responsibility of ensuring that their children receive appropriate services and treatment.
- The facilitated IEP meeting is used to complete a plan of work that addresses the needs of children with disabilities.

DISCUSSION QUESTIONS

1. Discuss a strategy, beyond those reviewed in this chapter, that you would use to facilitate the development and education of children with disabilities.

2. Review the challenges faced by families of children with disabilities. Identify the one challenge that you personally feel most prepared to address. Discuss your response with your peers.

3. **Your family involvement philosophy.** Return to the draft of your family involvement philosophy. Based on your reading of this chapter, what if any changes will you make to your philosophy statement? Discuss your answer to this question with your peers.

COMMUNITY OF LEARNERS' FIELD ASSIGNMENT

Develop a Professional Plan

Brainstorm a plan of action for developing one skill that will help you work with children with disabilities and their families. Begin by identifying professional journals and other materials you will read to learn about these skills. The Internet Resources section at the end of the chapter can help you in carrying out this task. Also think about how you can use community professionals within and outside a school to develop your skills. Share the results of your plan in class.

CAPSTONE ACTIVITIES

Activity 1: Review an IEP

Ask a school counselor or a teacher to review an IEP with you. Remember to remove the name of the child to protect his or her privacy. Talk with the counselor or teacher about the steps that were taken to develop and implement the IEP. Also ask the counselor or teacher for tips on working with families in completing the IEP. Share the results of your review in class.

Activity 2: Interview the Parent of a Child With a Disability

Ask the parent to describe positive and negative experiences he or she has experienced when working as part of an IEP team. How does the parent's responses compare to the information presented in this chapter? Ask the parent to give you tips for working with children with disabilities in the classroom. Also ask the parent about the language he or she uses to describe his or her child. For example, does the parent prefer the term *disability, exceptional, differently abled, developmentally delayed, special needs, at risk*, or another term or phrase?

Activity 3: Compile a Dictionary of Disability Terms

Learn more about the terms and phrases used by professionals who work with disabilities. Assign everyone in your class a disability to research. Define key terms and phrases associated with your assigned disability. Compile all the terms and phrases into a dictionary. Make copies for everyone to place in his or her teacher resource file.

INTERNET RESOURCES

You may find that some URLs have been altered by the webmaster. In these situations, try entering the name of the document or agency in a search engine. Alternatively, enter the domain name (e.g., http://www.xxxx.org). This should take you to the revised home page and associated links.

Council for Exceptional Children

http://www.cec.sped.org//AM/Template.cfm?Section=Home

This is an international organization devoted to improving the educational success of individuals with disabilities and/or gifts. The council advocates supportive policies, sets professional standards, and provides professional development. The council also sponsors a number of specialized divisions, publishes journals and newsletters, and conducts conferences. The council's website also includes a number of informational links, two of which include Supports for Teachers and Teachers' Blogs.

IFSP Web: Nebraska's Individual Family Service Plan

http://ifspweb.org/

This website provides information regarding the development of an IFSP. An example of the Nebraska IFSP is provided.

The National Early Childhood Technical Assistance Center (NECTAC)

http://www.nectac.org/topics/families/stateifsp.asp

Use this webpage to access information about IFSP guides and forms from various states.

Georgia Department of Education: Individualized Education Plan (IEP)

http://www.doe.k12.ga.us/DMGetDocument.aspx/IEP.pdf?p=6CC6799F8C1371F62DF15444679D354A EF963DEF8D6E4F4068F25B368692F236&Type=D

This is an example of an IEP from Georgia.

State of Washington, Office of Superintendent of Public Instruction, Special Education: Model Forms for Services to Students in Special Education

http://www.k12.wa.us/SpecialEd/Data/ModelStateForms.aspx

This link will take you to a variety of forms used to facilitate the IEP process in the State of Washington.

National Association for the Education of Young Children (NAEYC)

http://community.fpg.unc.edu/resources/articles/files/EarlyChildhoodInclusion-04-2009.pdf

Go to this webpage to read a position statement regarding early childhood inclusion. The position statement is published jointly by NAEYC and the Council for Exceptional Children.

National Association of Special Education Teachers

http://www.naset.org/

Under the "Resources" tab, click on the "Exceptional Students and Disability Information" link to read summaries about various types of disabilities.

National Dissemination Center for Children With Disabilities

http://www.nichcy.org/Pages/Home.aspx

As its name suggests, the purpose of this center is to disseminate a range of information to teachers and the general public about disabilities, special education and intervention services, research about educational practices, and other information related to IEPs, parenting, and professional organizations.

U.S. Department of Education: Building the Legacy: IDEA 2004

http://idea.ed.gov/

Visit this U.S. government website to learn more about IDEA.

A Village to Raise

http://www.avillagetoraise.com/

This website, established by a gay couple raising two children with mental challenges, provides members with opportunities to chat, support one another, socialize, and share resources related to raising children in general and children with disabilities in particular. Access to some links requires you to establish a username and a password. Other links are available without signing in. For example, click on "Resources" or "Articles" to gain access to a range of information related to disabilities.

STUDENT STUDY SITE

Log on to the Web-based student study site at **www.sagepub.com/coleman** for additional study tools including:

- eFlashcards
- Web Quizzes
- Links to SAGE Journal Articles
- Author-created Videos

- Learning Objectives
- Web Resources
- Family Involvement Portfolio Guides

CHAPTER 8

Immigrant Families and Families From Nondominant Cultures

Understanding the Adaptation Process

I n this chapter, we extend our examination of family diversity by looking at the challenges faced by children and families from nondominant cultures. We begin with an examination of different forms of cultural adaptation. Worldviews and their implications for parent-teacher and teacher-child interactions are then examined.

As you read this chapter, take notes on the following items. Use your notes to address the Reflections, Discussion Questions, Field Assignment, and Capstone Activities that you find in the chapter.

- Describe the differences among assimilation, acculturation, and enculturation.
- Describe the types of intergenerational conflict that immigrant families face.
- Describe the differences between individualistic and collectivist worldviews.
- Define the term *familism* and describe its importance to a collectivist worldview.
- Describe some ways that American teachers might misinterpret the behavior of children from collectivist cultures.
- Describe some classroom practices that are supportive of children and families from collectivist cultures.
- Explain why African American and Asian American parents are sometimes portrayed as more authoritarian in their parenting behavior than European American parents.
- Describe Poston's model of biracial identity development.

The information in this chapter supports the following family-school-community partnership standards. These standards are reviewed in Chapter 2

NAEYC Standards and Associated Key Elements	1b, 1c, 2a, 2b, 2c, 3b, 3c, 4b, 4c, 5c, 6c, 6d, 6e
ACEI Standards	1.0, 3.2, 4.0, 5.1, 5.2
PTA Standards	1, 2, 3, 4, 5, 6

Cultural Adaptation

In this section, we review one model of cultural adaptation that highlights the challenges faced by immigrant families who live in the United States. This model divides families' adaptation to a new culture into three categories (Tutwiler, 2005, p. 63). An immigrant family that steadfastly holds on to the cultural values and behaviors of its home country while also taking special care to ensure that those values and behaviors are followed by its children is described as embracing **enculturation**. In contrast, families who hold on to the cultural values and behaviors of their country of origin but also selectively incorporate elements of the dominant American culture into their daily lives are described as undergoing the process of **selective acculturation** (Glick, 2010; Pachter & Dumont-Mathieu, 2004). Finally, immigrant families who fully adopt American cultural values, behaviors, and customs are described as having **assimilated** the dominant culture. Working through the acculturation/assimilation process is dependent on a number of factors, including the following.

Transnational families. It is not uncommon for newly arrived immigrant families to be **transnational**, meaning family members are scattered across national borders (Zinn & Wells, 2000). Today, the relative ease of movement and communication between the United States and many other countries allows transnational families to remain connected, share resources, and maintain relationships (Glick, 2010). Nevertheless, the lack of direct access to a family support network can make it difficult for these families to negotiate the dominant American culture. In addition, unique challenges can arise. Consider, for example, children who are temporarily left behind in their home country. Such separation can threaten extended family and parent-child relationships (Landolt & Da, 2005) as well as introduce stress into the family system when, upon reunification, new family roles, rules, and relationships must be negotiated in order to accommodate work, educational, and social practices associated with the American culture (Glick, 2010).

Language differences. Even the presence of an immediate family network is no guarantee that immigrant families will escape the challenges of adapting to American culture. This is particularly true when that network consists of multiple generations (see Ishii-Kuntz, 2000a, 2000b; Pachter & Dumont-Mathieu, 2004; Silverstein, 2000; Wu, 2001; Zinn & Wells, 2000). Consider, for example, the acquisition of English among immigrant families.

Typically, children acquire a new language more quickly than their parents (Pachter & Dumont-Mathieu, 2004). This can interfere with family communication (Espinosa, 2010, p. 17), especially when elders view children's predominant use of English and English slang as a sign of disrespect.

Yet another example of how language differences can create family conflict is found among siblings. Younger children who are born closest to a family's immigration to the United States are more likely than their older siblings to master and make exclusive use of English versus their native language (Stevens & Ishizawa, 2007). Such language differences can in turn lead to the older child's being viewed as the "cultural preserva-tionist" who identifies with her or his parents' traditional cultural orientation while the younger and more assimilated child is seen as the "black sheep" of the family (Pyke, 2005, pp. 491, 510). To prevent this type of family conflict, it is important that teachers pay equal respect to immigrant children's use of their home language and their use of English. In turn, immigrant children are more likely to reap the short- and long-term academic and career benefits of being bilingual (Espinosa, 2010, p. 75; Hernandez, Takanishi, & Marotz, 2009).

Values surrounding the parent-child relationship. Immigrant children's exposure to American television and movies can lead them to adopt cultural values and behaviors related to parent-child relationship dynamics that are contrary to the expectations of their parents (see Reflection 8.1). For example, arguments can erupt over displays of disrespect, family roles, and communication patterns. The challenge of negotiating such arguments is compounded by the fact that children, just as they more readily acquire English proficiency, usually adopt new cultural values, attitudes, and behaviors more quickly than their parents (Pachter & Dumont-Mathieu, 2004).

REFLECTION 8.1   Identifying Sources of Intergenerational Conflict Among Immigrant Families

Provide specific examples of how, within immigrant families, the media and schools can lead to interpersonal conflict between generations.

Economic advancement. Upward economic advancement in successive generations of immigrant families can further divide the values of older and younger family members. Accepting a higher-paying job may require a move that threatens family cohesion. In addi-tion, an increase in income is likely to give children access to a wider range of American experiences and material possessions that run counter to the cultural experiences and values endorsed by older family members.

Life priorities. Families from cultures in which the family is the focal point may be frus-trated by American culture, in which children divide their time and loyalties among their families, friends, and youth groups. Tension also can arise when children begin to express their own life priorities rather than the priorities endorsed by their families. As you will dis-cover in the following section, these conflicts are grounded in different cultural worldviews about the relative importance of individual versus family priorities.

Cultural Worldviews

A **worldview** is a frame of reference for guiding our understanding of the world, our place in it, and our interpersonal relationships. Often, individuals from different countries and races share a worldview because of similar religious beliefs or histories that shape their behaviors, values, and social interactions. At other times unique worldviews can be identified, such as the indigenous worldview of Native Americans (Castagno & Brayboy, 2008), which overlap with more global worldviews. In this section, we will focus on two worldviews: individualism and collectivism.

An **individualistic worldview** is one in which the rights, interests, and needs of the individual are most important. Personal goals, independence, and self-fulfillment are emphasized, as are attempts to control events in one's environment (Chun, Moos, & Cronkite, 2006; Diller, 2004, p. 64; Rothstein-Fisch, Trumbull, & Garcia, 2009). An individualistic worldview is associated with the dominant European-American culture that characterizes traditional American values (Watts & Tutwiler, 2008, p. 47).

A **collectivist worldview** is one in which the rights and needs of the group are given priority over individual rights, interests, and needs. Cooperation, social conformity, group harmony, a sense of duty to others, and the fulfillment of assigned social roles are emphasized (Chun et al., 2006; Rothstein-Fisch et al., 2009). Interdependence is valued over independence (Chao & Tseng, 2002). A collectivist worldview is associated with traditional African, Asian, Hispanic or Latino, and Native American cultures.

Key characteristics of the individualistic and collectivist worldviews are summarized in FYI 8.1. Before we begin our examination of these characteristics, it is helpful to again note the dangers of ignoring Reality Check #4 (there is diversity within diversity) when describing the behavior and values of groups. As a reminder, Reality Check #4 is reflected in the following quote:

> there is usually as much variation in beliefs and behaviors within a cultural group as between groups. This point is important to recognize if one is to steer free of stereotypes. (Pachter & Dumont-Mathieu, 2004, p. 90)

The following examples highlight the significance of this warning:

- While Hispanics or Latinos are described as endorsing a collectivist culture, Cuban-Americans also display a sense of independence that reflects an individualistic worldview (Bevin, 2001).
- Indeed, some note that the concept of "familism," an individualistic cultural value (see the following heading), can be applied to Hispanics or Latinos of Mexican and Cuban origin more than to Hispanics or Latinos of Puerto Rican or Dominican origin (Cherlin, 2010).
- Among Mexican Americans, the concept of familism is of greater relevance to first-generation immigrants than to their second- or third-generation descendants (Oropesa & Landale, 2004).
- We might reasonably expect a middle-class Asian child who immigrated to the United States five years ago to display a stronger individualistic worldview than a child from an Asian country who only recently immigrated to the United States.
- Finally, scholars warn teachers not to ascribe a particular learning style to Native American children but to instead focus on the learning styles of individual children (Castagno & Brayboy, 2008).

FYI 8.1   Individualistic and Collectivist Worldviews

Individualistic worldviews:

- emphasize individual priorities
- emphasize the nuclear family
- are obsessed with time schedules
- are competitive
- emphasize independence
- focus on individual achievements

Collectivist worldviews:

- emphasize family priorities
- emphasize the extended family and fictive kin
- have a relaxed approach to schedules
- are cooperative and stress social harmony
- emphasize interdependence
- focus on group achievements

Individualism Versus Familism

Individualism, a hallmark of the individualistic worldview, emphasizes the priorities of individuals over those of the family unit. For example, there is no mention of the term *family* in the United States Constitution, and our country has no explicit family policy agenda (Bogenschneider, 2001, p. 16). Instead, laws are passed to address the rights of individuals. The reasoning behind this individualistic approach to legislation includes these ideas: (a) Individual well-being promotes family well-being and (b) the government should show restraint in passing legislation that interferes with private family lives.

Familism, a hallmark of the collectivist worldview, emphasizes the priorities of the family over those of the individual. Thus, not surprisingly, we are most likely to find families living close to one another or in multigenerational households in collectivist cultures (Chun et al., 2006; Dilworth-Anderson & Marshall, 1996, p. 73; Glover, 2001; McAdoo, 2001; Parke, 2004; Sarkisian, Gerena, & Gerstel, 2007; Tutwiler, 2005, p. 67; Zayas, Canino, & Suarez, 2001). In addition, families in collectivist cultures are more likely to make personal decisions for their children, while families from individualistic cultures are more likely to emphasize that it is important for children to make decisions on their own. As a cultural value and mind-set, familism promotes a sense of family solidarity, facilitates the delivery of emotional and financial support within the extended family, and promotes family responsibility for the care and guidance of children. As you will see, it can also influence how children and parents interact with educational institutions and social service agencies.

Familism, one characteristic of a collectivist worldview, emphasizes the priorities of the family over those of the individual.

Family Boundaries

Family boundaries are more permeable in collectivist cultures than in individualistic cultures. Thus, in Hispanic or Latino cultures, both the nuclear and extended families are seen as sources of loyalty, solidarity, and emotional and practical support (Espinosa, 2010, p. 17). For example, the importance of fictive kin is reflected in the life of one Hispanic scholar who, as a child growing up in Brazil, called her teachers aunts and considered them members of her family (Souto-Manning & Swick, 2006). Still other fictive kin, such as godparents, assume important child rearing roles in African American and Hispanic or Latino cultures (Crosbie-Burnett & Lewis, 1993; Dilworth-Anderson & Marshall, 1996; Parke, 2004; Tutwiler, 2005, p. 66; Zayas et al., 2001). Likewise, in Asian cultures the respect given to ancestors provides a sense of continuity across generations. Finally, Native Americans exhibit fluid family boundaries with tribal elders who help to guide, counsel, and teach children (Dilworth-Anderson & Marshall, 1996; Glover, 2001; Tutwiler, 2005, p. 67).

Because of the extensive family networks that result from a collectivist worldview, children from collectivist cultures may become confused if discussions about family life in the classroom focus only on the nuclear family. A simple remedy for this dilemma is to broaden these discussions to include extended and fictive kin (Smith, 1991). Indeed, this approach will benefit all children, since any family's adoption of individualistic versus collectivist behavior is not absolute but a matter of degree. Consider, for example, Reflection 8.2.

REFLECTION 8.2   How Does Your Family Life Reflect Individualism and Familism?

Think about the behavior, values, rituals, and traditions that your family followed when you were a child or that your current family follows. What elements of individualism and familism can you identify?

Engagement With Educational and Social Service Institutions

Families who follow a collectivist worldview may be hesitant to make full use of the services provided by schools and community agencies, instead relying on their family and neighborhood networks. This is especially true of families who have encountered cultural discrimination and thus may mistrust social institutions in general. As a teacher, you can play an important mediator role by linking immigrant families with community services and helping them advocate for their needs (Vesely & Ginsberg, 2011). For example, one Head Start teacher reported to the author of this textbook that she attended school enrollment meetings with families she felt might have problems communicating with school personnel because of cultural differences. During the meetings, the teacher helped families respond to questions, assisted them with paperwork, and made sure teachers were given information that would ease children's transition into their new classroom.

Another approach to encouraging immigrant parents' participation in their children's school activities is to offer school-based adult education classes. Consider, for example, the finding from one study that Mexican immigrant mothers who enrolled in adult education classes at their children's school also increased their involvement in their children's education (Crosnoe & Kalil, 2010). The researchers suggested that this finding was the result of mothers' becoming more familiar with the environment and language of the U.S. educational system. As a result, they gained a greater confidence in their ability to support and participate in their children's classroom work.

Time Management

Time management is of major importance to an individualistic worldview, reflecting a concern with predicting and controlling present and future events. In contrast, a collectivist worldview is less obsessed with schedules (Diller, 2004, pp. 64–65). One implication of these differences for the classroom is that children from collectivist cultures may take a more relaxed approach to completing tasks. It may also take them longer to understand the importance of following a daily schedule. Likewise, children who are accustomed to a relaxed time schedule at home are likely to experience problems readjusting to their more structured classroom schedule after having spent the weekend, a holiday, or a school vacation with their families (Bazron, Osher, & Fleischmann, 2005). Patience and a review of the classroom schedule will help reorient these children to their classroom environment.

Children's Classroom Behavior

Differences between individualistic and collectivist worldviews can at times lead teachers to misinterpret children's classroom behavior. Some examples are presented in FYI 8.2.

Let's examine how these differences might play out in the classroom, beginning with eye contact. Children who grow up in the dominant American culture are taught to assert their needs and views by speaking up for themselves and making direct eye contact. Such assertiveness reflects the individualistic values of self-expression, freedom of choice, and

FYI 8.2   Misinterpretations of the Behavior Displayed by Children From Collectivist Cultures

Children who are taught at home to	. . . may be viewed by American teachers as
• avoid eye contact as a sign of deference	• socially incompetent or defiant
• value cooperation over competition	• lacking self-initiative
• value listening over talking	• timid or fearful
• remain silent when admonished	• passive-aggressive
• take their time when completing tasks	• lacking time management skills

SOURCE: Adapted in part from Smith, D. E. (1991). Understanding some behaviors of culturally different children. *International Education, 24*(1), 31–40.

independent thinking. An individualistic worldview also encourages children to strive toward individual achievement by taking pride in their classroom accomplishments and to be proactive in shaping their environment to their liking (Diller, 2004, p. 65).

The behaviors and values endorsed by many collectivist cultures are just the opposite of those described earlier. Again, let's begin with eye contact. Hispanic or Latino children are taught that it is disrespectful to make direct eye contact when communicating with teachers, parents, and other authority figures (Espinosa, 2010, p. 15). It is not uncommon for teachers who are accustomed to individualistic norms to mislabel this behavior as a sign of social incompetence or disrespect, since they expect children to look at them when they are talking.

It is important that teachers consider the possible cultural basis behind children's classroom behavior.

Children in collectivistic cultures also are taught the importance of displaying cooperative behaviors, such as sharing work and working on behalf of the group rather than oneself. Asian children in particular are taught to maintain a modest demeanor, to avoid bringing attention to themselves, to listen more than speak, to speak in a soft voice, and to deemphasize individual accomplishments, since this is viewed as self-serving and offensive to others (Espinosa, 2010, p. 19; Shibusawa, 2001; Wu, 2001). They also are taught to comply with requests from authority figures (Diller, 2004, p. 65), who control their life choices (Chun et al., 2006). Other examples of how Asian cultural values can influence children's classroom behavior are presented in FYI 8.3. After reading FYI 8.3, complete Reflection 8.3.

Strategies for Supporting a Collectivist Classroom Environment

There are a number of steps you can take to support collectivist cultural values in your classroom. For instance, you might begin by following the example of teachers who participated in the Bridging Cultures Project in California. These teachers, some of whom self-identified as Hispanic or Latino and others as European American, met over a number of months to explore ways to incorporate both individualistic and collectivist values and practices into their classrooms (Rothstein-Fisch et al., 2009). They also arranged a series of breakfast and lunch meetings to share their reflections and experiences. The project yielded a number of positive results, as reflected in the following quote from a teacher raised in the individualistic culture of the United States (Rothstein-Fisch et al., 2009):

> It was a revelation that the parents weren't wrong, just different, because it never felt right to me to think they were wrong. Coming together [as part of the project group], it all made sense. It answered many of the questions I had. (p. 477)

FYI 8.3   Examples of Asian Cultural Influences on Children's Behavior

- *Decision making.* Unlike children who have grown up in the U.S., immigrant children from Asian cultures are likely to wait for directions from their teachers before taking action and to avoid volunteering an answer unless called upon (Espinosa, 2010, p. 19; Joshi, 2005). To accommodate these behaviors, provide the supportive structure these children need as they learn to adapt to their individualistic classroom culture.
- *Respect for authority.* An Asian child who smiles and nods in agreement with a teacher may do so even though she or he does not understand or agree with the teacher's request. This behavior reflects the Asian cultural norm that it is impolite to refuse to comply with a request from an authority figure. Gentle probing is thus needed to make sure a request has been properly communicated and agreed to. For example, after giving a child directions, you might state, "Please tell me what you will do."
- *Focus on the group.* A related Asian cultural norm is an emphasis on changing oneself rather than attempting to change a situation (Yeh, Arora, & Wu, 2006). This mind-set reflects the importance of personal restraint and social harmony, as summarized in the Japanese saying "The nail that sticks out gets hammered down" (Shibusawa, 2001, p. 288). As a result, Asian children may find it embarrassing to be singled out for an individual achievement. Indeed, parents in traditional Asian cultures are less likely to praise their children for good behavior and classroom grades (Cheung & Nguyen, 2001; Wu, 2001), since they place greater emphasis on effort (Espinosa, 2010, p. 19; Okagaki & Diamond, 2000; Shibusawa, 2001). Asian parents also fear that praising their children will encourage laziness (Lowinger & Kwok, 2001).
- *Commitment to academics.* Finally, teachers sometimes comment on the serious approach Asian children take to their academic work. It is helpful to remember that such seriousness reflects deeper cultural values where children's dedication to academic achievement is viewed less as a personal accomplishment and more as honoring their parents' sacrifices and expectations (Cheung & Nguyen, 2001; Watts & Tutwiler, 2008). Asian parents reinforce this mind-set by closely monitoring whether their children are exerting the effort needed to do well in school (Ng, Pomerantz, & Lam, 2007). One consequence of this cultural expectation is that Asian parents downplay their children's academic achievements and instead focus on their shortcomings (Ng et al., 2007). Of course, this mind-set is just the opposite of that of European-American parents, who promote their children's self-esteem by rewarding them for their academic achievements and downplaying their shortcomings.

REFLECTION 8.3   Anticipating Asian Children's Behavior

How might you avoid or respond to the following classroom situations that can arise when teaching Asian children who follow a collectivist worldview?

- A child stares at her lap when, after being presented with an award for her history project, she is asked to share her project with the class.
- A child remains silent during class meetings.
- A child is teased by other children about being the "teacher's pet" because he follows all your directions and requests without complaint.
- A child clearly does not understand how to approach a task, even though he said "yes" when you asked if he understood your directions.

Teachers raised in collectivist cultures also benefited from the project, as reflected in the following quote from a teacher raised in Mexico (Rothstein-Fisch et al., 2009):

> As an immigrant from Mexico myself I can see how I have had to fight my own collectivistic upbringing to be successful in U.S. schools. Those of us who jumped from one [cultural] orientation to another made the leap without even knowing it! Now we need to tap our cultural knowledge for the sake of our students. (p. 477)

We next turn to other examples of collectivist teaching and family involvement practices that are currently used by teachers (see Bazron et al., 2005; Rothstein-Fisch, et al., 2009; Sanacore, 2004; Wlodkowski & Ginsberg, 1995). You will have an opportunity to identify additional examples at the end of this chapter (see Capstone Activities 2 and 3).

Collaborative Learning

Collaborative learning is a type of teaching that encourages children to work together to accomplish a learning objective. In addition, lessons are structured in such a way that each child makes a meaningful contribution. For example, instead of asking children to report on their individual math projects, a group of children can work together to complete and present their collective math project. Small **literature circles** (Sanacore, 2004), where children explore a book together, are another example of collaborative learning. Children can also work together to build a model of a volcano. All of these examples reinforce the type of collaboration valued in Asian (Taylor, 2004), Native American (Castagno & Brayboy, 2008), and other collectivist cultures.

Role Plays

Role plays also fit well with the collectivist worldview, in which children are expected to learn about and conform to social norms. In addition, role plays make the actions and responsibilities of others more meaningful (Sanacore, 2004), thereby reinforcing the empathy, restraint, reflection, and other character traits highly valued in collectivist cultures. For example, assuming the role of a parent in a class play about family life on the American frontier encourages children to think about and practice meeting the needs of the family unit. Such role plays also build communication and interpersonal skills.

Collaborative learning is one example of a classroom practice that reflects a collectivist worldview.

Sharing Circles

Sharing circles are used at the beginning or end of the day to allow children to share with their peers something they feel is important. For young children, it is helpful to structure the sharing by identifying simple themes, such as a favorite classroom or home activity. Older children can be asked to share their plans for working on a homework assignment or their feelings about a current or historical event. Verbally affirming the value of each comment reinforces the collectivist values of group harmony and cooperation.

Peer Mentoring

Instead of pitting one student against another, **peer mentoring** encourages children to help each other. A simple statement such as "Madison and Abaeze, please talk with each other about your ideas" is all that is needed to encourage peer mentoring and, thereby, reinforce the collectivist cultural value of sharing and cooperation.

Assessment Portfolios

Assessment portfolios consist of carefully selected materials that document children's classroom achievements. Portfolios are especially useful in compensating for the cultural biases sometimes associated with standardized achievement tests (Walker-Dalhouse & Dalhouse, 2001). Portfolios also are useful in grounding children's achievements in a visible and real-life context that individuals from collectivist cultures, such as Native American cultures, value (Castagno & Brayboy, 2008).

Interpreting

The practice of **interpreting** is useful in helping children from different cultures understand each other's communication styles. For example, Kanya, a recent immigrant from Thailand, may smile while silently looking at John, who is experimenting with a small solar panel. Kanya's teacher can interpret this nonverbal form of communication by stating, "John, Kanya is smiling at you. I think he may like what you are doing. Will you invite him to work with you?"

Group Rewards

Acknowledging achievements through **group rewards** helps to avoid embarrassing children from collectivist cultures, in which, as noted earlier, bringing attention to oneself is viewed as self-centered and boastful. For example, following a class project, you might choose to balance individualistic and collectivist customs by giving each child an equally valued reward while reviewing all the tasks that were accomplished as a result of the children's working together. Also be sensitive to how you communicate with Asian parents about their children's achievements. For example, in addition to reporting a child's individual achievement, you might emphasize her or his hard work and contribution to the success of the class as a whole.

Social Mini-conferences

All parents benefit from an informal and personal relationship with their child's teacher. One simple but powerful way to build this type of relationship is through **social "mini-conferences."** For example, one teacher used morning arrival mini-conferences with her Latino and African American parents for the express purpose of socializing and building a close parent-teacher partnership (Trumbull, Rothstein-Fisch, Greenfield, & Quiroz, 2001).

Other teachers reported how they used home visits to develop comfortable and trusting partnerships with immigrant families (Vesely & Ginsberg, 2011). During their visits, teachers focused on learning about parents' goals for their children and families. They also focused on learning about families' cultures, including their experiences in coming to the United States. This allowed them to integrate cultural items (e.g., maps and flags), language (e.g., labeling of classroom items and areas), and experiences into the classroom environment.

Extending the Meaning of "Family"

Acknowledge the family-oriented strengths of collectivist cultures by inviting the whole family to attend family events. For example, one teacher announced that she planned to take family photographs during an open house as a means of encouraging attendance and validating the role extended family and fictive kin play in raising and educating children (Rothstein-Fisch et al., 2009).

Now that you have some ideas about how the collectivist worldview can be incorporated into your classroom, we examine how it can impact parent-teacher partnerships.

Parenting and Parent-Teacher Partnerships

As already reflected in some of the examples given in this chapter, cultural differences have a number of implications for understanding parenting behavior in general and guiding parent-teacher partnerships in particular. In this section, we examine these issues in further detail.

Home and Classroom Boundaries

Hispanic or Latino parents, as well as Asian parents, are accustomed to parent-teacher boundaries where teachers serve as authority figures and are responsible for making decisions about their children's education in the classroom (Espinosa, 2010, p. 15; Watts & Tutwiler, 2008). For example, Chinese American parents are more likely to support their children's education using in-home instructional practices versus volunteering at school (Diamond, Wang, & Gomez, 2006; Huntsinger & Jose, 2009). Likewise, rather than voicing their concerns about the quality of their children's classroom education, Chinese American parents may draw on family and community resources to provide their children with additional educational experiences (Diamond et al., 2006).

Families from cultures with structured home–school boundaries also are less likely to visit their children's classroom without first receiving a formal invitation to do so (Espinosa, 2010, p. 15; Lundgren & Morrison, 2003; Souto-Manning & Swick, 2006). Because of this mind-set, general invitations for families to visit their children's classroom may be viewed as mere courtesy gestures (Smith, 1991). Instead, extend invitations that are linked to specific activities or objectives. Also remember that, in some cases, immigrant families may be more open to home visits (see Chapter 12) or meeting with you in a familiar community setting.

Parent-Teacher Exchanges

It is not unusual for immigrant families to remain quiet during school meetings, since they may not know how or to whom to voice their concerns or questions (Bang, 2009). One simple way to address this issue is to explicitly invite all families to share their ideas and concerns with you. Also be explicit in explaining the purpose of parent-teacher conferences to immigrant families. This will help you avoid situations like the following:

> A parents' school visit in Korea means their children have misbehaved or gotten bad scores on tests. Therefore, I found that I had a negative preconception of participating in school even though American schools have lots of activities and meetings for parents to participate in and to be volunteers, irrespective of my children's problems. (Sohn & Wang, 2006, p. 129)[1]

To further facilitate immigrant families' participation in conferences, provide them with questions to ask during the conferences. One possible list of questions can be found in Chapter 13. Finally, remember to explain educational terms associated with the daily classroom routine (which children will no doubt talk about at home) and report cards.

Parenting Behavior

Within recent years, family scholars increasingly have come to appreciate the different parenting motivations associated with different racial and ethnic groups (Crosnoe & Cavanagh, 2010). In particular, African American and Asian American parents are sometimes portrayed as being more authoritarian in their parenting behavior than European American parents (Bigner, 2006, pp. 31–34; McLoyd, Cauce, Takeuchi, & Wilson, 2001), especially in their use of control. It is important that we not overstate this portrayal, since we also know that these parents use love and warmth in equal measure. Likewise, any comparison between parents from nondominant cultures and European American parents must be put within a proper social context.

African-American parenting. From an African American viewpoint, control and close supervision are used by parents to socialize children for life in a society characterized by racial profiling and other forms of discrimination. In short, African American families employ a form of **involved-vigilant parenting** (Berkel et al., 2009, p. 185) in which parents (especially mothers) teach children (especially sons) how to protect themselves from possible acts of discrimination while also providing them with support and understanding (Crowley & Curenton, 2011). Baumrind (1972) explains this line of reasoning best when she writes, "The fiercer the mother, the better protected [the child]" (p. 266). One result of involved-vigilant parenting is that sons especially report "a sense of tender connection with their mothers who listened to them and sustained their innocence" (Berkel et al., 2009).

African American socialization practices also involve parents' shielding children from and explaining negative stereotypes (Crowley & Curenton, 2011). Likewise, children are taught to maintain a wariness of social institutions (Parke, 2004; Watts & Tutwiler, 2008; Wilson &

Morgan, 2004), including schools (Pachter & Dumont-Mathieu, 2004) and the criminal justice system (Children's Defense Fund, 2011). Consider, for example, Case Study 8.1.

CASE STUDY 8.1   Racial Insensitivity

In 2010, a high school teacher and a middle school teacher addressed the topic of discrimination in the United States, during which some students were allowed to film a historical reenactment by dressing up in KKK sheets (Davis, 2010). Some in the community believed those who complained about the reenactment were overreacting. Others thought the teachers were insensitive. Still others labeled the reenactments as evidence of school-based discrimination. As a teacher, how might you structure a lesson on discrimination for preschool or elementary school children to avoid charges of racial insensitivity or discrimination?

Asian parenting. From an Asian viewpoint, control and the close supervision of children are viewed as signs of parental love (Watts & Tutwiler, 2008), as well as an indicator that children are being raised to internalize moral reasoning (Wu, 2001), social harmony (McLoyd et al., 2001), empathy with others, and a sense of reciprocity by which adults care for children and children in turn show respect and obedience to their families (Chao & Tseng, 2002, Ishii-Kuntz, 2000b; Lowinger & Kwok, 2001; Parke, 2004; Shibusawa, 2001; Wu, 2001). Some writers use the metaphor of plant cultivation to describe the use of control by Asian parents (Chao & Tseng, 2002, pp. 61, 80). To summarize, children, like plants, are cultivated through a careful and attentive process in which "inner tendencies" are permitted to unfold as parents indulge their children's demands and wishes. Such indulgence is permitted up to about age six, at which time parents begin to more forcefully shape children's behavior to prepare them for life in a collective society where individual interests are secondary to those of the family and community.

Racial Socialization

Discussions of race are approached differently among European-American parents and parents of color. While European American parents discuss race with their children to teach tolerance, African American and Native American parents pursue the additional objective of preparing children for bias and stereotyping (Crowley & Curenton, 2011; Glover, 2001; McAdoo, 2001; McLoyd et al., 2001). No doubt, discussions of race by Hispanic or Latino parents follow a similar theme.

Minority parents begin the racial socialization process early (Lesane-Brown, Brown, Tanner-Smith, & Bruce, 2010), using both overt strategies (e.g., talking to children about their heritage) and covert strategies (e.g., listening to music and wearing clothing grounded in ethnic and racial traditions) to boost their children's self-image and racial identity (Crowley & Curenton, 2011; Crosnoe & Cavanagh, 2010). In contrast, European-American parents are less likely to discuss their children's racial heritage (Brown, Tanner-Smith, Lesane-Brown, & Ezell, 2007; Lesane-Brown et al., 2010), or they do so indirectly and unintentionally (Lesane-Brown et al., 2010).

Poston's Model of Biracial Identity Development

Providing biracial children with a sense of "racial normalcy" necessitates their exposure to and involvement in multiple racial experiences that promote a sense of belonging and affirmation (Samuels, 2009). Otherwise, they are left with, and may even adopt, the following stereotypes: (a) Biracial children are socially maladjusted because of their inability to identify with a particular culture; (b) biracial children should identify with the parent of color because that is how society views them; and (c) biracial children do not like to discuss their racial heritage (Harris, 2002). The last stereotype is especially damaging, since discussions about race are essential in helping biracial children understand and deal with the strange looks and negative reactions they sometimes receive from others (Hud-Aleem & Countryman, 2008).

The importance of biracial experiences and open discussions about race is reflected in Poston's (1990) model of biracial identity development, a summary of which follows. As a teacher, you may find this model useful in helping families and colleagues understand the process biracial children go through in forming an integrated racial identity.

Personal identity. Children at this stage are very young, and their sense of group membership is often idiosyncratic and inconsistent. As a result, their "reference group orientation" is not fully developed, meaning they may not be aware of their biracial heritage. Beginning with this stage, it is important that adults not overreact to children's questions or concerns about their racial heritage. Instead, remember that being biracial in itself does not lead to emotional or relationship problems (Hud-Aleem & Countryman, 2008). Rather, the vast majority of biracial children make good life adjustments.

Choice of group categorization. At this stage, children begin to experience pressure to identify with one racial group in order to fully participate in their family or peer group. Three choices are typically available. Many children choose to make one racial heritage dominant over the other. Some children with sufficient cognitive maturity and exposure to empowering biracial experiences choose a biracial status that acknowledges the racial heritage of both parents. In rare cases, children may adopt a "transcendent identity" in which they view attempts to place them in a racial category as an "annoyance" and thus choose to ignore race altogether (Rockquemore & Laszloffy, 2005, pp. 8–9). Several factors influence the choice that is made, including a child's physical characteristics, the racial demographics of the local neighborhood, and the types of positive or negative influences exerted by peers and family members (Patel, 2009, pp. 11–15; Poston, 1990; Rockquemore & Laszloffy, 2005, p. 4).

Enmeshment/Denial. This stage is marked by confusion and guilt over having been forced to select a racial identity that is not fully representative of one's background. Children who selected a dominant racial identity in the previous stage may now feel alienated from the subordinate racial group. In addition, feelings of disloyalty may arise if the child is unable to embrace the racial heritages of both parents. Parent and teacher support is thus important in helping children to work through these feelings. For example, it is important that biracial children be allowed to have their own identity before having a racial identity (Kilson & Ladd, 2009, p. 108). Indeed, from a developmental perspective, we can argue that parents and teachers should encourage all children to fully explore and express their personal strengths and identities, independent of race, early in life. Developing confidence in oneself as a unique individual is crucial to withstanding the various labels that society ultimately ascribes to us based on our behavior, economic status, gender, and so on.

At this point, you may be wondering when biracial children are likely to have an awareness of how others perceive them racially. This usually occurs by kindergarten or first grade. It is thus important that biracial children at this age understand they are of two races (Kilson & Ladd, 2009, p. 108). A family climate characterized by open discussion of race and race-related matters can help facilitate such understanding (Kilson & Ladd, 2009, p. 109). For example, parents can listen sympathetically to children's comments about how others treat them. They also can make available books, videos, and artwork that present an affirming view of biracial individuals (Kilson & Ladd, 2009, p. 116). Your local librarian can assist you in identifying age-appropriate books to share with parents of biracial children.

Appreciation. At this stage, children begin to appreciate their biracial heritage and broaden their racial identity. While factors associated with the "choice of group" may still influence children's decision to adopt a particular racial identity, they also show greater interest in learning about their broader racial heritage. Thus, it is important that by at least middle childhood, parents begin to talk with their children about representations of race in movies, advertisements, and other media (Kilson & Ladd, 2009, p. 109). It is equally important that biracial children celebrate their "double rich" heritage (Hud-Aleem & Countryman, 2008; Kilson & Ladd, 2009, p. 116). For example, parents can identify cultural community events and groups in which all family members can participate. They can also provide crayons and art and craft materials that allow children to visually represent the skin tones, eye colors, and hair textures of different family members. As you will discover in Chapter 9, culturally responsive teachers also integrate these materials and self-expressive activities into the classroom.

Integration. As its label implies, children and adolescents at this stage recognize, appreciate, and feel secure in subscribing to a fully integrated biracial heritage. The importance of such integration is documented in findings that children with a true biracial identity grow up to be healthier than those with a single-race identity (American Academy of Child & Adolescent Psychiatry, 1999). Schools can facilitate this stage of identity development by promoting racial and cultural diversity (see Chapter 9). You may find the following website useful in helping your school with this task: www.multiracialsky.com/index.html. Additional resources are provided at the end of this chapter.

CHAPTER SUMMARY

- Upon moving to the United States, families from nondominant cultures may pursue assimilation, acculturation, or enculturation.
- The worldviews of individualism and collectivism influence not only individual behavior but also parent-child, teacher-child, and parent-teacher relationships.
- Teachers in the United Stated already employ a number of strategies that reflect a collectivist worldview: collaborative learning, role plays, sharing circles, and peer mentoring, among others.
- The vast majority of biracial children make good life adjustments.

NOTE

1. With the kind permission from Springer Science+Business Media. *Early Childhood Education Journal, 34*(2), 125–132, Sohn, S., & Wang, C. (2006). *Immigrant parents' involvement in American schools: Perspectives from Korean mothers.*

DISCUSSION QUESTIONS

1. Discuss the different ways an immigrant child or family might display assimilation, acculturation, or enculturation when interacting with teachers.

2. Discuss the social trends you see that suggest a strengthening of "familism" in contemporary American society. Discuss the appropriate balance between familism and individualism that American society should adopt.

3. **Your family involvement philosophy.** Return to the draft of your family involvement philosophy. Based on your reading of this chapter, what if any changes will you make to your philosophy statement? Discuss your answer to this question with your peers.

COMMUNITY OF LEARNERS' FIELD ASSIGNMENT

Addressing the Needs of Children From Migrant Farm Families

The Migrant Education Program (MEP) is a federally funded program that is represented in every public school district in the United States. Migrant Education coordinators ensure that children from migrant families receive appropriate developmental and educational services. Children are eligible for three years of service following each family move.

Your Task. Contact your local school board or your state MEP administrator (visit www2.ed.gov/ programs/mep/index.html) to identify the Migrant Education coordinator in your community. Invite this person to visit your class to make a presentation about her or his work. Also consider pooling class contributions to develop family backpacks for the coordinator to use when preparing children from migrant families for school. For example, some backpacks might contain educational activities designed to prepare children for their new school environment. Other backpacks might contain clothing, toiletries, and basic school supplies. Alternatively, your class might volunteer to help the Migrant Education coordinator with tutoring or other educational services. At the end of your volunteer work, discuss how your experiences prepared you to work with migrant farm families and their children.

CAPSTONE ACTIVITIES

Activity 1: Use Children's Books to Explore Worldviews

Select a children's book that reflects a behavior or value associated with a collectivist worldview and one that reflects an individualistic worldview. Bring the two books to class to share with your peers. How do the two books compare in terms of their themes, characters, and plots? How would you incorporate one or both books into a classroom lesson?

Activity 2: Plan a Cultural Learning Center

Assume you have accepted a teaching position in a community dominated by an African American, Asian American, Hispanic or Latino American, or Native American culture. Also assume the local school board has mandated that all teachers establish a "cultural learning center" in their classroom to highlight the historical and contemporary accomplishments of this culture. Describe the materials you will use in setting up your cultural learning center for any age group, prekindergarten through fifth grade. Describe how you will use the cultural learning center to reinforce respect for cultural diversity.

Activity 3: Collectivist Teaching and Family Involvement Strategies

In this chapter, you were introduced to examples of teaching and family involvement practices that reflect a collectivist worldview. Develop another example of a teaching or family involvement practice that supports a collectivist worldview. Compile your examples into a handout titled "Collectivist Teaching and Family Involvement Strategies." Make copies of the handout for everyone to place in her or his teacher resource file.

INTERNET RESOURCES

You may find that some URLs have been altered by the webmaster. In these situations, try entering the name of the document or agency in a search engine. Alternatively, enter the domain name (e.g., http://www.xxxx.org). This should take you to the revised home page and associated links.

African Studies Center, University of Pennsylvania

http://www.africa.upenn.edu/

The African Studies Center at the University of Pennsylvania serves those interested in gaining knowledge of contemporary and historical Africa. The above website provides links to information related to African countries, images, maps and flags, and K–12 lesson plans.

Asia Society

http://www.asiasociety.org/

The mission of the Asia Society is to strengthen relationships and promote understanding among people, leaders, and institutions of the United States and Asia. Visit this site to view the Asia Society Museum and to gain access to resources such as stories, games, and languages that you can use in your classroom.

Alaska Native Knowledge Network (ANKN): Guidelines for Preparing Culturally Responsive Teachers for Alaska's Schools

http://www.ankn.uaf.edu/Publications/teachers.html

Sponsored by the University of Alaska Fairbanks, the ANKN provides Native people, government agencies, educators, and the general public access to the knowledge base that Alaska Natives have acquired over millennia. Use this site to increase your knowledge about Alaskan Native American culture and to review resources for use in your classroom.

Native Languages of the Americas

http://www.native-languages.org/languages.htm

Native Languages of the Americas is a nonprofit corporation that works to preserve and promote endangered Native American languages. Included on the home page is a listing of Native American tribes. Click on each tribe to learn more about its language and to access links related to its history and culture.

Spanish Steps

http://www.spanishstepsonline.com/

This company provides tools for teachers and other professionals to assist them in communicating more effectively with Spanish-speaking parents. For example, the two booklets *Going Home With Spanish* and *Step Into English* include translations of words and phrases to assist teachers in communicating with Spanish-speaking parents verbally and in writing. Other products, such as bilingual notepads, facilitate common classroom communication needed for parent-teacher conferences, classroom celebrations, and notes of appreciation.

National Education Association: Lesson Plans

http://www.nea.org/tools/LessonPlans.html

Type the following phrases into the search box of this website to access classrooms lessons and/or information related to the following cultures: (a) "Lessons for Hispanic Heritage Month," (b) "Black History Month Lessons and Resources," (c) "Asians/Pacific Islanders: Education Issues," and (d) "American Indians/Alaska Natives."

Federal Resources for Educational Excellence

http://www.free.ed.gov/subjects.cfm?subject_id=171&toplvl=178

This site is sponsored by the U.S. Department of Education. Click on any of the appropriate links ("African Americans," "Asian Americans," "Hispanic Americans," "Native Americans") to gain access to Internet sources related to a particular culture and its history.

Association of MultiEthnic Americans, Inc. (AMEA)

http://www.ameasite.org/

This is an international association of organizations dedicated to advocacy and education. The AMEA offers support groups, a speaker's bureau, a newsletter, representation in Washington, D.C., and access to a national resource center.

Center for the Study of Biracial Children

http://csbchome.org/

The Center for the Study of Biracial Children produces and disseminates materials for and about interracial families and biracial children. The center also provides advocacy and training.

STUDENT STUDY SITE

Log on to the Web-based student study site at **www.sagepub.com/coleman** for additional study tools including

- eFlashcards
- Web Quizzes
- Links to SAGE Journal Articles
- Author-created Videos

- Learning Objectives
- Web Resources
- Family Involvement Portfolio Guides

CHAPTER 9

Adopting a Culturally Responsive Approach to Family Involvement

Two dramatic demographic shifts occurred during the 2000s. First, in 2007, the number of individuals in the United States from ethnic or racial minority groups reached more than 100 million, or about one third of the population (U.S. Census Bureau, 2007). Second, Hispanics overtook African-Americans as the largest minority group in the United States (U.S. Census Bureau, 2010). These historical announcements were accompanied by the projection that, in the decades to come, the percentage of white Americans in the United States will decrease while the percentage of other racial and ethnic groups will increase (U.S. Census Bureau, 2004). All of these trends support the need for a culturally responsive approach to working with children and their families. Subsequently, in this chapter we examine the process of becoming a culturally responsive teacher.

As you read this chapter, take notes on the following items. Use your notes to address the Reflections, Discussion Questions, Field Assignment, and Capstone Activities that you find in the chapter.

- Explain why scientists view "race" as a socially constructed concept rather than a biological reality.
- Explain how the term *minority* is fluid and relative.
- Define the difference between ethnocentrism and ethnorelativism.
- Explain what it means to be a culturally responsive teacher.
- Describe the four goals associated with the anti-bias education model.
- Describe the three approaches teachers might take when implementing a multicultural education curriculum.
- Describe some steps teachers can take to deconstruct stereotypes.

COMMUNITY LEARNING GUIDE

The information in this chapter supports the following family-school-community partnership standards. These standards are reviewed in Chapter 2.

NAEYC Standards and Associated Key Element	1b, 1c, 2a, 2c, 3c, 4b, 4c, 5c, 6c, 6d, 6e
ACEI Standards	1.0, 3.2, 5.1, 5.2
PTA Standards	1, 2, 3, 4, 5, 6

Diversity Concepts

Understanding the concepts associated with diversity is the first step in forming successful partnerships with children and families from different cultural and racial backgrounds. As you will discover, the following concepts underlie not only our identities but also our approach to looking at the world.

Culture

Culture has been defined as a learned value system of norms, beliefs, and attitudes that shape our behavior (Chun, Moos, & Cronkite, 2006; Espinosa, 2010, p. 15) and give meaning to our lives (Dilworth-Anderson, & Marshall, 1996; Espinosa, 2010, p. 15). Cultural knowledge and beliefs are passed from generation to generation and influence our choice of food, clothing, recreational pursuits, and aesthetic preferences (Diller, 2004, p. 4; Gadsden, 2004). They also influence our interpersonal relationships. Understanding the characteristics and influences of other cultures can be placed in a better context by examining our own culture. Complete Reflection 9.1.

REFLECTION 9.1   How Do You Define Your Culture?

- List the key values, beliefs, behaviors, artifacts, and so forth that you believe characterize your culture. Share your list with your peers.
- Identify similar and dissimilar responses among peers who share the same culture. Do the same for individuals from other cultures. Identify examples of how different cultures may share common values and beliefs.

Race

Race is typically defined by physical features such as our skin color, facial features, and the texture of our hair (Webb, 2001, p. 5). However, it is important to remember that scientists view such physical distinctions, and the idea of race in general, as superficial and arbitrary (American Anthropological Association, 1998; Burton, Bonilla-Silva, Ray, Buckelew, & Freeman, 2010; Samuels, 2009). In fact, genetic analysis reveals that there are greater physical variations within racial groups than between them (American Anthropological Association, 1998). This may be one reason why race has been given different degrees of importance and defined in different ways at different points throughout human civilization. In short, race is a socially constructed concept rather than a biological reality.

Perhaps the best example of how race is a socially constructed concept can be found in two changes the United States government made to the 2000 census form. First, for the first time individuals were permitted to report one or more racial designations (U.S. Office of Management and Budget, 1997). This resulted in 57 possible multiracial combinations (Williams, 2007) that government officials felt were needed to better reflect the diversity of our nation's population (U.S. Office of Management and Budget, 1997). Such flexibility is no doubt especially important for multiracial individuals who see themselves as representing a "racially different status" than their parents (Samuels, 2009). Today, 2.9% of individuals in the United States, just over 9 million, view themselves as belonging to two or more races (Humes, Jones, & Ramirez, 2011). We examined the socialization of biracial children in Chapter 8.

A second unique aspect of the 2000 census was that for the first time the United States government determined Hispanic individuals could be of any race. Also, due to geographic differences in termi-nology, the census form was changed to read "Hispanic or Latino." More specifically, the U.S. government determined that while the term *Hispanic* was commonly used in the

Scientists view race as a socially constructed concept rather than a biological reality.

eastern portion of the United States, the term *Latino* was more commonly used in the west-ern portion of the country (U.S. Office of Management and Budget, 1997).

Our obsession with race is unlikely to change anytime soon. Indeed, race is firmly embedded in our national mind-set and social institutions. For example, race is used as a basis for allocating federal funds to social programs and communities (Tutwiler, 2005, p. 51) and to ensure families have equal access to housing and employment (U.S. Office of Management and Budget, 1997). Likewise, under the No Child Left Behind Act of 2001, schools are required to disaggregate the results of achievement tests by race, the purpose of which is to ensure that children from all backgrounds are making adequate annual progress.

Ethnicity or Ancestral Origin

The terms **ethnicity** and **ancestral origin** are used to describe the connection we feel to others based on a shared ancestry and cultural heritage (McGoldrick, Giordano, & Garcia-Preto, 2005, p. 2; Webb, 2001, pp. 4–5). Based on one study by the United States Census Bureau (Brittingham & de la Cruz, 2004), the percentage of individuals reporting to be of German American, Irish American, or African American ancestral origin decreased between 1990 and 2000, while the percentage of individuals reporting to be Mexican American, Chinese American, Filipino American, or Asian Indian increased. This finding should not be surpris-ing. We need only to visit the international food aisle of our local grocery store to appreciate the diversity of cultural life found in our communities.

Still other evidence for the shift in the racial and ethnic makeup of American society comes from our schools, where the percentage of white students enrolled in K–12 classrooms decreased from 78% in 1972 to 56% in 2007 (Planty et al., 2009). At the same time, the percentage of students from other racial/ethnic groups grew from 22% to 44%, largely as a result of an increase in Hispanic or Latino students.

Ethnic Minority Status

The term **minority**, like *race*, is a social marker that is fluid and relative. For example, a Vietnamese child may be in the minority when in his or her classroom but in the majority when returning to his or her neighborhood that consists primarily of Vietnamese immigrants. Likewise, our status as a member of the majority or minority can change as we move among the different neighborhoods within a metropolitan area. Finally, it should be noted that some family scholars have refused to use the term *minority* in order to avoid the confusion and negative stereotypes that it can create (McAdoo, 2000, pp. F5, F7). Explore the relative meaning of ethnic minority by completing Reflection 9.2.

REFLECTION 9.2   When Were You in the Ethnic Minority?

Think about the different places you have lived, attended school, or visited. When have you been in the ethnic minority? How did you come to recognize your minority status? How did your feelings or behavior change as a result of this recognition?

Ethnocentrism

Ethnocentrism occurs whenever we hold our own culture to be superior to that of others and fail to recognize or honor different cultural standards and experiences (Diller, 2004, p. 274). An ethnocentric person frowns on, belittles, or dismisses the values, behaviors, and customs associated with other cultures (see Reflection 9.3).

**REFLECTION 9.3   Identifying the Characteristics
of Ethnocentrism**

Reflecting on the meaning and characteristics of ethnocentrism is an important part of becoming a culturally responsive teacher. Identify behaviors, artwork, advertisements, movies, television programs, or statements that you have seen or heard in the United States and/or when visiting another country that reflect ethnocentrism.

Ethnorelativism

Ethnorelativism is one hallmark of a culturally responsive teacher. This mind-set involves interpreting and judging behaviors and attitudes within their own cultural context (Diller, 2004, p. 274). In short, there are no good or bad cultural standards, only differences that as world citizens we strive to appreciate and learn from. Ethnorelativism also includes recognizing that our own cultural, racial, or ethnic identity is open to change as we compare our current personal life experiences and preferences to those of past generations (McGoldrick et al., 2005, p. 6). The importance of ethnorelativism will become clearer in the following section as we address the steps to becoming a culturally responsive teacher.

Becoming a Culturally Responsive Teacher

It is not uncommon for teachers to question whether they have the knowledge and experience needed to address cultural diversity in their classrooms (Daniel & Friedman, 2005). Others fear they may say or do something offensive. Fortunately, there are steps we can take to address these concerns.

We begin with a definition. Generally speaking, becoming a **culturally responsive teacher** means being able to appreciate, understand, and work with children and families from different cultures. Achieving this goal is not as simple as it perhaps appears, nor can it be accomplished in a short time. Thus, for example, learning "facts" about different cultures is not enough. Instead, it is more important that we make a long-term commitment to understanding and honoring cultural ideas, experiences, behaviors, and values (Diller, 2004, p. 12; Fine, Demo, & Allen, 2000; Han & Thomas, 2010; Lin, Lake, & Rice, 2008). This commitment requires us to remain reflective and open to examining our attitudes toward cultural beliefs and behaviors that differ from our own (Ford & Trotman, 2001; Han & Thomas, 2010; Hyland, 2010; McGoldrick et al., 2005, p. 32). That is why we begin with Reflection 9.4.

With this introduction, we are now ready to examine an anti-bias education model and three approaches to multicultural education—two related issues that are central to becoming a culturally responsive teacher.

The Anti-bias Education Model

The **anti-bias education model** can be summarized in two ways. First, it is founded on the idea that every child has the right to realize his or her full potential (Derman-Sparks & Edwards, 2010, p. 2). Second, it provides teachers with four goals for helping children acquire the attitudes, knowledge, and skills needed for a diverse social world (Derman-Sparks & A.B.C. Task Force, 1989, p. 5; Derman-Sparks & Edwards, 2010, p. 3). In this section, we review these four goals and their implications for practice (see Derman-Sparks & Edwards, 2010).

Goal 1: "Each child will demonstrate self-awareness, confidence, family pride, and positive social identities" (Derman-Sparks & Edwards, 2010, pp. 4, 22–23). The intent of this goal is to nurture children's

Becoming a culturally responsive teacher requires making a long-term commitment to understanding and honoring cultural ideas, experiences, behaviors, and values.

**REFLECTION 9.4   Reflecting on Your Experiences in
Dealing With Diversity**

Describe a situation in your personal or professional life where you felt unsure of what to do or say because of cultural differences. How did you handle this situation? Is there anything you would do differently today?

multiple social identities (e.g., gender, cultural, racial, economic class, etc.) in a way that reinforces their sense of self-worth. Armed with this foundation, children are better able to appreciate not only their own identities but the identities of others.

A tip. One typical way to reinforce social identities is through books. Your school librarian can help you select books that best match the identities of children in your classroom. In addition, visit the following websites:

- **University of Wisconsin Cooperative Children's Book Center.** Books are classified by age group and a number of categories. **www.education.wisc.edu/ccbc/books/bibBio.asp?publications=true**
- **A World of Difference Institute: Recommended Multicultural and Anti-bias Books for Children.** Books are classified by various categories. Also visit the link "Evaluating Children's Books." **www.adl.org/bibliography/default.asp**
- **Teaching for Change.** Visit the online store for teacher resources as well as early and upper elementary books. **www.teachingforchange.org/**
- **The Children's Peace Education and Anti-bias Library.** Recommended books are for children between one and six years of age. **www.childpeacebooks.org/cpb/Protect/ourProject.php**
- **Useful Links for Anti-bias Education.** This site provides links to a variety of books and other educational resources. **www.naeyc.org/publications/books/supplements/antibias**

Finally, when selecting books, look for those that depict individuals from different races and cultures engaged in everyday tasks rather than those that present stereotyped activities from the past (Roberts, Dean, & Holland, 2005; Shioshita, 1997). Other tips for selecting unbiased books, originally published by the Council on Interracial Books for Children (1980) and reproduced numerous times since 1980, include the following: Look for storylines that (a) depict minorities in active and powerful roles, (b) define success based on individual achievements versus standards endorsed by the dominant culture, (c) address the reasons behind poverty when it is part of the plot, (d) provide specific locations for photographs rather than making general statements such as, "In Africa . . . ," and (e) avoid assigning general personality traits such as "primitive," "lazy," "crafty," and "backward" to an entire group of people (see also Shioshita, 1997).

Goal 2: "Each child will express comfort and joy with human diversity; accurate language for human differences; and deep, caring human connections" (Derman-Sparks & Edwards, 2010, p. 4). A key theme of this goal is the importance of children's learning to appreciate not only their similarities but also their differences. For example, while it would be nice to assume a colorblind society where race can be ignored, in reality society is not colorblind and race especially continues to be a topic of controversy in many communities. Still other stereotypes are associated with gender-related behaviors, geographically based language patterns, cultural customs, developmental skills, income status, and religious practices. By addressing both the similarities and differences that exist within all these aspects of our social world, we lay the foundation for confronting stereotypes while learning to appreciate and treat everyone with fairness and respect.

A tip. To examine the similarities and differences within the human family, we must first make them equally visible. Unfortunately, this is not always easy because of **covertism**. This term refers to the hidden institutional advantages and disadvantages individuals receive based on their membership in some group, such as a dominant or nondominant culture, a majority or minority race, or a particular gender (Derman-Sparks & Edwards, 2010, p. 24).

Covertism comes in many forms, from schools that set policies with a "one size fits all" philosophy, to teachers who fail to consider the different ways that boys and girls respond to the materials used in a lesson, to assumptions about parent-teacher relationships that rely solely on the Western individualistic worldview. Consider, for example, the following quote from a Korean mother who felt invisible in her child's school:

> I think the relationship between American and Korean mothers is like that of oil and water, which cannot ever mix. Whenever I participate in PTA, I feel I am left out. (Sohn & Wang, 2006, p. 129)[1]

As a teacher, you can make similarities and differences equally visible by reflecting on your own attitudes and classroom behavior. Do you emphasize certain races, family structures, and/or genders more than others? How do you respond to children's questions about cultural similarities and differences? One way to examine these questions is by joining a parent-teacher group devoted to exploring diversity and equity issues within the classroom and community (Derman-Sparks & Edwards, 2010, p. 158). Any given group meeting may also include discussions about books or movies, explorations of new learning materials, and celebrations of achievements in giving equal value and respect to similarities and differences. Likewise, the group may share strategies for helping children and families from nondominant cultures feel visible and valued (see Tip Box 9.1). After reading Tip Box 9.1, complete Reflection 9.5.

Goal 3: "Each child will increasingly recognize unfairness, have language to describe unfairness, and understand that unfairness hurts" (Derman-Sparks & Edwards, 2010, p. 5). Critical thinking is as essential component of this goal, since it is through children's analyses of unfair situations that they learn to understand their negative consequences. Thus, children's questions, comments, and behaviors all represent teachable moments for discussing why and how we respond to intentional and unintentional acts of unfairness. It is equally important that teachers make use of planned lessons, projects, and daily class meetings to introduce activities and discussions designed to engage children's exploration of unfairness.

TIP BOX 9.1   Tips for Making Invisible Cultures Visible

- Create a World Art Gallery in the classroom that includes work by artists from around the globe.
- Read poems and sing songs written by contemporary figures from around the world.
- Create a bulletin board with the biographies of scientists and peacemakers from different cultures. Include quotes from these individuals.
- Provide children with different skin-tone crayons, paints, and collage materials that allow them to more realistically represent themselves and their families in their artwork.
- Address the interconnected aspects of our world by developing lessons that emphasize the importance of global cooperation in ensuring healthy national economies, launching and maintaining satellites, and facilitating the exchange of manufactured goods.

REFLECTION 9.5   Appreciating Similarities and Differences

Give an example of how a teacher might incorporate one of the activities in Tip Box 9.1 into a lesson that reinforces children's appreciation of similarities and differences.

A tip. For younger children, **persona dolls and puppets** provide teachers with a tool for teaching lessons about diversity and modeling how to use language and critical thinking to resolve unfair and discriminatory behaviors (Derman-Sparks & Edwards, 2010, pp. 49–51; Luckenbill, 2011; Pierce & Johnson, 2010). The concept of persona dolls was first introduced as part of the anti-bias curriculum (Derman-Sparks, 2004). As the label implies, each persona doll or puppet takes on a personality and has a personal background story that continues throughout the year, just like a real person. The teacher facilitates discussions between children and the persona doll or puppet to analyze unfair acts, discuss the feelings that resulted, and explore changes in attitudes, behaviors, and language that can create more respectful relationships.

For older children, the theme of unfairness can be critically explored through writing, music, or art projects. Alternatively, children may videotape public service announcements related to acts of unfairness. The class may in turn post their announcements on YouTube. In addition, a social science unit devoted to North America may include a research project in which children answer the simple question, "What do we know about the diverse lives of individuals who live in the United States?" (Derman-Sparks, 2004). Library and Internet resources can be used to research different aspects of this question in preparation for small-group poster or PowerPoint presentations.

Goal 4: "Each child will demonstrate empowerment and the skills to act, with others or alone, against prejudice and/or discriminatory actions." This final goal acknowledges what may for some be the most difficult aspect of anti-bias education. Having created an environment in which children demand self-respect, celebrate human diversity, and recognize acts of unfairness, they must also be willing and able to take corrective action.

A tip. Experiential class projects are an ideal way to meet this goal. For example, as part of a lesson on healthy living, children might petition a local television station to investigate the funding and operation of recreational facilities in different parts of their community. Part of an anti-bullying campaign might involve children's writing and reciting poems or songs. Finally, children might take turns writing a column for their classroom newsletter on a topic that is important to them and/or their families (e.g., dispelling stereotypes associated with their culture; social etiquette when using public transportation; the rewards of living with a single father).

Ideally, all of the above goals combine to create multicultural learning environments that promote the democratic ideals of equality, respect, and justice (Derman-Sparks & Ramsey, 2005). The significance of such a democratic learning environment is reflected in the following quote:

> Multicultural democracy means that our country will have to reflect the colors, the diversities, and the multilanguages of different groups and not get caught up in stereotypes. (McAdoo, 2000, p. F7)

Put another way, the importance of a true "multicultural democracy" is reflected in a view of our country where power and decision making are shared equally by multiple cultures. This view requires us to carefully consider how we address multicultural education.

Three Approaches to Addressing Multicultural Education

Teachers may approach multicultural education in one of at least three ways. First, some teachers use an **intervention approach** in that they teach lessons on cultural respect only after they observe children engaging in name calling or other discriminatory behavior. Obviously, this approach is limited by being reactive rather than proactive. This is why other teachers use a **multicultural festival** (Ladson-Billings, 1994) or **tour and detour** (Aldridge, Calhoun, & Aman, 2000; Derman-Sparks & Edwards, 2010, pp. 8–9) approach by using celebrations to teach children about different cultural customs. Unfortunately, this approach also has limitations, as demonstrated, for example, by a teacher who uses the Chinese New Year to teach children about traditional Chinese customs. Meanwhile, contemporary Chinese achievements, such as the staging of the 2008 Olympics and China's contribution to science, literature, art, and the modern global economy, are ignored. Such a limited focus **trivializes** the Chinese culture by reducing its complex heritage to one event. Two other potential dangers associated with a multicultural festival or tour and detour approach include the following:

- **Tokenism. Tokenism** occurs when teachers use one token item to represent an entire culture (Clark, DeWolfe, & Clark, 1992; Derman-Sparks & Edwards, 2010, p. 49). This can occur, for example, when a unit on "American families" includes one poster depicting Hispanic families amid numerous posters depicting Caucasian families. It can also occur when origami is used as a hallmark of Asian art in general.

- **Misrepresentation. Misrepresentation** occurs when teachers use materials and information that misinform or fail to fully inform children about a particular culture. For example, a teacher may limit his discussion about Native Americans to 19th-century battles featuring "American leaders." By itself this storyline is incomplete and misrepresents the historical events leading up to, during, and following this period of conflict.

As you may already have noticed, the multicultural festival, or tour and detour, approach not only trivializes a culture, but it can also lead to or support stereotypes (Aldridge et al., 2000). Subsequently, more is needed to help children appreciate the richness associated with any culture.

Teachers who adopt a **transformative approach** to multicultural education move children's understanding of cultural diversity beyond superficial comparisons of clothing and holiday celebrations (Ladson-Billings, 1994). Instead, cultural diversity is embedded in all aspects of children's daily learning experiences, activities are introduced that help children personalize the cultural experiences of others, and the similarities and differences among cultures are explored. In addition, children gain experience in considering the multiple perspectives represented within and between cultural groups (Morgan, 2009). All of these characteristics reflect the anti-bias education model reviewed above and thus best conform to a culturally responsive teaching style.

Consider how one teacher used a transformative approach to multicultural education by reading Case Study 9.1. Then read on to learn about other transformative multicultural practices you can use in your own classroom.

CASE STUDY 9.1   A Writing Project

Ms. Steel asks the children in her class to write poems about what they value in life. She is surprised to discover a wide range of values. One child writes about the value of love, another on self-respect, another on doing one's best, another on being a good citizen, another on protecting the environment, and another on being healthy and strong. As an extension of the writing project, children divide into small groups to share their poems. Ms. Steel joins each group, facilitating discussions about another value, the value of "respect." That is, Ms. Steel points out how the small groups are showing respect for different ideas, beliefs, and feelings. The theme of respect is further reinforced during subsequent discussions related to cultural diversity.

Personalize children's experiences with diversity. Make use of immigrant families' cultural assets to help them feel welcomed and engaged in the classroom (Hernandez, Takanishi, & Marotz, 2009). For example, survey families about the cultural artifacts used in their homes that are associated with games, daily routines, recreational pursuits, and other aspects of their daily lives. Use the results to engage families in establishing cultural learning centers in your classroom (Cohen, 2009). Then, use the centers as a basis for planning reading, writing, math, and science lessons.

Make your vacation an educational affair. When traveling in the United States, visit cultural centers to discover how values and behaviors are influenced by regional differences and local historical events. When overseas, pay attention to cultural differences related to hand gestures, the use of slang, and social greetings. If travel is not an option, make use of the many television programs that address cultural diversity. Travel, history, and science channels offer excellent opportunities to visit cultures from around the world in the comfort of your own home.

Use the Internet. Visit websites that provide information about the cultures represented in your classroom. For example, read online newspapers and blogs that address current issues of concern to cultural groups. Study the work of writers, musicians, and artists from different cultures. Start an Internet chat room and invite teachers from around the world to discuss their experiences with cultural diversity. Search for an Internet pen pal from another culture who is also a teacher. Search for lesson plans that address cultural diversity or use the Internet to plan your own lessons. Here are two examples:

- Help children explore the cultural origins of their names and gather information about their heritage.
- Explore different types of vegetables and fruit grown around the world. Make this exploration meaningful to contemporary events by addressing factors that influence food production, such as a plentiful source of water, a fairly paid labor force, and the use of pesticides versus other nonpoisonous strategies. Also address the farming industry's contribution to national economies.

Honor cultural beliefs regarding classroom celebrations. Some families may request that their children not participate in certain celebrations that violate their religious beliefs or run counter to their cultural values. Respect their requests by developing equally meaningful alternative activities for these children.

Help children and families assert their right to be heard. Teachers transform traditional ideas about power relationships when they provide daily opportunities for children from nondominant cultures to share their views and actively participate in classroom activities. As noted in Chapter 8, it is also important to encourage immigrant families to ask questions about their children's classroom performance and school policies, since the parent-teacher exchanges that many American parents take for granted can be confusing to parents from nondominant cultures. Consider, for example, the role ambiguity reflected in the following quote from a Korean mother:

> In Korean schools, parents usually respect teachers' opinions and they seldom insist on their own opinions. . . . However, American teachers listen to parents' voices and consider me as an equal partner. So I am confused about my role and attitude toward teachers in American schools and sometimes it makes me uncomfortable. (Sohn & Wang, 2006, p. 129)[1]

Asserting the right of immigrant families to be heard is a form of advocacy, a concept we reviewed in Chapter 2. Here is an example of an advocacy mind-set adopted by one family resource coordinator who works with migrant farm families (Lopez, Scribner, & Mahitivanichcha, 2001):

> This isn't a job where you punch in at eight and punch out at three. My parents know they can call me 24 hours a day, 7 days a week "para lo que necesiten" [for whatever they need]. They're like "familia" [family], you know? . . . They know I'm here for them. (p. 268)

Adopt a transformative teaching style. Developmentally appropriate practices (Copple & Bredekamp, 2009) call for a teaching style that matches instructional materials, languages, and methods to the cultures represented in a classroom. Teachers from around the world have observed and relied on this standard in a number of ways. For example, two teachers who visited classrooms on a Native American reservation learned that the "heartbeat" of drumming was used for a variety of purposes: dancing, singing, and to call children together (Gilliard & Moore, 2007).

Other teachers visiting Kenya noted the importance of storytelling as a culturally based instructional technique (Dunn, Mutuku, & Wolfe, 2004). In addition, they noted that while oral drill and rote practice would not be viewed as developmentally appropriate in the United States, these instructional strategies had greater significance in rural Kenya, where classrooms lacked the educational resources needed to carry out experiential learning activities (Dunn et al., 2004).

Still other teachers involved in a Head Start program discovered the value of developing lessons on topics of interest to children from migrant farm families (Duarte & Rafanello, 2001). Consider, for example, the many lessons that could be incorporated into a thematic unit on "Tomatoes." Children could be invited to (a) sort tomatoes and other fruits and vegetables into different bins; (b) compare the look and taste of different tomatoes; (c) study the impact of insects and the weather on tomato production; (d) read books and write about tomatoes; and (e) measure the growth of tomato plants.

Use classroom rules to reinforce respect. Help children set classroom rules that demonstrate respect for individual and cultural differences. Examples of three rules that reinforce the theme of respect include the following:

- We listen to each other.
- We talk with each other when we disagree.
- We help each other.

Before proceeding to the next section, review the above examples of a transformative approach to multicultural education. Then complete Reflection 9.6.

REFLECTION 9.6 Committing to a Transformative Approach to Multicultural Education

What one transformative teaching strategy are you most likely to implement? Work with one or more of your peers to brainstorm another transformative teaching strategy not addressed in this chapter. Share the two strategies from this reflection with your peers.

Deconstructing Stereotypes

Generally defined, **deconstruction** involves the critical examination of ideas. In this section we consider a few examples of how to deconstruct stereotypes and thereby prevent them from interfering with a culturally responsive classroom.

Remain Alert to Cultural Stereotypes

Stereotypes occur when descriptions of a cultural, racial, or other group are applied to everyone in that group and individual differences are ignored. You may already have noticed that this description represents a violation of Realty Check #4: There is diversity within diversity. Indeed, even positive descriptions of individuals become a stereotype when they ignore the uniqueness of those individuals (Derman-Sparks & Edwards, 2010, p. 49). For example, attributing the skills of African-American athletes to "good racial genes" is a stereotype since, as should be obvious, not all African Americans have such "good racial genes." Likewise, describing all Asian children as math wizards ignores the fact that some Asian children do not excel in math and discounts the contributions Asians make to the arts and humanities. Practice your skills at identifying and deconstructing stereotypes by completing Reflection 9.7.

Stereotypes occur when descriptions of a cultural, racial, or other group are applied to everyone in that group and individual differences are ignored. For example, not all Asian children are math wizards.

Avoid Ethnocentric Definitions of Achievement

Using only one type of academic assessment can provide results that stereotype certain children. For example, while achievement scores typically take precedence in American classrooms, other cultures place an equal emphasis on children's social skills. These skills include persevering in achieving a task, being helpful to others, listening to and displaying empathy with others, cooperating with others, and obeying teachers. Pay attention to these areas of achievement by addressing them in report cards and during parent-teacher conferences.

REFLECTION 9.7   Deconstructing Stereotypes

Give examples of stereotypes associated with the following groups: African Americans, Asian Americans, Hispanic or Latino Americans, Native Americans, and European Americans. As a teacher, how might you debunk the stereotypes you identify?

Personalize Your Experiences With Cultural Diversity

The importance of this step is reflected in the experiences of two teachers who, as noted earlier in this chapter, visited early childhood classrooms on a Native American reservation. To avoid misunderstandings, these teachers took care to talk with families, learn about their beliefs, and observe their way of doing things (Gilliard & Moore, 2007). As a teacher, you can adopt a similar approach by asking yourself the following reflective questions:

- What are the cultural beliefs and ethnic identities represented in my classroom?
- How can I learn more about how families in my classroom express their cultural identities?

A few practical strategies that can help you respond to these questions follow.

Become familiar with basic communication patterns. One basic step to personalizing cultural awareness is to ask parents (or a translator) to teach you how to pronounce each family member's name (Okagaki & Diamond, 2000). Also ask parents to share with you the words their children use or the behavior they exhibit when fearful, sick, frustrated, or angry. How does a child ask for assistance? How does a child handle conflict with other children? How does a child approach a new task? Use the information that results from these questions to personalize your communication with children and their parents.

Ask the parents of children who don't speak English to teach you words frequently used in the classroom, such as *bathroom*, *good*, and *listen*. Also look for resource books that provide English to Spanish (or other language) translations for common educational words like *reading*, *writing*, *recess*, *rest*, *transitions*, and *office*, as well as phrases like "José is making good progress" and "Seiko follows directions well" (see, for example, Bevere, 2002).

Pay attention to cultural activities and artifacts that have meaning for children. Which songs, games, books, and toys from a child's home country does he or she most enjoy? Is the child willing to share some of these with his or her peers for a show-and-tell? Is the child familiar with toys, games, or songs found in the United States? If so, make sure these are represented in your classroom.

Identify a cultural guide. Identify a member of the community who can answer your questions about working with children and families from another culture. Cultural guides can include community advocates, religious leaders, human service workers, parents, or other teachers. Attend meetings with your cultural guide that are conducted by cultural groups in your community. Following each meeting, discuss what you observed. For example, ask your guide to point out behaviors, gestures, or comments that can help you better understand the cultural nuances involved in interpersonal communication. Also jot down notes about the community resources that are discussed during the meetings.

Display empathy. Empathizing with the life experiences of immigrant children and families is important in building trust and respect, especially in situations where they have experienced discrimination or mistreatment because of their language, customs, religious practices, or the color of their skin. One way to display empathy is to allow families to self-define their culture for you. This also will help you avoid making broad generalizations about their lives (Okagaki & Diamond, 2000). Pay particular attention to indicators of cultural identity, such as those presented in Tip Box 9.2.

TIP BOX 9.2	Indicators of a Family's Cultural Identity

- **A child's name.** A child's name may reflect a family's expectations of that child, such as when a son shares his father's name or when a daughter's name carries a particular cultural meaning (Slonim, 1991, pp. 62–63). In contrast, an immigrant child may be given an "Americanized" name as a means of reinforcing the family's expectation that he or she will adopt the values and behaviors associated with the dominant American culture.
- **The family neighborhood.** Families who choose to live in a culturally diverse neighborhood may be making a statement about their desire to become integrated into American society. Other families may prefer the social support provided within an ethnically defined neighborhood (Slonim, 1991, pp. 66–67).
- **Eating practices.** Some families from nondominant cultures readily accept their children's eating American food. Others may request or provide special snacks that are in keeping with the health practices, eating habits, and/or religious practices of their home country (Slonim, 1991, pp. 74–76).
- **English proficiency.** Today there is enormous diversity in the degree of English spoken in immigrant children's homes (Hernandez et al., 2009). Some immigrant parents are English proficient, others are English learners, and still others speak little or no English. These differences can create a challenge for immigrant children who must learn to **code-switch** back and forth between English and their native language, depending on the particular situation (Ford & Trotman, 2001). Teachers also see code switching in the classroom when children who are learning to speak English begin a sentence in English and then intersperse words from their native language. Children may code-switch to show social identity with their culture, convey a specific meaning, emphasize a point, or emphatically state a need (Cheatham & Ro, 2010). For example, in the latter case, a child may first state that he wants more water in English but then repeat the request in his native language if he feels his original request was not heard.

CHAPTER SUMMARY

- The concepts of culture, race, ethnicity, and minority status are all important in a culturally responsive classroom.
- The concepts of ethnocentrism and ethnorelativism describe our interpretation of and respect for cultural diversity.
- Becoming a culturally responsive teacher involves more than "facts." It also involves a commitment to examining our attitudes toward cultural beliefs and behaviors that differ from our own.
- The anti-bias education model operates from the belief that every child has a right to develop his or her full potential.
- A transformative approach to multicultural education best conforms to a culturally responsive teaching style.
- The deconstruction of a cultural stereotype involves a critical examination of our and others' ideas about culturally based behaviors, customs, values, and beliefs.

NOTE

1. With the kind permission from Springer Science+Business Media. *Early Childhood Education Journal, 34*(2), 125–132, Sohn, S., & Wang, C. (2006). *Immigrant parents' involvement in American schools: Perspectives from Korean mothers.*

DISCUSSION QUESTIONS

1. Discuss how two classrooms may look and feel different based on a teacher's ethnocentrism versus ethnorelativism.

2. Discuss how a transformative approach to multicultural education fits with the Anti-bias education model.

3. **Your family involvement philosophy.** Return to the draft of your family involvement philosophy. Based on your reading of this chapter, what if any changes will you make to your philosophy statement? Discuss your answer to this question with your peers.

COMMUNITY OF LEARNERS' FIELD ASSIGNMENT

Develop a Classroom Cultural Dictionary

One suggestion made in this chapter is that teachers learn and practice using words and phrases to support their communication with children and families from different cultures. In this assignment you will have an opportunity to do this by developing your own cultural dictionary.

Your task. As a class, begin by identifying a comprehensive list of words and phrases you are likely to use with children during the classroom day. A few examples were given earlier in this chapter. Also identify words and phrases that you are likely to use with families during a parent-teacher conference. Next, assign each student or small group a foreign language. Translate the words and phrases identified by your class into your assigned foreign language. You can do this by using your own foreign language skills, a community translator, or visiting the Google Translate site: http://translate.google.com/#auto|de. Compile the different translations into a classroom cultural dictionary for everyone to place in his or her teacher resource file. Practice pronouncing the words and phrases in class.

CAPSTONE ACTIVITIES

Activity 1: Color Your Race

Paint a self-portrait. The level of realism is not important. Instead, focus on your skin tone. Use crayons, chalk, or watercolor to create a skin tone that closely matches your real skin. Bring your self-portrait to class and tape it to the wall. Examine your self-portrait and those of your peers. Do all your Caucasian peers have the same skin tone?

Do all your Hispanic or Latino peers have the same skin tone? Do all your African American peers have the same skin tone? Discuss how skin tone is used in society to label and promote different racial images.

Activity 2: Assess Cultural Responsiveness in a Classroom

As a class, use information from this and the previous chapter to develop a checklist for assessing the cultural responsiveness of a classroom in your community. Be specific, addressing not only classroom materials and lessons but also teacher-child interactions. Carry out a classroom assessment and share your results in class.

Activity 3: Incorporate Social Achievement Into Report Cards

The importance of social skills as a cultural value was noted earlier in this chapter. Assume you will add a section on "Social Achievement" to each child's report card. As a class, develop a list of words for completing this section of the report card. Some examples might include the following: *caring, determined, patient.* Use your list of words to write a sentence that addresses different types of social achievement. Compile all the social achievement words and sentences into a handout. Make copies of the handout for everyone to place in his or her teacher resource file.

INTERNET RESOURCES

You may find that some URLs have been altered by the webmaster. In these situations, try entering the name of the document or agency in a search engine. Alternatively, enter the domain name (e.g., http://www.xxxx.org). This should take you to the revised home page and associated links.

Teaching Diverse Learners: Principles for Culturally Responsive Teaching

http://www.alliance.brown.edu/tdl/tl-strategies/crt-principles.shtml

Sponsored by Brown University, the goal of this website is to help teachers work with English language learners. Visit the above link to read about seven principles of culturally responsive teaching, the first being "Positive Perspectives on Parents and Families."

EdChange

http://www.edchange.org/index.html

This website is devoted to issues of equity, diversity, multiculturalism, and social justice. Here you will find links to resources, workshops, and projects that contribute to multicultural education. For example, click on the link "Projects" and then "Teachers Corner" to access information and ideas about culturally responsive teaching.

National Association for Multicultural Education (NAME)

http://nameorg.org/

NAME brings together individuals and groups with an interest in multicultural education as well as representatives from businesses and communities. When visiting NAME's website, click on the link "Local Chapters" to identify the chapter in your geographic area. Click on "Resources" to gain access to multicultural educational information.

Cooperative Children's Book Center (CCBC)

http://www.education.wisc.edu/ccbc/default.asp

This center is operated by the School of Education at the University of Wisconsin–Madison. The CCBC supports teaching, learning, and research related to children's literature. Click on the "Books for Children & Young Adults" link to review a summary of books divided into a number of categories, including multicultural books.

Fulbright Teacher Exchange Program

http://www.fulbrightteacherexchange.org/

This program provides opportunities for teachers to exchange positions with colleagues from other countries for six weeks, a semester, or a full academic year. The purpose of the program is to promote mutual understanding between countries.

STUDENT STUDY SITE

Log on to the Web-based student study site at **www.sagepub.com/coleman** for additional study tools including

- eFlashcards
- Web Quizzes
- Links to SAGE Journal Articles
- Author-created Videos
- Learning Objectives
- Web Resources
- Family Involvement Portfolio Guides

SECTION III

Planning for and Facilitating Family Involvement

CHAPTER 10

Responding to the Challenges of Family Involvement

P lanning for family involvement, especially in the classroom, can involve a number of challenges. Fortunately, resourceful teachers can find solutions to almost any challenge. In this chapter we review common family involvement challenges as well as potential solutions to those challenges. We end by reviewing challenges faced by children from two unique families: military families and families with incarcerated parents. Included in this review are strategies for working with these children and their parents.

COMMUNITY LEARNING GUIDE

As you read this chapter, take notes on the following items. Use your notes to address the Reflections, Discussion Questions, Field Assignment, and Capstone Activities that you find in the chapter.

- Describe the benefits associated with a family survey.
- Describe the resource challenges associated with family involvement.
- Describe the attendance challenges associated with family involvement.
- Describe the personal challenges you might face when planning for family involvement.
- Describe a few strategies for helping children adjust to their military parents' pre-deployment, deployment, and post-deployment and reintegration.
- Describe the adjustment challenges faced by children whose parents are incarcerated.

The Family Survey

In Chapter 4, we reviewed the expectations families have of teachers. In other chapters, we addressed how factors such as income, family structure, and cultural background can challenge teachers to understand family expectations. In this chapter, we begin by examining one of the most efficient strategies for identifying and planning for family expectations: the **family survey.**

Although family surveys come in many different forms, they all support Reality Check #1: Teachers should be proactive in reaching out to families. In fact, there are at least three benefits associated with family surveys. First, they demonstrate teachers' respect for and commitment to family input. Second, family surveys serve the practical objective of allowing teachers to collect information about how best to communicate with families. Finally, family surveys allow teachers to plan family involvement activities that are linked to families' interests.

One example of a family survey is presented in FYI 10.1. The title "Family Survey" is used instead of "Parent Survey" to accommodate family members who are not biological parents. You will have an opportunity to develop your own family survey at the end of this chapter (see Capstone Activity 2). Some issues to consider as you develop your survey are presented after.

The information in this chapter supports the following family-school-community partnership standards. These standards are reviewed in Chapter 2.

NAEYC Standards and Associated Key Elements	1b, 1c, 2b, 2c, 4b, 5c, 6a, 6c, 6d, 6e
ACEI Standards	1.0, 3.2, 5.1, 5.2
PTA Standards	1, 2, 3, 4, 5, 6

FYI 10.1   A Family Survey

Dear Families

Please take a few minutes to complete this survey. Your responses will help me keep you informed about and involved in your child's education.

1. Name of family member or guardian: _____

2. Check all the ways you would like me to communicate with you about your child.

    ____ Phone _____ (Best time to reach you: _____)

    ____ Email _____

    ____ Mail

    ____ Notes home

    ____ During drop-off or pickup

    ____ Other _____

3. Check all the ways you would like to help with classroom activities. Activities marked with an asterisk (*) can be pursued in the classroom or at home.

    ____ Preparing classroom materials*

    ____ Helping with field trips

    ____ Helping to plan classroom parties*

___ Making bulletin boards*

___ Helping to keep the classroom organized

___ Sharing your hobby

___ Tutoring children

___ Helping with fund-raisers*

___ Helping put together fun and educational activities for use at home*

___ Helping with the classroom newsletter*

___ Helping to plan family workshops and other activities*

___ Other _____

___ I am not able to help at this time.

4. **Check the topics you would like to hear about during Family Workshops.**

___ Childhood health

___ Inexpensive family outings

___ Child guidance

___ Helping children with their homework

___ Age-appropriate home chores

___ Understanding classroom assessments

___ Make-and-take educational activities for use at home

___ Other topics: _____

5. **Please use the back of this survey to share other comments and ideas you have about your child's education.**

Thank you!

Ms. Adams

123-0006

adams@beaverschool.net

Contact Information. As noted in FYI 10.1, Ms. Adams begins her survey by asking for the name of the family member completing it. She next asks for contact information. Having this information on file will save Ms. Adams valuable time and energy when she needs to contact the parent or guardian.

Giving family members options for how they would like to be contacted shows respect for their privacy. Likewise, it sends the message that you do not follow a one-size-fits-all philosophy but instead recognize that each family is unique. Ms. Adams continues this theme by including an "other" line for other survey items, thereby allowing family members to share their own thoughts and suggestions.

Classroom and home-based activity options. Asking families to provide assistance in the classroom is a standard practice. However, as noted in an earlier chapter, such direct participation is not an option for those who have busy work schedules. Others may not find classroom work appealing. Some may even find it threatening. For these reasons it is important that the family survey include tasks that can be carried out at home. Note how Ms. Adams does this in her family survey.

There are many ways family members can support classroom activities at home, once they are given the appropriate materials and directions. For example, consider the prep work needed to carry out lessons or construct bulletin boards. These tasks usually involve cutting out patterns, collating materials, constructing props, and other organizational tasks that can be carried out in the classroom or at home. Likewise, family members can help research a topic for a classroom lesson by using electronic devices in their homes or borrowed from the school. For example, they might use their home computer to research the feeding behavior of local animals and/or use a cell phone to videotape animals feeding in their natural habitat.

In addition, family members usually are happy to send in materials from home to support a classroom lesson. Finally, family members can carry out follow-up tasks at home, such as compiling children's written work or artwork into a classroom scrapbook, repackaging patterns and other materials for use the following year, and making thank you notes to send to individuals who made classroom presentations. Use your creativity to identify opportunities for engaging families in the classroom and at home by completing Reflection 10.1.

REFLECTION 10.1   Involving Families in Activities

Consider the following activities that might appear on a family survey. Describe the specific tasks you would ask family members to work on at home or in the classroom to support these activities.

- Preparing materials for a classroom social science lesson on South America
- Putting together the weekly classroom newsletter
- Helping prepare for a "100 Days of Reading" classroom celebration
- Helping prepare a bulletin board devoted to children's study of volcanoes

---

Coordinating the schedules of volunteers. While this task typically is handled on a case-by-case basis, it may at times be possible to arrange for individuals with similar interests to work together. Regardless of how you arrange volunteers' classroom schedules, make sure you are available to oversee their work, answer their questions, and respond to their requests for assistance. Otherwise, their activities may interfere with other classrooms or violate school policies.

Family workshops. Surveying family members about their workshop interests can help ensure good attendance. Once identified, give the workshops catchy titles that will pique families' interest (see Tip Box 10.1). You will learn more about putting together a family workshop in Chapter 11.

TIP BOX 10.1	**Family Workshop Titles**

- Buyer Beware! Selecting Educational Software
- An Ounce of Prevention! Keeping Your Child Healthy During Flu Season
- There's a Monster Under My Bed! Responding to Children's Fears
- Read All About It! Fun Reading Activities for the Home
- The Next Step: Helping Your Child Transition to the Next Grade

List another family workshop title that would peak families' interest.

Administering the family survey. When and how you administer the family survey will depend on your situation. Many teachers prefer to administer the survey as part of the registration process. It can also be sent home during the first week of class. Still another option is to pass out the survey during your first family event. Whatever strategy you choose, remember to explain the purpose of the survey before asking for families' participation. This is usually all the encouragement families need to complete and return the survey. If, however, you feel additional encouragement is needed, attach a small piece of candy or a small thank you note to the survey. Such small gestures will go a long way in gaining families' cooperation.

The information you collect from family surveys will assist you in thinking through your family involvement ideas. It is equally important that you consider the resources available to support your family involvement ideas. This challenge is addressed in the following section.

Resource Challenges

No two schools have exactly the same family involvement resources. In some schools, administrators may build financial support for family involvement into the operating budget. Other administrators may provide you with access to school materials, space, and staff support. In still other situations, you may need to recruit at least some of your family involvement resources from the community. Conducting a community scan like the one described in Chapter 1 will help support your recruitment efforts.

In this section, we consider the resources of time, space, staff, and materials, which often are of greatest importance when planning classroom-based family involvement workshops and other activities. To begin, consider Case Study 10.1. Does the resource chart seem overwhelming? For most readers, the answer to this question is probably a definitive "Yes!" We can resolve this situation by remembering Reality Check #8: Begin small. Indeed, as first noted in Chapter 2, it is more important that you experience success with a limited number of family involvement activities requiring few resources than experience failure because of well-intentioned but overly ambitious activities. Make use of Reality Check #8 by completing Reflection 10.2.

CASE STUDY 10.1   A Resource Table for Creating a Butterfly Garden

Time Resources	1. Time devoted to researching plants to go in the garden
	2. Time devoted to building the garden
	3. Time devoted to caring for the garden
Space Resources	1. Storage space for equipment and materials
	2. Garden space to accommodate different lessons
Staff Resources	1. Administrator to approve the butterfly garden budget
	2. Secretary to process orders
	3. Custodian to assist with disposal of waste
	4. Family volunteers to assist with planting, weeding, and watering
	5. Family volunteers to assist with maintenance of gardening tools
Material Resources	1. Plants
	2. Soil
	3. Mulch
	4. Fertilizer
	5. Stakes and twine
	6. Water buckets
	7. Pruning shears
	8. Hoes, shovels and rakes
	9. Wheelbarrow
	10. Plant labels
	11. Water hose
	12. Butterfly nets
	13. Arts and crafts supplies for lessons
	14. Clipboards and pencils for recording observations
	15. Sundial
	16. Benches for observations and journaling

REFLECTION 10.2   Adapting the Butterfly Garden Resource Chart

It is unlikely that you will have the time, energy, or financial resources to oversee a fully operational butterfly garden like the one depicted in Case Study 10.1. Describe your ideas for revising this resource chart. Is there an easier way to involve children and their families in the study of butterflies?

A butterfly garden. Remember Reality Check #8 and begin small.

Time Resources

As you plan for family involvement, consider your **time resources** as you investigate the time commitments of families and community volunteers. For example, what is the level of interest shown for different activities? If families show little interest in an activity, scale it back like you did in Reflection 10.2, revise it to build greater interest, or drop it. On the other hand, if families show a great deal of interest in an activity, explore ways to extend it.

Remember, you do not have to carry out family involvement activities by yourself. Call on community volunteers for help. Honor their time commitments by assisting them in structuring their presentations so they are well received by families. This may involve attention to the pacing of a presentation, the alteration of props, the introduction of more hands-on activities, and/or a redefinition of technical concepts using everyday language.

Finally, it is equally important that you not overcommit your own time when planning family involvement activities. In particular, consider your professional and personal commitments when thinking through the number of family involvement activities you can offer throughout the year and the scope of those activities. For example, you will want to avoid scheduling in-depth family involvement activities on days when you must conduct mandated educational assessments, help with a school event, or deal with a personal family issue. Instead, think of more efficient ways to communicate with families or engage them in their children's education (see Reflection 10.3).

REFLECTION 10.3   Honoring Your Time Resources

Describe how you might engage families in supporting their children's understanding of the following classroom lessons, should time pressures prevent you from arranging classroom-based activities.

- Children's study of Arbor Day
- Children's study of their town's history
- Children's study of the Founding Fathers
- Children's study of line and bar graphs and pie charts

Space Resources

In most situations, teachers use their classrooms to carry out family involvement activities. There are some very good reasons for this arrangement. Teachers often feel most comfortable in their own classrooms, where they have easy access to materials and greater control over their use of space. In addition, conducting activities in the classroom allows families to experience their children's learning environment.

Despite these advantages, the classroom may not always be the best site for working with families and other **space resources** may be needed. Religious institutions, community centers, libraries, and other community locations may be more accessible to families, be more familiar to and thus more comfortable for families, or offer more space or more appropriate space for some activities. For example, suppose you plan to conduct a family workshop on pottery throwing as part of a classroom social science lesson on folk art. Such a workshop would be difficult to carry out in a classroom, since the pottery throwing process is messy and requires heavy and specialized equipment. A better option would be to conduct the workshop at a local art studio where pottery equipment and supplies are already in place. The studio director might even be willing to co-lead the workshop and/or reduce the user fee in exchange for help with cleanup.

Regardless of where you decide to locate a family involvement activity, it is important to keep the space needs of adults in mind. For example, adults need more space than do children because of their size and ability to participate in more elaborate activities. In addition, many adults have difficulty sitting at classroom desks and at low tables. This is especially true for adults with restricted movement. Finally, activities that involve several sessions will require an area where adults can store their work in progress.

Taking these considerations into account, remember that it may be more appropriate to conduct some family involvement activities in the school library, the teachers' workroom, or the cafeteria. There are still other options if you are limited to using your classroom space. For example, consider repeating a workshop on separate nights in order to avoid overcrowding. Designate adult storage areas when planning extended or elaborate activities. If adults will be moving among work stations, limit the number of rotations they will need to make. Finally, request that your custodian bring in adult-sized chairs to accommodate the needs of adults with limited movement, as well as large garbage cans to facilitate cleanup.

Staff Support

Family involvement activities often involve **staff support resources** other than family members and community volunteers. It is especially important to keep three staff members in mind when planning activities that involve the use of school facilities: secretaries, principals, and custodians.

Let's begin with the school secretary. Will this person be involved in making copies of handouts or reserving equipment? Will the secretary be sending out workshop notices or ordering supplies and snacks? Will the secretary be asked to attend the family involvement activity to help with registration, take attendance, or perform other administrative tasks? If the answer to any of these questions is yes, make sure the secretary's time and duties are approved by your principal.

Your principal also should be informed about your family involvement plans, as there may be insurance or legal issues that need to be addressed. Also, your principal may want to be present at some activities to show support for family involvement.

Finally, as caretakers of the school, custodians need to be informed about any activity that impacts their daily work. For example, consult with your custodian to determine who will be responsible for moving tables and making other arrangements in preparation for a family involvement activity. Likewise, determine who will be responsible for cleaning up your classroom, the hall, and/or restrooms following a family involvement activity.

Always check with custodians when planning family involvement activities.

Material Resources

The **material resources** needed to carry out family involvement activities are often the most difficult for teachers to address, especially if there is no budget for them. Some activities, like the butterfly garden in Case Study 10.1, require special materials. Other activities involve the use of more common materials, such as those that follow.

Consumable supplies. **Consumable supplies** frequently used in family involvement activities include art and craft materials, tape, pencils, and markers. Other consumable supplies include labels, envelopes, folders, computer supplies, and notebooks. While it may be tempting to pull these materials from your classroom, avoid doing so. Once supplies are borrowed from the classroom, you may find it difficult to replace them. Instead, maintain separate stocks of consumable supplies for classroom and family involvement activities.

Door prizes. You may decide to draw for door prizes as a means of encouraging family attendance at a classroom event. If so, you will need to purchase these items or seek donations from the community. Restaurants, gift stores, and large retailers are sometimes willing to donate gift certificates to show their support for teachers and schools.

Refreshments. Serving refreshments during family involvement activities not only helps to increase attendance but also creates a welcoming environment. In some cases your school may provide refreshments. In other cases a local church or civic group may volunteer to provide refreshments. Restaurants and fast-food chains also may be willing to donate food, drinks, plates, napkins, and cups. Otherwise, these are additional expenses that you will need to cover.

Rentals. Your family involvement plan may require the rental of special equipment, DVDs, videotapes, and so forth not available through your school.

Copying and printing charges. Consider both the types and number of handouts to be used during your family involvement activity. Can information be formatted to fit onto one page so fewer copies are needed? Can material be copied using a front/back format? Can handouts be printed on low-quality paper? Will local business run copies free of charge or at a reduced charge? There are still other strategies for locating free or inexpensive materials, equipment, and community services. Some examples follow:

- **Families.** Teachers often turn to families to help provide certain materials. For example, you might ask families to send in old magazines, milk cartons, family recipes, and so forth in support of family involvement activities. Remember, these items may need cleaning (a time resource). You also will need a storage area (a space resource).

- **Businesses.** Businesses often are happy to provide teachers with basic supplies. For example, one regional grocery story handed out to teachers packets of supplies valued at $48: copier paper, construction paper, hand sanitizer, dry-erase markers, facial tissues, and other items. As noted by the sponsor: "This event is designed to provide our educators with some of the basic classroom items they need to help instruct our children" (Coffee, 2010). When approaching businesses, focus on requesting gift certificates (for door prizes), refreshment supplies (e.g., plates, napkins, cups), and consumable supplies such as those listed above (e.g., folders, markers, art and craft materials). Stocking up on these items will help you meet the challenge of maintaining a stock of family involvement materials separate from your classroom materials.
- **Civic groups.** Civic groups frequently take on community projects as part of their service mission. Contact these groups to determine their willingness to raise funds to help offset the expense of carrying out family involvement activities. Alternatively, ask if they would prefer a hands-on approach, such as collecting children's books, gift certificates, and consumable supplies that you can use for door prizes and/or activities.
- **Garage sales and thrift shops.** When visiting garage sales or thrift shops, take along a list of the materials you need for upcoming family involvement activities. Use a thrifty mind-set as you complete Reflection 10.4.

REFLECTION 10.4   Make Your Garage Sale/Thrift Store Shopping List

Describe the materials you might add to your garage sale or thrift store list when planning the following family involvement workshops.

- **"Add It Up: Math at Home."** In this workshop families will learn how to use common household items to teach kindergarten math skills.
- **"Understanding the Benefits of Educational Games."** The purpose of this workshop is for families to assess the educational benefits of children's games.
- **"From Mountains to Beaches: Geography at Home."** In this workshop families will learn how to introduce children to landforms found in different regions of the United States.
- **"Understanding Your Child's Classroom Journal."** Come learn about the educational objectives associated with your child's classroom journal. Learn how you can support these objectives at home.

Family Attendance Challenges

Low attendance at family involvement activities and parent-teacher conferences is a concern for many teachers. As noted earlier in this textbook, families with limited education and low income present a unique challenge in that they face both logistical and psychological barriers to attending family involvement activities (Van Velsor & Orozco, 2007). In this section we examine common logistical challenges associated with family attendance along with suggestions for addressing them.

Families' Work Schedules

Family work schedules are perhaps the most common and difficult attendance challenge you will face. While the following suggestions can help, remember to adapt them to the lives of families in your classroom.

Plan for drop-in visits before or after school hours. This will allow working families to visit the classroom on their way to or from work and quickly gather information about their child's educational activities and progress. In fact, families may find such drop-in visits an attractive alternative to evening meetings, especially if they are promoted as a "breakfast stop" (e.g., juice, fruit, bagels) on the way to work or an "after-work chat and snack" (e.g., light refreshments) on the way home. Think about how drop-in visits might apply to the families in your community as you complete Reflection 10.5.

REFLECTION 10.5   Planning Morning and Afternoon Family Involvement Activities

- Describe a brief family involvement activity for families who drop in for a 10-minute "breakfast stop" on their way to work.
- Describe a brief family involvement activity for families who drop in for a 20-minute "after-work chat and snack" on their way home.

Conduct activities over time. As noted earlier in this chapter, not all family involvement activities have to be held on one day. Parent-teacher conferences are usually carried out over the course of a week. Similarly, science fairs, art exhibits, and other activities can be weeklong affairs, thereby giving families more flexibility in managing their work schedules.

Conduct Saturday family festivals. If a large number of families experience problems attending weekday events, consider schoolwide Saturday events as an alternative. Admittedly, Saturday events also can be accompanied by challenges. For example, you will need to make arrangements for opening and closing the building as well as limiting access to certain areas of the building. In addition, you will need to plan for setup and cleanup. Still, once these issues are addressed, Saturday events such as an "October Family Festival," a "Spring Family Fair," or a "Family Fun Day" (Phillips & Evanshen, 2006) can successfully combine entertainment and educational activities that encourage family attendance. Consider, for example, Case Study 10.2. You will have an opportunity to plan your own Saturday event in your Community of Learners' Field Assignment at the end of this chapter.

CASE STUDY 10.2   Plans for a Saturday Family Reading Festival

Entertainment Activities	Educational Activities
• Storytellers will perform for families	• Teachers will introduce families to classic and new children's books
• Papermaking and bookmaking activities	• Families will be given opportunities to read with their children
• Children will perform a story they have written in class	• Teachers will spend time talking with families about their children's reading activities in the classroom
• Door prizes (books, diaries, bags of writing and drawing materials)	• Families will complete a "story wall" made of large sheets of paper stapled to a wall. Families will be invited to add to the plot of a story the children began in class.

Take family involvement activities to the workplace. You may have a number of parents represented in your classroom who work at a local factory or other business. If so, contact their employer and ask if you might conduct family involvement activities or schedule parent-teacher conferences onsite during non-work hours. These can include the hours immediately before work, during lunch, or immediately following the workday. While at the workplace, use your observational skills to identify potential topics that can be incorporated into classroom lessons. Finally, remember to coordinate all workplace visits with your principal to ensure they follow school policies.

Undertake a community campaign in support of family involvement. Join with other teachers and family-teacher organizations to encourage employers to give parents time off to attend family involvement activities and parent-teacher conferences. Remind employers that such gestures are a good investment in both their current and future workforce. Use the research reviewed in Chapter 3 to provide employers with information about the short- and long-term value of family involvement for children. Or, if available, use quotes from state legislation (such as that presented in Case Study 10.3) to point out how family involvement builds human capital.

Feed them and they will come. The author of this textbook learned this lesson early in his career. Providing families with a free meal, such as a spaghetti or taco dinner, not only saves them time and money, but it also allows them to relax and socialize with teachers and other families. Grocery stores may be willing to donate food items for your family dinners or give you a discount. As noted earlier in this chapter, restaurants also are sometime willing to provide meals for family involvement activities at a reduced cost or as an in-kind service to your school.

Send families summaries of workshops and other activities. Keep families who are unable to attend family involvement activities informed by writing articles about the activities in

---

CASE STUDY 10.3   Georgia House Bill 901 (Parent Protection Act)

Although this bill (considered during the 2008 Georgia General Assembly) was not passed, portions are presented to highlight the attention being given to family involvement at the state level.

> The General Assembly finds that employees often have important family and medical needs that do not qualify for leave under the federal Family and Medical Leave Act of 1993. An employee who does not have available leave should be able to take time away from work to attend to family health needs and the educational achievement of children while protecting his or her employment status. The General Assembly finds that providing a state statutory mechanism for establishing a minimum amount of leave time available to employees for eligible family purposes under certain circumstances improves retention of students in school, improves retention of employees, increases productivity, and strengthens families. (Code Section 34-1-8)

A few details of this bill that relate to family involvement include the following:

- Parents would take leave to attend school conferences when they cannot reasonably be scheduled during the employee's non-work hours.
- The employee would be able to utilize accrued available leave time to attend classroom functions.
- The employee would provide reasonable notice to the employer prior to her or his absence and make a reasonable effort to schedule the absence so as not to unduly disrupt business operations.
- An employer could require employees to provide written verification of school appointments.
- An employer could require employees to take leave in increments of no less than two hours.
- Employers would annually notify employees of their eligibility to request leave to attend school functions and parent-teacher conferences.

How do you feel about this bill? Are there elements of the bill you would revise? Are there other family involvement issues that should be addressed in this bill?

---

your classroom newsletter. Include photographs to make the articles more meaningful. You may also choose to post your articles and photographs on your classroom Internet page (see Chapter 13).

Don't forget reminders. Given their busy schedules, families can easily forget the dates and times of family involvement activities. This is why it is a good idea to send out reminder notices. Suggest that the reminders be posted on the refrigerator door or some other visible spot in the home.

Lack of Transportation and Child Care

Transportation and child care are two additional reasons why families have difficulty attending parent-teacher conferences and other school-based activities. Addressing these challenges involves logistical and financial considerations.

Arrange transportation services. It may be feasible in some locations to use school vans or buses to provide transportation for families living along certain school routes. Another option is to check with religious institutions and community groups to determine if their vans can be used. Finally, if you live in a city, contact the metropolitan transit authority to determine if a free or low-cost fare can be arranged on days when your school conducts family involvement activities and parent-teacher conferences.

Arrange child care services. Approach civic groups as well as clubs at local colleges and universities to determine if they are available to provide free child care during family involvement activities. Remember to consult with state licensing representatives or other regulatory offices to determine if training is required for volunteers who provide this service.

Non-English-Speaking Parents

Parents' attendance at parent-teacher conferences and other family events will be difficult to achieve if they feel their involvement will be limited because of language differences. Some solutions for addressing this challenge include the following.

Learn key words and phrases. Learn to pronounce a few key words and phrases in all the languages represented in your classroom. This can have the practical effect of facilitating both parent-teacher communication and a welcoming environment.

Identify trustworthy interpreters. Ask your school social worker or the directors of community centers or religious institutions that serve non-English-speaking families to help you recruit volunteer interpreters. Make sure the translators can deliver trustworthy translations by using the following guide (see Cellitti, 2010):

- **Cultural awareness.** Make sure the interpreter not only demonstrates knowledge of a language but also is aware of cultural issues involving body language and the use of personal space.
- **Confidentiality.** Inform the interpreter about the importance of confidentiality.
- **Share the agenda.** Define educational terms and explain key components of the agenda so the interpreter is prepared to make appropriate translations.
- **Follow-up.** Ask the interpreter to share her or his observations following each meeting. Take this opportunity to increase your understanding of a family's home culture.

Translate written materials. Ask an interpreter to translate all handouts and other written materials that you will use during parent-teacher conferences and family involvement activities.

Monitor your eye contact and the pacing of your speech. Talk directly to the family, not the interpreter (Goldfarth, 1999). Also monitor the pacing of your speech. Give the interpreter enough time between sentences to translate your comments (Goldfarth, 1999).

Avoid using children as interpreters. Asking children to assume the interpreter role represents a form of parent-child role reversal that can threaten the family hierarchy (Goldfarth, 1999; Pachter & Dumont-Mathieu, 2004). In addition, it is unrealistic to ask children to correctly translate technical information, and it is unethical to ask them to translate news about their misbehavior or poor grades (Pachter & Dumont-Mathieu, 2004).

In the following section, we turn to the challenge of self-doubt.

Addressing the Personal Challenge of Self-Doubt

It is not unusual for beginning teachers to have doubts about their ability to work with families and plan interesting family involvement activities. Do not let such doubts discourage you. Use the following strategies to maintain a positive attitude.

Attend Family Involvement Workshops

Enrolling in professional workshops that allow you to improve your skills in working with families can have a positive impact on your attitude toward family involvement (Ginsberg & Hermann-Ginsberg, 2005). Such workshops are routinely offered at local, state, and national conferences. In addition, schools sometimes provide in-service trainings on family involvement. Don't be shy when attending these workshops and trainings. Ask questions. Collect handouts and other resources provided by speakers. If you hear an idea you like, ask the speaker for more information at the end of the workshop.

One way to address the challenge of self-doubt is to form a professional study group.

Keep a Journal

Document your interactions with families, both good and bad, in a journal. Use your entries to reflect and build on successful interactions while brainstorming new strategies for interactions that do not go so well. Also write down your reflections concerning families' responses to different types of family involvement activities.

Rely on Your Colleagues

The educational and professional experiences of colleagues are resources that too often are overlooked. When in doubt about a family involvement activity or when faced with a difficult challenge, turn to your colleagues for advice. For example, Knopf and Swick (2008) suggest that teachers form **professional**

study groups to share their experiences in working with families, explore ways to address family involvement challenges, and discuss strategies for empowering family-teacher partnerships. Practice this suggestion by joining your peers to address the professional dilemmas in Reflection 10.6.

REFLECTION 10.6   Professional Dilemmas

Work with your peers to address the following dilemmas:

- Today, Ethan's father yelled at him during drop-off. The other children were noticeably shaken by this experience, and Ethan was clearly embarrassed. How should you deal with this situation?
- Even though you have sent families a list of suggested nutritious snacks, Sydney's grandmother continues to pack candy bars for her morning snack. What else can you do to address this situation?
- One of your family volunteers frequently corrects you in front of the children. Her suggestions are sometimes on target; however, at other times they are inappropriate. What should you do?
- A father curses at you after you refuse to change his child's grade. You respond with words that you regret. What should you do?
- You use classroom portfolios to show parents examples of how their children's writing skills have improved. Some parents are unconvinced. What else can you do to help these parents appreciate their children's progress?

Perhaps nowhere is it more important that teachers overcome the challenge of self-doubt than when they are working with children from military families and those with incarcerated parents. In both situations, a calm and confident demeanor is needed. In the following and final section, we review the adjustment of children from these two families, along with steps that you as a teacher can take to assist children in coping with their respective life situations.

Challenges Associated With Military Families and Incarcerated Parents

Children of Military Families

There are currently 1.9 million children with a parent serving in the military, of which more than 700,000 have experienced one or more parental deployments (Interagency Policy Committee, 2011, p. 13). While military children in general handle their parents' initial deployment with resiliency, extended and multiple deployments can take their toll (Chandra, Martin, Hawkins, & Richardson, 2010; Interagency Policy Committee, 2011, p. 13), even after the deployed parent returns home (Lester et al., 2010). In fact, about one third of military children in two recent studies experienced or were at risk for experiencing adjustment problems (Flake, Davis, Johnson, & Middleton, 2009; Lester et al., 2010). A few examples of stress symptoms that these children may display are presented in FYI 10.2.

FYI 10.2   Examples of Childhood Stress Symptoms

- Clinging to people or a favorite toy
- Unexpected crying
- Preference for adults over same-age playmates
- Aggressive behavior or excessive shyness
- Difficulty sleeping (waking, bad dreams)
- Difficulty eating or a change in eating patterns
- Constant worrying about others' safety
- Somatic complaints with no underlying cause, such as stomachaches and headaches

SOURCE: U.S. Department of Defense. (2011, February). *Military deployment guide: Preparing you and your family for the road ahead* (p. 58). Washington, DC: Author.

Two factors seem especially significant in determining military children's level of functioning. First, greater parental distress is linked to greater stress in children (Flake et al., 2009; Lester et al., 2010). Second, military and community support are important coping resources (Chandra et al., 2010; Flake et al., 2009). In the following, we review the stages of deployment, children's reactions, and strategies for assisting children with their parents' absence.

Pre-deployment. **Pre-deployment** is the period leading up to a notice of deployment and ending when the military parent leaves home. One unique aspect of this period is that while service members typically are focused on, and may even be excited about, their training and bonding with unit members, family members are dealing with feelings of anxiety and dread (Laser & Stephens, 2011). It is at this stage that children can begin to show symptoms of stress. A few strategies to employ during this stage include the following:

- **Be truthful and reassuring about the deployment** (U.S. Department of Defense, 2011, p. 53). This gives children time to work through their emotions. It also allows parents to address children's fears and misinformation. For example, it is important to reassure children that their parents have been well-trained for their mission and will do everything possible to remain safe.
- **Avoid ignoring children's feelings.** Instead, give them opportunities to name and explore their feelings (Laser & Stephens, 2011). For example, teachers can work with school or community counselors to form support groups. During group meetings, counselors may use techniques such as "feeling thermometers" and "narrative timelines" from the Families Overcoming Under Stress program developed for military families (Lester et al., 2011). The former technique allows children to document and reflect on their daily stress levels. It also allows parents and counselors to monitor and

if necessary intervene when stress levels rise. The latter technique involves having children write short narratives about their concerns throughout the different stages of deployment (Lester et al., 2011).

- **Monitor television viewing.** Some news stories about war may be too graphic and legitimize children's fears (Laser & Stephens, 2011). At a minimum, news stories about a war need to be discussed with a parent.
- **Plan for communication between children and their military parents.** This will help maintain the parent-child bond. The plan may include sharing photos, drawings, or videos (Laser & Stephens, 2011). It may also include e-pals (see Chapter 13). Other creative strategies include developing a parent-child secret code for writing letters and exploring the use of puzzle letters (i.e., cutting a letter into pieces to form a puzzle; U.S. Department of Defense, 2011, p. 54).
- **Provide children with a sense of control.** Invite children to help their parent pack for deployment. Include a drawing or photograph that shows the child and parent together. Children may also enjoy making a calendar or some other prop (e.g., a paper chain) to mark the days of deployment. These types of activities will help give children a sense of control over their parents' deployment (U.S. Department of Defense, 2011, pp. 55, 101).

Deployment. **Deployment** is the period during which parents are away from home. Even with pre-deployment planning, it is only natural for families to experience a sense of loss once the service member leaves home (Laser & Stephens, 2011; U.S. Department of Defense, 2011, p. 97). The reaction of children during this stage can vary depending on factors such as their age, personality, type of pre-deployment support, and previous experiences with deployment (U.S. Department of Defense, 2011, pp. 97, 99).

The stress symptoms children exhibited during pre-deployment may continue (U.S. Department of Defense, 2011, p. 97), along with or substituted by other behaviors such as whining, irritability, and complaining (Laser & Stephens, 2011; U.S. Department of Defense, 2011, p. 98). Fortunately, some of the strategies initiated during the pre-deployment stage can be continued and adapted during deployment (U.S. Department of Defense, 2011, pp. 99–100).

- **Continue open and honest discussions.** Opportunities to express our concerns and feel supported are essential in the coping process.
- **Continue giving reminders.** A news story or other event may lead children to fixate on their military parent's safety. If so, parents can remind their children of the training that took place during pre-deployment. It is also important to alert the military parent of the child's concerns so she or he too can provide reassurance.
- **Make home chores therapeutic.** To provide a sense of normalcy and reinforce the parent-child bond, invite children to assume some aspect of their military parent's home chores. This can also serve as a point of ongoing parent-child communication during deployment.
- **Keep children involved in community life.** Part of the coping response involves remaining engaged in community life. Thus, it is important that military children remain active in community clubs and sports. Likewise, they can participate in community-military partnership programs designed to support military families (Huebner, Mancini, Bowen, & Orthner, 2009).

Post-deployment and reintegration. The **post-deployment and reintegration** period involves the military parent's return home. While the days immediately following post-deployment can be joyful, attention must also be paid to reintegrating the military parent into the family system (U.S. Department of Defense, 2011, p. 203). A few strategies for addressing post-deployment and reintegration include the following:

- **Be patient.** It may take time for the parent-child bond to reestablish itself (Laser & Stephens, 2011: U.S. Department of Defense, 2011, pp. 225–226). For example, having grown accustomed to one set of parent-child interactions, children may at first resist being parented by the military parent. Recreational activities can help to reinforce the bond, as can acknowledging the child for her or his "good job" in keeping the household running (U.S. Department of Defense, 2011, pp. 225–227).
- **Be realistic.** Maintaining a healthy family takes work, especially following a separation. An open discussion about family roles and rules, as well as home chores and routines, can help family members avoid the trap of assuming everything will be as it was before deployment.
- **Take care of personal feelings.** To ensure an overall healthy family climate, it is important that military parents give themselves time to grieve losses experienced during their deployment (Laser & Stephens, 2011). Equally important, military spouses should make plans to reinforce their marital relationship (U.S. Department of Defense, 2011, p. 207).

The resources at the end of this chapter provide additional information about military families and their children. You may find these resources useful in your role as a teacher. For now, we turn our attention to the challenge of working with children whose parents are incarcerated.

Children of Incarcerated Parents

The number of children with a parent in state or federal prison increased from fewer than 1 million in 1991 to just over 1.7 million in 2007, accounting for 2.3% of all children in the United States (Glaze & Maruschak, 2010). Rather than representing the beginning of problems for children, parental incarceration is more likely to represent a continuation or exacerbation of other family stressors (Kjellstrand & Eddy, 2011). Indeed, one researcher found that a majority of children of incarcerated parents were exposed to four or more risks factors, including living with never-married mothers with less than a high school education (Poehlmann, 2005). Just under one half of these children had also experienced prenatal substance abuse exposure, along with complications during their mother's pregnancy or delivery. Finally, just over one half of the children were being cared for by a single caregiver dependent on public assistance.

Similar findings have been found in other studies (Glaze & Maruschak, 2010; Poehlmann, 2005), along with parents' personal struggles with depression and their use of ineffective parenting strategies (Kjellstrand & Eddy, 2011). Given these multiple family life stressors, it is not surprising that children of incarcerated parents experience adjustment challenges.

Childhood challenges. A number of studies reveal that, across time, children of incarcerated parents exhibit higher levels of antisocial behavior (e.g., persistent arguing, fighting, lying), delinquent behavior (e.g., destructive behavior, arrests, physical attacks), mental health problems (e.g., anxiety and depression), and cognitive delays (Kjellstrand & Eddy, 2011; Murray, Farrington, Sekol, & Olsen, 2009). Furthermore, many of these challenges last into adulthood (Murray & Farrington, 2005).

Some of these challenges are also reflected in interviews with teachers who noted that children of incarcerated parents expressed concerns about the instability of their caregiving environments and, subsequently, what might happen to them (Dallaire, Ciccone, & Wilson, 2010). For example, one teacher noted the "disturbances of attachment" that a child experienced as a result of having multiple caregivers.

A second theme noted by teachers was that children experienced a number of behavioral and emotional disturbances that impacted their academic performance. For example, one teacher noted a child's "emotional block" as he struggled to deal with a range of feelings related to his father's pending release from prison. Other teachers reported that children exhibited a low threshold for frustration that led them to easily "fall apart." Some children acted out in the classroom and had problems interacting with their peers.

Finally, although teachers felt it was helpful to know about a parent's incarceration, they also reported that such knowledge could result in some colleagues' holding lower academic expectations of children.

Steps teachers can take. Rather than adopting low expectations of children whose parents are incarcerated, teachers should keep two points in mind. First, not all children with incarcerated parents exhibit adjustment problems (Kjellstrand & Eddy, 2011; Mackintosh, Myers, & Kennon, 2006). Second, teachers can help children and their caregivers cope with a parent's incarceration in a number of ways. A few suggestions follow.

- **Be honest.** Provide children with age-appropriate and honest explanations of their parents' incarceration (Dallaire et al., 2010; Murray et al., 2009).
- **Help build resiliency.** Focus on developing the type of stable, warm, and accepting teacher-child relationship that children need to remain resilient (Mackintosh et al., 2006).
- **Monitor children's adjustment.** Many states do not provide formal systems for monitoring the adjustment of children with incarcerated parents (Poehlmann, 2005). Work with school or community social workers to perform this task at school so appropriate services can be sought in a timely fashion.
- **Build on positive caregiver-child relationships.** Despite the financial and other challenges they may face, caregivers care deeply for the children in their care (Dallaire et al., 2010; Mackintosh et al., 2006). Join with school counselors and social workers to build on this strength by offering individual assistance and group workshops related to building responsive, stimulating, and safe home environments (Poehlmann, 2005). For example, provide caregivers with information and support aimed at helping them cope with child guidance challenges and other life stressors they may be confronting (Mackintosh et al., 2006).
- **Help support prison visits.** Children can find the logistics of prison visits frustrating, awkward, or frightening (Clopton & East, 2008a). Join with school administrators and

prison officials to establish visitation programs that support parent-child attachment (Murray et al., 2009). Strive to adopt policies that are flexible enough to meet the needs of each child. This applies to both physical and electronic visits.

- **Establish a school support program.** One such program lasted across eight sessions and involved having children journal about their feelings, explore coping strategies, and develop social skills and peer group support systems (Lopez & Bhat, 2007).
- **Avoid demeaning language.** Be careful when making general references to "good guys" and "bad guys" (Clopton & East, 2008a). Make sure such phrases are clearly explained within the context of a specific historical or current event.
- **Share books.** A number of books are available that deal with parents in prison (see Clopton & East, 2008b). Make these available to children and their caregivers. Also consider establishing a book exchange between incarcerated parents and their children (Clopton & East, 2008b). This can take many forms, including parents' making an audio or video recording of themselves reading a book that is then sent to their children. Develop tip sheets to educate parents about techniques they can use when making their recordings to support their children's reading skills.

Chapter Summary

- Several issues must be considered when planning a family survey, including its content and administration.
- Teachers face four resource challenges when planning family involvement activities: time, space, staff, and materials.
- Teachers face three attendance challenges when planning family involvement activities: work schedules, transportation and child care, and non-English-speaking parents.
- To deal with their personal doubts about carrying out family involvement activities, teachers can consider attending workshops, keeping a journal, and relying on their colleagues for support and advice.
- Strategies exist for helping children cope with their military parents' deployment as well as absences that result from parents' incarceration.

Discussion Questions

1. As a class, develop a list of the "Top 10 Steps" that teachers can take to ensure successful school-based family involvement activities.

2. Discuss your ideas for how teachers might structure a professional study group like the one described in this chapter. What topics would be discussed? How often would the group meet?

3. Discuss your ideas for structuring a school-based support group for children of deployed military parents and/or incarcerated parents.

4. **Your family involvement philosophy.** Return to the draft of your family involvement philosophy. Based on your reading of this chapter, what if any changes will you make to your philosophy statement? Discuss your answer to this question with your peers.

Community of Learners' Field Assignment

Plan a Saturday Family Involvement Event

Review Case Study 10.2. Divide into small groups to identify a number of annual events that you as teachers might carry out on a Saturday from 10 A.M. to 2 P.M. Think about how you would combine entertainment and educational activities at these events. Also think about how you could involve businesses, museums, civic groups, theatrical groups, nature centers, firefighters, and other community groups in your plans. Use the outline that follows to organize your ideas.

Entertainment Activities	Educational Activities

Capstone Activities

Activity 1: Survey a Teacher About Her or His Family Involvement Challenges

Interview a teacher about the challenges she or he has faced when planning school-based family involvement activities. How did the teacher handle these challenges?

Activity 2: Design a Family Survey

Design your own family survey and share it with your peers. Note the similarities and differences among the resulting surveys.

Activity 3: Advocate Family Involvement

Using the information from this and earlier chapters, develop an informational flyer that explains why and how businesses should work with teachers to support families' involvement in their children's education. Compile everyone's informational flyers into a booklet. Place your booklet in your teacher resource file for future reference.

INTERNET RESOURCES

You may find that some URLs have been altered by the webmaster. In these situations, try entering the name of the document or agency in a search engine. Alternatively, enter the domain name (e.g., http://www.xxxx.org). This should take you to the revised home page and associated links.

Teachers Count

http://www.teacherscount.org/teacher/

This website posts information about teaching awards and competitions, conference listings, and a variety of programs designed to aid teachers inside and outside the classroom. Click on the "Grants" link to browse the different foundations and organizations teachers can apply to for classroom financial assistance.

MilitaryHOMEFRONT

http://www.militaryhomefront.dod.mil/portal/page/mhf/MHF/MHF_HOMEPAGE

MilitaryHOMEFRONT is the Department of Defense website for official Military Community and Family Policy (MC&FP) program information. The site is designed for troops and their families, leaders, and service providers.

Tragedy Assistance Program for Survivors (TAPS)

http://www.taps.org/about.aspx

TAPS is a tragedy assistance resource for those who have suffered the loss of a military loved one. TAPS offers comfort and care through services and programs that provide peer-based emotional support, casework assistance, crisis intervention, and grief and trauma resources.

National Resource Center on Children and Families of the Incarcerated (NRCCFI) at Family and Corrections Network (FCN)

http://fcnetwork.org/

The mission of the NRCCFI/FCN is to raise awareness about the needs of children of incarcerated parents by providing information derived from a combination of research and the experiences of families and practitioners. Visit this site to locate programs in your home state that serve families of incarcerated adults. The site also includes a library with information for families and service providers.

Children of Incarcerated Parents: A Bill of Rights

http://www.fcnetwork.org/Bill%20of%20Rights/billofrights.pdf

Developed by the San Francisco Partnership for Incarcerated Parents, this brochure highlights eight rights of children with incarcerated parents.

STUDENT STUDY SITE

Log on to the Web-based student study site at **www.sagepub.com/coleman** for additional study tools including

- eFlashcards
- Web Quizzes
- Links to SAGE Journal Articles
- Author-created Videos

- Learning Objectives
- Web Resources
- Family Involvement Portfolio Guides

CHAPTER 11

Empowering Families Through Family Involvement

E mpowered families are defined by their self-confidence and demand for respect and fair treatment from others. As a teacher, you can count on empowered families' advocating for their children's best interests. In contrast, disempowered families lack the confidence needed to participate in family involvement activities and to make decisions about their children's education. In this chapter we begin with a review of the characteristics associated with strong and at-risk families. We then examine principles and strategies for empowering families.

The information in this chapter supports the following family-school-community partnership standards. These standards are reviewed in Chapter 2.

NAEYC Standards and Associated Key Elements	1b, 1c, 2a, 2b, 2c, 3b, 3c, 5c, 6a, 6c, 6d, 6e
ACEI Standards	1.0, 3.2, 4.0, 5.1, 5.2
PTA Standards	1, 2, 3, 4, 5, 6

Strong Versus At-Risk Families

Like individuals, families develop and change over time. Some families are able to take life changes in stride while other experience dysfunction. Understanding the characteristics of strong and at-risk families will provide you with insight into how family life experiences can impact parents' participation in their children's education.

Characteristics of Strong Families

Strong or **resilient families** respond positively to life stressors and emerge feeling strengthened, more resourceful, and more confident

(Simon, Murphy, & Smith, 2005). In the 1980s, two researchers (Stinnett & DeFrain, 1985) studied a number of families from around the world to identify a set of characteristics that make families resilient and strong, even when faced with life challenges.

Commitment. Members of strong families are dedicated to and want the best for each other. They value family goals over individual goals. For example, the father or mother of a strong family would be unlikely to agree to a job transfer if it threatened family unity.

Appreciation. Members of strong families take delight in showing their appreciation for each other. Appreciation may be demonstrated through verbal statements ("I love you" or "I appreciate your hard work") or through daily deeds such as volunteering to run an errand or help with a task.

Communication. Members of strong families exhibit good communication skills and keep in touch with each other. Their conversations can be trivial or deep. Even when they travel, it is not uncommon for family members to communicate daily through telephone calls or emails. Of these two forms of long-distance communication, which do you think the members of strong families prefer?

Family time. Members of strong families enjoy being together. They are proactive in setting aside family time and protecting that time from work and other outside demands. The time family members spend together does not necessarily involve lots of money or planning. Instead, it is as likely to involve simple routines and recreational pursuits such as taking a walk, eating dinner together, or working on a family project or hobby (see Patterson & Kirkland, 2007).

Spiritual wellness. Members of strong families have a sense of a greater good or power in life. They care about their world and community. They also have compassion for others. Their expressions of spirituality may involve faith in God, faith in humanity, or some other form of spiritual faith that provides them with a sense of optimism and meaning about the purpose of their lives.

Coping. Members of strong families view life crises as opportunities for growth. Rather than giving up in the face of a crisis, they rally together to plan and pursue a course of action. No matter how dire their life situation, strong families are able to identify a silver lining and maintain a family spirit of hope and togetherness.

A recent review of research on family resiliency added still other characteristics (e.g., a small family structure, a stable marital relationship, supportive parent-child interactions, and a stimulating home environment, among others; Benzies & Mychasiuk, 2009). In addition, the researchers took an ecological perspective by documenting individual and community factors that contributed to family resiliency. Individual factors included an ability to regulate one's emotions, a sense of self-reliance, and a stable health status, among others. Community factors included family involvement in the community, a safe neighborhood, and access to quality schools and health care, among others.

Many of the family involvement principles and strategies reviewed in this and other chapters directly or indirectly help to support many of the above family strengths. Before continuing on to at-risk families, apply the characteristics of strong families to your own life by completing Reflection 11.1.

REFLECTION 11.1   Identifying Your Family Strengths

Describe a situation where your current or childhood family relied on one of the preceding family strengths to maintain a cohesive family system. How did this family strength contribute to your development and/or education?

Characteristics of At-Risk Families

At-risk families are defined by their display of ineffective behaviors when faced with life adversities. These behaviors can include a lack of self-esteem, a breakdown in family relationships, poor parenting skills, poor problem solving skills, and a fatalistic belief that things will never get better (Bemak & Cornely, 2002; Swick & Graves, 1993, pp. 44–45). In extreme cases, these behaviors can impact the lives of children. For example, children may report an absence of birthday celebrations, a lack of family support, or little encouragement from their parents (Patterson & Kirkland, 2007). They may also talk about or draw pictures of their parents yelling, crying, and so forth. Some families are at risk because they are unable to develop the characteristics of strong families. Other families succumb to a pileup of normative and/or nonnormative stressors.

Normative stressors. Stressors that many if not most families experience during the family life cycle are called **normative stressors**. It is easy to understand why some normative stressors create family distress. For example, the death of a family member and a family move, while normal happenings of life, are still stressful and in some situations can disrupt family stability.

Other normative stressors, such as a child's entering school or a family vacation, may seem like causes for celebration. Nevertheless, each of these events involves some degree of financial or relationship stress. As a child enters school, parents must adapt to his or her growing independence by adjusting family roles and rules. Otherwise, family conflict can erupt. Even family vacations can become stressful when arguments arise over where to go, how much to spend, and how much time to spend together. Think about how normative stressors have impacted your own family life by completing Reflection 11.2.

REFLECTION 11.2   Recalling a Family Normative Stressor

Give an example of a normative stressor that your family experienced while you were growing up or that your current family has experienced. How did your family handle this normative stressor and maintain a state of equilibrium?

Fortunately, most families are able to cope with normative stressors by adjusting their roles, rules, boundaries, and climates. It is only when a number of normative stressors occur at the same time or in quick succession that families begin to feel overwhelmed and show signs of vulnerability. Consider, for example, Case Study 11.1.

CASE STUDY 11.1   The Smite Family

The Smite family recently moved from a rural town in Michigan to San Francisco so that Mr. Smite could accept a better position with a new company. Two weeks after arriving in San Francisco, Ms. Smite gave birth to the family's second child. One month after this happy event, their eldest child, Kelsey, entered kindergarten. Unfortunately, things have not gone well for Kelsey. She dislikes her family's new condominium, her kindergarten teacher, and her new classmates. She complains about the snacks served in her classroom, and she has adopted what her parents describe as a "negative attitude" toward her new sibling. As Kelsey's teacher, help her parents identify the pileup of normative stressors that Kelsey has experienced over the past year. What suggestions can you offer to help Kelsey and her family make a positive adjustment?

Nonnormative stressors. **Nonnormative stressors** are associated with events that are extreme and outside a family's control. Earthquakes, hurricanes, and tornadoes are examples of nonnormative stressors that not only threaten families' basic needs (e.g., housing and clothing) but also have serious emotional consequences.

Nonnormative stressors can also result from discrimination and living in high-crime neighborhoods. Likewise, prolonged periods of family financial insecurity and a family member's mental illness represent nonnormative stressors that can challenge family stability over time. As reflected in Case Study 11.2, even a normative stressor like the death of a family member can become a nonnormative stressor when the death is traumatic or unexpected.

CASE STUDY 11.2   The Death of Jake's Mother

Jake, a five-year-old, is a curious and friendly child. Unfortunately, his mother recently passed away following her battle with cancer. Jake's father is understandably shaken and feels unprepared to deal with Jake's crying and constant stream of questions. For now, Jake is staying with his grandparents so his father has time to mourn and plan for his and Jake's future. Jake's father has asked Ms. Connelly, Jake's teacher, to help him understand the feelings he is experiencing. Ms. Connelly begins by reading Jake the book *I'll Always Love You* (Wilhelm, 1985). The book is about a boy and his dog. One day the dog dies. The boy must come to accept this but knows his dog will always love him. Ms. Connelly is relieved when, upon completing the book, Jake states that he will always love his mom even though she is no longer with him and his father. However, Ms. Connelly is surprised when, the following week, Jake begins to frequently ask for kisses and hugs. Clearly, more needs to be done to address the trauma Jake is experiencing. The major stressor, the death of Jake's young mom, is evident. Less evident are the stressors that were introduced into Jake's life following his mom's death. Identify those stressors. What suggestions might Ms. Connelly offer the father to help Jake cope with this stressful situation?

In responding to Jake's grief, Ms. Connelly no doubt remembered the stress responses of young children to a family loss. These can include withdrawal, aggressive behavior, a decline in classroom performance, reverting to more immature behavior such as thumb sucking, asking many questions about the loss, and expecting a replacement for the parent who is away or deceased (Perkins & Mackey, 2008; Wood, 2008). In preparing Jake and his classmates for life losses and other stressful events, Ms. Connelly might use strategies like those presented in Tip Box 11.1 to help them develop positive coping skills. After reading Tip Box 11.1, continue on to read about principles for empowering families.

TIP BOX 11.1   **Strategies for Helping Children Cope With a Loss and Other Stressful Life Events**

- **Literacy experiences.** Introduce children to books that deal with loss (Perkins & Mackey, 2008). These can help comfort children, provide positive models of coping behavior, and facilitate children's expression of feelings through spoken language, dramatic play, writing, and art (Roberts & Crawford, 2008). Your local librarian can assist you in identifying age-appropriate books.
- **Feeling pictures.** Invite children to draw and color shapes or pictures that represent different feelings such as happiness, fear, anger, and sadness (Wood, 2008). For example, you might begin by drawing a picture of the sun and putting a smiley face in the center. Use the children's drawings as discussion launchers to help them put their feelings into words.
- **Meaningful tasks.** Following a crisis, children, like adults, sometimes have a difficult time concentrating. Providing them with tasks related to the crisis at hand can help to focus their attention and give them a sense of purpose (Ableser, 2008). For example, following a destructive earthquake, children might help raise money for the homeless by putting on a play, planting trees, or performing some other service-related task. Likewise, they can participate in campaigns sponsored by groups like UNICEF (see www.unicef.org) and Heifer International (see www.heifer.org), both of which provide support materials to teachers (Miller, 2010).
- **Paintings.** Provide children with photographs of paintings that depict different emotions. For example, select paintings that reflect themes of loss and separation. Play a game of "I spy" (Eckhoff, 2010). Ask children to work in small groups to identify the emotions being displayed by figures in the paintings. Follow up with discussions about the possible reasons behind the emotions and how to cope with them.
- **Your turn.** Describe another activity you would recommend to Ms. Connelly and families to help children express their feelings when coping with a loss or another stressful life event.

Principles for Empowering Families

Empowering families can be facilitated by establishing what Swick (1997) calls a "caring community that embraces the lives of parents, children, and teachers" (p. 154). At the heart of a caring community is a realignment of power (Bemak & Cornely, 2002) where teachers treat families as equal partners (Christenson & Sheridan, 2001, p. 163). This principle of power realignment reinforces Reality Check #9: Families do in fact care about their children's learning activities and are willing to work with teachers when invited to do so. Some other principles for empowering families are presented in this section.

Collaborate Rather Than Direct

Reject the role of an expert who dispenses directives about what is best for children. Instead, collaborate with families by involving them in discussions about their children's development and education. Set a collaborative tone by using words such as *we*, *our*, and *us* instead of *you*, *me*, and *my* (see Tip Box 11.2; Christenson & Sheridan, 2001, p. 125). Such language ensures that both positive and negative results from any plan of action will be shared equally between yourself and families. The following quote summarizes the empowerment benefits of parent-teacher collaboration:

> Collaborative planning provides a context for validating the expertise that parents bring to the relationship and may enhance their sense of efficacy as an essential partner in connection with the educational setting. (Sheridan, Clarke, Marti, Burt, & Rohik, 2005)

TIP BOX 11.2	Using Win-Win Collaborative Language
Noncollaborative Language	**Collaborative Language**
"You need to be more assertive with Hannah."	"Let's brainstorm how we might be more assertive with Hannah."
"This is an important issue for you to consider."	"This is an important issue for us to consider."
"Trust me. I have a great deal of experience in this area."	"We can work this out. What are your thoughts about how to proceed?"

Instill Hope

Hope is essential to empowerment. Families who have hope in their futures and their children's futures are more likely to show a willingness to work through life challenges. The simple act of listening to and acknowledging families' concerns about their children is a first step in promoting this positive mind-set. Also, project your confidence in and hope for families by maintaining a cheerful and positive attitude (Swick, 2004).

Instilling a sense of hope in families can also be achieved by remembering Reality Check #3: Look for and remind families of their strengths. For example, add a **strengths report** to each report card to remind families of their children's strengths (Bemak & Cornely, 2002). Use the strengths report to share something positive about children's social behaviors ("Chloe is always the first to volunteer"), unique interests ("Alonso is showing a strong interest in our study of maps"), classroom contributions ("Noah took charge of decorating our holiday door"), or academic skills ("Sophia's reading skills are improving").

Reframe Self-Defeating Messages

It is easy for families who are under stress or who have lost hope to interpret events only from a negative perspective. Unfortunately, this can lead to self-defeating behaviors that in turn reinforce a negative view of life. Break this cycle of defeatism by **reframing** comments so they are more realistic and empowering (Christenson & Sheridan, 2001, p. 124). Consider, for example, Reflection 11.3.

REFLECTION 11.3   Reframing Negative Messages

Reframing sometimes involves addressing demeaning labels and negative messages that reflect developmentally inappropriate assumptions about a child's skills, a lack of appreciation for individual differences, or a lack of faith in a family's strengths. Reframe the following negative labels and messages to make them more positive.

- Ryan's mother states, "I got your note about Ryan talking back to you and the other teachers. Unfortunately, he's stubborn, just like me."
- A grandmother states, "I'm fed up with Francisco's sissy behavior. He's too old to let others pick on him. We need to make a man out of him."
- Mr. Pellegrino states, "I've told Angelo that he cannot take part in the after-school soccer team. I know he's disappointed, but he has to learn that we are just poor simple people who need to stick to the basics of life."

Know Your Strengths and Limitations

You may already have observed that teachers' work with families can at times take on dimensions of counseling. Therefore, it is important that you recognize the limits of your expertise and training. In your role as teacher, it is sufficient that you use appropriate communication skills (see Chapter 13), display empathy with the stressors families face, reframe negative messages, and use your community scan to make families aware of community counseling programs (Swick & Graves, 1993, p. 71).

Admittedly, it can be difficult to define the fine line between being a teacher who is supportive of families and being a school social worker or counselor. This is why it also is important to establish a network of colleagues to whom you can turn when you have questions about your professional responsibilities. For example, and as first noted in Chapter 10, you may want to help coordinate weekly study groups with your colleagues where classroom and family-teacher partnership challenges can be discussed and possible solutions explored.

In the following section, we add to our knowledge of empowerment by reviewing specific empowerment strategies. As a teacher, your task will be to decide how these strategies best apply to your classroom environment.

Family Empowerment Strategies

As you read this section, think about how the following family involvement strategies empower families and how they fit with your family involvement philosophy. This will help you to further refine your philosophy statement so that it matches your family involvement practices.

Family Resource Centers

Family resource centers empower families by providing them with their own space where they can read books, magazines, and other materials related to child development and childhood education. Family resource centers also contain educational materials and games that families can check out and work on at home with their children. Examples of two family resource centers are presented in the photos on this page and the next. Factors to consider when putting together and managing a family resource center are presented in this section.

Using a small storage area as a family resource center.

Developing a Family Resource Center

Identify a space. Family resource centers may be small or large. Examples of small spaces include a corner of a classroom or a classroom bookcase. Large spaces include a section of the school library or a converted storage area or teacher workroom. Still another option is to approach the administrator of a public library or community center to determine if space is available there for a family resource center.

Decide who will be involved in operating the center. You may decide to set up a separate family resource center in your own classroom. Alternatively, you may choose to join with other teachers to set up a grade-specific family resource center. In some cases, a family resource center may be established for an entire school.

Select materials. The exact composition of your family resource center will vary depending on the availability of materials. Unfortunately, it is rare that teachers get everything they want in a family resource center. Instead, they must prioritize a list of materials, using their family involvement philosophies as a guide. Examples of categories to use in prioritizing your own search for materials are presented in FYI 11.1. After reading about these materials, complete Case Study 11.3.

Just as you need to think creatively to acquire space for a family resource center, creativity is required for gathering materials. Businesses, thrift stores, civic groups, families, and even you, the teacher, represent possible sources from which to obtain donated materials and equipment. Think about your own community as you complete Reflection 11.4.

Identify volunteers to maintain the center. Without constant attention, a family resource center can quickly disintegrate into a disorganized mess. Use parent volunteers to make sure materials are kept in their proper place, damaged items are identified, and consumable

Using a hallway bookshelf as a family resource center.

supplies such as crayons, construction paper, and markers are restocked. If parent volunteers are not available, turn to community volunteers. Contact service clubs at high schools, universities, and colleges to determine if their members are interested in volunteering their time. Also seek out senior citizen volunteers.

Consider a virtual center. Developing a **virtual family resource center** negates the need for physical space, since families instead link to the Internet to access online information, educational games, and ideas for home-based learning activities. A few websites are listed below to get you started. As you visit the different sites, identify one activity that might interest parents. What tip sheets, workshops, or other supports might parents need to help their children successfully complete this activity?

FYI 11.1   Materials Found in a Family Resource Center

- **Adult publications.** Select books, brochures, and magazines that provide parents with information about child guidance, child development, and childhood health and safety.
- **Children's books.** Provide parents with different genres of children's books to check out for home use. These can include grade level reader books, fiction and nonfiction books, informational books, large books, wordless picture books, rhyming books, and concept books with themes like ocean animals or island nations.

Treasure Island: Front of activity folder.

- **Encyclopedias, dictionaries, atlases, and maps.** These reference materials allow parents to support their children's personal interests and classroom assignments. For example, parents may help their children use an encyclopedia to learn more about hummingbirds that live in different countries. They then may show their children how to use a world map to locate those countries.
- **Family backpacks.** As reviewed in Chapter 3, backpacks provide parents with the materials and directions needed to carry out home-based educational activities. The family resource center provides a perfect space for storing backpacks and promoting their availability.

- **Educational activity idea books.** Select activity books with simple and inexpensive educational games and other projects that parents can make at the resource center and use at home.
- **Activity folders.** Develop your own educational **activity folders** for your family resource center. One example, using a standard office file folder, is presented in the photo on page 224 (front of folder), the photo at top of this page (inside

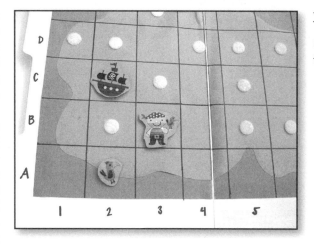

Treasure Island: Inside the activity folder.

folder), and the photo below (back of folder). Directions from the back of the folder are reprinted in FYI 11.2. Make sure you set aside one copy of each folder you develop in case it is lost or damaged. (The Treasure Island activity folder was developed by Dinna Duong, a Master of Arts in Teaching student at the University of Georgia, Athens.)

- **Art and craft materials.** When combined with activity idea books and activity folders, art and craft materials provide parents with everything they need to develop their own educational games and learning activities for use at home. Remember that you will need a source of support, either financial or through donations, to replenish these materials.
- **Computers, printers, and educational software.** Check with businesses and local government offices to determine if they have surplus pieces of equipment to donate to your family resource center. Connect the computer to the Internet so families can carry out research on educational topics that interest them and their children.

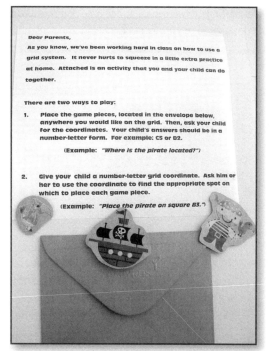

Treasure Island: Back of activity folder.

- **Videotapes, DVDs, and CDs.** These might include educational lessons designed for parents (e.g., English or GED study guides). They also might include songs and other activities for children. You can purchase commercially produced videotapes, DVDs, and CDs or make them yourself using simple recording devices. The latter option not only will be more cost efficient but also will allow you to match the content of your recordings to the educational needs and interests of children and families in your classroom. Do not worry about the lack of a flashy production. Children and parents will appreciate the personal touch you bring to your recordings.

FYI 11.2   Treasure Island: Directions From Back of Activity Folder

Dear Parents,

As you know, we've been working hard in class on how to use a grid system. It never hurts to squeeze in a little extra practice at home. Attached is an activity (Treasure Island) that you and your child can do together.

There are two ways to play:

1. Place the game pieces, located in the envelope below, anywhere you would like on the grid. Then ask your child for the coordinates. Your child's answers should be in a number-letter form (for example: C5 or D2).

   (Example: "Where is the pirate located?")

2. Give you child a number-letter grid coordinate. Ask him or her to use the coordinate to find the appropriate spot on which to place each game piece.

   (Example: "Place the pirate on square B3.")

SOURCE: The Treasure Island activity folder was developed by Dinna Duong, a Master of Arts in Teaching student at the University of Georgia, Athens.

CASE STUDY 11.3   Design a Family Resource Center

You and your colleagues have been given a one-time grant of $1,500 to start a small family resource center for the five fourth-grade classrooms at your school. The space you are to occupy was previously used as a large storage closet. The closet can accommodate the work of two people at one time and contains a bookshelf and a small table. Use classroom supply catalogs and the Internet to select other materials for the center.

REFLECTION 11.4   Acquiring Donated Materials for a Family Resource Center

Now that you have spent the $1,500, identify two additional items you would like to include in your family resource center. Identify community sources from which you might recruit these items as donations.

- **National Library of Virtual Manipulatives.** This site provides online math activities for all grade levels: **http://nlvm.usu.edu/**
- **Scholastic Teaching Resources.** This site provides online language arts, social studies, and science activities for all grade levels: **www2.scholastic.com/browse/learn.jsp**
- **Utah Education Network: Writing for Grades K–2.** This site provides online writing activities for Grades K–2: **www.uen.org/k-2interactives/writing.shtml**

- **PBS Kids.** This site, sponsored by the Public Broadcasting Service, provides games, stories, videos, and other online educational activities: **http://pbskids.org/**

If you decide to pursue a virtual center, remember to periodically check the content of your Internet links to make sure they remain relevant to the children in your classroom.

Managing a Family Resource Center

Publicize the center. Making families aware of the family resource center and its purpose, location, and hours of operation is essential to its success. Consider at least two options. First, if the center is large enough, invite families to an open house at the beginning of the school year. If the center is small, use your classroom newsletter to inform families about its contents. Also use your classroom newsletter to update families about new additions to the center and describe the activities that are being conducted there.

Display examples of parents' work. Put up displays of the artwork, educational games, books, and other products created by parents using materials from the family resource center. Publish photographs of these items in your classroom newsletter or website. Also include tip sheets on how to make the items.

Set center hours. To be worthwhile, the family resource center needs to be open for a sufficient amount of time each week so parents have multiple opportunities to visit. This usually is not a problem if the center is located in your own classroom. Simply set up a classroom or online calendar where parents can reserve a time slot. This will avoid overcrowding. If, on the other hand, the center is located outside your classroom, then volunteers may be needed to answer parents' questions and provide them with assistance. In this situation, the schedules of volunteers will determine center hours.

Limit children's access to the center. As noted earlier, family resource centers are designed to empower families by providing them with their own space. For this reason it is best to avoid taking items from the center for use in your classroom. Likewise, avoid using the resource center as a second classroom to carry out special activities. Otherwise, additional volunteer time and financial resources will be needed to keep the center organized, the equipment in good repair, and consumable materials fully stocked.

Family Portfolios

Family portfolios are similar to classroom portfolios in that both are used to collect samples of children's work that documents their developmental and educational progress. For example, when developing classroom portfolios, children work with their teachers to select samples of work that represent their progress in meeting spelling, math, reading, and other learning objectives. The same task is associated with family portfolios, except in this situation children work with their parents to select items produced at home. A comparison of the two portfolios can provide insight into children's ability to transfer knowledge and skills from the classroom to the home and vice versa.

The process of putting together a family portfolio empowers families as equal partners in their children's education. Family portfolios also serve as supplements to standardized testing, thereby providing a more personalized picture of children's learning. This is especially important for minority children, who tend to perform less well on standardized tests (Walker-Dalhouse & Dalhouse, 2001), as well as for children who experience test anxiety or who exhibit learning or developmental challenges. Finally, family portfolios boost children's pride and reinforce their efforts as they reflect on concrete examples of their skills and knowledge (Harris, 2009).

Developing and Managing Family Portfolios

Any piece of documentation placed in a portfolio should tell a story about the educational significance of a child's learning experience (Gilkerson & Hanson, 2000; Seitz, 2008). Parents will need training in how to carry out this process (Weldin & Tumarkin, 1998/1999); otherwise, items may be selected without much thought as to how they reflect specific skills.

Begin the training by showing parents an example of a family portfolio. Explain its purpose. Then use the information presented in Tip Box 11.3 to write tip sheets or articles for your classroom newsletter or website on selecting family portfolio items. Also consider conducting workshops to provide parents with practice in putting together their family portfolios. After reading Tip Box 11.3, continue on to learn about a few additional guides for developing and managing family portfolios.

Focus on one skill area at a time. Once the logistics of developing a portfolio are understood, work with each family to identify one skill area that they and their child will focus on during the upcoming quarter (e.g., reading, writing, math, artistic expression). Limiting the family portfolio to one skill area will help keep the selection of items more manageable.

Include children. Give children practice in putting together their classroom and family portfolios. Begin in the classroom by choosing a specific skill, such as using correct punctuation. Next, lay out a number of writing samples that children have produced. Finally, ask the children to discuss which items they think should go in their portfolios as a demonstration of their progress in using correct punctuation. Such practice in the classroom will help the development of a family portfolio at home go more smoothly.

Consider packaging and storage. Alert families to the different ways they can package and store their portfolios. Possibilities include portfolio folders, large pizza boxes, notebooks, shoeboxes, scrapbooks, and large plastic storage bags.

Provide support. It may take time for families to become comfortable working with family portfolios. For example, some families may at first select too many items to go in their portfolios. Others may select items that go beyond the one skill area they identified as a focal point. Be patient and provide guidance as needed. For example, conduct workshops to boost families' confidence and skills in managing their portfolios. Also consider including a regular column in your classroom newsletter devoted to answering families' questions about their portfolios.

TIP BOX 11.3	Examples of Items That Can Go in a Family Portfolio

- **Writing samples.** Parents can document changes in children's writing skills by collecting notes they write on birthday and holiday cards as well as their artwork. In addition, encourage parents to collect writing samples from their children's homework assignments. Encourage them to look for changes in spelling, punctuation, organization, and neatness.
- **Artwork.** Children's artwork documents more than just their artistic skills. It also documents changes in their eye-hand coordination, planning, creativity, academic skills, and emotional state. For example, young children may demonstrate their ability to use triangles, squares, circles, and other geometric shapes. Older children may use the same shapes to design a building or neighborhood.
- **Photographs.** Photographs can be used to document children's motor, social, and problem solving skills during a group game. They also can be used to document the planning that went into a complex project (e.g., helping to build a tree house).
- **Backpack and activity folder activities.** Products resulting from these two home-based activities are perfect candidates for inclusion in family portfolios.
- **Checklists or rating scales.** In some cases, teachers may ask parents to use simple checklists or rating scales to document children's behaviors and skills at home (Harris, 2009). These items also can be considered for placement in family portfolios.

Don't force it. Because portfolios take time to put together, not all families will show the same level of interest in pursuing this type of project. Some may decide from the very beginning not to participate, while others may begin a portfolio but then decide to drop out. Accept each family's decision. For families who choose not to participate, let them know they can join in later if they change their minds. Practice helping families put together their family portfolios by completing Reflection 11.5.

Thank You Notes

Thank you notes empower parents by acknowledging and honoring the contributions they make to their children's development and education. Follow Reality Check #6 (reinforce family efforts, not just their successes) by giving parents thank you notes for attending a parent-teacher conference, for helping with events (see photo below), and for helping with general classroom activities. (The thank you note in the photo was developed by Shannon Bruns, a Master of Arts in Teaching student at the University of Georgia, Athens.) Still other examples where thank you notes can be used to reinforce family involvement are listed below.

- Thank parents for providing you with updated information about their child's health.
- Thank parents when they share a new community resource with you.
- Thank parents for asking you questions about their child's classroom performance.
- Don't forget about community volunteers. Give them thank you notes for helping with classroom activities and making classroom presentations.

REFLECTION 11.5 Helping Families With Their Selection of Family Portfolio Items

Suppose the families of children in a given age group, prekindergarten through fifth grade, ask you for examples of how to document their children's progress in one of the following curriculum areas. What examples might you give?

- Language
- Science
- Art
- Math
- Fine Motor Skills
- Large Motor Skills
- Social Science
- Reading
- Social Skills

Thank you note: Field trip.

Developing and Managing Thank You Notes

Design your own thank you notes. Use simple and inexpensive materials like cardstock and art and craft materials to make your thank you notes. The time and thought you devote to creating your own notes will have a much greater impact on parents and volunteers than those you purchase at a store. Likewise, think carefully before emailing Internet thank you notes, as they are not very personal. Even an animated Internet thank you note can't compete with a handmade note. In addition, some parents may refuse to open email attachments. Try your hand at creating your own thank you note by completing Reflection 11.6.

Make copies of thank you notes. Design two or more versions of thank you notes for events such as those mentioned at the beginning of this section. Then make copies so you have easy access to the notes as you need them.

REFLECTION 11.6 Your Turn! Design a Thank You Note

Identify a situation that lends itself to a thank you note, other than the examples already given in this chapter. Use your creativity to design a thank you note for this situation that can be reproduced in batches and stored for later use.

Deliver thank you notes in a timely manner. The greater the time lapse between the need for a thank you note and its delivery, the more diminished its significance.

Personalize each note. Avoid writing the same message when sending out thank you notes. Instead, mention the specific behavior or assistance for which the thank you note is intended. Also remember to personally sign each note. See Tip Box 11.4 to read how the publication of a classroom magazine can result in a number of personalized thank you notes.

TIP BOX 11.4	**Personalizing Thank You Notes for Help Received on a Classroom Magazine**

"Thank you for sending in your old magazines. They helped us in learning about different types of publications."

"Thank you for helping the children with their spelling as they worked on their classroom magazine. We hope you enjoy reading our magazine articles."

"Thank you for helping the children with their poetry for our classroom magazine. It is one of our favorite sections."

"Thank you for helping the children with their background research for their magazine articles. We could not have succeeded without your assistance."

"Thank you for helping the children to design a logo for our classroom magazine. We think it's very clever!"

"Thank you for teaching the children how to take photographs for our magazine. We are very proud of our end product."

Take advantage of children's creativity. Ask children to think of all the ways families and community volunteers helped with a classroom activity or event. Then provide them with art and craft materials so each child can make a personal thank you note. Finally, ask the children to sign their thank you notes. Parents and community volunteers will appreciate receiving these special handmade notes.

Family Workshops

Family workshops empower families by providing them with opportunities to learn new information and develop new skills. There are at least three types of family workshops to consider: informational, educational, and make-and-take workshops. Any workshop can include one, two, or all three types.

Informational workshops involve the delivery of factual information about a topic related to children's development, education, or general well-being. They also may be used to update families about school policies as well as health and safety issues. While informational workshops often are one-time events, they can be extended to multiple sessions if families show sufficient interest.

Educational workshops focus on increasing parents' knowledge and skills. The parent education curricula you read about in Chapter 4 are usually conducted as educational workshops. Other examples include adult computer, financial planning, and English-as-a-second-language workshops. Because educational workshops often involve practice in skill development, they usually require multiple sessions over a period of time.

Finally, **make-and-take workshops** engage parents in making educational games and other instructional products for use at home. Demonstrations are provided on how to use the products to achieve educational objectives. Examples of a few make-and-take workshop titles are provided in FYI 11.3.

FYI 11.3 Examples of Make-and-Take Workshop Titles

- Math in a Folder: Fun and Simple Math Games You Can Make at Home
- It's Not Rocket Science: Making and Using Bubbles to Teach Science at Home
- Just in Time for the Holidays: A Papermaking Workshop
- Pretty as a Picture: Constructing and Using an Inexpensive Pinhole Camera

Planning Your Family Workshop

Begin by surveying parents and talking with them informally to identify a workshop topic that interests them. Also consult with your colleagues to learn about popular workshop topics from years past. Once a topic is identified, be proactive in reminding parents about the workshop. Begin a month in advance by including a column about the workshop in your classroom newsletter. Follow up by sending home individual invitations a week before the workshop. In addition, publicize the workshop on your classroom Internet site. Also, don't forget to mention the workshop to families as you talk with them informally.

Finally, remember refreshments and door prizes. As noted in Chapter 10, both will help to boost attendance. Practice putting this suggestion into practice by completing Reflection 11.7.

REFLECTION 11.7 Your Turn! Develop a Refreshment Menu and a List of Door Prizes

- List the refreshments you will include in your workshop invitation. Remember, you will want a menu that lends itself to easy preparation, service, and cleanup. Finger food is usually the best option.
- Assume that the families who will attend your workshop include men and women, young and middle-aged parents, and families from different economic, ethnic, racial, and religious backgrounds. List three donated door prizes that will interest everyone in this group of people.

Writing Your Workshop Plan

Family workshop plans are important for a number of reasons. They serve as a roadmap to guide you in setting up your room, carrying out activities in a logical sequence, and assessing outcomes. In addition, the very act of writing a plan often results in the identification of challenges which, if not addressed, can doom your workshop. Finally, workshop plans allow others to fill in for you at the last minute if you become sick or are called away because of a family emergency. An example of a family workshop plan is presented in FYI 11.4. Details of each component of this workshop plan are presented next.

FYI 11.4   Family Workshop: Egg Unit

Grade: Third – Fifth Grade
Title: *Engineering an Egg Drop*
Audience: All Families
Length: 1 hour
Goal: Families will learn about their children's study of engineering.

Objectives:

1. Families will review their children's classroom activities.

2. Families will carry out and analyze the educational significance of one engineering activity conducted by their children.

Room Arrangement: Tables and chairs arranged around the room.
Materials:
_____ Name tags

_____ Computer, projector, and screen (for PowerPoint presentation)

_____ Small box or basket

_____ Pens/pencils/markers

_____ Raw eggs

_____ Baggies. Each baggy will contain the following materials:

    _____ Five cotton balls

    _____ Two paper towels

    _____ Ribbon or yarn (24 inches)

    _____ 12-inch ruler

    _____ Small sheet of construction paper

    _____ Tape (one roll)

_____ Large sheet of paper to record results of egg drop (Attachment A)

_____ Large sheet of blank paper to summarize families' observations

_____ "Engineering Skills" recording sheet (Attachment B)

_____ Door prizes

_____ Evaluation form (Attachment C)

Procedure:

1. Introduce yourself and state the purpose of the workshop (see goal and objectives).

2. Divide family members into small groups based on the color of their name tags. Ask the individuals in each group to introduce themselves by sharing something they built (e.g., "engineered") as a child (e.g., damming a stream or building a kite, tree house, or something else using Tinkertoys, unit blocks, or computer software).

3. Give a PowerPoint presentation showing the engineering activities children have pursued in the classroom.

4. Give each small group a bag of materials and a raw egg.

5. Tell the family members they are engineers. Their assignment is to protect their egg so it does not break when dropped from a predetermined height. Ask the group to identify the height criteria.

6. Ask each group to (a) explain their design, (b) drop their egg from the predetermined height, and (c) observe and record the results on a large sheet of paper (Attachment A).

7. Ask the small groups to discuss what they learned as engineers, using the "Engineering Skills" recording sheet (Attachment B). Summarize their observations on a large sheet of paper. Review.

8. Follow up by showing PowerPoint slides of children engaged in the egg drop activity. Explain how the skills listed on the "Engineering Skills" recording sheet are reflected in each slide.

9. Ask family members to place their nametags in the small box or basket. Thank the families for coming. Draw for door prizes.

10. Pass out the evaluation form (Attachment C).

Extension:

- Ask the group to identify other "engineering" projects they would like to work on at home with their children. Use these ideas to create a family backpack.
- Provide families with a list of children's books related to engineering.
- Plan a family field trip to an engineering office or field site.

References: None

Attachment A

What We Observed

Group	Results
Group 1	
Group 2	
Group 3	
Group 4	
Group 5	

Attachment B
Engineering Skills

Discuss how your group used the following engineering skills in this activity.

1. We used our **senses** to explore materials and the environment: _____

_____

2. We used **language** to communicate with other engineers: _____

_____

3. We used our **memory** and past **observations** to make informed decisions: _____

_____

4. We **classified** objects according to their characteristics (light/heavy; soft/hard): _____

_____

5. We used **math** to measure width, length, circumference, etc.: _____

_____

6. We used our **creativity** to think about how best to protect our egg: _____

_____

7. We made **hypotheses** about the usefulness of different designs in protecting our egg: _____

_____

8. We **observed** and **thought about** the results of our design: _____

_____

9. We **cooperated** in carrying out the project: _____

_____

Attachment C

Evaluation Form

Your Feedback Is Important!

How helpful was this workshop? (Check one)

_____ 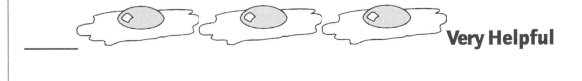 **Very Helpful**

_____  **Somewhat Helpful**

_____  **Not Very Helpful**

Thanks for coming! Please share any thoughts you have about this workshop.

_____

Grade. Begin your workshop plan by specifying the grade level(s) of children whose parents will be attending the workshop.

Workshop title. Develop a clever but descriptive title that will catch parents' attention.

Target audience. Since the target audience for most workshops will include all the families represented in your classroom, keep the content general enough to reach everyone who attends. Invite those who want additional information to see you at the end of the workshop. This will allow you to address their specific interests.

At other times your workshop may need to be tailored to the needs of a particular audience. For example, a parenting workshop for young parents will be different from a workshop for grandparents who have assumed parenting responsibilities.

Length. Specify the length of the workshop. One to one and a half hours is the norm for most family workshops.

Goal. Keep the workshop goal simple by writing a one-sentence statement about what you hope to achieve by conducting the workshop. Note the example given in FYI 11.4.

Objectives. Write a few objectives that describe the specific outcomes you expect to achieve at the end of the workshop. For example, objectives may address the need to explain new concepts, build skills, increase knowledge, make families aware of something, or provide them with support. Usually, two or three objectives are sufficient.

Room arrangement. Begin this section of your workshop plan by identifying an appropriate seating arrangement. There are at least three options to consider, each of which has a unique purpose.

- Rows of chairs or desks are suitable for informational workshops where parents listen to a presentation and ask questions of the presenter.
- A semicircle of chairs lends itself to educational workshops where ideas are shared and discussed.
- Tables located around the room are needed for hands-on workshops. In some cases, parents may visit different tables to work on different projects. In other cases they may remain seated at one table.

Also pay attention to the room environment. Create a homey and relaxing space. This will help to focus family members' attention on the information being presented (Bentham, 2008). Place posters and samples of children's artwork on the walls. Place plants around the room. Place tablecloths and baskets of art supplies on the worktables. Put a sign outside the room that reads, "Quiet, please. Workshop is in session." Soften the lighting of the room to reduce eyestrain and set the thermostat at a comfortable temperature. Play soft background music as families arrive.

Materials and other resources. There is nothing more frustrating than beginning a workshop only to discover you have forgotten a vital piece of equipment, a handout, or another resource. To avoid these oversights, write down everything you will need, no matter how small, to carry out each step of your workshop procedure. Prior to the workshop, conduct a quality check of computers and other electronic devices. Likewise, contact guest speakers to determine if they need assistance in setting up their materials and equipment.

Procedure. In this section, describe step by step how your workshop will flow. Begin with an explanation of the purpose of the workshop. You may also want to include an icebreaker activity, especially if families have not previously met. Once these preliminary steps are completed, continue to summarize other procedural details of the workshop that support your objectives. Expect to make a number of revisions before finalizing a plan that you feel comfortable implementing. Use the questions in Tip Box 11.5 to facilitate development of this part of your workshop plan.

Extension. Use this section to briefly describe how you might extend the workshop, should families show an interest in learning more about the topic presented.

TIP BOX 11.5	Questions to Ask When Developing the Procedure for a Family Workshop Plan

- Will I include hands-on activities in my workshop?
- Will I have speakers?
- Will I use electronic devices? Do I know how to use these devices?
- Will I use demonstrations or role plays? Will I have an opportunity to practice these before the workshop?
- How will I divide my time among different components of the workshop? As a general rule, you will want to limit lectures to 10- to 15-minute segments (any longer and parents will get bored). Adults, like children, gain the most from doing rather than from listening. Discussion groups, hands-on activities, question-and-answer sessions, games, and role plays represent a few strategies you can use to facilitate parent participation.

The Highlighter Award.

References. Provide reference citations for any resources you used in developing your workshop plan. Include background readings as well as other sources from which activity ideas were drawn. This section will prove useful if you need to recheck the accuracy of the information you are sharing with families or if you need to revise your workshop plan.

Other Empowerment Strategies

A number of other practical family empowerment strategies are summarized in this section. Some are easy to implement while others require a bit more work.

Random acts of kindness awards. **Random acts of kindness awards** are a specialized version of thank you notes. Use them to practice "random acts of kindness" throughout the year. Instead of recognizing parents for special achievements or their help, send home an award to let them know how much you enjoy having their child in your classroom and to acknowledge the many contributions they make to their child's well-being (see the photo on page 238). (This random act of kindness award was developed by Lauren Shinn, a graduate student in the Department of Child and Family Development, University of Georgia, Athens, under the direction of the author.)

The surprise factor associated with random acts of kindness awards is what makes them so empowering. In short, the awards recognize the worth of individuals rather than their accomplishments. Keep track of the awards you send out so each parent receives an equal number during the year. Make the awards fun and creative. Some other examples are presented in FYI 11.5.

FYI 11.5   Other Examples of Random Acts of Kindness Awards

- The "Parent Power" Award. (Attach a small action figure or a small battery to the award). "Please accept this award as thanks for being a 'powerful force' in your child's life."
- The "Well Rounded" Award. (Attach a round piece of candy to the award). "Thanks for helping your child become a 'well-rounded' individual."
- The "Measure Up" Award. (Attach a small ruler to the award). "Thanks for being a great parent! Use this ruler to 'measure' all the ways you support your child's development and education."
- The "Money" Award. (Attach a quarter to the award). "When it comes to your child's development, 'our money is always on you!' Thanks for all you do for your child."
- The "Coupon" Award. (Attach a few coupons to the award). "You're the greatest! Hopefully, you can use one of these coupons to 'cash in' on being such a great parent."

Family certificates. An alternative to random acts of kindness awards are **family certificates**. The idea behind these is borrowed from a school where parents of children who had perfect attendance were sent a certificate (Lopez, Scribner, & Mahitivanichcha, 2001). The certificates were given to honor parents for their commitment to their children's education. For example, you might write the following message on a family certificate in recognition of a child's perfect classroom attendance:

"Please accept this family certificate in honor of your child's classroom attendance this past month. This achievement would not have been possible without your support."

Family clubs. You may find that some parents in your classroom or school share the same hobby. If so, determine their interest in forming a **family club**. In addition to providing a venue for socializing and learning from each other, family interest clubs can help you develop new learning opportunities for children. For example, you might ask members of a family art club to help you develop classroom lessons on teaching children different drawing techniques. Think about how family interest clubs might contribute to your classroom by completing Reflection 11.8.

REFLECTION 11.8   Transforming Family Clubs Into Classroom Resources

Describe the classroom lessons you might develop by working with the following family clubs: (a) golf, (b) numismatics (collecting coins and studying their history), (c) organic gardening, (d) square dancing, (e) camping.

Family support groups. When families are under stress, talking to others who are experiencing a similar situation can be comforting and empowering. As noted earlier in this chapter, while your training as a teacher does not prepare you to facilitate **family support**

groups, you can still be of assistance by helping to find a school or community counselor to serve in this role. The counselor in turn might invite participants to share their stories, examine different approaches for addressing a common challenge, or establish mentoring relationships (O'Nell & Giannoni, 2010). In some cases, families may decide to facilitate their own group. Consider, for example, Reflection 11.9.

REFLECTION 11.9   Assisting Family Support Groups

A recent national newscast highlighted a family support group that formed to help its members cope with the emotional and financial stress of home foreclosures. The members chose to facilitate their own meetings. List all the community professionals you could put in touch with this group to serve as guest speakers.

Family fun nights. Not all school-based family gatherings have to be serious. Families also need to see their children's classroom as a place where they can relax, enjoy themselves, and get to know the teachers and other families (Van Velsor & Orozco, 2007). For example, hold a "Potluck Dinner" so families can socialize with one another. Arrange a "Family Recreation Night" where families can come together to enjoy a variety of games. Hold a "Family Talent Night" and invite parents and children to share a skit, musical number, or some other performance with those in attendance. Use thank you notes or family certificates to recognize each family.

Family fun nights, while seemingly simple, serve an important function in strengthening family resilience. Indeed, the sharing of fun and positive experiences such as those described above contributes to a sense of cohesiveness within the family system. The result is that children and their parents are better able to cope with life challenges (Bagdi & Vacca, 2005).

Policy briefing updates. Each year the United States Congress, state legislatures, and local governments create thousands of policies that impact our lives. As a teacher, you can empower families to advocate for their children's interests by providing **policy briefing updates:** brief updates on early childhood policies you learn about when reading professional journals and attending workshops. Also invite local officials to speak to families about their efforts to support children and families.

Community education updates. Use your community scan to develop **community education updates** to keep families informed about new educational opportunities and family services in your town or city. Invite representatives from community agencies to speak to families about their services. Alternatively, ask them to write a column about their services for your classroom newsletter.

As a final reflection, review all the family empowerment strategies presented in this chapter. Then, complete Reflection 11.10.

> **REFLECTION 11.10   Which Empowerment Strategies Will You Use?**
>
> Identify the one family empowerment strategy you are most likely to try. Why did you choose this strategy? Compare your selection with those of your peers.

CHAPTER SUMMARY

- Strong families possess several characteristics: commitment, appreciation, communication, family time, spiritual wellness, and coping skills.
- All families can experience normative and nonnormative stressors.
- At the heart of family empowerment is a "caring community" in which families and teachers share power.
- Practical strategies for empowering families include family resource centers, family portfolios, thank you notes, and family workshops.

DISCUSSION QUESTIONS

1. Discuss how the characteristics of strong families might contribute to children's classroom performance. How do these characteristics contribute to the family-teacher partnership?

2. Discuss whether teachers are prepared to carry out the empowerment principles reviewed in this chapter. What types of support are needed to assist teachers in carrying out these principles?

3. **Your family involvement philosophy.** Return to the draft of your family involvement philosophy. Based on your reading of this chapter, what if any changes will you make to your philosophy statement? Discuss your answer to this question with your peers.

COMMUNITY OF LEARNERS' FIELD ASSIGNMENT

Practice Responding to Parents' Requests for Assistance

In this assignment, you will have an opportunity to implement one additional empowerment principle: "Information is power."

Your task. Divide into small groups and research the following information requests that teachers sometimes receive from parents at the end of the school year. Share your results in class.

- "Can you help me find an after-school program for my child that offers more than sports?"
- "I would like my child to do more reading this summer. Can you give me some book recommendations or suggest kid-friendly Internet magazines?"

- "My child likes adventure. Can you suggest some unusual summer programs for my child?"
- "Can you suggest some child-friendly vacation spots that are within a two-hour drive of our town [or city]?"

CAPSTONE ACTIVITIES

Activity 1: Develop an Activity Folder

Develop an activity folder to go in your family resource center. Share your folder with your peers.

Activity 2: Design a Random Act of Kindness Award

Use a bite-sized piece of candy or other small object to design a random act of kindness award. Share the resulting awards in class.

Activity 3: Design Your Own Classroom Family Resource Center

Assume your school has no money or space to support a family resource center. Furthermore, you have only two open shelves in the one bookcase in your classroom. Turn these two shelves into a family resource center. Begin by including your activity folder from Capstone Activity 1. What other materials will you place on the two shelves that can be made, donated, or obtained from a yard sale or thrift store? Share your list in class. Compile a handout of everyone's ideas for a no-cost, classroom-based family resource center. Place your handout in your teacher resource file for future reference.

INTERNET RESOURCES

You may find that some URLs have been altered by the webmaster. In these situations, try entering the name of the document or agency in a search engine. Alternatively, enter the domain name (e.g., http://www.xxxx.org). This should take you to the revised home page and associated links.

Mathematica Policy Research: Building Strong Families

http://www.buildingstrongfamilies.info/

The mission of this project is twofold. First, it provides workshops on building positive marital relationships. Second, the project helps couples identify community services related to employment, physical health, mental health, and substance abuse that support family stability.

University of Nebraska–Lincoln Extension:
How Strong Families Manage Stress and Coping

http://www.extension.unl.edu/c/document_library/get_file?folderId=3099192&name=DLFE-19757.pdf

Visit this site to review a community-based lesson that makes use of the six family strengths reviewed at the beginning of this chapter. The purpose of the lesson is to help families reflect upon their strengths.

Family Ties: Your Family Strengths

http://www.edu.pe.ca/southernkings/familystrengths.htm

This webpage is part of a family support website sponsored by a Canadian school district. Nine family strengths are presented, each of which is briefly explained and accompanied by brief activity ideas.

STUDENT STUDY SITE

Log on to the Web-based student study site at **www.sagepub.com/coleman** for additional study tools including

- eFlashcards
- Web Quizzes
- Links to SAGE Journal Articles
- Author-created Videos

- Learning Objectives
- Web Resources
- Family Involvement Portfolio Guides

CHAPTER 12

Creating a Welcoming Environment for Families

The importance of creating a welcoming classroom environment has been mentioned a number of times in this textbook—and for good reason. Families who feel welcomed in their children's classrooms are more likely to attend and actively participate in parent-teacher conferences and other activities. They also are more likely to communicate with you, as a teacher, about their questions and concerns. The five welcoming strategies that we review in this chapter are summarized in FYI 12.1.

COMMUNITY LEARNING GUIDE

As you read this chapter, take notes on the following items. Use your notes to address the Reflections, Discussion Questions, Field Assignments, and Capstone Activities that you find in the chapter.

- Explain the purpose behind writing two letters of welcome at the beginning of the school year. Share some tips for writing each letter.
- Explain how the registration process is also part of the welcoming process.
- Explain the purpose behind making a home visit. Also describe the steps involved in carrying out successful home visits.
- Explain how teachers can address parent-child separation anxiety. Consider both the child and parent's perspective.
- Share some tips for facilitating parents' observations in the classroom.

Letters of Welcome

The welcoming process begins with two letters of welcome, one for families and a second for children. Both letters serve the important function of establishing a positive first impression. The letters need not be long or detailed. They should, however, be informative and designed with visual appeal in mind.

The information in this chapter supports the following family-school-community partnership standards. These standards are reviewed in Chapter 2.

NAEYC Standards and Associated Key Elements	1b, 1c, 2b, 2c, 3b, 3c, 5c, 6a, 6c, 6d, 6e
ACEI Standards	1.0, 3.2, 4.0, 5.1, 5.2
PTA Standards	1, 2, 3, 4, 5, 6

FYI 12.1   Strategies for Structuring the Welcoming Process

Component	Objectives
Letters of Welcome	• Building rapport • Sharing information about yourself and the classroom • Gathering information for welcoming children into the classroom
Registration and Orientation	• Facilitating introductions • Completing paperwork • Touring the classroom • Introducing the family handbook
Home Visits	• Demonstrating a commitment to families • Empowering families • Observing children in a familiar context
The First Day of Class	• Helping children make a smooth transition • Reassuring families that their children will be okay • Helping children and families to separate
Classroom Observations	• Reinforcing the theme that families are always welcome • Encouraging repeated visits to the classroom • Facilitating meaningful observations

In their letter, families will appreciate receiving information about the registration process and how to prepare their children for the first day of class (see FYI 12.2 for one example). In their letter, children will want to know a little about you, their teacher, and their new classroom. They also will appreciate reading about how much you look forward to having them in your classroom. For younger children who are just beginning to read, use a **picture letter** to share drawings and photographs that depict you and your classroom (see FYI 12.3). Finally, remember to invite families to bring their children with them to registration, the objectives of which are explained in the following section.

The welcoming process begins with two letters, one for families and a second for children.

Registration and Orientation

In addition to the logistics of completing paperwork, registration can be viewed as a "get-to-know-you" meeting and an opportunity to orient families and children to the classroom. Just

FYI 12.2 Letter of Welcome to Families

3 – 2 – 1 . . . Countdown to Kindergarten

Dear Ms. Westgate:

The first day of school is almost here! I look forward to working with you to make this an exciting year of discovery for **Ava.** Here are a few "countdown" tips families often find helpful in preparing for their child's first day of school.

3. **Get Ready** . . . **Begin preparing your child.** Talk to Ava about how much fun she will have at school. What does she think her new classroom will look like? What might she learn about this year? These types of questions will help to prepare Ava for the beginning of school.

    Help Ava get used to her new morning routine. This may involve getting up earlier and following a more structured breakfast schedule. Ava also may want to practice collecting her school materials. Begin practicing the new morning routine one week before classes begin. This will help leaving for school go more smoothly for you and Ava.

2. **Get Set** . . . **Don't forget school supplies.** When shopping for school clothes, don't forget classroom supplies. Stimulate Ava's interest in school by allowing her to help pick out the following:

    - Supply container
    - Pencils
    - Crayons
    - Ruler
    - Extra eraser
    - Markers
    - Glue stick

1. **Go** . . . **Attend registration.** I look forward to meeting with you during registration. The school will be open to receive families **August 18.** Please contact me at 503-503-5030 or adams@beaverschool.net to set a date and time for us to meet. We should need no more than **20 to 30 minutes.** I will have a small gift for you that hopefully will be of help during this school year. I also would like to take you on a brief tour of the classroom, if you have time.

Feel free to bring **Ava.** I will have a few learning centers set up so she can get a feel for her classroom.

Sincerely yours,

Ms. Adams

FYI 12.3 Letter of Welcome to Kindergarten Students

Dear Ava:

I am very [smiley] to be your teacher this year. I have a cute [cat] named [carrot]

at [house] . I enjoy [person] and [sun/pencils] . I **LOOK** forward to

learning more about **YOU** ! We are going to have a great time at [school] ! We

are going to use [crayons] and [pencils] to write stories. We are

going to have **FUN** with [books] .

Your Teacher,

Ms. Adams

Families: Please work with your child to complete the following items. Bring this page with you to registration. I will use it to welcome your child on the first day of class.

_____

Ava:

- What is your favorite color? _____
- What is your favorite animal? _____
- Draw a picture or yourself on the back of this page.

as you used letters of welcome to make a good first impression, make a lasting impression by incorporating the activities that follow into the registration and orientation process.

Conduct a Tour of the Classroom

Following registration, take families on a tour of the classroom. Note the locations where lunch menus, the class schedule, and safety rules will be posted. Point out the location where children will store their belongings (cubbies, desks, lockers, etc.). Also point out any additional areas of the classroom that you think are important. Pay close attention to the comments family and children make during the tour. Likewise, pay attention to questions parents and children ask about objects, schedules, and learning centers. Such information will prove useful as you begin to assess individual children's educational experiences, interests, and needs.

Set up a few learning centers where children can explore the materials they will be using in the classroom. Alternatively, set up an interactive bulletin board (see Chapter 13) or an area where children can work with activity folders (see Chapter 11) or other hands-on activities. Finally, keep in mind that some families may request a meeting with your school counselor, nurse, or nutritionist in order to discuss issues surrounding their children's health, development, or education.

Review the Family Handbook

The family handbook can serve as the "small gift" mentioned in your letter of welcome to families (see FYI 12.2). It sometimes may be necessary to develop different versions of the handbook for families with limited reading skills or those who do not speak English. If so, make sure basic information and visual appeal are maintained. Guidelines for putting together a family handbook are available on the "Family Involvement Portfolio" page of the student study site accompanying this textbook.

Using the family handbook as a welcoming gift serves multiple objectives. First, it sends the message that you are organized and professional. Second, it serves as a resource for families throughout the year when they need to contact someone or need information about classroom or school policies. Finally, the handbook provides information about your plans for engaging families in their children's education. Think of other practical gifts for families as you complete Reflection 12.1.

When reviewing the family handbook, it is not necessary to carry out a detailed review of all sections. Instead, explain the purpose of the handbook and note the table of contents. Also

---

REFLECTION 12.1 *Brainstorming Practical Registration Gifts for Families*

Other than the family handbook, what other practical gifts might you use to assist families in learning about their children's classroom or school? Share your ideas with your peers.

note your availability to discuss questions about the handbook that might arise during the year. Then, decide which sections need only a mention and which require more detailed attention. For example, the section of the handbook dealing with contact information is straightforward and requires little discussion. Plan to spend more time discussing the following sections of the handbook, which are of greatest interest to families.

The daily classroom schedule. Families will be interested in hearing about how their children will spend their day. A review of this section will also give families the opportunity to tell you about any special considerations you need to make concerning their children's strengths and challenges.

Classroom behavior management. Most families will be interested in learning about your classroom rules and how you handle misbehavior. Because this can be a sensitive topic, give yourself enough time to discuss families' questions about your behavior management style. Likewise, reassure families that you are open to suggestions for how best to work with individual children.

Health and safety. Also take time to review information in the health and safety section of the handbook. Note the importance of families' sharing information about changes in their children's health status. Explain how medical emergencies and medications are to be handled. Explain how to schedule vision and hearing tests, if these are conducted at your school. Take notes as parents describe particular health issues about which you should be aware. Place these notes in the child's folder and discuss them with the school nurse so you both are prepared to respond in case of a health emergency.

Family-teacher communication. To facilitate this part of your review, make a display of classroom newsletters, family notes, daily folders, and/or other communication strategies that are reviewed in Chapter 13. Also show families the school website. Close your review of communication strategies by restating your commitment to keeping families informed about classroom activities and their children's educational progress.

Community resources. It is important to at least introduce this section of the handbook to families. Then, use their reactions as a guide for discussing particular resources. For example, families with higher incomes are unlikely to ask questions. In contrast, families with lower incomes or those facing life stressors may have a number of questions.

The family survey. One good way to end your discussion of the family handbook is to review the family survey. Explain its purpose and, if time permits, ask families to complete the survey before leaving the classroom. Otherwise, ask them to complete the survey at home and return it to you.

Take Photographs of Children and Their Families

Consider taking photographs of children and their families as they explore the classroom. As you will discover later in this chapter, the photographs can be used to address the anxiety that some children experience during the first week of class. Before taking photographs, remember to check with your supervisor to determine if parents need to sign a photograph permission form. When introducing the form, explain that the photographs you take will only be used for classroom purposes.

Home Visits

A survey of kindergarten through second-grade teachers revealed the many benefits of making **home visits** (Meyer & Mann, 2006; see Reflection 12.2). First, teachers felt they gained a better understanding of children's strengths and challenges after observing their living conditions at home. For example, when making your own home visits you might have opportunities to assess the quality of parent-child relationships, the presence or absence of educational materials, and environmental factors that may interfere with children's homework assignments (e.g., high noise level or overcrowding).

Second, home visits allowed teachers to develop a deeper level of empathy with children whose home life was in some way lacking. For example, during your home visits you might find that some parents cannot write or that they show their children little affection. Such observations will assist you in making plans to give these children extra help and attention in the classroom.

Third, teachers were able to establish rapport with parents by giving them their full attention and responding to their particular concerns and questions. Such rapport can prove especially helpful in promoting family-teacher partnerships among immigrant families (Inger, 2001; Lopez, Scribner, & Mahitivanichcha, 2001) and refugee families (Szente, Hoot, & Taylor, 2006), who may otherwise be hesitant to reach out to teachers or who are unfamiliar with negotiating the family involvement process as practiced within American culture. Indeed, because home visits are conducted on families' home turf, families in general are more likely to feel empowered and, as a result, discuss sensitive issues that might otherwise be avoided (e.g., a child's weight or lack of assertiveness).

Finally, teachers felt home visits helped them develop a positive relationship with children. This in turn facilitated a smoother transition into the school year.

REFLECTION 12.2   Benefits of Home Visits

Other than those already listed, what ways might home visits benefit families, children, and teachers?

Preparing for the Home Visit

The success of home visits rests on both the family's and the teacher's accepting the idea. This can be challenging if neither has experienced home visits in the past. Careful planning is therefore key to ensuring successful visits. Begin by completing Reflection 12.3. Then consider the tasks that follow to learn about preparing for successful home visits.

> **REFLECTION 12.3   Examining Anxieties Associated With Home Visits**
>
> - Describe an anxiety that families may experience prior to or during a home visit. How will you reduce their anxiety?
> - Describe an anxiety that you or a fellow teacher might experience when making a home visit. How will you reduce your own anxiety?

Establish the objectives of the visit. As already noted, one objective associated with any home visit is to socialize and build positive family-teacher partnerships. Other objectives include sharing information about your classroom, completing forms, and reviewing children's educational progress. Whatever objective(s) you identify for making home visits, it is important that families know what will take place. Also remember to involve families in setting home visitation objectives by asking if they have issues they would like to discuss (see Reflection 12.4).   *The Why*

> **REFLECTION 12.4   Identify an Objective for Your First Home Visit**
>
> Use your family involvement philosophy statement to identify one objective you might pursue when planning your first home visit. Compare your objective to those of your peers.

Avoid wearing out your welcome. A 20- to 30-minute home visit is usually sufficient, although some (Bouhebent, 2008) recommend visits of 60 minutes or more. Ultimately, the length of your home visits will be determined by their purpose and the schedules of the families you visit. Another good rule of thumb is to monitor families' level of interest as the visit progresses. It is better to cut a visit short if families begin to show signs of discomfort or boredom than to risk wearing out your welcome.   *Don't overstay*

Decide on the number of visits. Hopefully, your first home visit will be followed by others. The exact number of visits you make during the year will depend on your family involvement philosophy, the interest of families in taking part in home visits, and the needs of the families you are visiting. For example, at-risk families who are experiencing a pileup of stressors may require more visits than strong families (Bouhebent, 2008). This is another example of the importance of treating families fairly rather than equally, a reality check we first examined in Chapter 2.

The number of home visits you make during the year also will be influenced by your other professional obligations and the availability of colleagues to accompany you on visits. As a safety precaution, it is best to take a school colleague with you when making home visits. One never knows when the colleague will be needed to help deal with an emergency or a safety issue.   *Don't visit too often*

Be prepared. In preparing for your first home visit, review the information you collected and the notes you took during registration. Make sure you know the names of family members and their relationship to the child whose home you are visiting. Finally, visit the Internet or the library to read about the cultures of immigrant families whose homes you are visiting. This will allow you to place their language, behavior, and social customs within an appropriate cultural context.

know what to talk about

Prior to making subsequent home visits, review your notes from previous home visits and parent-teacher conferences. Also review the child's classroom portfolio as well as the results of standardized assessments. This will help you to prioritize the objectives of your visit. It will also assist you in responding to parents' questions.

Confirm your driving route. Ask families for directions to their residence. Alternatively, use the Internet or the global positioning system in your car. If you use the Internet, check at least two different sites to make sure both are in agreement as to mileage and directions. If you still get lost or encounter another problem that leads to a delay, call before arriving. Ask if it is still okay to make the visit or if the family would prefer to reschedule. Finally, when making more than one home visit per day, leave plenty of time between visits. Arriving late at the home of one family because you stayed too long visiting the previous family will not set a good tone, especially if your late arrival impinges on a family's schedule.

be on time

Give yourself and families reminder notes. Send families a reminder note one week prior to your visit. Also be sure to log the visit in your personal calendar. Finally, let your supervisor know the dates, times, and locations of your home visits.

Don't forget

Facilitating the Home Visit

You have two roles to play during a home visit, those of guest and teacher. A balance is thus needed between observing social niceties while also sharing and collecting information. Some suggestions for achieving this balance are presented below.

Begin with small talk. Ease into the visit by commenting on something positive you noticed about the home (e.g., furniture, flowers, wall decoration) or neighborhood. As with any parent-teacher meeting, share something positive about the child. If your first home visit occurs before classes begin, use the bottom half of the "Letter to Children" (see FYI 12.3) to guide your opening comments. Or, share something positive you observed about the child or the parent-child relationship during registration. Then, briefly restate the purpose of your visit. For practice, complete Reflection 12.5.

REFLECTION 12.5   Planning for Small Talk

Some of us are better at small talk than are others. Work with your peers to develop a list of small-talk topics you can use to put parents at ease during home visits.

Conduct an informal visit. Avoid asking a stream of questions or following a strict agenda or scripted interview. Instead, use your observational skills and ask a few open-ended questions, such as those presented in Tip Box 12.1. If the questions you ask are met with discomfort, quickly explain your reason for asking them. This will help avoid the perception that you are invading the family's privacy.

TIP BOX 12.1	**Questions to Facilitate Parent-Teacher Conversations During Home Visits**

- "What is the one thing you would like me to know about Rosario that would help her make a smooth transition into her new classroom?"
- "We all have unique preferences. Does Rosario have any unique food, communication, or other preferences that I should know about?"
- "I have a terrible fear of snakes. Does Rosario have any special fears? I would not want to do something in class that would scare her."
- "I've found that children express their feelings in different ways. Some stop talking. Others are very verbal or physical when expressing their emotions. What types of behavior should I look for in Rosario when she is feeling sad? When she is sick? When she is angry? When she is embarrassed?"
- "What else should I know about Rosario in order to help her make a smooth transition into the classroom?"

Expect the unexpected. Remain calm if something unusual happens. For example, your chair might break, you may be served food you do not recognize, or your conversation with a parent might be interrupted by loud noises from an adjoining apartment. Use your skills as a good guest to accommodate these situations. Graciously accept the food and drink you are offered. If there is limited furniture in the home, be proactive by nonchalantly taking a seat on the floor. These and other accommodating gestures will go a long way in creating a relaxed and successful visit.

Dress appropriately. A casual form of dress is best when making home visits. However, avoid jeans, T-shirts, and shorts. You do want to look professional.

Avoid bringing special gifts. Bringing a toy with you to your first home visit can be distracting. It can also lead children to expect other special gifts during future home visits. Instead, tie a ribbon around a crayon, pencil, ruler, or some other small item that is used in the classroom. Present this item to children as a means of structuring a discussion about their classroom environment and the learning activities in which they will be participating.

Following the first home visit, show your appreciation when making other visits by decorating an item from the child's classroom portfolio. For example, construct a simple cardstock frame for a writing sample from the child's portfolio. Use this item to structure your discussion about the child's writing skills and the social or language skills the child displayed when sharing the writing sample with others. Another option is to frame a photograph from the child's classroom portfolio that depicts her or him working on a science project. Use the photograph to structure your discussion about the child's math and problem solving skills. Before continuing, use your creativity to complete Reflection 12.6.

> **REFLECTION 12.6   Identify a Practical Home Gift**
>
> Assume you are making your second or third home visit. Identify the child's grade level, prekindergarten through fifth grade. Describe a practical gift you could use to facilitate a discussion about the child's progress in a particular subject area.

Be proactive in dealing with attention seeking behavior. Some children will want to dominate your time while you are in their home. Paying special attention to them at the beginning of the visit can help contain this behavior. For example, you might ask them to show you their pet or tell you about their day. Then, give them an activity to work on while you talk with their parents. For younger children, this can be as simple as laying out crayons, paper, and a few art and craft materials. Ask children to use these materials to make a picture for their parents. For older children, bring along a new backpack or an activity folder for them to explore (see Reflection 12.7). Leave the backpack or folder with the children so they can share it with their family.

> **REFLECTION 12.7   Dealing With Attention Seeking Behavior**
>
> Identify specific examples of attention seeking behaviors you might encounter during a home visit. Brainstorm strategies for dealing with these behaviors.

Discuss observations made by families. Discussing families' observations of their children can be enlightening. For example, you may learn about skills that you have not observed in the classroom. Alternatively, you may discover that the skills you observe in the classroom are not being transferred to the home environment. Families also may ask about whether specific behaviors their children display are age appropriate. One way to structure this discussion is to give families a simple **child development survey**, such as the one presented in FYI 12.4. You can create your own survey by reviewing the standards for different subject areas published by your state department of education.

Plan for closure. Let families know when your visit is about to end. Ask if there is anything else they would like to discuss. If so and time permits (and families are willing), extend the visit. If this is not possible, make plans to address their issues in a timely fashion. This may mean making an additional home visit or scheduling a classroom parent-teacher conference.

Following Up on the Home Visit

Complete the home visit by making notes about your observations and social interactions with family members. Use these to carry out the following tasks.

FYI 12.4   A Child Development Survey for Kindergarten

Listed below are some of the skills we will work on this year in kindergarten. To what degree does your child display each of these skills at home? Your child is not expected to be an "expert" in every area or even most areas. Each child has her or his own unique strengths.

1 = My child does not yet display this skill

2 = My child is beginning to display this skill

3 = My child already displays this skill

4 = I'm not sure if my child displays this skill

Language Skills

___ Follows simple directions

___ Accurately describes her or his daily activities

___ Uses complete sentences when speaking

Math Skills

___ Counts objects up to 30 or more

___ Names the days of the week and their order

___ Names the four seasons and their order (fall follows summer)

___ Recognizes geometric shapes (square, triangle, circle, and rectangle)

___ Understands concepts of time, such as morning, afternoon, yesterday, and year

Reading Skills

___ Understands that written words have meaning

___ Distinguishes among letters, words, and sentences

___ Recognizes lowercase and uppercase letters of the alphabet

___ Understands that some words can have multiple meanings

___ Answers questions about the beginning, middle, and end of stories

Social-Emotional Skills

___ Cooperates with others

___ Expresses feelings using appropriate words

___ Greets others

___ Shares with others

___ Takes turns

___ Thinks before acting

Please describe any issues you would like to discuss during our visit.

Send thank you notes. Continue your role as a guest by sending families and children a thank you note for allowing you to visit with them. Personalize each note by mentioning a highlight of the visit.

Reflect on your observations. How did your expectations about the home visit differ from your actual experiences? What aspects of your visit worked well? What can you change to make future visits even more successful? Record your reflections to these questions in a journal for future reference.

Make plans for integrating your observations into your classroom. Look through your notes and journal reflections to identify objects, events, interactions, and other bits of information that can be used to make your classroom lessons more meaningful for children. Likewise, use your observations to think about whether you need to adjust your expectations of, or your interactions with, individual children. For example, did a home visit help you better understand a child's behavior? Did you observe child guidance or instructional strategies that can be adapted for use in your classroom?

Before continuing to the next section, return to Reflection 12.3 (Examining Anxieties Associated With Home Visits). Based on what you have read so far, would you make any changes in your responses to this reflection?

The First Day of Class: Making a Smooth Transition

The first day of class can be hectic for children and their parents, even following letters of welcome and the personal contacts that were made during registration and home visits. It is thus important not to rush this transitional period. Since the transition process typically is more of an issue for younger than older school-age children, the following strategies are designed specifically for them. However, some of the strategies also can be adapted for use with older school-age children.

The first day of class can create anxiety for children and their parents.

Making a Smooth Entry Into the Classroom

Help children make a smooth entry into their classroom by reacquainting them and their families with the welcoming experiences associated with their registration and home visit. For example, you may choose to follow the suggestion made earlier in this chapter to take photographs of children and their families during their registration visit. If so, post the photographs on a large display board for families and children to view when entering the classroom on the first day of class. Alternatively, use information and drawings from the picture letter (see FYI 12.3) to make a welcome display.

Songs, poems, books, and bags. Send a couple of songs or poems home for families to sing or read with their children. Use these during the first week of class to provide children with a sense of continuity between their home and classroom environments. You may also choose to send parents a list of suggested books that address children's entry into different grades. Many bookstores display these types of books a few weeks before school begins. Librarians at your school or the public library may do the same.

Finally, give each child a paper bag. Ask them to work with their parents to identify a few objects (or drawings or photographs) for their bags that reflect something about their interests or daily life (Steen, 2011). During the first week or two of class, ask children to periodically share something from their bags with others. Such sharing can facilitate children's understanding of each other.

Puppets. During registration or the home visit, give each child a packet containing a sock or small paper bag. Also include art and craft materials in the packet. Invite each child to make a puppet for the first day of class. During their first class meeting, invite children to use their puppets to introduce themselves. Also lead the children in a puppet parade so they learn how to stay together when walking to and from the classroom. Finally, use the puppets to write a short story that children can read together.

Flowers. During registration or the home visit, help children plant and water a few seeds of an inexpensive and multicolored flower that is easy to grow. Marigolds are one good choice. Invite children to bring their flowers to school. Compare the different colors and blooms. Also ask children to share information about how they cared for their flowers.

Find your cubby. Post the names and photographs of children above their respective cubbies. Alternatively, use the drawings children made of themselves (see FYI 12.3). As families arrive, suggest a game where parents help children find their cubbies by looking for their names, photographs, and/or drawings. Once they are found, let parents show children how to put away the items they brought from home.

The treasure hunt. Mount photographs of various objects found in your classroom on card-stock. Ask children to help their families find each object. Use the back of the photographs to give families pointers for talking with their children about the purpose of each object. The last photograph can depict a large treasure chest. Invite children to open a real treasure chest and select a healthy snack.

Family Separation Anxieties

For most families, the first day will be a fairly routine one. They will make an uneventful exit after they help their children get settled. For other families, the exit process will take longer. At least a few families are likely to remain in the classroom for a time to reassure themselves that their children are truly settled. Some may repeat this routine for the first few days of class. Give these families the following pointers to move the separation process along in a positive direction (DeSteno, 2000).

Provide help only as needed. Ask families to give children plenty of space to explore the classroom on their own. Likewise, explain why it is important to let children work independently of adult interference, even if it takes them a little longer to accomplish a task. Ask that families provide just enough support to help their children understand and become acquainted with new materials and activities.

Stay in the background. In the case of shy children, families can play the role of mediator by introducing themselves and their children to others. Once these introductions are made, encourage families to ease into the background. This will allow children to assert their own personalities and get to know their peers on their own terms.

Saying good-bye. Ask families not to sneak away from the classroom if they fear their children will begin crying upon their departure. This can lead to resentment and mistrust, making future departures even more difficult. Instead, identify a plan for how to turn separation anxiety into a growth experience. Strive to give children as much control as possible in saying good-bye. For example, some children will be satisfied helping to direct their parents' departure (e.g., "Help me finish this; then you can go"). Other children will need greater reassurance that their parents will return. For example, you might help a child set a large clock showing the time when his grandmother will return. You might help another child write a note to place in her father's pocket or tape to his shirtsleeve reminding him when he is to return. Think about the different types of separation anxiety you are likely to encounter as a teacher. Then complete Reflection 12.8.

> **REFLECTION 12.8 Brainstorming Parent-Child Separation Strategies**
>
> Other than those already listed, what parent-child separation strategies can you suggest? Share your ideas with your peers.

Facilitating Children's Adjustment to the Classroom

Children's adjustment to the classroom is essential in helping families feel comfortable with the classroom environment. Like other transition issues, this one is particularly important for younger children. A few strategies for facilitating the adjustment process are presented.

Be patient and provide reminders. Be patient in helping children understand the importance of following arrival routines and rules. Remember that younger children in particular will need a little time to assimilate this information. Be prepared to provide repeated and gentle reminders.

Point out new choices. Children may not always see the choices that are available to them when they first enter a classroom. Point out existing and new possibilities. Tweaking one or two learning centers just a little each day makes separation easier as children begin to look forward to new learning opportunities (see Reflection 12.9). Remember to make only small changes, since children also need a sense of continuity in their lives.

Pair up children. Arrange for children to work in pairs on simple tasks like putting away materials, gathering classroom assignments, and caring for the classroom pet. These joint activities can lead to new friendships. Friendships in turn provide a source of emotional support that can be especially helpful in facilitating children's adjustment to their classroom.

> ## REFLECTION 12.9   Tweaking Classroom Learning Centers
>
> Identify a learning center in a prekindergarten or kindergarten classroom. Brainstorm the differ-ent ways you can tweak this center each day during the first week of classes in order to facilitate children's classroom adjustment. Repeat this activity for a learning center that might be found in a first- through fifth-grade classroom.

Provide separation supports. Provide emotional supports to help children deal with the anxiety that accompanies separation from their families. Soft cushions in the reading center can serve as a temporary retreat until children feel like joining their friends. An item from home, like a cap or a stuffed toy, stored in a young child's cubby also can be comforting. Some children who are feeling anxious respond well to an adult who reads or sings to them.

Set up a family mailbox. Place the mailbox in the hallway next to the classroom door. Invite families to write encouraging notes to their children and place them in the mailbox during morning drop-off. Families also can place notes in their children's daily folders (see Chapter 13) for them to put in the mailbox. The notes can be shared during snack, a class meeting, or individually with each child. Of course, not all families may choose to send in notes. In these situations, fill the void by writing generic encouraging notes to share with children (see Reflection 12.10). When delivering the notes, introduce them with a general statement such as the following: "These notes are from your families and teachers."

> ## REFLECTION 12.10   Writing Notes for Families
>
> Assume that a family chooses not to participate in the family mailbox activity. Give an example of a generic and encouraging note you might write to a child.

Facilitating Classroom Observations

Since parents need and deserve full access to their children, it is important that you maintain an open-door policy. At the same time, it is important that you manage the number of visi-tors in your classroom at any one time. Make parents' visits to your classroom a success by using the following guidelines.

Manage the Number of Visitors in the Classroom

If, upon arrival, parents find others already observing, ask them to wait a few minutes before entering the classroom. Explain that this will help maintain an orderly learning environment for children. Suggest activities for parents to pursue while they wait. For

[handwritten margin note: Don't have many people visit at the same time TOG]

example, invite them to visit the interactive bulletin board outside your classroom (see Chapter 13). Encourage them to view the new books on display in the library. Provide them with a new activity folder (see Chapter 11) from the family resource center.

There are at least two ways to avoid overcrowding in the classroom altogether. First, encourage parents to eat lunch with their children. This is a time when space constraints are less an issue. In addition, lunch is a perfect time for parents to observe their children's social interactions. Second, communicate with parents in multiple ways (see Chapter 13) and on multiple occasions about their children's classroom activities and educational progress.

Alert Parents to Schedule Changes

[handwritten margin note: keep parent informed]

Parents understandably become frustrated when they arrive to observe their children only to find that the daily schedule has been altered. To prevent this from happening, publish a monthly calendar that specifies when the daily schedule will be altered to accommodate classroom celebrations, assessments, and other events. A week before each event, send a note to parents explaining how it will impact the daily schedule.

Provide Observational Guides

Parents will get the most out of their classroom observations if they understand the educational significance of the activities they see taking place. This usually is not a problem for parents of older elementary school children, since the classroom environment most likely will reflect pretty much what they expect to see. Parents may have more difficulty understanding the educational significance of what they observe in prekindergarten and kindergarten classrooms. Address this challenge by developing observational guides that summarize the educational objectives associated with both the short-term and standing learning centers represented in your classroom.

Construct Observational Notepads

Provide parents with notepads for taking notes about their observations. Create a simple notepad by stapling together 5 to 10 small pages. Place a small logo at the top of each page. Encourage parents to place key notes in their family portfolios (see Chapter 11) so they can be discussed during parent-teacher conferences. Before reading about other welcoming strategies, complete Reflection 12.11.

REFLECTION 12.11 Planning for a Welcoming Environment

Quickly review the five components of the welcoming process summarized in FYI 12.1. Then explain which components you are most and least likely to implement. Discuss your responses with your peers.

Other Welcoming Strategies

The five components of the welcoming process offer a glimpse into how creating a comfortable environment for families involves not only physical materials, such as letters of welcome and observational notepads, but also an emotional environment that is warm and supportive. Other welcoming strategies that can be used to create this type of environment are reviewed in this section.

Family Involvement Storybooks

Use family involvement storybooks to facilitate families' awareness of the benefits associated with supporting their children's education at home, in the classroom, and in the community (Mayer, Ferede, & Hou, 2006). Place the storybooks on a display table in your classroom or in the family resource center. Also list them on your school website. To learn more about family involvement storybooks, visit the Storybook Corner at the Harvard Family Research Project website: www.hfrp.org/family-involvement/projects/family-involvement-storybook-project-completed-project/storybook-corner

The Family Reception

Just as there is power in numbers, there is also empowerment in numbers. Families who feel they are part of a greater good are more likely to come together to support school and classroom activities. Encourage this sense of community by conducting a family reception at the beginning of the school year. Keep the reception informal. Invite families to drop by between designated hours to enjoy light refreshments, view children's work, and chat with teachers and other families. Build on this initial event by planning additional family fun nights and workshops throughout the year (see Chapter 11).

Family Telephone and Email Directories

At times, families may prefer to communicate directly with each other rather than have you, the teacher, serve as a mediator. You may choose to support this type of networking by setting up a parent telephone or email directory. Ask each parent for her or his permission before including her or him in the directory. Once established, the directory will need to be revised at various points throughout the year as new children are enrolled in your classroom, families move, and some families request that their names be removed from the directory. One word of caution is in order regarding this last point. Families will ask to be removed from the directory if they feel it is being used in ways that are abusive. To prevent this from happening, establish some ground rules. Explain that the directory is being developed so families can exchange information and discuss issues associated with their children's development and education. It should not be used to discuss the behavior of others, solicit donations, promote sales, or endorse election campaigns.

Bumper Stickers

You may have seen bumper stickers celebrating a "super student," an "honor student," or a particular school. A variation of these bumper stickers can be used to celebrate families as children's protectors, supporters, teachers, and so forth. Try your hand at developing a bumper sticker by completing Reflection 12.12.

REFLECTION 12.12   Your Turn! Create a Family Bumper Sticker

Design a bumper sticker that celebrates families. As a class, see how many different designs and supportive messages you can create.

Family Mentors

Family mentors provide assistance to families who are working to overcome challenges similar to ones they themselves have experienced. This type of personal assistance in turn creates the type of welcoming environment that is especially important for at-risk families. For example, a Mexican American parent in your classroom might volunteer to assist another parent who recently immigrated from Mexico. Her role as mentor might include explaining the daily classroom routine, making introductions within the Latino community, explaining American customs, and helping the parent complete the paperwork needed to receive school, health, and social service assistance.

CHAPTER SUMMARY

- Letters of welcome are important in forming positive first impressions. For this reason, keep them brief, informative, and visually appealing.
- Beyond the completion of paperwork, beginning-of-the-year registration serves two other objectives. It allows parents and teachers an opportunity to meet face to face in a "get to know you" meeting. It also provides an opportunity for teachers to orient parents and children to the classroom.
- Your family handbook reflects both your organizational skills and your commitment to providing families with information they can use throughout the year.
- Home visits serve multiple purposes. Some benefit teachers (e.g., making informal assessments of children in their home environment). Some benefit both parents and teachers (e.g., interpersonal rapport), and some benefit children (e.g., developing a positive relationship with their new teacher).
- Preparing for a home visit requires multiple considerations. Some are practical (e.g., identifying objectives for the visit; confirming the driving route) and some are administrative (e.g., reviewing each child's file before the visit; sending home a reminder note regarding the date and time of the visit).
- Facilitating a home visit involves two roles, that of guest and teacher.
- Following up on home visits is as important as preparing for and facilitating them.
- Teachers should be prepared to help both children and parents make a smooth transition into the classroom at the beginning of the school year.
- Observational guides are helpful in communicating an open-door policy and facilitating informal family visits.

DISCUSSION QUESTIONS

1. Of all the information reviewed in this chapter, identify one bit of information or a strategy that you feel is most important in helping children feel welcomed in their classroom. Do the same for families. Compare your selection with those of your peers.

2. Pair up with one of your peers. Write a short scenario of something unexpected that could occur during a home visit. Exchange your scenario with another pair of peers. Discuss how you will respond to each of the two scenarios.

3. Identify an object, routine, center, or lesson in the classroom that families may not understand. Discuss how teachers might explain its significance to families during registration or an observational visit.

4. **Your family involvement philosophy.** Return to the draft of your family involvement philosophy. Based on your reading of this chapter, what if any changes will you make to your philosophy statement? Discuss your answer to this question with your peers.

COMMUNITY OF LEARNERS' FIELD ASSIGNMENT

Home Visits: Advice From a Panel of Experts

As noted earlier in this chapter, the home visit represents a worrisome task for many teachers. The purpose of this field assignment is to allay some of your anxieties concerning home visits.

Your task. As a class, work with your instructor to identify a date and time for a panel presentation on making home visits. Begin by listing a few questions you would like panel members to answer. Some examples follow.

- What are some tips for making a safe home visit?
- What are some things I can do to break the ice upon arriving at a home?
- What topics should I cover during a home visit?
- What topics should I avoid?
- How long should each home visit last?
- What other tips can you give for making a successful home visit?

As a class, identify individuals who can respond to your questions. Options include one or more parents, a police officer, a school or community social worker, a teacher with experience in making home visits, and a school principal. Divide into small groups, each group taking responsibility for inviting one person to serve on the panel. Finally, consider the following logistics to make sure the panel presentation goes well:

- Give each invited guest the names of the other panel members.
- Make arrangements for free parking.
- Give each panel member written directions for getting from the parking area to your classroom.
- Ask each panel member how she or he would like to be introduced.

- Identify one person from your class to serve as the panel moderator. That person will be responsible for keeping track of time, asking the questions identified by your class, ensuring that each person has an opportunity to share her or his views, moderating follow-up questions, making concluding remarks, and verbally thanking the panel for their participation.
- Following the presentation, send each panel member a thank you note signed by everyone in the class.

Capstone Activities

Activity 1: Collect Welcoming Strategies From the Field

Interview a teacher about the strategies she or he uses to help families feel welcomed in the classroom. What strategies have worked best? Were any strategies tried and dropped? If so, why were they dropped? Are there special strategies the teacher uses to welcome non-English-speaking families?

Activity 2: Develop a Picture Letter

Draw or take a small photograph of yourself. Use this as a starting point to make a one-page picture letter to welcome preschool or kindergarten children into their new classroom. What messages will you write on the back of your letter to help families translate it for children?

Activity 3: Design Your Own Welcoming Strategy

Consider the welcoming strategies you read about in this chapter. Also visit the Internet resources listed in the following section to learn about other welcoming strategies. Then, think creatively to design a new welcoming strategy. Compare your strategy to those of your peers. Compile a handout of everyone's ideas. Place your handout in your teacher resource file for future reference.

Internet Resources

You may find that some URLs have been altered by the webmaster. In these situations, try entering the name of the document or agency in a search engine. Alternatively, enter the domain name (e.g., http://www.xxxx.org). This should take you to the revised home page and associated links.

National Parent Teacher Association (PTA): Welcoming All Families Into the School Community

http://www.pta.org/2757.asp

"Welcoming All Families Into the School Community" is the first of six standards endorsed by the National PTA (see Chapter 2). Click on "Standard 1—Welcoming All Families" to learn more about this standard.

Wake County Public School System, North Carolina: Wake County Schools Work to Welcome Families Into Schools

http://www.wcpss.net/news/2008_nov20_welcome_families/

This website provides an example of how one school district implemented the National PTA standard of "welcoming all families into the school community."

University of California, Los Angeles (UCLA), School Mental Health Project: Welcoming Strategies for Students and Their Families

http://smhp.psych.ucla.edu/atyourschool/sept02.htm

The authors of this website provide teachers with a number of strategies for helping children and families feel welcomed in the classroom.

National Education Association: Creating a Professional Image

http://www.nea.org/tools/creating-a-professional-image.html

Visit this website to learn about practices teachers can use to create a positive image and advance the family-teacher partnership.

Quail Run Elementary School, San Ramon, California

http://www.qres.srvusd.k12.ca.us/index.html

Providing parents with a range of information about child development and early childhood education is one way to ensure they feel welcomed in their child's school. Quail Run Elementary provides a good example of this basic rule. Using the above URL, go to the link "Resources" and click on "Parenting Resources." Then click on the link "School Success Ideas for Parents." Here you will find videos, parent guides, educational quizzes, and other materials developed specifically to send the message that parents are important to the success of their children's well-being and education.

STUDENT STUDY SITE

Log on to the Web-based student study site at **www.sagepub.com/coleman** for additional study tools including

- eFlashcards
- Web Quizzes
- Links to SAGE Journal Articles
- Author-created Videos

- Learning Objectives
- Web Resources
- Family Involvement Portfolio Guides

CHAPTER 13

Communicating With Families

I t is impossible to overstate the importance of communication in building positive family-teacher partnerships. As a teacher, you will be expected to communicate with parents about their children's classroom performance and respond to questions about classroom routines, rules, and lessons. Unfortunately, these tasks are not always easily accomplished. Indeed, communication has been identified by at least one educator as the most common source of conflict between parents and teachers (McEwan, 2005, p. 8). Results of national surveys conducted with parents (Olson & Hyson, 2005) and teachers (Olson & Hyson, 2003) lend support to this observation. In both surveys, communication between families and teachers was viewed as an area of teacher training that needed greater attention. Subsequently, in this chapter you will learn about a number of strategies for communicating with families in your classroom.

COMMUNITY LEARNING GUIDE

As you read this chapter, take notes on the following items. Use your notes to address the Reflections, Discussion Questions, Field Assignment, and Capstone Activities that you find in the chapter.

- Why is communication a dual responsibility?
- Describe some practical strategies you will use to communicate with families.
- Describe the steps you will take to facilitate a smooth parent-teacher conference.
- Summarize the guidelines for reviewing report cards with parents.

Facilitating Constructive Communication

Communication is often characterized as a dual responsibility. The person speaking has the responsibility of sending a clear message. In turn, the receiver of the message has the responsibility of listening to and acknowledging receipt of that message. Communication problems occur when either of these responsibilities is ignored. Some techniques for facilitating constructive communication are reviewed in this section.

Control Your Private Thoughts

Even though we may not always be aware of it, we often conduct private conversations with ourselves when listening to others talk. Think back to the last time you were engaged in a serious conversation with someone. What types of thoughts were running through your mind? They might have included something like the following:

- "Why is she telling me this?"
- "This person is really upset."
- "What am I going to say when she stops talking?"
- "I wish I had avoided this person."
- "I feel sad about this person's situation."

The information in this chapter supports the following family-school-community partnership standards. These standards are reviewed in Chapter 2

NAEYC Standards and Associated Key Elements	1b, 1c, 2c, 3b, 3c, 4b, 6c, 6d, 6e
ACEI Standards	3.2, 4.0, 5.1, 5.2
PTA Standards	1, 2, 3, 4, 5, 6

While such thoughts are normal, they nevertheless prevent us from focusing on what the other person is communicating. To address this challenge, keep the following three rules in mind. **STOP** your private thoughts, **LOOK** at the parent who is speaking, and really **LISTEN** to what the parent is saying.

Pay Attention to Feelings That Accompany Words

When considered alone, words can mask the feelings behind a message. To fully understand what a parent is communicating, also pay attention to how words are spoken. For example, different voice tones add meaning to communication, as do the pacing and volume of speech, pauses in speech, repetitive speech, and even the loss of a thought midsentence. Paying attention to the types of body language noted in FYI 13.1 adds still more information to what is being communicated. After reading FYI 13.1, complete Reflection 13.1.

FYI 13.1 Types of Body Language

Here are a few examples of body language that we use to communicate our thoughts and feelings:

- Facial expressions like smiling, frowning, grimacing, and squinting our eyes
- Fidgeting movements like tugging at our shirt, looking at our watch, and tapping our fingers on the table
- Body positions like crossing or uncrossing our arms, rocking back and forth, and stooping versus standing straight
- Hand gestures like clinching our hands, gesturing with our index finger, and waving our hands in the air

---

Signal That You Are Listening

We can signal that we are listening both passively and actively. Usually, both approaches are needed to facilitate a meaningful communication exchange.

REFLECTION 13.1   Interpreting Body Language

Describe the body language a parent might display when having the following thoughts during a parent-teacher conference:

- "I'm not sure the teacher is being totally honest with me."
- "I am so bored. Will this meeting never end?"
- "I'm feeling nervous about what she is telling me."
- "Please, let me speak. I have questions that need to be answered."
- "I feel comfortable with this teacher."

Listening passively. Generally defined, **passive listening** means not speaking and only listening (Gordon, 2000, p. 44). We also signal that we are listening passively by putting down our work, matching our facial expression to the emotional state of the speaker, periodically writing down a quick note as needed, and gently nodding our heads to signal our attentiveness (see Reflection 13.2). Of course, it is important that we not take passive listening too far or that we use it as a way of withdrawing from uncomfortable conversations. This is why active listening is equally important (see the next section).

REFLECTION 13.2   Let Parents Know You Are Listening

Other than the examples already given, describe some ways to signal that you are listening to parents during a parent-teacher conference.

Listening passively can be more difficult than it seems, especially when we feel the need to acknowledge the speaker's statements by interjecting our own statements of understanding, support, or disagreement. Nevertheless, interrupting prematurely can result in misunderstanding. Instead, wait until the speaker has completed his or her thoughts. Then, use **door openers** to encourage further communication and ask for clarification (Gordon, 2000, p. 56). Door openers include short statements like the following:

- "Tell me more about that."
- "Please continue. I'm listening."
- "I'm not sure I understood. Please go over that again."

Listening actively. Listening actively (also called **active listening**) involves a give-and-take exchange in which the receiver of a message reflects his or her interpretation of that message back to the sender. This allows the receiver to confirm that he or she has interpreted the message correctly. Here is one example of an active listening exchange:

- Ms. Scott: "I'm concerned about David's test scores."
- Teacher: "I see. You're fearful that he may be getting behind?"

- Ms. Scott: "No, that's not it. I'm concerned that he's getting bored with school and not applying himself."
- Teacher: "Oh, I misunderstood. What have you noticed about David's behavior that indicates he is bored with school?"

In this active listening exchange, the teacher reflected her interpretation of Ms. Scott's statement, which Ms. Scott then corrected. Note that the teacher did not simply state, "You feel . . ." and repeat Ms. Scott's statement verbatim. This approach, which is sometimes used by individuals just learning about active listening, is too rigid. Instead, follow the teacher's approach by using door openers and adding other personal touches to keep communication exchanges diplomatic and natural. Consider, for example, the rigid versus more personal touch used in FYI 13.2. Then complete Reflection 13.3.

FYI 13.2 Personalizing Active Listening

Statement	Rigid Active Listening Response	Adding the Personal Touch
"No one listens to me."	"You feel you're not being heard."	"Not being heard can be frustrating. Tell me more."
"I hate doing all this work by myself."	"You don't like doing all the work by yourself."	"I can hear the frustration in your voice. What type of assistance would you like to receive?"
"I am very concerned about Hunter's academic work."	"You're worried about Hunter's grades."	"Tell me more about your concerns. Are there particular subjects we should discuss?"
"I am very angry about how you handled Savannah's situation."	"You're angry with me."	"Thank you for being honest about your feelings. Please tell me more so we can work this out."
"I am so happy with Brooke's project."	"You feel happy about Brooke's classroom work."	"Thank you for sharing your thoughts with me. What in particular did you like about Brooke's project?"

REFLECTION 13.3 Practicing Active Listening

You may find FYI 13.2 helpful as you complete this Reflection. Practice personalizing your active listening skills. First, give an example of a rigid active listening response to the following statements. Then add your personal touch to make your active listening response more diplomatic and natural.

- "Johnny tells me that you pick on him."
- "I think you are overreacting to Jamie's behavior."
- "Thank you for taking so much time with me today."

Ask Clarification Questions

At times you may question whether you are communicating effectively with a parent. If so, ask clarification questions such as the following:

- "Does my explanation help?"
- "Is there anything else about this issue we should discuss before proceeding?"
- "Am I addressing your concern?"

Control Your Emotions

Our emotions can get the better of us during heated conversations. As difficult as it may be, focus on remaining calm when confronted with an angry parent. You will be surprised at how your calm demeanor helps to bring the emotions of the parent under control. One way to present a calm demeanor is to use a soft voice tone. Also, use active listening to acknowledge the parent's anger. This too can help diffuse a tense situation.

It is equally important that you remain in control of your emotions when dealing with parents who react to bad news with tears. While it is certainly important to empathize with tearful parents, creating a sense of calmness is also essential to promoting a productive dialogue.

Keep an Open Mind

If you begin a conversation with negative assumptions about the outcome, chances are you will achieve just that. Keep an open mind and think about how the parent might be feeling. This can prevent unfortunate situations, such as the one reported in the following quote from a Korean mother:

> My son's teacher is a new one who just graduated from the College of Education. She speaks English very fast. When she does not understand my English, she is impatient and quite irritated. It makes me really upset and uncomfortable. (Sohn & Wang, 2008, p. 128)[1]

Also remember to avoid jumping to conclusions about the cause of a parent's angry or tearful outburst. Things are not always as they seem. For example, not all parents have someone in their lives with whom they can talk or vent their frustrations. In these situations it may be easier for parents to vent their emotions to teachers they view as supportive and understanding. Similarly, a parent's anger over a classroom incident may be less about the incident than about his or her feelings of being ignored or disrespected by school staff.

Select Your Words Carefully

You may have heard the statement "Those are fighting words." Because words can carry more impact that we realize, pay attention to the words you use when communicating with parents. Asking parents if they are willing to "consider" doing something is very different than telling them they "must" do something. Telling a parent that her son needs to work on his "eye-hand coordination" is different from telling the parent her son is "clumsy." Before communicating with parents, think about the language you plan to use and decide if a more diplomatic phrase or word is needed. For practice, consider Reflection 13.4.

REFLECTION 13.4   Word Choices

How would you rephrase the following to make them more diplomatic?

Instead of saying Jesse is   **I would say Jesse. . .**

- an academic failure   • _____

- mean   • _____

- lazy   • _____

- defiant   • _____

- timid   • _____

- immature   • _____

- a cheater   • _____

- sloppy   • _____

- selfish   • _____

Avoid Technical Jargon

Avoid using professional abbreviations and technical labels that have little meaning for parents. For example, most parents will not understand the acronym NAEYC used by teachers referring to the National Association for the Education of Young Children. Instead, use the complete title. Also, clearly define educational concepts to prevent the type of frustration expressed by a Korean mother when her child's teacher failed to use appropriate language:

> I don't know educational terms in English. For example, I did not know these English words like "curriculum," "substitute teacher," "time-out," and so on. So when I have to use these kinds of educational terms, I feel stuck. (Sohn & Wang, 2006, p. 128)[1]

Visit the following website for a parent's glossary of educational terms used by the Cincinnati Public Schools (click on "Parent Glossary"): www.cps-k12.org/parents/parents .htm.

Remain Focused

It is easy to drift from topic to topic when engaged in a conversation. When you sense that a discussion is wandering, diplomatically note this and ask if the discussion regarding the original topic is finished. If not, suggest that the conversation return to the original topic so a decision can be reached regarding what, if any, steps should be taken.

Before continuing, complete Case Study 13.1 to see if you can put the communication strategies reviewed above into practice. As you complete Case Study 13.1, remember that there is no one correct way to address a communication block. Rather, different situational contexts and personalities will require different approaches.

CASE STUDY 13.1 Addressing Communication Blocks

In what ways are the following exchanges being blocked? How can you unblock them?

Situation #1

Teacher: "Abby is having difficulty following directions in class. Is this just a classroom issue or do you have the same experience at home?"

Ms. Nowak: "Sometimes I think she just doesn't want to hear. Maybe she has poor hearing. Can we schedule a hearing assessment through the school?"

Situation #2

Ms. Smith: "I feel the classroom is overcrowded. Could some of the equipment be moved to storage so the children have more room to move around?"

Teacher: "I understand your frustration. Unfortunately, there are no other options. I'm sorry you can't be more patient like the other parents."

Situation #3

Mr. Lenley: "I'm concerned about Nicole's academic progress this year."

Teacher: "I agree. Academically, Nicole is the slowest student in the class."

Manage Conflict by Word and Action

Together with the communication techniques reviewed so far, the following suggestions can help you manage parent-teacher conflict in a respectful and productive manner.

Accept conflict as part of any relationship. Some people feel uncomfortable addressing conflict, preferring to avoid it. This can be damaging to relationships as concerns go unanswered and resentment builds. It is therefore best to accept conflict as part of any relationship and use your communication skills to work through it.

Focus on the issue, not the person. One natural response when feeling threatened is to verbally attack the individual with whom we are communicating. This is sometimes exhibited through name calling, something we usually regret. When you are the target of name calling, ignore the attack and redirect the conversation back to the issue at hand. If you are called "incompetent," respond with an active listening statement such as "I can understand your anger over Jacob's bruised arm. Here is what happened." You might also redirect name calling with an invitation for cooperation. If you are called "mean" because of a grade you assigned, reply by stating, "I too am concerned about Lauren's grade. I would like to discuss a plan for helping her raise her grade." Note that this statement ignores the personal attack while refocusing the discussion on a plan of action.

Look for a win-win outcome. When confronted with a conflict, avoid making global statements such as "You are always misinformed about the facts of a situation." This statement reflects a defensive stance that blocks communication. Instead, begin by validating a parent's concern. Then, engage the parent in exploring ways to address that concern. For example, if a parent accuses you of withholding information, you might diplomatically state, "The concern you raise is indeed important. In fact, I addressed it a few months ago in the classroom newsletter. Let me get a copy of the newsletter so we can review the information. I think that will help to clarify things." This type of nondefensive language will go a long way in encouraging parents to join you in seeking win-win outcomes.

Assume personal responsibility for your views. At times you might be tempted to defend your views by pointing to others who you feel share those views. For example, if a parent challenges your teaching practices, you might be tempted to state, "All the other parents are happy with my performance as a teacher." The problem with such a statement is that the parent in question may follow up by contacting the other parents to challenge their assessment of you. Obviously, this would put everyone in an awkward situation. It is better to assume personal responsibility for your views by stating something like, "I feel I am following professional teaching standards. I'll be happy to review those standards with you so we can address your concerns."

Be persistent. It is easy to give up when an initial discussion fails to resolve a conflict. Avoid taking this easy way out. Instead, express your interest in keeping up a dialogue until a workable solution is achieved. Sometimes, points raised during an initial discussion can lead to new insights after a few days spent in reflective thought. Practice using this and the other conflict management techniques by completing Case Study 13.2.

CASE STUDY 13.2   Managing Parent-Teacher Conflicts

Use the communication and conflict management strategies reviewed in this section to revise the teachers' responses to the following conflicts.

Conflict #1

Parent: "I've been talking to some other parents and we agree that the strategies you use to communicate with us are not very effective."

Teacher: "I don't how to respond to that. I spend a great deal of time preparing children's daily folders. Just tell me what you want and I'll do it."

Conflict #2

Parent: "I don't think the parents who prepared the workshop room did a very good job. I rearranged the tables and chairs."

Teacher: "I know you meant well, but your actions were not helpful."

Putting it all together. In this section you had opportunities to practice using various communication strategies. This is important because the process of communication is subtle, often not well understood, and frequently involuntary (e.g., body language, facial expressions). Thus, because "practice makes perfect," we end this section with one final practice session. Join your peers to complete the communication role plays in Capstone Activity 3 at the end of this chapter. When you are done, turn your attention to the following section where we examine the use and management of practical strategies for communicating with parents.

Practical Communication Strategies

We begin this section by addressing the general communication environment. Use the following strategies to establish an environment that fosters honest and open communication.

Make contact with each family during the first week of class. Let them know how things are going and how much you enjoy having their child in your classroom. Reinforce your availability to meet with families.

Set up a rotating system of contacts. After the first week of class, establish a rotating schedule in which you make contact with a few families each week. Provide a brief comment about each child's behavior or educational progress. Establish a log to track your communication across time (see FYI 13.3).

Communicate both good and bad news. Regular communication with each family about positive aspects of their child's behavior and classroom performance helps to lessen their anxiety if at some point you must share unpleasant news.

When a problem arises, immediately contact families. Otherwise, if the problem escalates it will be difficult to explain why you did not contact them in a more timely fashion.

Admit your mistakes. Most families are forgiving and will respect your honesty.

FYI 13.3   Log for Documenting Rotating Family Contacts

– Contact six parents this week
Type of contact: P = Phone E = Email L = Letter N = Note O = Other

Date	Parent Contacted	Type of Contact	Purpose of Contact	Notes

Next, we review a number of specific communication strategies. Some strategies require a bit more time and planning than others. Nevertheless, these expenditures are more than offset by the good will that comes from demonstrating your commitment to providing families with regular updates about their children's education.

Brief Face-to-Face Communication

This traditional type of communication takes place during morning drop-off and afternoon pickup. Four communication objectives are associated with these daily routines.

- Social greetings that reinforce the family-teacher partnership (e.g., "Good morning! How are you today?") are exchanged.
- Families are reassured of your interest in their children as they experience your greeting and welcoming them into the classroom.
- Families make brief inquiries about upcoming classroom activities or children's classroom work or behavior.
- Families are given materials that otherwise must be mailed, emailed, or sent home with children.

To successfully carry out face-to-face communication, make yourself available to families by staying close to the classroom door during morning drop-off and afternoon pickup. If you have a paraprofessional or volunteer, assign him or her the responsibility of facilitating children's activities during these times so you are free to interact with families. If this is not possible, multitask by continuing your work with children while also waving and saying hello and good-bye to families.

Telephone and Cell Phone Calls

The telephone represents a traditional communication device that is still useful today when parents and teachers need to discuss a child's behavior or classroom performance. The cell phone makes these exchanges even easier. When initiating a call, remember to use the family survey to identify times when families are available to receive your call. Also remember to document your conversations, and who initiated them, by keeping a log in each child's file (see FYI 13.4).

The telephone can be used in still other ways. For example, some teachers record general messages for families to retrieve by dialing a special telephone number. Examples include reminders about upcoming classroom meetings, tips for helping with homework assignments, and updates on school policies.

Email and Texting

Email and texting offer an appealing alternative to the telephone, since both can save time. For example, you can set up a classroom email listserv to send out announcements and distribute electronic classroom newsletters. Remember, however, that some families may not have easy access to email or a cell phone. For these reasons, some have suggested that teachers make any technology-based communication available to families in hard copy as well (Mitchell, Foulger, & Wetzel, 2009).

FYI 13.4 Log for Individual Family Contacts

Purpose of Call: _____

Person Initiating Call: _____ Date: _____

Summary of Conversation:

Actions Taken:

Equally important, consider your own schedule and privacy needs. Are you prepared to respond to numerous emails and tweets throughout the day? Chat with administrators and other teachers at your school about their experiences with email and texting. Also follow established school policies to ensure your efficient use of these communication strategies.

Social Networking

You may also choose to use social networking sites such as Myspace and Facebook to communicate with families. If so, consider both the positive and negative implications. On the positive side, social networking sites can be used to build online communities with families who share a teacher's interest in a particular classroom, school, and community. Sharing photos, videos, and blogs concerning these common interests enriches family-teacher partnerships and creates a denser social network that builds social capital. In short, parents themselves benefit from having ties to other parents both within and outside their children's schools (Wanat, 2010).

Teachers can also make practical use of social networking to publicize and create excitement about upcoming classroom activities (Carter, Foulger, & Ewbank, 2008). Finally, social networking within the teaching profession builds teachers' reflective skills and sense of self-efficacy as they share and receive ideas, resources, and emotional support (Carter et al., 2008; Greenhow, 2009).

On the negative side, not all families have equal access to the technology needed for social networking. In addition, teachers in various states have lost their jobs because of inappropriate postings (e.g., racy photos or language; venting about school administrators or parents; Carter et al., 2008). In at least one case a student was denied a teaching certificate because of the "drunken pirate" photos she included in her Myspace profile (Carter et al., 2008).

In all these cases, the individuals shared their private lives within a public domain, thereby creating a virtual identity that violated the high public standards to which teachers are held (Barrett, 2007; Carter et al., 2008). While it is true that teachers enjoy the same free speech rights as everyone else, two Supreme Court rulings, collectively referred to as the **Pickering/Connick balancing test**, allow school administrators to discipline teachers for speaking out publicly against their school when that speech interferes with the efficient operation of the school (Carter et al., 2008). In addition, state certification language often warns teachers against engaging in conduct that discredits the teaching profession (Carter et al., 2008). Thus, it is essential that teachers consider the guidelines in Tip Box 13.1 when managing their social networking sites.

TIP BOX 13.1	**Guidelines for Teachers' Social Networking Sites**

While participation in most social networking sites require children to be at least 13 years of age (Davis, 2010), younger children and/or their parents may still gain access to your site. Thus, it is important that your profile and postings reflect well on your professional role in the community. The following guidelines can help.

- **Be judicious in what you post.** One rule of thumb is to consider how you would feel if your Myspace page was posted for everyone to see during an open house night at your school (Barrett, 2007). Would you feel embarrassed over what parents saw?
- **Check your "friends'" profiles.** Ask them to remove any photos that reflect badly on your professional standing as a teacher (Barrett, 2007).
- **Make your profile private.** This will allow only "friends" whom you have granted permission to view and post on your page (American Federation of Teachers, 2010; Barrett, 2007).
- **Think and write like a teacher** (Barrett, 2007). Limit personal postings to generic recreational pursuits, hobbies, and family life, devoting more space to your professional life. You might include, for example, your reflections about a book you recently read, lessons learned from a trip you took, ideas that teachers can use in their classrooms, and tips that families can use to reinforce classroom learning experiences.

Finally, keep two other points in mind regarding emailing, texting, and social networking. First, while all of these communication strategies can make our lives more efficient, they are not a substitute for face-to-face communication and therefore should not be used to deliver negative news or avoid personal contact with families. Second, it is easy to misinterpret email, text messages, and social networking postings because they lack direct visual and auditory cues. Subsequently, email, texting, and social networking should be avoided when complex or sensitive topics are to be discussed. These also require face-to-face conversations.

Family Notes

Family notes represent another traditional and valuable communication strategy that can be used to request a meeting or obtain information from families about a child's behavior or medical condition. They can also be used to deliver brief information about a child's classroom performance. As a teacher, you may even use notes to encourage families to reinforce their children's developmental and educational milestones. Consider, for example, the note one teacher sent home to reinforce a child's achievement (see FYI 13.5).

Daily Folders

Daily folders are used to exchange materials between the classroom and home. Visit the Internet Resources section at the end of this chapter to view one teacher's daily folder. Common components of the daily folder are presented in FYI 13.6 (also see the photo on page 280). (The daily folder was developed by the author.) These components can be adapted for use in **weekly folders** (e.g., Friday Folders), if you prefer.

FYI 13.5   A Family Note

Front of Note

Give me a pat on the back. (turn me over) ▶

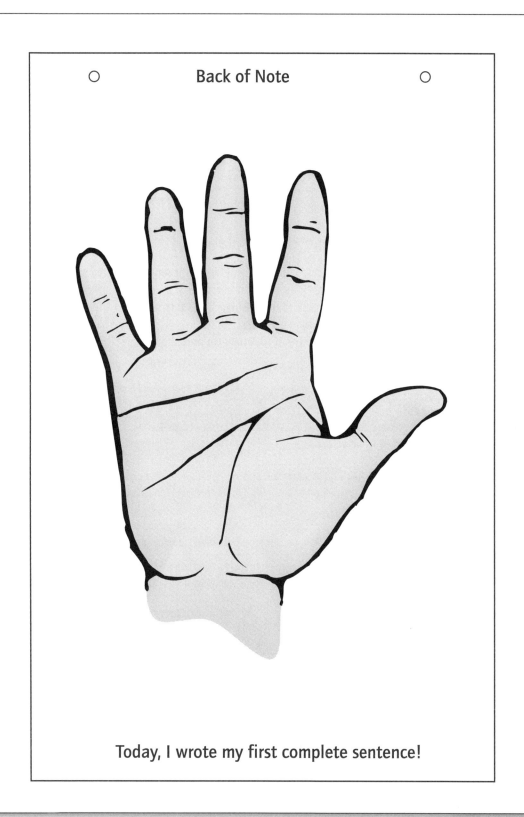

Back of Note

Today, I wrote my first complete sentence!

Outside cover page of Dan's Daily Folder.

Finding time in your schedule to deal with daily folders need not be an obstacle to their use. Consider, for example, the task of collecting daily folders. Some teachers sit at their classroom doors each morning to collect daily folders as they greet children and families. Other teachers have children place their daily folders in a special crate. Once the folders are collected, teachers look through them, gather materials to put in them, and insert new materials at different points during the day. For example, they may carry out these tasks while children are at lunch or recess or while they are participating in lessons conducted by another teacher. Still other teachers train a paraprofessional or a community volunteer to assist with these tasks. Children themselves can assist with inserting materials into their daily folders at the end of the day or after completing a lesson.

Classroom and Hall Displays

One indicator of a quality learning environment is the presence of children's work in the classroom. Take every opportunity to display children's work on tables, bookshelves, doors, and other surfaces as permitted by the fire and safety policies at your school. Make sure the displays are located at or near children's eye level. This will encourage them to reflect on and share their work with others.

FYI 13.6 Inside Cover Page of Dan's Daily Folder

Dear Families,

No more lost notes and books! Your child's daily folder will allow us to keep all of these materials organized. The daily folder will be sent home with your child at the end of each day. Please have your child bring it back to the classroom the following morning.

Money Pocket	Place money and checks in this pocket for book orders, lunch, field trips, etc.
Class Materials	You will find a number of items in this pocket: notes to and from parents, the classroom newsletter, forms that require your signature, samples of your child's classroom work, and invitations to classroom events.
Behavior Chart	Use this chart to track your child's daily classroom behavior. Please review the chart with your child each night, initial it and, if you like, add comments.
Home Assignments	Your child's homework assignments will be placed in this section of the daily folder. At times, you may also find a parent-child homework assignment. Have fun as you join your child in completing these assignments. We will review them in class.
Reading Log	Your child will enjoy coloring in a picture for each five minutes he or she spends reading to you during the week.
Pocket Book	Each Monday, your child will select a book to read at home. Please listen to your child read each night. On Friday, place the book back in the book pocket and return it to the classroom.

Change classroom and hall displays often so parents and visitors see the learning activities taking place in your classroom. For similar reasons, display children's work during parent-teacher conferences and when conducting family workshops or other family events.

Interactive Bulletin Boards

Jazz up the traditional bulletin board by turning it into an **interactive bulletin board**. As the title suggests, interactive bulletin boards require some type of action on the part of the viewer. An example of an interactive bulletin board is presented in this photo and FYI 13.7. (The interactive bulletin board was developed by Lauren Shinn, a graduate student in the Department of Child and Family Development, University of Georgia, Athens, under the direction of the author.)

An interactive bulletin board.

Classroom Newsletters

Consider the **classroom newsletter** a multipurpose informational outlet. It can be used to provide families with information about birthdays and other classroom events, summaries of field trips, explanations of new school policies, words of the week, lesson highlights, reminders about upcoming parent-teacher conferences and family workshops, reports from classroom committees, and general items of interest concerning children's development and education.

Newsletter formats can include sheets of paper, pamphlets, booklets, or electronic newsletters sent by email. Newsletters also can vary in length from one to multiple pages. Regardless of their format and length, add visual appeal to your newsletters by including drawings, photographs, and clip art. Also identify a newsletter title and logo. Some teachers involve children in these tasks.

Finally, it is important that your classroom newsletter be published according to a consistent schedule: weekly, biweekly, or monthly. Form a committee of parents and community volunteers to assist in the publication and distribution of the newsletter. A few examples of prekindergarten/kindergarten and fourth-/fifth-grade newsletters can be found by visiting the Internet Resources section at the end of this chapter.

Photo Newsletters

Photo newsletters represent a variation on written newsletters. Instead of printed columns, photo newsletters primarily contain photographs of children engaged in classroom lessons and other activities. Photo newsletters are especially useful for families with limited reading skills as well as those with busy work schedules. They also are useful following holidays and classroom celebrations when there are many photographs to share with families. Remember to summarize the significance of each photograph. For example, you may choose to comment on a learning objective or a social behavior. Finally, remember to check with your principal to determine if photo releases are needed.

FYI 13.7   Directions to Parents for the Interactive Bulletin Board

PARENTS!

This week we have been learning about animal habits. See how much we have learned! Ask your child the following questions about this bulletin board.

1. What type of *habitat* is this?
2. Show me an animal that is *camouflaging* itself.
3. Why is the animal camouflaging itself?

Use the craft materials on the table and work with your child to create an animal that lives in this habitat. Be as creative as you like! Be sure to camouflage your animal!

Internet Sites

Many if not most schools today already use the Internet to communicate with families. Links found on these sites may include staff directories, various forms, family handbooks, announcements, menus, calendars, lesson summaries, and family resources for supporting children's homework and classroom learning objectives. Some schools also include a private "family portal." Each family is assigned a password so its members can enter the portal and review teacher comments about the child's academic work, review the results of academic assessments, make payments, track the child's attendance, and/or arrange parent-teacher conferences. The Internet offers still other options.

- Link a classroom video camera to your website. Invite families to use their password to view live shots of their children's classroom activities.
- Establish an Internet chat room for families who prefer not to be listed in a telephone or email directory but would still like to stay in touch with other families.
- Post a "tip of the day" that elaborates on the materials placed in children's daily folders. Post a "Q&A" link to respond to frequently asked questions.
- Also post a "supply list" link to assist families in shopping for school materials.
- Create a series of electronic photo stories with captions, music, and narration that capture the problem solving, communication, and social processes associated with classroom projects. Again, remember to check on the need for photo releases. Visit the following website to download a free software package: www.microsoft.com/windowsxp/using/digitalphotography/PhotoStory/default.mspx.

Support families in using your website by conducting workshops to explain its content and the steps to take when maneuvering through different links. Provide tip sheets for families who cannot attend the workshops along with information about locations in the community that provide free or inexpensive access to the Internet (e.g., libraries and community centers). Examples of different school-sponsored websites are presented under the Internet Resources section at the end of this chapter. You will also have an opportunity to put your own Internet ideas to work in your Community of Learners' Field Assignment at the end of the chapter.

Parent Diaries

Parent diaries are especially useful in facilitating communication within family support groups like those presented in Chapter 11. For example, at the end of a group meeting concerning childhood diabetes, the leader might assign a topic for diary entries. The resulting entries can be shared during the next meeting as a means of structuring group discussion.

Home-Classroom Dialogue Journals

Home-classroom dialogue journals are especially useful when parents and teachers must keep in close contact. For example, a physician may ask that a child's medical condition be tracked at home and in the classroom. Likewise, a school counselor may ask a parent and teacher to compare their observations of a child's behavior across home and classroom settings. Email, a notebook, a notepad, or some other document can be used to make brief entries (see FYI 13.8).

Podcasts

A **podcast** is an audio or video feed that can be downloaded over the Internet or through use of a portable media player, such as an iPod. Podcasts are now being used for classroom projects beginning at the elementary school level (see Lucina, 2008). Examples of popular classroom podcasts include children's oral presentations, class discussions, musical performances, and interviews. Visit the Internet Resources section at the end of this chapter to discover how one school in Burlington, North Carolina, makes use of audio and visual podcasts.

Communication Cartoons

Some have suggested that teachers use a cartoon format to explain classroom procedures to immigrant parents who do not read English (Szente, Hoot, & Taylor, 2006). This communication strategy would be equally useful for parents from the United States who have limited reading skills. The development of **communication cartoons** involves arranging small drawings or staged photographs in a sequential order to visually communicate a routine or policy. For example, cartoons might be used to visually show the routine that children follow when entering the classroom each morning, to explain classroom rules, or to depict the daily schedule.

E-Pals

Consider **e-pals**, a modern-day version of pen pals. Family members can, with a parent's approval, sign up for email newsletters and photographs that keep them current on activities being carried out by their grandchildren, nieces, or nephews (Ray & Shelton, 2004). This communication strategy is especially useful for family members living in other regions of

FYI 13.8 A Home-Classroom Dialogue Journal

Teacher	Parent
January 12 *Jen continues to be withdrawn in class. I implemented our plan to look for opportunities to encourage her to interact and communicate with her peers. I also reinforced all her efforts (no matter how small) with smiles and hugs.*	January 19 *Thanks for the update. Jen's second play therapy session seemed to go well. The counselor told me to be patient. It will take time. We should continue reinforcing any small improvements we see.*
January 26 *This week, Jen displayed a little progress. She is now asking me a few questions. However, she still refuses to talk about her work with the other children. I'm following the counselor's advice to be patient.*	February 2 *Thanks for your positive thoughts. Jen asked about her next appointment with her "play doctor." I hope that means she is benefiting from her counseling sessions.*
February 9 *I think this is the week you visit what Jen calls her "play doctor." I hope things go well. I continue to reinforce Jen's developing social skills. She has been a bit more verbal. ONE NEW DEVELOPMENT.* *Yesterday, Jen played with another child. We were careful not to overdo our attention, but we made sure they sat next to each other at lunch. The other child is also shy. I am hopeful this is the beginning of a new friendship.*	February 16 *Jen had another good "play" session. I shared our journal with the counselor. She would like us to continue communicating every week for a while longer . . . if that is ok with you.*

the country or abroad. For example, you might invite a military father who is serving in a foreign country to be an e-pal with his daughter. You might also work with transnational families to set up e-pal exchanges. If photographs are included in the exchanges, make sure they depict only the target child. Alternatively, seek releases from the parents of the other children shown in the photographs.

We now turn to what is perhaps the most common form of family-teacher communication: the parent-teacher conference. As you will see, there are a number of considerations to keep in mind when carrying out a successful conference.

Parent-Teacher Conferences

Parent-teacher conferences serve multiple purposes beyond review of children's report cards:

- They provide opportunities for parents to share information about changes in children's personal lives that can impact their classroom performance.
- They provide opportunities for parents and teachers to discuss classroom practices and school policies.
- They provide opportunities for parents and teachers to discuss and make plans for addressing children's interests, strengths, and challenges.

- They allow parents and teachers to engage in social conversations and build positive partnerships.

In this section, three aspects of parent-teacher conferences are examined. First, the steps involved in planning a parent-teacher conference are reviewed. Then issues related to facilitating the conference are addressed. Finally, guides for reviewing report cards with parents are presented.

Planning the Conference

The exact number of parent-teacher conferences you conduct each year will vary depending on the school where you teach. Regardless of their frequency, careful planning is required to ensure each conference goes smoothly. Guides for planning parent-teacher conferences are presented in this section.

Arrange a conference date and location. Schedule a mutually convenient date and time to meet. In most cases you will want to conduct the parent-teacher conference in your classroom so parents can see their children's learning environment. Some parents will prefer to meet early in the morning on their way to work while others will prefer to meet late in the afternoon on their way home from work. Although it is never ideal, it may at times be necessary to conduct parent-teacher conferences using email or cell phones. At still other times you may need to meet in a child's home, at a parent's work site, at a community center, or at some other safe location. If so, try to conduct the conference in as private and quiet a space as possible.

Prepare the meeting location. Regardless of the meeting space, make it comfortable and conducive to an exchange of information and ideas. For example, keep the seating arrangement open. Arrange chairs so they face each other or, better yet, place chairs around a table where everyone has easy access to the materials that are to be reviewed. Avoid sitting behind a desk as this projects a power hierarchy. Keep distractions to a minimum by clearing the table of all materials except those needed for the conference. Ideally, the materials and assessments you select should reflect the development and education of the whole child. Finally, if parents choose to develop a family portfolio, encourage them to bring it with them to the conference.

Set a realistic conference schedule. Allow enough time during the conference for a review and discussion of portfolio materials. Usually, 15 to 20 minutes will suffice (Seplocha, 2004), although in some cases more time may be needed. Include 5 to 10 minutes between conferences to accommodate parents who may arrive late, give yourself enough time to summarize your notes from the previous meeting (Seplocha, 2004), review materials for the next meeting, and make a quick visit to the bathroom.

Know who is coming. One or both parents may attend the parent-teacher conference. As noted in earlier chapters, some parents may bring along relatives or caregivers. Identify who is coming to the conference so you can greet everyone by name and arrange sufficient seating.

Send out a confirmation note with an agenda. Include information about the date, time, and location of the conference. Summarize the purpose of the conference and invite parents to provide you with topics they would like to include on the conference agenda. One example of a confirmation note is presented in FYI 13.9.

FYI 13.9   Confirmation of a Parent-Teacher Conference

[Date]

Dear Mr. and Ms. Tully:

I look forward to our conference on [date]. We will meet in Alex's classroom from 4:00 to 4:15 p.m. We will review Alex's work and share our thoughts about his progress. Below, I have listed a few items I would like to discuss during our conference. Let me know if you have items you would like to add to this list. I will be happy to add them.

- Welcome
- Discuss issues of importance to Mr. and Ms. Tully
- Review Alex's report card and classroom portfolio
- Set goals for classroom and/or home
- Final questions and review of conference

I look forward to our conference on [date]. Please let me know if you plan to bring others with you so I can provide enough chairs.

Sincerely yours,

Ms. Adams

Provide families with questions they might like to ask. This will help facilitate an active dialogue, especially in situations where parents do not feel comfortable interacting with a teacher. The questions, like those in Tip Box 13.2, can go in the family handbook or on a tip sheet you attach to the confirmation note.

TIP BOX 13.2   Questions Parents May Want to Ask Teachers

Below are a few questions parents sometimes ask me about during parent-teacher conferences. These are just examples. Feel free to ask your own questions.

- "What are my child's strengths?"
- "What can I do at home to reinforce these strengths?"
- "Are there areas where my child needs to show improvement?"
- "What can I do to help my child improve in these areas?"
- "How do you assess my child's academic progress?"
- "How well does my child follow classroom rules?"
- "Does my child cooperate with others?"

SOURCE: Adapted from Coleman, M. (1991). Planning for the changing nature of family life in schools for young children. *Young Children, 46*(4), 15–20. Reprinted with permission from the National Association for the Education of Young Children (NAEYC). www.naeyc.org.

Facilitating the Conference

The day of the conference has arrived! Facilitate a smooth conference by keeping in mind the communication practices we reviewed at the beginning of this chapter. They will ensure everyone is heard, statements are clarified, and questions are answered. Also remember that each parent-teacher conference has a beginning, middle, and end.

The beginning: Set a positive tone. There are a number of ways to do this. First, be prompt. Avoid keeping parents waiting, as this will reflect badly on your professionalism. Second, remember to welcome everyone by name. Third, conduct a quick tour of the classroom if time permits. If not, use classroom displays like those noted earlier in this chapter to quickly point out children's classroom activities. Finally, begin the meeting with a positive statement about the child. This is standard practice for any parent-teacher conference. The positive statement may involve some aspect of the child's classroom work, a social skill, a unique talent, something humorous the child did in the classroom, or a courtesy the child extended to others.

The middle: Communicate efficiently. This is where most of the conference work gets done. Begin by passing out and reviewing the agenda. Then let parents go first, since you will have placed their issues at the top of the agenda. If parents do not raise issues prior to the conference, ask again if they have questions or concerns they would like to discuss. Next proceed to a review of the report card. We will examine this task later in this section.

Monitor the amount of time you spend talking versus listening. Facilitate an open dialogue by letting parents know you are eager to hear their views. Also take notes on important points, especially those that require follow-up. However, avoid taking long or too many notes, as parents may feel you are not listening to them. Give parents a three- to five-minute alert before the conference ends. Ask if they have any final questions or concerns.

In some cases it may be necessary to develop a plan of action that addresses an academic or behavioral challenge. This most likely will require an additional meeting. When developing the plan, identify the steps to be taken at home and in the classroom. Also establish a schedule for reporting back on how the plan is going.

The end: Focus on the positive. All the work done during the parent-teacher conference can be undone if there is a lack of attention to details at the end. Consider using the following guidelines. First, summarize the major points discussed during the conference. Ask parents if they agree with your summary or if they have other interpretations of what was discussed. Second, summarize your understanding of goals that were set. Again, do parents agree with your summary? If not, more discussion is needed. Third, end on a positive note, even if disagreements arose during the conference. Thanking parents for their time and input is one way to end the conference. Another approach is to mention something positive about the conference, whether it be a suggestion made by a parent, an insightful comment, or the sharing of new information. Fourth, send parents a summary of the conference. This can be done via email, a letter, or a thank you note (see FYI 13.10).

Finally, follow through on anything you promised during the conference, no matter how small. This might be a promise to research a topic, check with an administrator about a question that was raised, or begin work on a goal that was set. Failure to follow through on any of these or other promises will raise questions about your dependability as a teacher.

FYI 13.10   Thank You Note Following a Parent-Teacher Conference

Thank You!

[Date]
Dear Ms. Tully:

Thank you for taking time from your busy schedule to attend Alex's parent-teacher conference. I enjoy working with Alex and was delighted to learn that he is eager to talk about his classroom activities at home. We both agreed that Alex is making good progress in all his subjects. As we discussed, I will encourage Alex to slow down when writing. We both will reinforce Alex's efforts at writing neatly.

I look forward to our next conference. In the meantime, don't hesitate to contact me should you have questions or concerns about our conference, Alex, or the classroom.

Sincerely yours,

Ms. Adams

Reviewing the Report Card

For the typical parent, reviewing the report card will be the most important component of the parent-teacher conference. It is thus important that you practice reviewing this document. Begin by considering the following guidelines. They will round out the communication strategies and tips covered earlier in this chapter. Then complete the role plays in Case Study 13.3.

- **Identify priorities.** You may not have time to cover every part of a report card, especially if it is lengthy. Provide balance by leading with a few areas where the student shows strength. Then focus on areas where improvement is needed.
- **Explain the grading system.** This is important because your school's report card may include letter or number grades, visual elements such as bar graphs, or some other type of grading system. For example, suppose a report card includes the grades "ES = exceeds standards," "MS = meets standards," and "NI = needs improvement." It is important that you explain the exact meaning of these designations before reviewing the report card. In some cases, this may involve a review of state standards. If so, provide parents with a user-friendly version of this document.
- **Give specific reasons for the grades a child received.** Was the decision based solely on class exams? Do any of the grades include bonus points, homework assignment points, project points, or other considerations?
- **Support grades with other assessments and explanations.** For example, some teachers pair children's portfolios with their report cards to emphasize the level of progress between grading periods. Also review the steps you took between grading periods to alert children to their performance, assist them in making progress, and keep parents informed and engaged.
- **Encourage parental input throughout the process.** Ask parents to interrupt you to ask questions and seek clarification at any point. Otherwise, they may leave the conference confused or angry.

- **Provide supports.** For each child, identify a tip sheet, backpack, activity card, Internet source, or other item that parents can take home with them. Explain how it will help parents maintain or support their children's academic strengths and/or challenges.

CASE STUDY 13.3   Role Plays: Reviewing Report Cards

For this case study, collect report cards from local elementary schools. If this is not possible, visit the following websites and print out the report cards posted by various schools. Divide into groups of three. Each person should take turns rotating through three roles: parent, teacher, and observer. Before meeting with the parent, the teacher should complete a report card that reflects the performance of an imaginary child. Then use the information from this chapter to review the report card with the parent. The parent should ask questions as the conference unfolds. At the end, the observer should summarize his or her thoughts about the conference in general and the teacher's review of the report card in particular.

- Issaquah School District 411, Issaquah, Washington: www.issaquah.wednet.edu/academics/fieldtest.aspx
- Jefferson County Public Schools, Golden, Colorado: http://sc.jeffco.k12.co.us/education/components/docmgr/default.php?sectiondetailid=229213&catfilter=ALL#showDoc
- Murrieta Unified School District, Murrieta, California: www.murrieta.k12.ca.us/site/Default.aspx?PageID=83
- Department of Education and Early Childhood Development, Victorian State Government, Melbourne, Victoria, Australia: www.education.vic.gov.au/studentlearning/studentreports/samples/default.htm

---

CHAPTER SUMMARY

- Communication is a dual responsibility. In this chapter, a number of strategies were reviewed for helping the listener and speaker meet their responsibilities.
- A few practical tips that teachers can use to facilitate family-teacher contact include, among others, making contact with all families during the first week of class, setting up an ongoing system of contacts, and communicating good news as well as bad news.
- There are a number of communication strategies available to teachers, making it much easier to stay in touch with families.
- Practice makes perfect. Take every opportunity to practice the communication strategies and skills reviewed in this chapter.

NOTE

1. With the kind permission from Springer Science+Business Media. *Early Childhood Education Journal, 34*(2), 125–132, Sohn, S., & Wang, C. (2006). *Immigrant parents' involvement in American schools: Perspectives from Korean mothers.*

DISCUSSION QUESTIONS

1. Based on your personal observations and experiences, discuss whether or not teachers receive adequate communication training.

2. Which communication strategies are you most likely to use? Which strategies are you least likely to use? Discuss the reasoning behind your selections.

3. **Your family involvement philosophy.** Return to the draft of your family involvement philosophy. Based on your reading of this chapter, what if any changes will you make to your philosophy statement? Discuss your answer to this question with your peers.

COMMUNITY OF LEARNERS' FIELD ASSIGNMENT

Design a Classroom Internet Site

Divide into small groups and have each group represent a specific grade level, prekindergarten through fifth grade. Design a classroom website for your grade level. You may find it helpful to visit the sites listed under the Internet Resources section of this chapter. Then visit the free Google site at the following Internet address: www .google.com/sites/overview.html. This site provides a number of free and ready-made templates, including a template for classrooms. Share your results in class.

CAPSTONE ACTIVITIES

Activity 1: Develop an Interactive Bulletin Board

Working in small groups, put up separate interactive bulletin boards or use trifold posters to create mobile interactive bulletin boards. Critique each bulletin board.

Activity 2: Review Classroom Newsletters

Collect classroom newsletters from teachers in your community. Post the newsletters on the walls around your classroom. Compare the different newsletter formats and columns. What are the strengths of the different newsletters?

Activity 3: Communication Role Plays

Join with a peer to role-play the following communication scenarios. One person can assume the role of parent and the other the role of teacher. As you take turns, allow each parent to round out and elaborate on each scenario. For example, each parent may assume different emotions (e.g., whining, angry, sad, happy, calm, hyperactive, confused). Each parent may also adopt different approaches (e.g., rational, nonsensical, vague, detailed, reasonable, unreasonable, pleading, threatening, cooperative). As the teacher, use the following communication review guidelines to facilitate a productive exchange:

1. Begin by listening to what is said while also assessing the parent's emotional demeanor.

2. Clarify the reasons behind the parent's demeanor and storyline.

3. Remain diplomatic throughout your exchange by, for example, focusing on the issue and not the person.

4. Check that your communication has been appropriately received.

5. Persevere if you at first encounter difficulties.

6. Regardless of the nature of the exchange, end by thanking the parent for his or her request, statement, or complaint.

- Role Play Scenario #1: A parent asks that you allow her child to retake a math test
- Role Play Scenario #2: A parent states that she would prefer that her child be taught by another teacher
- Role Play Scenario #3: A parent asks that you personally tutor her son three days a week after school
- Role Play Scenario #4: A father presents you with a medical bill, explaining that his son's inner ear infection resulted from inappropriate care at school
- Role Play Scenario #5: A parent complains that you gave her son a B on his science project

INTERNET RESOURCES

You may find that some URLs have been altered by the webmaster. In these situations, try entering the name of the document or agency in a search engine. Alternatively, enter the domain name (e.g., http://www.xxxx.org). This should take you to the revised home page and associated links.

Center for Appropriate Dispute Resolution in Special Education (CADRE): Educating Our Children Together: A Sourcebook for Effective Family-School-Community Partnerships

http://www.directionservice.org/cadre/EducatingOurChildren_01.cfm

When visiting this website, click on "Strategy 4: Developing family-friendly communication." Here you will find case studies of how schools have used various communication strategies, many addressed in this chapter, to communicate with families.

PTA National Standards for Family-School Partnerships Assessment Guide

http://www.pta.org/National_Standards_Assessment_Guide.pdf

You will recall from Chapter 2 that "communicating effectively" is the second of six family involvement standards endorsed by the National PTA. The above link takes you to the assessment guide for all six PTA family involvement standards, including the standard of "communicating effectively."

George Mason University, Graduate School of Education: Improving Student Achievement by Increasing School-Family Communication and Family Involvement

http://gse.gmu.edu/research/lmtip/arp/vol3/

Visit this webpage to read about the results obtained by two elementary school teachers who studied family-school communication strategies at their school. Scroll down to the Family Involvement heading. Then look for the teacher entry from Carlin Springs Elementary.

#Edchat

http://teacherbootcamp.edublogs.org/2009/07/30/what-is-edchat/

Join this site to tweet about educational issues. Among other benefits, you can learn about new resources, collaborate with others in solving a school-based problem, and gain tips on conducting parent-teacher conferences and family workshops.

Examples of Kindergarten and Prekindergarten Newsletters

Visit the following websites to view the content and format of different classroom newsletters.

Tallula Elementary, Petersburg, Illinois: Ms. Lambert's Classroom Newsletter

http://www.porta202.org/vnews/display.v/ART/47502650a9e00

Rochester City School District, Rochester, New York: Prekindergarten News

http://www.rcsdk12.org/rcsd/site/default.asp

Clink on PreK Information, then Prekindergarten and finally Prekindergarten Newsletter.

Vestal Universal Pre-kindergarten News

http://www.vestal.stier.org/pdf_downloads/UPK/news/UPKNews910.pdf

Examples of Fourth- and Fifth-Grade Newsletters

Mitch Charter School, Tigard, Oregon: Fourth-Grade Newsletter

http://www.mitchcharterschool.org/

Click on "School Life" and then on "Classes." Select a grade and read their newsletter.

Wilson's Creek 5th–6th School, Battlefield, Missouri

http://sps.k12.mo.us/wilsonscreek/

Scroll over the "Academics" tab and click on "5th Grade" to view the monthly newsletter. Also check out the "5th Grade Supply List."

Teacher- and Elementary-Sponsored Internet Sites

Visit the following websites to get a feel for communication strategies used by teachers and elementary schools around the United States.

Welcome to Mrs. Holmberg's Third Grade Class

http://www.cedargrove.k12.nj.us/south/3eweb/index.htm

Visit this website to see the content of a New Jersey teacher's classroom Internet home page. Click on the "Friday Folders" link to see how the teacher introduces parents to this communication device.

Greenbrook Elementary School, Kendall Park, New Jersey

http://www.sbschools.org/schools/gb/school_information/friday_folders/index.php

Visit this website to see the electronic Friday Folders posted by teachers from this New Jersey elementary school.

Delaware City Schools, Delaware, Ohio

http://www.dcs.k12.oh.us/delawarecs/site/default.asp

Click on the "For Parents and Students" link to see the different type of information this school shares with parents.

Blanchard Elementary School, Cape Girardeau, Missouri

http://www.cape.k12.mo.us/blanchard/

This school's webpage includes a number of links that will interest families. Note especially the following links: "Supply Lists by Grades," "Dates to Remember," "Blanchard Reads," and "Parent Resources." Finally, click on "Classroom Web Pages." Here you will find websites for prekindergarten through fourth grade. Pay special attention to the "2nd Grade Web Page," where you will find an example of a "notebook folder" that is sent home twice a week (click on the "T.I.G.E.R.S. Notebook" link). The purpose of this folder is to improve parent-teacher communication.

Kingsley Elementary School, Evanston, Illinois

http://kingsley.district65.net/home%20page

Click on "Parents" and then click on "e-Packets." Here you will find examples of electronic Friday Folders.

Almond Elementary School, Los Altos, California

http://www.almondschool.org/

Click on the link "Parent Information" to review various school events, activities, and supports that will interest families.

Marvin B. Smith Elementary School, Burlington, North Carolina

http://mse.abss.k12.nc.us/

Click on the "Video Page" link to view examples of how this school makes use of audio/visual podcasts to communicate with families about classroom learning activities and school projects.

O'Hara Elementary School, Pittsburgh, Pennsylvania

http://www.fcasd.edu/j_ohara/

Click on the various links to view the information shared with parents by the administrators and teachers at this school.

Wilson Elementary School, Petamula, California

http://www.wilsonschoolpetaluma.org/

Click on the "Parents" link and then the "Parent Forums" link to read a brief discussion of how this school uses the Internet to facilitate parent discussions and projects. Please note that you will not be able to see the forum in action, since the school requires a registration process in order to protect the privacy of parents who choose to participate in this type of communication.

STUDENT STUDY SITE

Log on to the Web-based student study site at **www.sagepub.com/coleman** for additional study tools including

- eFlashcards
- Web Quizzes
- Links to SAGE Journal Articles
- Author-created Videos

- Learning Objectives
- Web Resources
- Family Involvement Portfolio Guides

CHAPTER 14

Organizing Your Family Involvement Program

You have been introduced to a number of family involvement strategies in this textbook, all of which can empower family-teacher partnerships. On the other hand, making effective use of these strategies requires an organizational plan. In this chapter we examine three models that meet this objective. We begin with a narrow curriculum-based model (family involvement webs), then look at a broader model that uses various family involvement roles, and finally review a comprehensive school reform model (Comer's school development program model). It is up to you to decide which of the models you prefer. This chapter is designed to help you make that decision.

COMMUNITY LEARNING GUIDE

As you read this chapter, take notes on the following items. Use your notes to address the Reflections, Discussion Questions, Field Assignment, and Capstone Activities that you find in the chapter.

- Describe the steps involved in developing a family involvement web.
- Give examples of activities that are associated with support, teacher, student, advocate, protector, and ambassador family involvement roles.
- Describe the purpose of James Comer's school development program model as well as its structure, process, and operations.
- Describe steps teachers can take to facilitate families' participation in brainstorming family involvement activity ideas.

Model 1: Webbing Family Involvement

Family involvement webs follow a curriculum-based planning approach. More specifically, they provide a visual picture of linkages between classroom- and home-based activities, all of which are tied to a central educational theme (Coleman & Wallinga, 2000) In this section, we review the benefits of family involvement webs. We also review the structure of family involvement webs and steps for constructing them.

The information in this chapter supports the following family-school-community partnership standards. These standards are reviewed in Chapter 2.

NAEYC Standards and Associated Key Elements	1b, 1c, 2c, 6c, 6d
ACEI Standards	5.1, 5.2
PTA Standards	1, 2, 3, 4, 5, 6

Benefits of Using Family Involvement Webs

One example of a family involvement web devoted to the theme of transportation is presented in FYI 14.1. Another example of a web devoted to the theme of fall can be found at Ms. Adams's family involvement portfolio on the student study site accompanying this text (see Section IV). These family involvement webs fulfill a number of objectives:

- They allow teachers to document the link between classroom lessons and family involvement activities.
- They visually demonstrate teachers' commitment to planning for families' engagement in their children's education.
- They can be incorporated into parent-teacher conferences as a means of comparing children's use of concepts and skills in the classroom and at home.
- They reinforce the message that both the teacher and the family have important roles to play in helping children master new skills and knowledge.
- They promote the importance of the classroom community's coming together for the good of all children. That is, families are able to see how their participation in a particular family involvement activity relates to other activities in the web.

The Structure of Family Involvement Webs

As demonstrated in FYI 14.1, family involvement webs are simple to construct. In short, they consist of a center point and two rings.

- The **center point** contains the name of a thematic unit (e.g., Transportation) that is surrounded by lessons from two or more subject areas (see FYI 14.1). Alternatively, you may choose to make the center point a learning theme (e.g., Bodies of Water) that is surrounded by lessons from just one subject area (e.g., Geography). In this chapter, we use a thematic unit focus.
- The **inner** or **first ring** contains classroom lessons that support the thematic unit.
- The **outer** or **second ring** contains family involvement activities that support the classroom lessons.

FYI 14.1   Family Involvement Web: Thematic Unit—Transportation

Classroom Newsletter Column:

"Ideas for Teaching Your Child About Traffic Signs"

↑

Classroom Lesson #1: Social Studies

Traffic Sign Safety

↕

Classroom Lesson #3: Math & Geography   *Classroom Lesson #2: Social Studies*

Maps ◄——► TRANSPORTATION ◄——► Emergency Vehicles

↓   ↓

Family Backpack: **Classroom Visit:**

Mapping Your Neighborhood   Parents who are first
                                                                              responders will bring their
                                                                              vehicles to school

Unit Goal. Children will be introduced to transportation issues in their local community.

Classroom Lesson #1: Traffic Sign Safety. Children will learn the purpose of traffic signs and how to respond to them.

   Family Involvement: Classroom Newsletter Column. A newsletter column will be written about children's study of traffic signs. Tips will be provided on how families can reinforce children's understanding of traffic signs within their neighborhoods.

Classroom Lesson #2: Emergency Vehicles. Children will learn about the purpose of emergency vehicles.

   Family Involvement: Parents' Visit to the Classroom. Ask Ashley's dad (a police officer) and William's mom (a paramedic) to visit the classroom to give a demonstration on how they use their vehicles to carry out their jobs as first responders.

Classroom Lesson #3: Maps. Children will learn how to use a legend to interpret maps related to transportation. For example, they will learn how to distinguish among different types of roads; how to identify buildings, railroad lines, and airports; and how to estimate distances between locations.

   Family Involvement: Family Backpack. Families and children will develop a map of their respective neighborhoods. An interactive bulletin board will be created using the returned maps. Families and children will use the interactive bulletin board to identify specific locations and measure distances between locations.

Constructing Family Involvement Webs

Step 1: Identify a theme. As noted earlier, web construction begins with the identification of a central theme that in turn guides lesson development. Note that in FYI 14.1 transportation is used as the thematic unit. For a further explanation of thematic units, visit Ms. Adams's family involvement portfolio on the student study site accompanying this text (see Section III, the Family Handbook, Subsection D). Finally, remember to start small and be selective when identifying units to accompany family involvement webs. For example, work on developing webs for one or two units during your first year of teaching. Then develop webs for a few additional units in following years.

Step 2: Identify classroom lessons to link to the thematic unit. Just as not all units need a family involvement web, not all classroom lessons associated with a thematic unit need to be represented in a web. This would be too much to reasonably manage, even for a seasoned teacher. Instead, follow Reality Check #8 by selecting only a few lessons that reinforce key learning objectives. This will make it easier to tie those objectives to family involvement activities.

Now return to FYI 14.1. Note that the teacher selected three classroom lessons for inclusion in this family involvement web. The first lesson is on traffic sign safety, the second deals with emergency vehicles, and the third involves the study of maps. While other lessons will be taught as part of the transportation theme, the teacher wisely focuses on keeping the family involvement web manageable and practical by focusing on only three lessons.

Step 3: Identify family involvement activities to support classroom lessons. Web construction concludes with the planning of family involvement activities that will be linked to the classroom lessons from Step 2. Thus, as noted in FYI 14.1, three family involvement activities complete the transportation web, one for each of the three lessons represented in the first ring of the web. These activities include writing a column for the classroom newsletter on what children are learning about traffic signs, inviting two parents to bring their first responder emergency vehicles to school, and developing a family backpack for families and children to complete at home.

Deciding on which family involvement activities to include in a web is guided by two general rules. First, include only activities that you can realistically support. Use the information in Chapter 10 to guide you. Second, consider the interests of families by engaging them in the planning process. We return to this topic at the end of this chapter. For now, consider how you might use different roles to organize your family involvement activities.

Parents may assume many different roles within and outside the classroom.

Model 2: Family Involvement Roles

This broader-based model matches the skills and interests of individual parents to different family involvement roles that can be played out at home, in the classroom, and in the community. Brief descriptions of six family involvement roles are presented in FYI 14.2, along with descriptions of the types of parents who are likely to show an interest in assuming each role. As you will no doubt discover as you read on, any given family involvement activity can be assigned to more than one role, depending on how it is defined and structured.

Some parents may enjoy assuming a particular family involvement role while others may prefer multiple roles. Remember, however, that not all roles have to be represented in your family involvement plan. It is better to use a few well-selected roles that meet families' interests than to overwhelm them with roles they find uninteresting.

FYI 14.2   Family Involvement Roles

Role	Description of Role	Parents Who Might Enjoy This Role
Support	Parents assume a behind-the-scenes role to support the teacher in preparing for or carrying out classroom lessons and other activities. Support can be provided in the classroom or at home.	• Those who do not yet feel comfortable working directly with children • Those with busy work schedules or who travel as part of their job • Those whose personal preferences best match a behind-the-scenes role
Teacher	Parents work directly with children to carry out learning activities in the classroom, at home, or in the community.	• Those who work with their children on family backpacks, activity calendars, and other activities sent home by the teacher • Those who enjoy tutoring individual children • Those who enjoy sharing their hobbies with children • Those who enjoy helping the teacher develop and/or carry out classroom lessons
Student	Parents attend workshops or classes to advance their knowledge and skills, thereby improving the well-being of their families.	• Those who seek life enrichment experiences as part of the lifelong learning process • Those who seek new technical skills to advance their careers • Those who seek to advance their formal education • Those who seek workshops devoted to child guidance or strategies for promoting their children's education
Advocate	Parents take part in activities that promote the best interests of their children and the children of other families.	• Those who have specific concerns about their child's rights, education, and well-being • Those who are concerned about the rights, education, and well-being of children in general
Protector	Parents help to ensure the physical and emotional safety of children.	• Those who have an interest in childhood health and safety issues • Those who have an interest in contemporary social topics such as bullying, violence, and social justice
Ambassador	Parents help to facilitate positive relationships between families and teachers.	• Those who serve as translators for non-English-speaking families • Those who enjoy facilitating the work of parent committees • Those who enjoy serving on advisory committees to help the teacher think through classroom policies and practices

SOURCE: Adapted from Coleman, M. (2007). A family bill of rights. *Democracy and Education, 16*(4), 6–14; Coleman, M., & Wallinga, C. (2000). Connecting families and classroom using family involvement webs. *Childhood Education, 76*(4), 209–214.

Parents in the Support Role

The **support role** involves working behind the scenes to help teachers prepare for upcoming activities and events. Examples of traditional and contemporary activities associated with this role are summarized below.

Traditional Support Role Activities

- Helping with fundraisers such as bake sales and raffles
- Putting up informational bulletin boards
- Helping to prepare educational materials for use in the classroom
- Making copies of handouts, educational materials, and classroom newsletters
- Helping to organize the teacher's desk
- Taking classroom attendance
- Helping with classroom celebrations
- Sending in materials from home to support classroom lessons
- Helping to put up tables and chairs for family workshops
- Preparing refreshments for classroom celebrations and family workshops

Contemporary Support Role Activities

- Helping to keep the family resource center organized
- Staffing the family resource center and providing help to visitors
- Writing articles, taking photographs, or making drawings for the classroom newsletter
- Using the teacher's lesson plan to organize classroom materials
- Helping the teacher take inventory of and order classroom supplies
- Gathering information about television programs and community events to share with other families
- Helping the teacher put together daily folders, podcasts, Internet content, and classroom displays
- Helping the teacher make random acts of kindness awards, family certificates, and thank you notes
- Using the teacher's family workshop plan to gather materials and organize a room in preparation for a workshop
- Summarizing evaluation forms from family workshops and family backpacks

While some of the above traditional support activities may seem outdated, this is not true. Today, even more than in the past, administrative paperwork and committee tasks eat away at teachers' time. Behind-the-scenes support gives back to teachers the time they need to plan and carry out instructional tasks. Likewise, teachers continue to look to traditional fundraising events, such as bake sales, as an avenue by which to finance many of the family involvement strategies reviewed in this textbook.

It is important to remember that support role activities can be carried out in the classroom as well as at home, providing both teachers and parents with a great deal of flexibility. The support role also represents a nonthreatening way to help parents transition into more active roles. Consider, for example, the following quote from a teacher involved in a family involvement program serving migrant families:

> When we were walking in, you probably saw two ladies at a bulletin board. Those were parents. Migrant parents. They feel ownership of what they're doing. They take pride that they're fixing the bulletin board outside the parent center. We didn't tell them to do it. They did it by themselves. (Lopez, Scribner, & Mahitivanichcha, 2001, pp. 269–270)

Parents in the Teacher Role

Parents assume the **teacher role** when they facilitate children's learning experiences in the classroom or at home. The manner by which parents assume the teacher role can vary, just as it can for the support role. For example, some parents may choose to work with individual children or small groups of children in the classroom, while others may prefer to work with the entire class. Some parents may prefer activities that can be accomplished within one classroom visit, while others may prefer to take on a classroom project that extends over a period of weeks. Some parents may prefer to assist the teacher in carrying out existing classroom lessons, while others may prefer to help develop new lessons. Finally, some parents may prefer to limit their teacher role activities to helping their own children in their own home.

Whatever their preference, everyone benefits from parents serving as teachers. Children benefit from the extra support they receive from adults, including their own parents. Parents benefit by gaining confidence in their ability to contribute to the education of their children and the children of other families. Teachers benefit from becoming more familiar with families and using their unique skills and talents to enrich the classroom learning environment. A sampling of teacher role activities that parents can carry out in the classroom, at home, or in the community are presented below:

- Teaching children new skills and hobbies
- Helping to plan and carry out field trips
- Reading to children and listening to children read
- Checking children's classroom assignments and providing them with feedback
- Telling children stories
- Facilitating children's learning activities and projects
- Tutoring individual children
- Listening to and talking with children about their learning experiences
- Providing encouragement to children with unique needs or interests
- Helping students who have been absent make up missed lessons
- Helping the teacher develop and demonstrate family backpacks, activity calendars, activity cards, and other home-based educational materials

Parents as teachers in the classroom. You will want to prepare parents who volunteer to help in the classroom. Some basic preparation tasks include letting parents know what types of clothes they should wear, providing them with name tags, asking parents to observe you working with children on a task before inviting them to assist, and educating parents about the classroom schedule and classroom rules (Desteno, 2000). Also show parents how to use classroom materials and equipment. Share with them the strategies you use to get children's attention, redirect their behavior, and help them make smooth transitions. Give parents examples of common abbreviations, words, and phrases that are used in the classroom. Finally, alert parents to any unique behaviors or communication patterns exhibited by individual children so that misunderstandings are avoided.

Parents as teachers at home. Not all parents are aware of the many educational opportunities associated with the home environment. For example, parents with limited resources may need help in identifying how common household materials and daily routines can be used to support children's education. Reinforce and extend parents' views of themselves as teachers by providing them with a tip sheet of inexpensive in-home learning opportunities, such as the ones presented in Tip Box 14.1. Encourage parents to share their home activities with others during family workshops, in the classroom newsletter, or on the classroom website.

TIP BOX 14.1   Parent-as-Teacher Activities for the Home: A Tip Sheet

- **Waiting for the bus.** While waiting for the bus, ask your child to identify the types of vehicles that pass (cars, dump trucks, ambulances, police cars, garbage collection trucks). Why are these different types of vehicles needed? Are the vehicles traveling fast or slow? Are their speeds justified? These questions are especially helpful for teaching young children about community life and civic responsibilities (e.g., pulling your car over to the side of the road when the lights on an ambulance are flashing).
- **Family routines.** Use your daily routine to teach your child educational concepts. For example, invite older children to help sort garbage into different recycling bins. Count and graph the types of items that are placed in each bin. Use the graph to compare and track the types and amount of garbage your family is recycling. For younger children, note the different geometric shapes that are formed as your child helps you fold napkins and clothes (squares, triangles, rectangles). Encourage your child to count the number of plates, cups, and utensils she or he places on the table before a meal. Encourage your child to practice subtraction skills as she or he clears the table.
- **Talk to and sing songs with children.** These activities will help build your child's language skills.
- **Watching television with children.** Watching television with your child presents an ideal opportunity to talk about appropriate and inappropriate behavior displayed by TV characters.
- **Milk and juice cartons.** Make these into planters by cutting them in half, washing them, and punching holes in the bottom for drainage. Plant an inexpensive window or patio garden for your child to care for and observe as part of a home-based science lesson. For example, ask older children to draw each plant at different stages of maturity (the drawings do not have to be perfect or pretty!). Place the drawings in a "nature notebook" for a review of changes in each plant's foliage and/or flowers. Identify and record the insects, birds, or butterflies that visit each plant.
- **Socks.** Young children can use socks to learn how to name and classify colors, to order items by their length, and to compare different textures and uses.
- **Boxes of different shapes and sizes.** Younger children can use empty shoe, cereal, and other household boxes to construct tunnels, highways, and buildings. Encourage your child's creativity, math, and problem solving skills by asking her or him to construct buildings of different lengths, heights, and widths. Provide a ruler or measuring tape to reinforce your child's understanding of measurement instruments.
- **Family photographs.** Use family photographs to tell your child stories about the family and to encourage her or him to ask questions and talk about her or his own life. Help your child begin her or his own family picture album.
- **Nature walks.** As you walk, talk about the importance of exercise and/or the importance of protecting the environment. Take along a bag to collect garbage. Ask younger children to name the different shapes and colors of plants, trees, and flowers. For older children, check out a plant and tree reference book from the local library. Use the reference book to identify and compare different plants and trees. Alternatively, check out a bird reference book and use it to identify and compare different species of birds.

Parents in the Student Role

Parents assume the **student role** when they take advantage of learning opportunities to advance their own knowledge and skills. Some parents already may be accustomed to taking evening or weekend classes as a means of expanding their education, keeping up with changes in technology as part of their job requirements, learning a second language, or improving their financial or time management skills. A few examples of student role activities you might help to arrange at your school are presented in Tip Box 14.2.

Parents in the Advocate Role

Families assume the **advocate role** by promoting the best interests of their children in both small and big ways. For example, a parent's simple act of briefly chatting with a teacher about a child's educational progress is a type of advocacy. Attendance at a more formal parent-teacher conference is also an important type of advocacy. Likewise, participating in a campaign to raise community awareness about child abuse is a type of advocacy, as is voting for a political candidate who a parent believes is supportive of children's issues. Examples of other family advocacy role activities are presented.

TIP BOX 14.2   **Workshops and Classes to Support the Parent-as-Student Role**

- **Make-and-take workshops.** Show parents how to make inexpensive activity folders like those described in Chapter 11. Conduct art and craft workshops so parents can have fun while making inexpensive decorations, cards, and gifts.
- **Life enrichment classes.** Collaborate with instructors at nearby colleges and universities, museums, history centers, libraries, art and craft centers, floral shops, home gardening centers, and art studios to offer classes on topics of interest to parents. For example, work with a librarian or bookstore owner to arrange monthly book club meetings. Make arrangements for a floral designer to offer a workshop on arranging flowers. Work with travel agents to conduct classes on local, state, national, and international locations of cultural and historical interest. Invite a nutritionist to conduct a demonstration on how to reduce fat and salt in our diets.
- **Technical education classes.** Collaborate with instructors at nearby technical schools, high schools, and labor departments to offer classes on technical skills related to computer software, home or auto repairs, carpentry, and other topics that can benefit parents in their workplace or at home.
- **Career classes.** Collaborate with instructors at nearby colleges, universities, and technical schools to offer GED classes, foreign language classes, and workshops designed to improve parents' résumés and their communication and job interview skills.
- **Parenting classes.** Work with community parent educators to offer general parenting classes. Also consider arranging child guidance classes for parents whose children display specific behavioral challenges or who are experiencing difficulty coping with family life stressors.
- **Family bulletin board.** Develop a family bulletin board for the hall, family resource center, or classroom website. Post brochures, newspaper columns, and magazine articles about current child and family development issues, job fairs, and community events. Some parents may enjoy helping to research materials for the bulletin board.

- Helping the teacher adapt classroom routines and lessons so they are applicable to all children
- Participating in family telephone or email directories
- Writing letters to the local newspaper about issues important to families
- Helping develop files for the family resource center with information about financial, food, clothing, furniture, nutritional, and other resources
- Attending community forums related to children's issues and summarizing the outcomes in the classroom newsletter
- Working with the teacher and other parents to write informational pamphlets about contemporary issues such as peer pressure, food allergies, and immunizations
- Helping identify representatives from community social service agencies to speak at family night workshops

A parent advisory committee is another advocacy activity you might consider pursuing. Parents who serve on this committee perform an important function in helping you think through classroom policies and practices on issues such as selecting classroom books and other materials, revising the family handbook, and planning family involvement activities. These and other committee activities not only empower families as advocates for their children, but they also reinforce your image as someone who is sincere in asking for families' input.

As a teacher, your role on the advisory committee is to facilitate thoughtful discussions and empower parents by listening to and seriously considering their suggestions. This may at times require you to compromise or take other steps. For example, if a suggestion made by the committee is not practical because of a school policy, explain the policy and help the committee explore other options. If a disagreement arises among committee members, make sure everyone is heard and discussions about the disagreement are conducted in a respectful manner.

Of all the roles available to families, the advocate role is perhaps the least understood and most threatening to parents and teachers. Think about how you might promote this role among families in your classroom by completing Reflection 14.1.

REFLECTION 14.1   Think Through an Advocate Role Activity

Identify an advocacy activity that you might offer to families. How will you explain the importance of this activity to families? Identify a challenge that you might face in planning or facilitating this activity. How will you address this challenge?

Parents in the Protector Role

The **protector role** combines elements of support, teaching, and advocacy to address the physical and emotional safety of young children. Some activities associated with the protector role are presented below. One specific example of how dads can assume the protector role is presented in Case Study 14.1.

Physical Safety

- Conducting safety inspections of classroom and playground equipment
- Repairing broken equipment
- Monitoring children's outdoor activities
- Escorting children to and from the bathroom, playground, and other school locations
- Introducing children to first-aid procedures so they know what to expect during emergencies
- Helping children practice preventive health skills, such as washing their hands and brushing their teeth
- Helping children understand what happens (and why) in a doctor's office and a dentist's office
- Helping with fire, earthquake, tornado, or tsunami drills
- Monitoring traffic, pollution, and noise levels around the school

Emotional Safety

- Helping the teacher offer verbal reinforcement to children for following classroom rules of behavior
- Helping the teacher conduct life skills activities such as dealing with strangers, discussing disagreements among peers, and identifying appropriate ways to express one's feelings
- Helping children make get well cards for sick classmates
- Helping the teacher with classroom activities that promote positive communication skills
- Learning about and teaching children noncompetitive games to help them learn how to work together to achieve a common goal

---

CASE STUDY 14.1   180 Days for 180 Dads

This program allows dads to carry out simple but important tasks throughout the school year (see Staples, 2009). For example, some dads might meet buses in the morning or help buses safely depart from school in the afternoon. Other dads might serve as crosswalk guards. Some dads might hold doors and welcome children as they enter the building. Still other dads might supervise children during breakfast, lunch, or recess. While these tasks serve multiple family involvement roles, they are especially helpful in reinforcing dads' view of themselves as "protectors" of children, families, and communities.

Parents in the Ambassador Role

Parents who assume the **ambassador role** help teachers navigate among the various family backgrounds and interests represented in a classroom. For example, the importance of recruiting translators to work with parents who do not speak English was addressed in an earlier chapter. Likewise, immigrant parents can provide you with information about parent-child relationships in their culture of origin, help you better understand the stressors immigrant families face in your community, and suggest ways to help immigrant children adapt to their new classroom.

Other ambassador activities extend beyond cultural issues. For example, some parents may have the professional training needed to facilitate support groups like those discussed in Chapter 11. Still other examples of ambassador role activities are presented below:

- Researching books and music that have to do with a particular culture or historical event
- Organizing field trips that introduce children to different cultures
- Sharing family cultural traditions with children and other families
- Coordinating an Earth Day event, a musical production, or some other school event that requires organizational, diplomatic, and leadership skills
- Serving on a planning committee whose purpose is to plan a collaborative school-community service learning project
- Helping to welcome and assist visitors who make presentations for children or families

Charting Family Involvement Roles

It is helpful to chart family involvement roles and their associated tasks so you can establish a visual summary of your planning work. Such charts also help you to think through the amount of time needed to facilitate family involvement tasks. For example, parents who sign up for support role tasks most likely will need little assistance once you show them what is to be done. On the other hand, parents who commit to working directly with children will need more assistance as they plan for and carry out their instructional responsibilities. One example of a planning chart is presented in FYI 14.3. Note that the teacher did not tie every family involvement role to every activity. Rather, he was selective in matching a few roles to a few activities, as suggested earlier in this chapter. This resulted in a more manageable family involvement plan. After reading FYI 14.3, complete Reflection 14.2. Then turn your attention to a third and final family involvement model.

Model 3: James Comer's School Development Program

Dr. James Comer of Yale University created the **school development program model** (SDP) in 1968 to address the needs of children who, because of a number of disadvantageous community, family, and school factors, were being denied a chance to participate in the U.S. economic and social mainstream (Comer, Haynes, & Joyner, 1996, pp. 1–4). In this section, we review key assumptions of this comprehensive planning model as well as its structure, processes, and operations. We end with two reflections aimed at helping you integrate family involvement webs and roles into the SDP model.

Assumptions of the School Development Program

Comer places children's development as the "keystone" to academic achievement and life success (Comer, Joyner, & Ben-Avie, 2004, pp. 16–17). Furthermore, he identifies six "developmental pathways" as laying the foundation for learning: cognitive, psychological, language,

FYI 14.3 Charting Family Involvement Roles

This chart summarizes family involvement roles associated with the three family involvement web activities from FYI 14.1.

Classroom Theme: Transportation

Family Involvement Activity ▶	Article in Classroom Newsletter	Classroom Visit From Two Parents	Family Backpack on Maps
Description of Activity ▶	*An article will be written to help parents teach children about traffic signs.*	*Parents who work as first responders will be invited to school to talk about how they use their vehicles to carry out their jobs.*	*Parents and children will construct maps of their neighborhoods.*
Support Role ▶	*Parent volunteers* will make copies of the newsletter for distribution to families. They also will help insert copies into children's daily folders.	*Parent volunteers* will prepare refreshments for the first responders and the children.	*Parent volunteers* will (a) help make copies of the backpack, (b) check returned backpacks to identify missing or torn items, (c) collect and summarize backpack evaluations, and (d) use the maps returned by parents to make an interactive bulletin board.
Teacher Role ▶	*Parent volunteers* will (a) work with the teacher to develop tips for parents on teaching their children about traffic signs and (b) search the Internet for traffic safety websites to include in the newsletter column. *All parents* will teach their children about traffic signs, using tips from the newsletter.	*Ashley's dad* (police officer) will make a class presentation that includes his squad car. *William's mom* (paramedic) will make a class presentation that includes her emergency vehicle.	*All parents* will help their children complete the backpack activity.
Student Role ▶	*All Parents* will learn about traffic safety by reading the newsletter column.		
Advocate Role ▶		*Ashley's dad and William's mom* will serve as advocates for the promotion of children's safety.	

Family Involvement Activity ▶	Article in Classroom Newsletter	Classroom Visit From Two Parents	Family Backpack on Maps
Protector Role ▶	*All parents* will help protect their children from pedestrian accidents by talking about traffic signs in their neighborhood.		*All parents* will help protect their children from pedestrian accidents by talking about the traffic signs associated with their neighborhood map.
Ambassador Role		*Ashley's dad and William's mom* will serve as ambassadors for community police officers and paramedics.	

REFLECTION 14.2   Matching Parents to Family Involvement Roles

Identify a thematic unit for any grade level, prekindergarten through fifth grade. Outline three classroom lessons that support this unit. Next, outline three family involvement activities that support each of the three classroom lessons. Finally, develop a chart that shows how different family involvement roles might be tied to the three family involvement activities.

social, ethical, and physical. Reflected in these six pathways is the **whole child perspective** that emphasizes the multiple ways children grow and develop. Comer also takes an ecological view of development, acknowledging that parents, school administrators, teachers, school support staff, and community members all have an important contribution to make in preparing children for a successful life.

Finally, the SDP model reflects the social capacity model we first examined in Chapter 1. In short, Comer and his colleagues acknowledge that community support and involvement is essential for children to develop adequately (Comer et al., 2004; Emmons, Comer, & Haynes, 1996). Put in social capacity terms, Comer recognizes the importance of a community's collective efficacy in building human capital.

The Structure, Processes, and Operations of the School Development Program

As noted earlier, the SDP model is built on three structures and three processes that are used to mobilize adults to support children's learning and overall development (Comer et al., 2004, p. 18). The model also includes three operations.

SDP structure. The hallmark of the SDP model is its three teams (Comer et al., 1996, 2004, p. 18).

- **School planning and management team.** The **school planning and management team** is the central organizing body and is responsible for developing a comprehensive school plan to address a range of goals that include the development and education of children, staff development, and family and community involvement. It also provides oversight for the coordination and monitoring of programs and activities related to established goals. Members of this team include administrators, teachers, school support staff, and parents.
- **Student and staff support team.** The **student and staff support team** is responsible for promoting a school climate that fosters students' adjustment and addresses individual student needs. Members include school support staff (e.g., counselors, school nurses) and individuals from the community with child development and mental health knowledge and experience. The team works from a preventive rather than reactive stance by, for example, meeting weekly to deal with any number of issues. These issues can include, among others, assisting classroom teachers with behavior challenges, accessing student services outside the school, and providing training workshops for teachers and school support staff on child-related topics identified as important to a particular school (e.g., bullying, Internet threats, children of military families).
- **Parent team.** The **parent team** includes parents who help plan family involvement strategies and activities at all levels of school life. For example, the team selects representatives to serve on the school planning and management team. Care is also taken to recruit participation by families who in the past may have felt uncomfortable in the school environment. One key objective behind this team is to empower parents as advocates for their children. Another objective is to provide children with social and educational continuity between their home and classroom lives. To achieve these and other objectives, the SDP model recommends three levels of parent and family involvement. We examine all three levels later in this section.

SDP processes. Three core **processes** serve as ground rules for social interactions within and between the above three teams (Comer et al., 1996, 2004, p. 18; Haynes et al., 1996).

- **No-fault.** Almost all groups experience disagreements when planning and implementing a plan of action. Often, one or more people are blamed for setbacks or other problems. The no-fault process avoids the disruptive effects of blame by asserting that mistakes result from misunderstandings, misinterpretations, or miscommunication and not deliberate attempts to offend others. In addition, the no-fault process facilitates the idea that everyone on a team is accountable for problem solving and decision making.
- **Consensus.** Team members are also trained to work toward consensus using dialogue and understanding. This means everyone on a team commits to hearing the viewpoints of others. Everyone also commits to embracing and acting upon team decisions, with the understanding that decisions can be adapted or dropped should they prove ineffective. One key to building consensus is a focus on the best interests of children.
- **Collaboration.** As its label implies, collaboration encourages team members to work together. This means respecting the respective roles and responsibilities of each

member. The importance of collaboration is made clear when one considers the vastly different responsibilities found within the three SDP teams, some of which are nonnegotiable or not easily altered.

SDP operations. The parent team and the student and staff support team provide input to members of the school planning and management team as they plan for, implement, and evaluate three **operations** (Comer et al., 1996, 2004, p. 21).

- **Comprehensive school plan.** This plan addresses all aspects of school improvement, including curriculum, instruction, assessment, and the overall climate of the school.
- **Staff development.** Staff development plans are coordinated with the overall comprehensive school plan. The purpose of this operation is to further school improvement goals by meeting the professional development needs of teachers and school support staff.
- **Assessment and modification.** This operation makes use of assessment data to advance the comprehensive school plan, including modifying the plan as needed. It is through ongoing assessments that schools can ensure continuous improvement.

Family Involvement Within the School Development Program Model

As reflected in the preceding discussion, family involvement is a key element of the SDP model (Jackson, Martin, & Stocklinski, 2004). In particular, family involvement activities are grouped into three overlapping categories or levels (Comer et al., 1996; Jackson et al., 2004).

Broad participation and support. This is the broadest level and includes many general ways for families to support their children's education at home and at school. Examples include physically preparing children for school (e.g., adequate rest and nutrition), encouraging children to commit themselves to their school work, providing enrichment activities outside of school, joining organizations and teams that support home–school connections, and taking part in school activities. As you may have already noted, all of these examples reflect activities covered in this and previous chapters, including those contained in Epstein's family-school-community partnership model. This is also true of other activities represented in the following two SDP categories or levels.

Active participation in schools. At this level, parents and other family members become engaged in the day-to-day life of the school. For example, they may assist teachers in the classroom by working directly with children, helping prepare materials for lessons, or helping in the school office, library, or cafeteria.

Participation in school management. At this level, parents may assume a leadership role in parent organizations or support groups. They may also serve on the school planning and management team, speak to community leaders or school board members, or take part in teacher-parent leadership workshops. Finally, they may assist with assessment and monitoring activities as well as help write or revise the comprehensive school plan.

Because of the comprehensive nature of the SDP model, it cannot be achieved overnight. Rather, it is an ongoing process that requires time and training (Comer et al., 1996; Jackson et al., 2004). In fact, a five-year commitment is needed to fully implement the SDP model and become a certified SDP school (Comer et al., 2004, p. 21). Keep this requirement in mind as you complete Reflections 14.3 and 14.4. Then read the final section of this chapter.

REFLECTION 14.3   Assess Your Role in the School Development Program Model

As a teacher, consider your own role in the SDP model by responding to the following questions: Which of the three teams would you want to join? What strengths would you bring to this team? What types of training would you like to receive in order to carry out the SDP model?

REFLECTION 14.4   Applying the School Development Program Model

How might the two family involvement planning models we reviewed earlier in this chapter (i.e., family involvement webs and family involvement roles) be integrated into the structure, processes, and/or operations of the SDP model?

Engaging parents in the family involvement planning process is empowering. Parents are more likely to participate in activities they helped to plan.

Engaging Parents in the Planning Process

Regardless of which model you choose to help you organize your family involvement activities, it is important to assess the interests of parents by engaging them in the planning process. Otherwise, those who have had few or no family involvement experiences may feel overwhelmed. Others may resent having a family involvement plan forced upon them without consultation. In addition, engaging parents in the planning process is empowering and makes it more likely they will participate in the activities. Steps for facilitating a brainstorming planning session include the following:

- *Introduce the purpose of the session.* Begin by explaining that the purpose of the brainstorming session is to provide parents with an opportunity to tell you, the teacher, about the types of family involvement activities that interest them.
- *Explain the theme that will drive family involvement planning.* Develop a handout, display, or PowerPoint presentation to explain the thematic unit that you will use to plan classroom lessons. Give a few brief examples of specific lessons.

- *Invite parents' participation.* Invite parents to suggest family involvement activity ideas they would like to see implemented in support of the classroom lessons. To get the process started, share a few examples of family involvement activities that have been used in previous years. During your first year of teaching, use examples borrowed from your colleagues. Thereafter, use your own examples. Invite parents to work in small groups as they write down their ideas on large sheets of paper. Avoid making comments about specific suggestions. This will ensure that everyone feels empowered to participate.
- *Protect feelings and provide explanations.* Thank parents for their participation in the brainstorming session. Explain that while it may not be possible to implement all the ideas that were shared, you will take them all into consideration. Remember to explain that the activities selected for implementation may need to be adapted to conform to school polices and to reflect available resources.
- *Make the activity ideas visible to parents.* To demonstrate your sincerity in using the ideas shared by parents, post them in your classroom or in the family resource center. Send out thank you notes to parents thanking them for their ideas. Also remember to point out how parents' ideas are represented in the family involvement activities that are implemented.

At times, a family involvement plan may require families to work together. In these situations, your leadership is important in avoiding accusations of preferential treatment and conflict over how best to carry out an assigned task (see Hu, 2007). Thus, it is important that you remain engaged in families' work. Be prompt in answering questions and offering assistance as needed. If a certain task requires a special skill, help parents master that skill by conducting a hands-on training session. Alternatively, provide parents with a tip sheet that summarizes each step in carrying out the task (see Reflection 14.5).

REFLECTION 14.5   Preparing Parents for Volunteer Work

Identify a task that parents have volunteered to assist with in support of a family involvement activity. Develop a tip sheet that describes the specific steps families are to take in carrying out that task.

Also remember that even with detailed explanations, it is likely that parents' interpretation of any given task will be somewhat different from your own. Unless their actions are unsafe or developmentally inappropriate, allow parents to carry out their own interpretation of the task. This will help build their self-confidence, creativity, and ultimately their participation in other family involvement activities.

CHAPTER SUMMARY

- Family involvement webs provide a visual picture of your plans for linking classroom- and family-based learning activities.
- Charting family involvement roles is useful in matching the skills and interests of individual parents to different tasks and activities.
- The school development program model is a comprehensive school improvement model that relies heavily on family involvement.

DISCUSSION QUESTIONS

1. Discuss the advantages and disadvantages of the three models presented in this chapter.

2. Discuss the benefits of seeking family input when planning family involvement activities.

3. **Your family involvement philosophy.** Return to the draft of your family involvement philosophy. Based on your reading of this chapter, what if any changes will you make to your philosophy statement? Discuss your answer to this question with your peers.

COMMUNITY OF LEARNERS' FIELD ASSIGNMENT

Gain Practice in Facilitating a Parent Meeting

In this assignment you will have an opportunity to facilitate a parent meeting, during which parents will help you brainstorm family involvement activities.

Your task. As a class, identify a thematic unit for a given grade level. Next, identify three classroom lessons that support your unit. Finally, identify a teacher in the community who will help you recruit a small focus group of three to five parents. Use the information in this and previous chapters to lead the parents in brainstorming family involvement activity ideas that will support your classroom lessons. Following the parent meeting, review your observations.

- How well did the parents work together? Were there disagreements?
- How will you integrate the parents' ideas into a family involvement web or family involvement role chart?
- What lessons did you learn as a result of this field assignment?

CAPSTONE ACTIVITIES

Activity 1: Brainstorm Other Family Involvement Planning Ideas

In this chapter, you were introduced to three family involvement planning models. As a class, brainstorm other ideas for how you might go about planning family involvement activities that meet the interests and needs of diverse families.

Activity 2: Interview a Teacher About Family Involvement Planning

Interview a teacher about how she or he plans for family involvement activities. For example, does the teacher (a) use a parent advisory committee, (b) consult with other teachers, (c) survey families, (d) plan alone, or (e) use another strategy? Share the results of your interview with your peers.

Activity 3: Create a Family Involvement Web

Identify a thematic unit for a particular age group, prekindergarten through fifth grade. Use this thematic unit to create a family involvement web. Remember to summarize the classroom and family involvement activities that appear in your web, as shown in FYI 14.1. Share your web with your peers. Compile everyone's webs and make copies for the class. Place your copy in your teacher resource file for future reference.

INTERNET RESOURCES

You may find that some URLs have been altered by the webmaster. In these situations, try entering the name of the document or agency in a search engine. Alternatively, enter the domain name (e.g., http://www.xxxx.org). This should take you to the revised home page and associated links.

Harvard Family Research Project: Concepts and Models of Family Involvement

http://www.hfrp.org/publications-resources/browse-our-publications/concepts-and-models-of-family-involvement

Here you will find case studies that demonstrate how different family involvement concepts and models can be used to build family-teacher partnerships.

University of Connecticut, Children, Youth and Families Educational Research Network: Supporting Family Involvement in Children's Learning: Trainer Module

http://www.cag.uconn.edu/ces/bestpractices/Trainer%204-14-03.pdf

Although this family involvement manual is designed to train professionals and volunteers working in informal educational settings, the information presented is also applicable to teachers working in schools and other educational environments. Of particular note is the review of various family involvement models.

Comer School Development Program

http://childstudycenter.yale.edu/comer/index.aspx

Visit this site to learn more about James Comer's school development program model and associated resources, programs, and services.

STUDENT STUDY SITE

Log on to the Web-based student study site at **www.sagepub.com/coleman** for additional study tools including

- eFlashcards
- Web Quizzes
- Links to SAGE Journal Articles
- Author-created Videos

- Learning Objectives
- Web Resources
- Family Involvement Portfolio Guides

SECTION IV

Promoting the Well-Being of All Children

CHAPTER 15 Protecting Children's Health and Safety

C hildren's health and safety influence every aspect of their lives, including their ability to learn, play, and form meaningful friendships. It is thus important that teachers monitor children's health and safety in the classroom as well as work with families and community professionals to ensure children's overall well-being. In this chapter, we begin with a review of what it means to lead a healthy lifestyle. Then we examine childhood infectious illnesses and childhood obesity. We end with a review of child maltreatment.

COMMUNITY LEARNING GUIDE

As you read this chapter, take notes on the following items. Use your notes to address the Reflections, Discussion Questions, Field Assignment, and Capstone Activities that you find in the chapter.

- What does it mean to be healthy?
- Why are children especially susceptible to infectious illnesses?
- As a teacher, how can you prevent the spread of infectious illnesses in your classroom?
- Distinguish between childhood overweight and childhood obesity.
- Describe some of the consequences of being overweight or obese.
- Describe the biological, environmental, and behavioral factors that contribute to childhood overweight and obesity.
- Describe the rules of thumb for assessing possible child maltreatment.
- Describe steps teachers should take when they suspect child abuse or neglect.

Defining a Healthy Lifestyle

The World Health Organization (2006) defines **health** as a "state of complete physical, mental and social well-being and not merely the absence of disease or infirmity." This definition fits nicely with a holistic focus on children's physical, psychological, and social-emotional well-being (Pollack, 1994; U.S. Department of Health and Human Services, Centers for Disease Control and Prevention, 2008). One example of how a holistic concept of health may play out in the classroom can be found in Case Study 15.1.

Case Study 15.1 reflects two additional factors that are important to remember when defining health. First, health exists along a continuum. Our daily definition of health can change, depending on how well we manage our physical, social, and cognitive well-being. Second, some if not most of our physical ailments, stressful relationships, and life disappointments can be tied to the choices we make in life. Rather than just thinking about exercising, healthy people set aside time to engage in rewarding physical activities. They also take steps to avoid infectious illnesses.

The information in this chapter supports the following family-school-community partnership standards. These standards are reviewed in Chapter 2.

NAEYC Standards and Associated Key Elements	1b, 1c, 2b, 2c, 3b, 3c, 5c, 6a, 6b, 6c, 6d, 6e
ACEI Standards	1.0, 2.6, 2.7, 3.2, 4.0, 5.1, 5.2
PTA Standards	2, 3, 4, 5, 6

CASE STUDY 15.1 Defining Health

Jason is severely asthmatic. However, he takes care to follow his doctor's directions and is sensitive to his surroundings and diet. Likewise, he is quick to alert you to situations that may trigger an asthma attack. Jason encounters few asthmatic episodes during the school year.

Eric has no physical ailments. However, he is socially immature and has poor impulse control. As a result, Eric often rushes into situations without considering the potential danger they present. As a result, Eric has had a number of accidents that required visits to the emergency room.

Which child, Jason or Eric, is healthier? To answer this question, think about not just the physical child but also the social-emotional and cognitive child.

Controlling Infectious Illnesses

To prevent infectious illnesses we must first understand how they come about. To summarize, all infectious illnesses result from the transmission of germs such as viruses, bacteria, parasites, and fungi (Aronson & Shope, 2005, p. 9). Germs are spread in various ways: (a) through the respiratory system (e.g., during coughing and sneezing), (b) through direct touching of an infected individual or object, or (c) through touching body fluids such as mucus, saliva, urine, fecal matter, or blood (Aronson & Shope, 2005, pp. 3–9; Aronson & Spahr, 2002, pp. 3, 10).

Children are especially susceptible to infectious illnesses for at least three reasons. First, their immune systems are still developing, making them more vulnerable to infections (Aronson & Shope, 2005, p. 3). Second, children lack the social and cognitive skills needed to consistently remember and carry out preventive health practices such as hand washing and covering one's nose when sneezing. Finally, children lack the life experiences needed to fully appreciate the negative consequences that accompany infectious illnesses.

In this section, we focus on general principles for preventing and managing infectious illnesses. To research information about specific infectious illnesses and other health conditions, visit the following two Internet Resources at the end of this chapter: (a) the Mayo Clinic and (b) the Centers for Disease Control and Prevention (CDC).

Preventing the Spread of Infectious Illnesses in the Classroom

Teachers follow four primary strategies in preventing the spread of infectious illnesses in the classroom. First, they make sure children have received their immunizations. Second, they implement a hand washing routine in the classroom. Third, they sanitize classroom surfaces. Finally, they exclude from the classroom children who are sick (National Health and Medical Research Council, 2005, p. 3).

Strategy #1: Immunizations. Immunization requirements are set by each state and automatically become classroom policy. Teachers and administrators are responsible for ensuring that each child's family presents immunization documentation as part of the registration process. You can find the immunization requirements for your state on the National Network for Immunization Information website: www.nnii.org/vaccineinfo/index.cfm?l=1.

Strategy #2: Hand washing and other preventive behaviors. Health professionals consider hand washing to be an essential practice in preventing the spread of infectious illnesses. To be effective, hand washing should follow a specific routine, a summary of which is provided in FYI 15.1.

Although studies document the effectiveness of hand washing training programs (Tousman et al., 2007), there are certain challenges to their successful implementation. One common challenge is that it takes time for children (and even adults) to memorize the hand washing routine. In addition, some children will, over time, forget parts of the routine. Likewise, young children in particular may have difficulty timing the recommended

---

FYI 15.1   Hand Washing

When Should Children Wash Their Hands?

- When they first arrive in the classroom
- Before eating food
- Before, during, and after handling food
- After going to the toilet
- After touching body fluids such as nose secretions, blood, and vomit
- Before going home

How Should Children Wash Their Hands?

- Begin by wetting your hands with running warm or cold water.
- Apply soap and rub your hands together to create a lather.
- Rub your hands quickly for at least 20 seconds. Remember to scrub the backs of your hands, your wrists, between your fingers, and under your fingernails.
- Rinse your hands well.
- Dry your hands with a clean or disposable towel or air dry your hands.
- Use a paper towel to turn off the faucet to avoid the potential for reinfection.

SOURCE: Adapted from U.S. Department of Health and Human Services, Centers for Disease Control and Prevention. (n.d.). *Stopping the spread of germs at home, work & school.* Retrieved November 9, 2011, from http://www.cdc.gov/flu/protect/stopgerms.htm. (Other hand washing tips and educational campaigns listed by the CDC also can be found at this website.)

20 seconds of hand washing (Vessey, Sherwood, Warner, & Clark, 2007). To address these challenges, some teachers use a simple song, chant, or poem (see Reflection 15.1).

> **REFLECTION 15.1   Managing the Hand Washing Routine**
>
> Create a song, chant, or some other strategy to help children spend at least 20 seconds washing their hands.

Teachers also sidestep the above challenges by using antibacterial hand sanitizers. These have been shown to be effective in reducing absenteeism due to illness when used alone (Vessey et al., 2007) or combined with hand washing (Lennell et al., 2008). Nevertheless, it is worth noting that some wonder if overuse of antibacterial agents may lead to the evolution of bacteria that are resistant to these products, making them less effective in the future (Mayo Clinic, 2010).

Still other behaviors that help to prevent the spread of infectious illnesses include teaching children to cough or sneeze away from others (see Reflection 15.2), teaching them to immediately dispose of tissues, and establishing a classroom rule that we do not share our personal items, such as jackets and eating utensils, with others (Aronson & Spahr, 2002, p. 4).

Strategy #3: Sanitizing surfaces. Cleaning, sanitizing, and disinfecting refer to different levels of germ control (Aronson & Shope, 2005, p. 15; National Resource Center for Health and Safety in Child Care and Early Education, 2007). **Cleaning** involves the removal of soil

> **REFLECTION 15.2   Give Germs a Cold Shoulder**
>
> "Give germs a cold shoulder" is a popular phrase used by teachers to teach children to cough and sneeze away from others. Use your own creativity to develop another phrase, chant, or quick song for teaching children to turn away from others when coughing or sneezing.

and dirt with water and soap. **Sanitizing** involves not only the removal of soil and dirt but also the removal of some germs with additional chemical agents. Cleaning and then sanitizing classroom surfaces reduces germs to a level that minimizes the spread of infectious illnesses. **Disinfecting** involves the use of still additional chemical agents and procedures that remove virtually all germs.

Most teachers use a sanitizing procedure to reduce the population of classroom germs. The most popular sanitizing agent is a mixture of household bleach and water. The standard formula is 1 tablespoon of bleach added to 1 quart of water (or ¼ cup of bleach added to 1 gallon of water; Aronson & Shope, 2005, p. 15). When applying this solution, spray it on surfaces that have been cleaned with soap and water until the entire surface is wet (Aronson & Shope, 2005, p. 15). Then allow the solution to air dry for two minutes.

Strategy #4: Excluding sick children from the classroom. Some common exclusion criteria include the following: (a) The child has a fever, (b) the illness prevents the child from actively participating in classroom activities, (c) the severity of the illness requires care that is beyond what can be provided in the classroom, (d) the illness can be easily spread to others, and (e) the child's inability to follow hygiene precautions places himself or herself and others at risk (American Academy of Pediatrics, 2010; Aronson, 2002, pp. 4–5; Aronson & Shope, 2005, p. 27; National Health and Medical Research Council, 2005, p. 6). Armed with these general criteria, you may want to consult your local or state health department to indentify exclusion criteria for specific childhood illnesses, such as those found on the following websites.

- Texas Department of State Health Services
  www.dshs.state.tx.us/idcu/health/schools_childcare/resources/ ChildCareChartNotes.pdf
- Flint Community Schools, Flint, Michigan
  http://flintschools.schoolfusion.us/ (Click on "Departments," then "Health Services," and finally "Communicable Disease Information.")
- *The New Mexico School Health Manual*
  www.nmschoolhealthmanual.org/shm_int.pdf

While infectious illnesses have been a long-standing topic of concern for teachers, parents, and school administrators, in the past decade a new type of health threat has taken on equal importance: the growing number of children who are overweight or obese. We address this threat in the following section.

Childhood Overweight and Obesity

The prevalence of overweight children in the United States not only has increased across all racial-ethnic, age, and gender groups (Sothern & Gordon, 2003), but has also become an "epidemic" (Council on Sports Medicine and Fitness and Council on School Health, 2006, p. 1839; Olshansky et al., 2005, p. 1139). In this section, we begin by distinguishing between the concepts of overweight and obesity. We then examine the causes of overweight and obesity. We also review the consequences of being overweight and obese. We end by looking at what you can do in your classroom and by working with families to address childhood overweight and obesity.

Defining Overweight and Obesity

While the phrase "childhood obesity" is often used to refer to children who are overweight, it is important to note the technical distinction between obesity and overweight when communicating with health professionals. While both terms are based on a measure referred to as **body mass index (BMI)**, which is a measure of a child's weight in relation to his or her height, they differ in degree. For children and adolescents (ages 2 to 19 years), **childhood overweight** is defined as a BMI at or above the 85th percentile and lower than the 95th percentile for children of the same age and sex (U.S. Department of Health and Human Services,

CDC, 2009b). In contrast, **childhood obesity** is defined as a BMI at or above the 95th percentile for children of the same age and sex. In general, both overweight and obesity are the result of a basic energy imbalance where children take in too many calories and do not get enough physical exercise to burn off those calories (Anderson & Butcher, 2006; U.S. Department of Health and Human Services, CDC, 2009b).

The CDC provides a website for calculating children's BMI (http://apps.nccd.cdc.gov/dnpabmi/Calculator.aspx). However, a word of warning is in order regarding the use of this calculator. Some parents may object to teachers' tracking their children's weight, viewing it as an invasion of personal privacy rights. For example, parents may worry about their children being bullied should weight results be made public. To address these concerns, share the above Internet link with parents for them to use on their own at home. Other tips for working with families to address childhood overweight and obesity are addressed in an upcoming section of this chapter.

Causes of Childhood Overweight and Obesity

No one factor is responsible for childhood overweight and obesity. Instead, a number of biological, behavioral, and environmental factors work together to promote unhealthy eating patterns and inhibit daily physical activities.

Biological factors. There are a few medical syndromes that are clearly associated with childhood overweight and obesity. For example, Prader-Willi syndrome is a potentially life-threatening genetic disorder that causes, among other things, low muscle tone, a chronic feeling of hunger, and a metabolism that causes the body to utilize fewer calories than normal (Prader-Willi Association, 2010). In addition, research studies show that our genetic makeup can predispose us to being overweight, although the exact way by which genetics and environmental factors interact to influence this outcome is not clearly understood (Nammi, Koka, Chinnala, & Boini, 2004; Sothern & Gordon, 2003).

Food environment factors. The easy availability of fast foods and sugary soft drinks are major topics in the overweight and obesity discussion (Anderson & Butcher, 2006; Davis et al., 2007). In addition, portion sizes continue to increase, leading children and adults to take in more calories with each snack or meal (Anderson & Butcher, 2006; Cawley, 2006; Davis et al., 2007; Young & Nestle, 2002). Finally, food labeling and advertising can be confusing and at times misleading. For example, not all prepackaged foods are as "heart healthy" as their advertisements might suggest. Calls for clearer definitions of calorie- and fat-related labels such as *reduced, fewer,* and *light* continue (see Federal Trade Commission, 2010).

Behavioral factors. The most obvious examples of behavioral factors that contribute to childhood overweight and obesity include a sedentary lifestyle and an increase in food consumption. Other behaviors are more subtle, such as when children use food to cope with feelings of anxiety or depression (Anderson & Butcher, 2006). Children also may mimic the poor eating and physical activity habits of their parents. For example, parents with busy schedules may choose convenience over quality by relying on prepackaged foods that require little time to prepare, can be purchased during sales and stored for weeks or months, are available at any time and from multiple sources, and appeal to the tastes of family members. Unfortunately, such convenience foods are often high in fat and calories (Schumacher & Queen, 2007, p. 15). In addition, parents have no control over the amount of fat, salt, and sugar that go into prepackaged foods the way they would for homemade meals. The same is true for parents who rely on fast foods as a meal plan of choice for themselves and their children (Cawley, 2006).

The built environment. A range of environmental factors contribute to childhood overweight and obesity. Consider, for example, technology. The time children spend watching television, playing video games, and surfing the Internet detracts from the time they spend playing outdoor games and pursuing other recreational pursuits. To make matters worse, it is not uncommon for high-fat snack foods and high-sugar sodas to accompany television viewing, video games, and Internet surfing.

Urban sprawl also contributes to overweight and obesity (Anderson & Butcher, 2006). Indeed, some argue that communities today are designed more for vehicles than for walking and biking (Fierro, 2002), making it difficult if not impossible for families to walk or bike to schools, grocery stores, libraries, and neighborhood parks. Other environmental factors that prevent children and their parents from pursuing outdoor recreation include missing or damaged sidewalks, heavy traffic, too few or unsafe highway crossing points, and high-crime areas.

Consequences of Childhood Overweight and Obesity

Some of the negative consequences associated with being overweight and obese include the following:

- **Type 2 diabetes** (American Diabetes Association, 2011; Daniels, 2006)
- **Cardiovascular risk factors** such as high blood pressure and high cholesterol (Daniels, 2006; Freedman, Dietz, Srinivasan, & Berenson, 1999)
- **Respiratory problems** that inhibit one's ability to breathe (Nammi et al., 2004)
- **Gastroesophageal reflux** in which increased abdominal pressures causes the stomach's contents to flow back into the esophagus (Daniels, 2006; Denney-Wilson & Baur, 2007)
- **Orthopedic problems** in the lower extremities that make it awkward or painful to walk, and that make children susceptible to ankle sprains (Denney-Wilson & Baur, 2007)
- **Psychological and social issues**, which can include depression, anxiety, a low self-esteem, and difficulties with peer relationships (S. M. Byrne & Puma, 2007; Daniels, 2006)

Three points are noteworthy regarding these health problems. First, they previously were associated only with adults (Daniels, 2006). Second, their occurrence during childhood makes them more difficult to control over time (Daniels, 2006; Schumacher & Queen, 2007, p. 12). Finally, not all the preceding consequences involve biological systems. Some involve children's social and psychological well-being.

Addressing Childhood Overweight and Obesity in Educational Settings

A review of multiple studies finds that school-based obesity prevention programs can be effective when they take a sustained and comprehensive approach to changing nutrition and sedentary behaviors (Cook-Cottone, Casey, & Feeley, 2009; Prelip, Slusser, Lange, Vecchiarielli, & Neumann, 2010; Yetter, 2009). Specific recommendations follow.

Restructure the food environment. One important component of any food environment is the training provided to those responsible for preparing and serving meals. The CDC recommends the following national agencies and organizations as resources for ensuring that food service workers receive appropriate training (Wechsler, McKenna, Lee, & Dietz, 2004).

- United States Department of Agriculture, Food and Nutrition Service, Team Nutrition
  www.fns.usda.gov/tn
- School Nutrition Association
  www.asfsa.org
- University of Mississippi, National Food Service Management Institute
  www.nfsmi.org

Another option is to take advantage of the Farm to School Network. One goal of this network is to improve student health by bringing local farm-grown foods to community schools. To learn more about this network, its programs, and how it operates in your state, visit the following website: www.farmtoschool.org/.

Finally, restructuring the food environment must include teachers themselves. In particular, it is important that teachers model eating behavior they would like children to adopt. In some cases this may lead to a ban on all soft drinks and candy within a school. In other cases teachers may decide to restrict the consumption of these items to adult-only areas, or they may adopt other measures that reinforce a healthy food environment.

Restructure the physical activity environment. Physical education and/or recess are being reduced or cut altogether in many schools. In fact, one national study found that 30% of third graders had less than 15 minutes of recess each day (Barros, Silver, & Stein, 2009). As you might suspect, these trends are in opposition to national guidelines set by the National Association of Sport and Physical Education (2010a). According to this association, preschoolers should engage in at least 60 minutes of structured physical activity each day along with at least 60 minutes and up to several hours of active free play. Likewise, school-age children ages 5 to 12 should engage in at least 60 minutes (and up to several hours) of vigorous physical activity on all or most days of the weeks (National Association for Sport and Physical Education, 2010b).

There is a growing call for schools to help address the childhood overweight and obesity epidemic.

Fortunately, the call for a return of both recess and physical education is growing. As a teacher, you may be asked to help design or select a physical education curriculum. If so, keep in mind the following guidelines recommended by the CDC (Wechsler et al., 2004). First, focus on more than skill development by including activities that promote problem solving, reflection, and strategic thinking. Second, design programs that meet the needs of all students, including those who are overweight or display learning or other challenges. Third, follow developmental guidelines to keep students active during most of each class period (see FYI 15.2). Finally, focus on activities that students enjoy, including the use of flexible rules, practice time, and brief instructional periods (Council on Sports Medicine and Fitness and Council on School Health, 2006).

FYI 15.2 Guidelines for Planning Developmentally Appropriate Physical Activities

Preschool and Young Elementary School–Age Children (4–6 Years)	Elementary School–Age Children (7–10 years)
• Encourage children's participation in nonstructured physical activities based on the pleasure of the movement experience versus a need to demonstrate a competitive advantage over peers (Georgia Department of Education, 2008). Rather than observing children's play, actively join them to model your enjoyment of physical activities (Pica, 2006).	• Continue to encourage nonstructured play while introducing games and dances that involve social interactions, cooperation, and an ability to respond to directions and make movement adaptations in relation to a partner (Georgia Department of Education, 2008)
• Encourage experimentation with motor skills that are the building blocks for more complex movements (Pica, 2006). For example, encourage fundamental motor skills like bending, turning, dodging, hopping, running, and jumping (Georgia Department of Education, 2008).	• Introduce more sophisticated activities that combine fundamental motor skills such as throwing at a target, moving in tempo to different rhythms, catching moving objects at different speeds, striking objects, and dribbling (Georgia Department of Education, 2008).
• Focus on 10- to 15-minute fitness "bouts" rather than activities that require sustained exertion (Pica, 2006).	• Assist children in learning to moderate the duration and intensity of their physical activities by paying attention to physiological indicators such as breathing, heart rate, and muscular endurance (Georgia Department of Education, 2008).
• Incorporate movement into indoor activities that keep children active throughout the day (Pica, 2006). This may include large-group time, transitions, and indoor lessons. For example, ask children to count the number of times they jump in place as part of a math lesson. During transition from small group to large group, invite children to walk in place until they are called to take their place at the group meeting space.	• Help children begin to refine their individual skills and interests (Georgia Department of Education, 2008). For example, encourage activities that allow children to transfer concepts from one skill or game to a new skill or game. Help children analyze their own skills, as well as those of others, in a supportive manner.

SOURCE: Adapted from Georgia Department of Education. (2008). *Georgia performance standards for physical education.* Atlanta, GA: Author; Pica, R. (2006). Physical fitness and the early childhood curriculum. *Young Children, 61*(3), 12–19. Reprinted with permission from the National Association for the Education of Young Children (NAEYC). www.naeyc.org.

Take students' preferences into account. While it is ultimately adults' responsibility to ensure the quality of physical activities and food environments, it is also important to consider the views of students. Otherwise, all your efforts may be in vain. For example, one study of preschool playgrounds found children spent less time in sedentary activities and more time in moderate to vigorous physical activities when there were fewer fixed pieces of equipment (e.g., swings and slides), more portable playground equipment (e.g., balls and tricycles), and a larger playground space (Dowda et al., 2009).

Model an active lifestyle. Pay attention to your own behavior during recess. Promote an interest in physical activities by joining with children rather than sitting or standing on the sidelines (Cardon et al., 2008; Pica, 2006). Such active involvement not only will motivate children to participate with you, but will also provide you with a more intimate assessment of the physical, cognitive, and social learning taking place on the playground.

Issue a health report card. Some schools include a measure of children's health, often weight, in their report cards. Before deciding to pursue a similar course of action, keep one warning in mind. As mentioned earlier in this chapter, some parents may object to their child's being weighed, and for that reason you will want to seek parental input when determining whether or not to include a health indicator in your school's report card.

Working With Families to Address Childhood Overweight and Obesity

Like most other aspects of children's lives, healthy eating and physical activity begin at home (Lindsay, Sussner, Kim, & Gortmaker, 2006; Schumacher & Queen, 2007, p. 16). In fact, it is through the home that families model eating and physical activity patterns of behavior for their children to follow (Coleman, Wallinga, & Bales, 2010; Eliassen, 2011). The importance of modeling is reflected in the following quote from a parent:

> I think that it all comes back down to the parents because if they let them sit there and do nothing, well of course they're just going to sit there and do nothing. . . . I am an outside person and so is my husband . . . we're not telly people. So I guess that sort of has rubbed off on my kids. (Dwyer, Higgs, Hardy, & Baur, 2008, p. 5).

The importance of family influences is also reflected in obesity prevention and intervention programs, many of which follow a family systems perspective (Kitzmann, Dalton, & Buscemi, 2008). In short, these programs recognize the limited impact of any program that does not involve the entire family system. The following strategies reflect a family systems approach, as well as an ecological approach, to preventing overweight and obesity.

Help parents form realistic expectations about children's eating behavior. Parents' attempts to control their children's eating behavior often focus on external cues such as "**clean plate club**," where children are expected to eat everything on their plate. Unfortunately, this approach usually leads to parent-child conflict. Additionally, focusing on external food cues can interfere with children's ability to pay attention to internal hunger cues and, subsequently, their ability to self-regulate their eating behavior (Birch & Fisher, 1998). This can in turn lead to overeating or undereating (Francis & Susman, 2009; Johnson, 2000). One way to address this issue is for parents and teachers to help children recognize hunger and fullness cues as well as help them find releases from boredom or anxiety that do not involve food.

Parents may also attempt to totally ban children's consumption of "bad" food. Unfortunately, such attempts often involve mixed messages, as, for example, when sweets are banned in one setting but permitted in another setting (Birch & Fisher, 1998). In addition, children may become preoccupied with the very foods that parents forbid (Eliassen, 2011). Subsequently, a total prohibition on cake, candy, or soft drinks may in itself be ineffective. Instead, parents should focus on making these foods a "sometimes" treat served on special occasions.

Finally, health professionals remind us that children's food preferences are influenced by associating food flavors with eating environments (Savage, Fisher, & Birch, 2007). Thus, they suggest that parents serve a variety of appealing foods in a pleasant environment and allow children to determine how much they would like to eat of those foods (Eliassen, 2011; Satter, 1996). It is also important that parents be patient when introducing a new food, as it may take 10 to 16 offerings to increase a child's acceptance of that food (Savage et al., 2007).

Encourage families to take a community preventive approach. Some communities strive to create healthy school environments by partnering with families and the community at large (Prelip et al., 2007). As a teacher, you can follow their lead by working with families to lobby parks and recreation officials to establish community walking trails, playing fields, garden plots, playgrounds, and fitness courses designed for adults and children of different ages. In some cases, it may even be possible to establish these amenities around a school, thereby providing opportunities for before- and after-school family programs.

Point out ways that families can model healthy living. For example, suggest that parents (a) limit their children's media time to no more than one to two hours per day (American Academy of Pediatrics, 2001); (b) schedule daily family recreation time (see, for example, FYI 15.3); (c) avoid using candy as a reward and withholding food as punishment; (d) encourage children to choose fresh fruit, vegetables, and water by making them readily available in a bowl that children themselves have decorated (Coleman et al., 2010); and (e) establish a family rule that there is no eating or drinking while watching TV, playing video games, or using the computer.

In the following and final section, we address a unique threat to children's well-being that teachers should be prepared to recognize and address: child maltreatment.

Children often model the physical activity patterns shown by their parents and teachers.

FYI 15.3   A Family Activity Calendar

A Month of Fun Physical Activities for Your Child and Family

Theme	Mon	Tue	Wed	Thu	Fri
Practice Fundamental Motor Skills	Trapping. Sit on the floor and roll a large ball back and forth. Roll it to one side, then the other side. Roll it slowly, then quickly.	Catching. Help your child practice catching a large ball by rolling it down a slide or chute. Then, toss the ball back and forth to each other.	Hopping. Hop like a rabbit or grasshopper. See how long you can hop on one foot.	Weaving. Weave through an obstacle course of chairs or sheets hung over an outdoor line.	Throwing. Practice throwing a ball through a hula hoop from different distances and angles.
Encourage Creative Movement	Attach a large scarf to your child's pants or around her waist. Do the same for yourself. Pretend you have been swept up by the wind and are floating in the sky. What do you see below?	Observe how bugs move on the ground. Take turns making up your own creative bug movements.	Use ribbons attached to your wrists as butterfly wings. Fly around and visit your favorite flowers and plants.	Some communities have free introductory dance classes. Take your family to different classes. Which ones do family members enjoy the most?	Put on a fast song. Everyone make up a silly dance. The sillier the better.
Family Relaxation and Recreation	As a family, take a stroll around the neighborhood after dinner. Using hints, play a game of "guess what I see."	As a family, color and decorate heavy paperplates. Use them as Frisbees. Aim for a tree or play toss and catch.	Read a book with or to your child. Make up a story together. Be sure to write it down and draw pictures so you can enjoy it again later.	Use the internet or library to look up dances from different cultures. Try a new dance each week.	As a family, bowl, play a round of putt-putt golf, ride bikes, dance, etc. Don't make it competitive. Just have fun.
Movement Games	Try walking in a straight line while balancing a balloon or foam ball in your hand. Repeat, this time walking in a circle or along a winding path.	Play "Simon Says" by directing your child to move in different ways. Repeat, with your preschooler giving you directions.	Make up your own family movement game. Remember to keep it simple so everyone can play and have fun.	Divide into pairs and play a game of opposites. If your partner hops forward, you hop backward. If your partner crouches on her knees, you jump up in the air.	As a family, form a line and play a movement game of follow the leader. Take turns being the leader.

SOURCE: Coleman, M., Wallinga, C., & Bales, D. (2010). Engaging families in the fight against the overweight epidemic among children. *Childhood Education, 86*(3), 150–156.

Child Maltreatment

The CDC (U.S. Department of Health and Human Services, CDC, 2009a) defines **child maltreatment** as acts of abuse or neglect by a parent or other caregiver that result in harm, the potential for harm, or the threat of harm. A recent report from the U.S. Department of Health and Human Services (2010, pp. 21, 35) found that 702,000 children were victims of child maltreatment in 2009. In this section, we review four types of maltreatment, selected demographics associated with maltreatment, teachers' responsibilities for responding to child maltreatment, the treatment process, and the impact of domestic violence on children.

General Types of Child Maltreatment

A summary of four types of child maltreatment is presented in FYI 15.4. When reviewing this table, keep the following rules of thumb in mind. First, consider any extreme and sudden change in a child's appearance, emotional state, or behavior as cause for concern. Second, consult with a counselor to determine if a pattern of behavior suggests maltreatment versus some other cause (e.g., a physical illness, emotional disorder, missed meal, or life stressor).

FYI 15.4 Types of Child Abuse and Neglect		
Type of Maltreatment	Some Examples	Examples of a Pattern: Ask the following questions to determine if you see a pattern or behavior that suggests abuse or neglect.
Neglect refers to the failure of a parent or caregiver to provide for the basic needs of a child (Crosson-Tower, 2003, p. 16).	Physical, emotional, and educational	• Is the child dressed in soiled clothing? • Does the child have an unpleasant body odor? • Does the child hoard food? Does he or she constantly complain of hunger? • Does the child report caring for or being cared for by underage siblings? • Does the child complain of sleep deprivation at home? • Does the child have health needs that are being ignored?
Physical abuse (separate from sexual abuse) refers to the nonaccidental infliction of pain or injury (Crosson-Tower, 2003, p.14).	Kicking, beating, slapping, burning, and biting	• Do bruises appear on soft tissue areas of the body (e.g., belly and buttocks)? These areas usually are not bruised during falls that accompany children's play. It is more reasonable to assume that bony areas of the body, such as elbows, knees, and chins, would be bruised during accidental falls. • Do bruises show imprints of bite marks, brushes, cords, belts, buckles, or other objects? • Are there unexplained or changing stories about the cause of burns or injuries?

(Continued)

(Continued)

Type of Maltreatment	Some Examples	Examples of a Pattern: Ask the following questions to determine if you see a pattern or behavior that suggests abuse or neglect.
Sexual abuse refers to the exploitation of children for sexual gratification (Aronson & Spahr, 2002, p. 173).	Forcing, encouraging, or allowing children to participate in adult sexual behavior	• Does the child complain of genital or anal itching, pain, or bleeding? • Is the child withdrawn and unusually secret about his or her life? • Does the child display a knowledge of sexual behavior beyond what is age appropriate? • Does the child show anxiety over being in certain locations or with certain people?
Emotional or **psychological abuse** refers to a pattern of punitive verbal statements and behavioral acts that damage children's self-worth and self-confidence.	Name calling, belittling comments, intentional embarrassment, and verbal threats	• Does the child show extreme behaviors, such as being manically happy, depressed, compulsive, or preoccupied? • Does the child display self-destructive behavior, such as cutting his or her arms or legs? • Does the child display destructive behavior or cruelty toward others? • Does the child show regressive behavior, such as thumb sucking or bedwetting?

Demographics of Child Maltreatment

A report by the U.S. Department of Health and Human Services (2010) noted a number of demographic data that have remained stable for several years. First, younger children were the most vulnerable to child maltreatment, with just over one third being under the age of 4, just over one fifth being between the ages of 4 and 7, and just under one fifth being between the ages of 8 and 11 (p. 22). Second, certain factors placed children at risk for maltreatment. For example, 11% of maltreated children had a disability (pp. 24, 49) and 18.4% were exposed to domestic violence (pp. 24, 50). Boys were the victims of maltreatment 48.2% of the time and girls were victims 51.1% of the time (pp. 22, 43). Over one third (37.7%) of children were maltreated by their mother, just under one fifth (18.8%) by their father, just under one fifth (18.0%) by both their mother and father, and 4.5% by a male or female relative (pp. 22, 39).

In a separate federal report, a larger percentage of children were found to have experienced some form of neglect (61%) than abuse (44%; Sedlak et al., 2010, p. 5). These percentages, as well as those that follow, were greater than 100% because some children experienced more than one type of maltreatment. Thus, of all the children who were neglected, just under one half experienced educational neglect (47%), more than one third experienced physical neglect (38%), and one fourth experienced emotional neglect (25%; Sedlak et al., 2010, p. 5). Of all the children who were abused, a majority experienced physical abuse (58%), slightly over one quarter experienced emotional abuse (27%), and slightly under one quarter experienced sexual abuse (24%; Sedlak et al., 2010, p. 5).

Steps Teachers are Required to Take

Despite the publication of professional standards that require teachers to, in part, "understand their legal and ethical obligations to recognize and report suspicions of abuse"

Teachers are professionally and legally mandated to report suspected cases of child abuse and neglect.

(National Association for the Education of Young Children, 2004), they are at times hesitant to make such reports. Such hesitancy is associated with a lack of preservice or in-service training (Kenny, 2004), a resulting uncertainty about what constitutes child maltreatment, questions about legal guidelines for reporting suspected cases of maltreatment (Hinkelman & Bruno, 2008), fear that the parent-teacher relationship will be damaged (Crosson-Tower, 2003, p. 34; Hinkelman & Bruno, 2008), dissatisfaction with the "mandated reporter" role (Kenny, 2004, p. 1316), and concern over whether any action will be taken following a report (Crosson-Tower, 2003, p. 35).

These barriers can be addressed in two ways. First, it is vital that schools provide in-service training on child abuse and neglect. A few facts that typically are included in such training are provided in Tip Box 15.1. A list of questions for structuring in-service training is presented in FYI 15.5. Because answers to the questions in FYI 15.5 can vary based on state laws and/or local procedures, visit the **Child Welfare Information Gateway** Internet resource at the end of this chapter to find answers to some of the questions for your state. Two of the many topics addressed at this website include state-based definitions of child abuse and neglect along with responsibilities of mandatory and other reporters.

A second way to address barriers to reporting suspected cases of child maltreatment is for schools to establish a child protection team (Crosson-Tower, 2003, p. 34). The purpose of this team is twofold: (a) to facilitate in-service training and (b) to serve as a support network for reporters. The latter point is important, since confidentiality laws place limits on who reporters can talk to about their concerns. Thus, a network of colleagues who have permission to listen to and support reporters is essential not only for encouraging reports of suspected child maltreatment but also for alleviating the anxiety associated with such reports.

Treatment of Maltreated Children

Abused and neglected children often need assistance in developing new ways to think, feel, and behave (Stien & Kendall, 2004, p. 182). In the following, we review some of the issues that therapists are likely to address when working with maltreated children. As a teacher, you may be asked to take part in the treatment process by observing children's behavior and/or providing some of the other types of support addressed.

Safety and stabilization. Therapists first strive to establish a sense of safety for children (Gimpel & Holland, 2003, pp. 152–155; Stien & Kendall, 2004, pp. 141–147). For example, they may work with social workers to make sure the home environment is safe. In some cases

TIP BOX 15.1	Facts About Child Abuse and Neglect for Teachers

- Every state legally mandates that teachers, as well as other community professionals who work with children, report suspected cases of child abuse and neglect. Failure to do so can result in prosecution.
- Teachers are not required to have absolute proof of child abuse and neglect, only a "reasonable suspicion" (p. 24). All states provide reporters with immunity under a "good faith" clause, meaning they made the report with the sincere intention of protecting a child (p. 10).
- Not every report of child abuse and neglect necessarily results in an arrest. Investigators follow state guidelines in assessing evidence of abuse or neglect and deciding on the most appropriate steps to take.
- Some abused children may invite punishment by acting out. This usually occurs as children "test" teachers' affection or because they have come to believe this is the only type of attention they are entitled to receive from adults.
- Children do not always admit to abuse or neglect out of fear they will be taken away from their parents.
- It is best to let community professionals handle all child and family interviews. As a teacher you want to listen to children and acknowledge their concerns. At the same time, it is important not to ask leading questions or attempt to intervene on your own.

SOURCE: Adapted from Crosson-Tower, C. (2003). *The role of educators in preventing and responding to child abuse and neglect* (pp. 10–13, 15, 24). Washington, DC: U.S. Department of Health and Human Services, Office of Child Abuse and Neglect.

FYI 15.5 Questions to Address During In-Service Training on Child Abuse and Neglect

- How does the state define child abuse and neglect?
- How soon after suspecting child abuse and neglect must I make a report?
- Am I to personally report suspected cases of child abuse and neglect to the appropriate community authorities, or do I report to a designated person in my school?
- If I must report personally, to which agency do I report? What is the telephone number or email address for making the report?
- What information should I include in my report?
- What types of documentation should I keep regarding my suspicion of child abuse or neglect? Should I take notes? How should I write my notes?
- How do I respond if a parent asks me if I reported them to the authorities?
- When does a parent's corporal punishment become physical abuse?

this may mean removing certain individuals from the household. In addition, children are given age-appropriate explanations as to why they are visiting with a therapist. Other goals may include providing children with alternative behaviors and incentives aimed at stopping self-destructive or other dysfunctional behavior and correcting children's faulty assumptions (e.g., self-blame) about why the abuse occurred.

Regulating emotions. Children may be taught physical and mental relaxation exercises aimed at helping them to control their emotions when upset (Stien & Kendall, 2004, p. 147). Adults, including teachers, may be asked to help by giving gentle touches, using a calm voice, and reminding children to refocus their attention on pleasant thoughts or objects (Stien & Kendall, 2004, p. 148). These tasks are essential to helping children learn to trust and accept their emotions, to trust and accept comfort from others, and to build their self-esteem and self-control.

Problem solving skills. Abused and neglected children sometimes lack the problem solving skills that allow them to assess and think through new situations (Stien & Kendall, 2004, p. 169). Therapists teach children how to define problems, consider possible alternatives, anticipate consequences, and take action that is not based on conditioned fear or mistrustful responses. As a teacher, you may be asked to help support this process in the classroom.

Social skills training. Maltreated children have been shown to be more aggressive, to be more withdrawn, and to engage in more antisocial behavior (Jaffee, Caspi, Moffitt, & Taylor, 2004). These behaviors help to explain why maltreated children are less accepted by their peers (Anthonysamy & Zimmer-Gembeck, 2007). Overly aggressive children are likely to scare their peers while withdrawn children often lack the skills needed to assert their personalities and engage their peers in meaningful exchanges. Therapists address these challenges by teaching children how to approach and initiate socially appropriate interactions. Modeling and role playing are just two examples of strategies used to teach maltreated children appropriate social skills. Again, therapists may ask teachers to use certain types of modeling and/or role playing in the classroom.

Working with parents. Child neglect and abuse, regardless of whether it originated inside or outside the family system, can damage the parent-child relationship. For this reason, parents are essential players in the treatment process. Some examples of issues therapists may address with parents include modifying family roles, introducing new parent-child communication skills, implementing activities designed to strengthen the parent-child bond, providing parenting education, and helping parents understand therapy objectives and their role in facilitating those objectives at home. In some cases, individuals within the family may be helped to accept responsibility for contributing to a child's abuse or neglect either as perpetrators or because they failed to provide sufficient protection (Stien & Kendall, 2004, p. 136).

Managing stress. A few "stress busters" for helping all children learn to manage stress, including those who have experienced maltreatment, are presented in Tip Box 15.2. These strategies, along with those previously presented in Chapter 11 (see Tip Box 11.1), may be incorporated into an abused or neglected child's treatment plan following consultation with the child's therapist and parents.

TIP BOX 15.2	Stress Busters for the Classroom

- **Use a graffiti board.** Cover a bulletin board with paper. Invite children to anonymously write down or draw their frustrations and feelings rather than act on them. This can be a stand-alone board or incorporated into lessons about expressing feelings in a positive manner. The graffiti board will also provide teachers with information about the types and levels of stress represented in their classrooms.
- **Teach children relaxation strategies.** Ask the school or a community counselor to teach you how to use breathing and muscle relaxation techniques with children. Invite the counselor to class to conduct an art or music class aimed at helping children manage their anxiety.
- **Give children a sense of control over their classroom learning environment.** Make sure children have their own desks, materials, and storage space. As noted in previous chapters, engage them in setting classroom rules. These acts will help to promote children's sense of self-worth and control over their personal property.
- **Maintain a warm and empathetic demeanor.** All children, regardless of their life experiences, have good and bad days. Maintain a calm demeanor as you engage children in discussions about their misbehavior and deliver appropriate consequences. Your calmness will help to maintain a respectful classroom environment. In contrast, arguing with children or raising your voice will only escalate feelings of anxiety and resentment.
- **Introduce a feelings barometer.** This device, which can be made out of cardstock or cardboard, allows children to physically move an arrow to show how they feel. For very young children, numbers can be accompanied by smiling, frowning, crying, or angry faces. For all children, the act of moving the indicator helps them to own their feelings. It also provides an opening for teachers to talk with children about their feelings.
- **Encourage problem solving and creative thinking.** As noted above, problem solving can be difficult for abused and neglected children. Discussing age-appropriate "what if" social dilemmas gives children practice in using their creativity and logical thinking skills to think through interpersonal problems. Persona dolls and puppets (see Chapter 9) can also be used as safe surrogates for structuring problem solving discussions about interpersonal problems (see Pierce & Johnson, 2010). Consult a school or community counselor for tips on facilitating discussions of social dilemmas in your classroom.
- **Keep in touch with the caseworker, therapist, and parents.** It is important to coordinate an abused or neglected child's classroom work with his or her caseworker, therapist, and parents. Their input will ensure that activities implemented in the classroom support the therapeutic objectives being carried out in the therapist's office and at home.

SOURCE: Adapted from Crosson-Tower, C. (2003). *The role of educators in preventing and responding to child abuse and neglect* (pp. 39–41). Washington, DC: U.S. Department of Health and Human Services, Office of Child Abuse and Neglect; Fallin, K., Wallinga, C., & Coleman, M. (2001). Helping children cope with stress in the classroom setting. *Childhood Education, 78*(1), 17–24.

Domestic Violence

The information we have reviewed so far does not address domestic violence. Yet a review of numerous studies (Kitzmann, Gaylord, Holt, & Kenny, 2003) as well as teacher and social worker interviews (Byrne & Taylor, 2007) reveals that children who witness domestic violence are also at risk for a range of psychosocial adjustment problems, including externalizing behavior (e.g., loudness and aggression), internalizing behavior (e.g., withdrawal and somatic complaints), psychological problems (e.g., poor attention and self-esteem), social problems (e.g., poor peer relationships) and academic problems.

Teachers can best support children who live in homes characterized by violence and conflict by creating a nurturing and safe classroom environment, promoting healthy teacher-child interactions, reinforcing children's self-esteem and life skills, and compensating for behaviors and experiences that may be absent at home. Examples of basic teaching strategies that accomplish these objectives (many of which we have addressed in previous chapters) include the following (Baker & Cunningham 2009):

- Help children master new skills so they gain a sense of self-control.
- Use active listening to validate children's feelings.
- Validate children's sense of independence by giving them choices.
- Model and give children opportunities to practice problem solving and conflict resolution skills.
- Maintain a positive outlook on life and display respectful attitudes toward others.
- Reinforce children's self-worth by showing your admiration of their unique interests and skills.

Chapter Summary

- Health exists along a continuum and is influenced in part by the choices we make in life.
- Children are at a greater risk for infectious illnesses because of their developing immune systems, their incompletely developed cognitive and social skills, and their lack of life experiences.
- Many factors contribute to childhood overweight and obesity. Some are biological, others environmental, and still others behavioral.
- When assessing suspected cases of maltreatment, follow two rules of thumb: (a) Look for extreme and sudden changes in a child's behavior, and (b) look for a pattern of symptoms that excludes other possible explanations for the child's behavior.

Discussion Questions

1. Discuss the policies you think schools should adopt regarding teachers' consumption of soft drinks and candy at school.

2. Discuss how you would respond both emotionally and pragmatically should you discover that a child in your classroom has been neglected or abused.

3. **Your family involvement philosophy.** Return to the draft of your family involvement philosophy. Based on your reading of this chapter, what if any changes will you make to your philosophy statement? Discuss your answer to this question with your peers.

Community of Learners' Field Assignment

In-Service Training: Invite a Nurse to Class

To learn more about childhood illnesses and their implications for the classroom, it is important that you hear from a community or school nurse.

Your task. A few health-related questions teachers often ask about are presented below. As a class, brainstorm other questions. Your class will be responsible for arranging and facilitating a visit by a nurse who can respond to your questions.

- What precautions should I take when a child presents with the diagnosis of diabetes? What about asthma? Allergies?
- How do I use an Epipen to treat an allergic reaction?
- How do I carry out a head lice check? At what point should a child with head lice be excluded from the classroom?
- What should go into a classroom first-aid kit?
- What first-aid techniques are teachers most often asked to perform?
- What types of childhood injuries are most likely to occur in a classroom and on a playground? How do I respond when these injuries occur?
- Is it unhealthy to keep certain pets in the classroom?

Capstone Activities

Activity 1: Research a Specific Childhood Illness or Injury

Visit the CDC and/or Mayo Clinic website at the end of this chapter to identify and read about the causes, symptoms, prevention, and treatment of any one childhood illness or injury. You may also choose to interview a nurse or another health professional in your community. Write a tip sheet to educate parents about this illness or injury. Make a handout of your tip sheet for your peers to place in their teacher resource file.

Activity 2: Practice Developing a Home-Based Healthy Living Activity

Develop a healthy living backpack, activity calendar, or activity card to send home.

Activity 3: Make an Assessment of Children's Behavior

As a class, discuss whether the following situations would lead you to suspect possible child maltreatment. Ask a school or community counselor to comment on your assessments. Also invite the counselor to make a class presentation on identifying and responding to suspected cases of child abuse and neglect.

- Elizabeth comes to class with a distinct odor. The odor is so unpleasant that children refuse to sit next to her. You have not noticed this odor before.
- Christopher has given way to angry outbursts since the beginning of school, especially when frustrated. His mother has dismissed your concerns, describing Christopher as an "overly sensitive" child. This morning, a

teacher gently patted Christopher on the knee to remind him to pay attention. He responded violently by striking out at everyone within reach.

- Miranda quietly whispers in your ear, "Uncle Ted touched me."

INTERNET RESOURCES

You may find that some URLs have been altered by the webmaster. In these situations, try entering the name of the document or agency in a search engine. Alternatively, enter the domain name (e.g., http://www.xxxx.org). This should take you to the revised home page and associated links.

Readability Calculators

Use the following sites to calculate the reading level of health-related and other written materials that you send home to families. Use the resulting information to revise the material so its reading level matches that of your target audience.

Text Readability Scores

http://www.addedbytes.com/code/readability-score/

Tests Document Readability

http://www.online-utility.org/english/readability_test_and_improve.jsp

Readability Index Calculator

http://www.standards-schmandards.com/exhibits/rix/

Mayo Clinic: Children's Health

http://www.mayoclinic.com/health/childrens-conditions/CC00059

Visit this site to read about the top five health reasons why children miss school. You may choose to use the information provided by the Mayo Clinic to write a tip sheet or newsletter column for families. Click on the "Diseases and Conditions" link for information about specific illnesses.

Centers for Disease Control and Prevention: Diseases & Conditions

http://www.cdc.gov/DiseasesConditions/

Visit this site to learn about a range of health conditions and infectious diseases.

American Academy of Pediatrics

http://www.aap.org/

Although aimed primarily at pediatricians, this website includes a link to information for parents as well as information about various health topics that you will find helpful.

U.S. Department of Agriculture: ChooseMyPlate.gov

http://www.choosemyplate.gov/

The food pyramid has been replaced by a dinner plate: "Choose My Plate." Visit this site to learn about food groups, interactive tools, and other resources for promoting healthy eating patterns.

U.S. Food and Drug Administration

http://www.fda.gov/Food/default.htm

Visit this site to collect information on food labels, food safety, and dietary guidelines to share with parents.

National Association for Sport and Physical Education (NASPE)

http://www.aahperd.org/Naspe/

The NASPE has established physical activity guidelines for children of different ages. The NASPE's website also includes links for parents and professionals.

American Association for the Child's Right to Play

http://www.ipausa.org/index.html

Visit this link for resources that can help you advocate children's play.

Kids Walk-to-School

http://www.cdc.gov/nccdphp/dnpa/kidswalk/

This site is sponsored by the Centers for Disease Control and Prevention to support communities in their efforts to reinforce children's need for daily physical activity. It offers a number of resources that schools can use to coordinate a community walk-to-school program.

The Food Trust

http://www.thefoodtrust.org/index.php

The mission of this organization is to improve the health of children and adults, promote good nutrition, increase access to nutritious foods, and advocate better public policy. Click on "Our Projects" to discover the various school- and community-based programs associated with this organization.

Child Welfare Information Gateway: State Laws on Child Abuse and Neglect

http://www.childwelfare.gov/systemwide/laws_policies/state/can/

Visit this site to learn more about child abuse and neglect laws in your state. The site allows the reader to click on multiple issues, making the search for targeted information much easier than reading entire pieces of legislation.

STUDENT STUDY SITE

Log on to the Web-based student study site at **www.sagepub.com/coleman** for additional study tools including

- eFlashcards
- Web Quizzes
- Links to SAGE Journal Articles
- Author-created Videos

- Learning Objectives
- Web Resources
- Family Involvement Portfolio Guides

Position Statement: NAEYC Code of Ethical Conduct and Statement of Commitment

Section II: Ethical Responsibilities to Families

Families* are of primary importance in children's development. Because the family and the early childhood practitioner have a common interest in the child's well-being, we acknowledge a primary responsibility to bring about communication, cooperation, and collaboration between the home and early childhood program in ways that enhance the child's development.

Ideals

I-2.1—To be familiar with the knowledge base related to working effectively with families and to stay informed through continuing education and training.

I-2.2—To develop relationships of mutual trust and create partnerships with the families we serve.

I-2.3—To welcome all family members and encourage them to participate in the program.

I-2.4—To listen to families, acknowledge and build upon their strengths and competencies, and learn from families as we support them in their task of nurturing children.

I-2.5—To respect the dignity and preferences of each family and to make an effort to learn about its structure, culture, language, customs, and beliefs.

I-2.6—To acknowledge families' childrearing values and their right to make decisions for their children.

I-2.7—To share information about each child's education and development with families and to help them understand and appreciate the current knowledge base of the early childhood profession.

I-2.8—To help family members enhance their understanding of their children and support the continuing development of their skills as parents.

I-2.9—To participate in building support networks for families by providing them with opportunities to interact with program staff, other families, community resources, and professional services.

Principles

P-2.1—We shall not deny family members access to their child's classroom or program setting unless access is denied by court order or other legal restriction.

P-2.2—We shall inform families of program philosophy, policies, curriculum, assessment system, and personnel qualifications, and explain why we teach as we do—which should be in accordance with our ethical responsibilities to children (see Section I).

P-2.3—We shall inform families of and, when appropriate, involve them in policy decisions.

P-2.4—We shall involve the family in significant decisions affecting their child.

P-2.5—We shall make every effort to communicate effectively with all families in a language that they understand. We shall use community resources for translation and interpretation when we do not have sufficient resources in our own programs.

P-2.6—As families share information with us about their children and families, we shall consider this information to plan and implement the program.

P-2-7—We shall inform families about the nature and purpose of the program's child assessments and how data about their child will be used.

P-2.8—We shall treat child assessment information confidentially and share this information only when there is a legitimate need for it.

P-2.9—We shall inform the family of injuries and incidents involving their child, of risks such as exposures to communicable diseases that might result in infection, and of occurrences that might result in emotional stress.

P-2.10—Families shall be fully informed of any proposed research projects involving their children and shall have the opportunity to give or withhold consent without penalty. We shall not permit or participate in research that could in any way hinder the education, development, or well-being of children.

P-2.11—We shall not engage in or support exploitation of families. We shall not use our relationship with a family for private advantage or personal gain, or enter into relationships with family members that might impair our effectiveness working with their children.

P-2.12—We shall develop written policies for the protection of confidentiality and the disclosure of children's records. These policy documents shall be made available to all program personnel and families. Disclosure of children's records beyond family members, program personnel, and consultants having an obligation of confidentiality shall require familial consent (except in cases of abuse or neglect).

P-2.13—We shall maintain confidentiality and shall respect the family's right to privacy, refraining from disclosure of confidential information and intrusion into family life. However, when we have reason to believe that a child's welfare is at risk, it is permissible to share confidential information with agencies, as well as with individuals who have legal responsibility for intervening in the child's interest.

P-2.14—In cases where family members are in conflict with one another, we shall work openly, sharing our observations of the child, to help all parties involved make informed decisions. We shall refrain from becoming an advocate for one party.

P-2.15—We shall be familiar with and appropriately refer families to community resources and professional support services. After a referral has been made, we shall follow up to ensure that services have been appropriately provided.

*The term *family* may include those adults, besides parents, with the responsibility of being involved in educating, nurturing, and advocating for the child.

Section IV: Ethical Responsibilities to Community and Society

Early childhood programs operate within the context of their immediate community made up of families and other institutions concerned with children's welfare. Our responsibilities to the community are to provide programs that meet the diverse needs of families, to cooperate with agencies and professions that share the responsibility for children, to assist families in gaining access to those agencies and allied professionals, and to assist in the development of community programs that are needed but not currently available. As individuals, we acknowledge our responsibility to provide the best possible programs of care and education for children and to conduct ourselves with honesty and integrity. Because of our specialized expertise in early childhood development and education and because the larger society shares responsibility for the welfare and protection of young children, we acknowledge a collective obligation to advocate for the best interests of children within early childhood programs and in the larger community and to serve as a voice for young children everywhere. The ideals and principles in this section are presented to distinguish between those that pertain to the work of the individual early childhood educator and those that more typically are engaged in collectively on behalf of the best interests of children—with the understanding that individual early childhood educators have a shared responsibility for addressing the ideals and principles that are identified as "collective."

Ideal (Individual)

I-4.1—To provide the community with high-quality early childhood care and education programs and services.

Ideals (Collective)

I-4.2—To promote cooperation among professionals and agencies and interdisciplinary collaboration among professions concerned with addressing issues in the health, education, and well-being of young children, their families, and their early childhood educators.

I-4.3—To work through education, research, and advocacy toward an environmentally safe world in which all children receive health care, food, and shelter; are nurtured; and live free from violence in their home and their communities.

I-4.4—To work through education, research, and advocacy toward a society in which all young children have access to high-quality early care and education programs.

I-4.5—To work to ensure that appropriate assessment systems, which include multiple sources of information, are used for purposes that benefit children.

I-4.6—To promote knowledge and understanding of young children and their needs. To work toward greater societal acknowledgment of children's rights and greater social acceptance of responsibility for the well-being of all children.

I-4.7—To support policies and laws that promote the well-being of children and families, and to work to change those that impair their well-being. To participate in developing policies and laws that are needed, and to cooperate with other individuals and groups in these efforts.

I-4.8—To further the professional development of the field of early childhood care and education and to strengthen its commitment to realizing its core values as reflected in this Code.

Principles (Individual)

P-4.1—We shall communicate openly and truthfully about the nature and extent of services that we provide.

P-4.2—We shall apply for, accept, and work in positions for which we are personally well-suited and professionally qualified. We shall not offer services that we do not have the competence, qualifications, or resources to provide.

P-4.3—We shall carefully check references and shall not hire or recommend for employment any person whose competence, qualifications, or character makes him or her unsuited for the position.

P-4.4—We shall be objective and accurate in reporting the knowledge upon which we base our program practices.

P-4.5—We shall be knowledgeable about the appropriate use of assessment strategies and instruments and interpret results accurately to families.

P-4.6—We shall be familiar with laws and regulations that serve to protect the children in our programs and be vigilant in ensuring that these laws and regulations are followed.

P-4.7—When we become aware of a practice or situation that endangers the health, safety, or well-being of children, we have an ethical responsibility to protect children or inform parents and/or others who can.

P-4.8—We shall not participate in practices that are in violation of laws and regulations that protect the children in our programs.

P-4.9—When we have evidence that an early childhood program is violating laws or regulations protecting children, we shall report the violation to appropriate authorities who can be expected to remedy the situation.

P-4.10—When a program violates or requires its employees to violate this Code, it is permissible, after fair assessment of the evidence, to disclose the identity of that program.

Principles (Collective)

P-4.11—When policies are enacted for purposes that do not benefit children, we have a collective responsibility to work to change these practices.

P-4-12—When we have evidence that an agency that provides services intended to ensure children's well-being is failing to meet its obligations, we acknowledge a collective ethical responsibility to report the problem to appropriate authorities or to the public. We shall be vigilant in our follow-up until the situation is resolved.

P-4.13—When a child protection agency fails to provide adequate protection for abused or neglected children, we acknowledge a collective ethical responsibility to work toward the improvement of these services.

NAEYC. 2011. NAEYC Code of Ethical Conduct. Reaffirmed and Updated. Washington, DC: Author.
   www.naeyc.org/files/naeyc/file/positions/Ethics%20Position%20Statement 2011.pdf
Excerpted and reprinted with permission from the National Association for the Education of Young Children (NAEYC).

   Copyright 2011 by NAEYC. Full-text versions of all current NAEYC position statements are available at www.naeyc.org/positionstatements

GLOSSARY

A Nation at Risk: A 1983 report that focused on how public schools were failing to prepare children for productive lives in a new world economy. A "word to parents" was given at the end of the report to encourage parents to support their children's education.

Active listening: This involves a give-and-take exchange in which the receiver of a message reflects his or her interpretation of that message back to the speaker.

Activity calendars: These serve two purposes: (a) They remind families about upcoming classroom and family involvement events and (b) they contain simple at-home educational activities that are linked to classroom lessons.

Activity cards: These index or other types of cards are used to deliver brief home-based educational activities. Activity cards typically are easier to construct and implement than other home-based family involvement strategies.

Activity folders: These manila or other types of office folders are used to make inexpensive educational activities. Activity folders may be used in the classroom or a family resource center. They may also be sent home.

Advocate role: A family involvement role in which parents take part in activities that promote the best interests of children.

Ambassador role: A family involvement role in which parents help to facilitate positive relationships between families and teachers.

Anti-bias education model: A model of education operating on the belief that every child deserves to develop to his or her full potential. Objectives of this model include promoting children's respect for themselves and human differences, recognizing different types of bias, and correcting biased behaviors and statements.

Assessment portfolio: Carefully selected materials that document children's classroom achievements. Portfolios ground children's academic achievements in a visible and real-life context.

Assimilation: A mode of cultural adaptation in which immigrant families fully adopt American values, behaviors, and customs.

At-risk families: These families display ineffective behaviors when faced with life adversities, including, among others, a breakdown in family relationships and a fatalistic belief that things will never get better. At-risk families stand in opposition to **strong** or **resilient families**.

Authoritarian parents: These parents exhibit a high level of demanding behavior but a low level of responsiveness. They expect blind obedience from their children.

Authoritative parents: Sometimes referred to as democratic parents. These parents are responsive to their children's wishes and ideas but also demand that agreed-upon rules be followed. Children of authoritative parents exhibit responsible and adaptive behavior.

Binuclear family: The living arrangement of children who divide their time between the households of their divorced biological parents.

Biological parents: Parents who are genetically related to a child.

Body mass index (BMI): A measure of a child's weight in relation to his or her height.

Child development survey: A survey used by parents to describe their children's development and educational skills. The survey may also be used as a beginning point from which to address parents' questions about age-appropriate behaviors.

Child maltreatment: Acts of abuse or neglect by a parent or other caregiver that result in harm, the potential for harm, or the threat of harm.

Child Welfare Information Gateway: An Internet site that summarizes child abuse and neglect laws, policies, and responsibilities for each state.

Childhood obesity: A BMI at or above the 95th percentile for children of the same age and sex.

Childhood overweight: A BMI at or above the 85th percentile and lower than the 95th percentile for children of the same age and sex.

Chronic poverty: Long-term poverty associated with factors such as ongoing physical or mental disabilities, discrimination, and a lack of education or work skills.

Chronosystem: A concept associated with Bronfenbrenner's ecology theory. The chronosystem reflects the changes that occur in our human ecology over time.

Civil union. A type of legal union between gay and lesbian partners granted by some states. Unlike same-sex marriages, civil unions provide gay and lesbian couples with many, but not necessarily all, of the rights given to heterosexual couples. Like same-sex marriages, civil unions are not recognized by the federal government. In addition, the U.S. Defense of Marriage Act (DOMA) does not require civil unions to be recognized outside the states in which they take place.

Classroom newsletters: A multipurpose outlet used to provide families with information about classroom events, field trips, school policies, words of the week, lesson highlights, upcoming parent-teacher conferences, reports from classroom committees, and general items of interest concerning children's development and education.

Clean plate club: The expectation that children are to eat everything on their plate. Nutritionists do not consider this strategy helpful in addressing childhood overweight and obesity.

Cleaning: Removal of soil and dirt with water and soap, as opposed to sanitizing and disinfecting.

Communication cartoons: These are useful in explaining classroom procedures to immigrant parents who do not read English and to English-speaking parents with limited reading skills.

Code switching: Children code-switch when speaking by going back and forth between their native language and a new language they are attempting to master.

Collaborative learning: A collectivist teaching practice that encourages children to work together to accomplish a learning objective.

Collective efficacy: The ability of a community to mobilize its social capital to improve the lives of others.

Collectivist worldview: Worldview in which the rights, interests, and needs of the group are given priority. Cooperation, social conformity, group harmony, a sense of duty to others, and the fulfillment of assigned social roles are emphasized. This worldview is associated with traditional African, Asian, Hispanic or Latino, and Native American cultures.

Community: A location defined by the quality of life provided through its institutions, services, cultural events, and the cohesion of its neighborhoods.

Community education updates: These are used to update families about new educational opportunities and family services in their town or city.

Community scan: An informal strategy teachers use to assess a community's social capacity.

Confrontive coping: A problem-focused coping strategy that involves asserting one's needs and expectations, expressing one's feelings, and taking chances in order to explore new life experiences.

Consent laws: Laws that allow grandparents to give legal consent for their grandchildren to receive educational and community services.

Consumable supplies: Classroom supplies that are "consumed," such as construction paper, paint, crayons, tape, pencils, markers, glue, labels, envelops, computer supplies, and notebooks.

Costs: A concept associated with social exchange theory. Costs include anything that we find punitive or unrewarding in our social relationships.

Covenant marriage: Couples voluntarily enter covenant marriage with the understanding that their state will grant a divorce only in a limited number of situations. Premarriage counseling is often mandated as part of a covenant marriage.

Covertism: Refers to the hidden institutional advantages and disadvantages individuals receive based on their membership in some group, such as a dominant or nondominant culture, a majority or minority race, or a particular gender.

Culturally responsive teacher: A teacher who is able to appreciate, understand, and work with children and families from different cultures. Becoming a culturally responsive teacher involves more than learning "facts." It also involves time and an examination of our attitudes toward different cultural beliefs and behaviors.

Culture: A learned value system of norms, beliefs, and attitudes that shape our behaviors. Cultural values are passed from generation to generation.

Culture of poverty: A view in which families living in poverty are characterized by defeatist attitudes, a lack of initiative, and a lack of intelligence, all of which keep them from making economic advancements. In short, the poor are themselves to blame for their poverty. This is an outdated view as it overlooks other economic and social factors.

Daily and **weekly folders:** These are used to exchange a range of materials and information between the classroom and home (e.g., money, notes and other class materials, reading logs).

Deconstruction: Generally, the critical examination of ideas. The deconstruction of cultural stereotypes can be accomplished by remaining alert to stereotypes, avoiding ethnocentric definitions of achievement, and personalizing our experiences with cultural diversity.

Deployment: The period during which the military parent is away from home.

Disinfecting: Involves the use of chemical agents and other procedures that remove virtually all germs, as opposed to cleaning and sanitizing.

Distancing behaviors: A destructive coping strategy that involves denying or trying to forget about the presence of stress as well as making light of stressful situations.

Door openers: Statements a listener uses to encourage the speaker to provide more information (e.g., "Tell me more about that.").

Education for All Handicapped Children Act: This act required teachers to join with parents and community professionals to design lessons and classroom environments that accommodated the skills and needs of handicapped children.

Educational workshops: Workshops that focus on increasing parents' knowledge and skills (e.g., GED and English as Second Language workshops).

Emerging families: Family arrangements that are becoming more visible and gaining recognition in American society.

Emotional or psychological abuse: A pattern of punitive verbal statements and behavioral acts that damage children's self-worth and self-confidence.

Enculturation: A mode of adaptation in which immigrant families attempt to hold on to the cultural values and behaviors of their home country.

e-Pals: A modern-day version of pen pals. This form of communication is especially useful for family members living in other regions of the country or abroad.

Escape-avoidance behaviors: A destructive coping strategy that involves behaviors such as hoping for miracles, using food or drugs, and avoiding other people.

Ethnicity: Also known as **ancestral origin**, ethnicity describes the connection we feel to others based on a shared ancestry and cultural heritage.

Ethnocentrism: Holding one's own culture as superior to that of others and failing to recognize or honor different cultural standards and experiences.

Ethnorelativism: Interpreting and judging behaviors and attitudes within their own cultural context.

Exosystem: A concept associated with Bronfenbrenner's ecological theory. The exosystem includes social systems in which children do not directly participate but are nevertheless influenced by the decisions of those who do participate. Examples include school administrative bodies, community agencies, businesses, and the federal government.

Extended family: The nuclear family as well as immediate relatives such as grandparents, aunts, uncles, and cousins.

Extended parents: Relatives of a nuclear family who assume parenting responsibilities.

Externalized behavior problems: These occur when children externalize their frustrations in unhealthy ways. Examples include destructive behavior, aggression, and acting-out behavior.

Families of choice: Also known as **network** or **friendship families**, families of choice are formed when individuals who are not related join together to provide each other with emotional and/or financial support.

Familism: Emphasis on the priorities of the family over those of individuals.

Family backpacks: These are designed to reinforce classroom learning experiences in the home environment. Backpacks contain all the materials and directions parents need to complete an educational activity at home with their children.

Family boundaries: A concept associated with family systems theory. Family boundaries function like gates in controlling the flow of information and social interactions between the family system and the outside world. Family boundaries are generally characterized as "open," "closed," or "permeable."

Family certificates: These certificates, which can be given to parents at any time, honor parents' commitment to their children's education.

Family climate: A concept associated with family systems theory. The family climate refers to the emotional environment in which family members live.

Family clubs: Clubs formed among parents in a classroom or school who share similar interests or hobbies. Family clubs provide a venue in which parents can socialize and learn from each other. They can also lead to new learning opportunities for the classroom.

Family equilibrium: A concept associated with family systems theory. Family equilibrium is defined as a state of normalcy where everyone in a family knows what is expected of him or her. Families attempt to maintain or return to a state of equilibrium after they encounter challenges to their family life.

Family fun nights: Social events where parents can relax, enjoy themselves, and get to know teachers and other families. Family fun nights can help facilitate family resiliency.

Family household: A type of household in which at least one individual is related to the householder by birth, marriage, or adoption.

Family involvement: A broadly defined concept that includes activities connecting children's home and classroom learning experiences, as well as activities addressing the total needs of children and their families. This broad definition is best reflected in Joyce Epstein's family-school-community partnership model.

Family involvement web: Center point: The part of a family involvement web that contains the name of a thematic unit.

Family involvement web: Inner (first) ring: The part of a family involvement web that contains descriptions of the classroom lessons that support the thematic unit.

Family involvement web: Outer (second) ring: The part of a family involvement web that contains descriptions of the family involvement activities that support classroom lessons.

Family knowledge: Knowledge based on the life experiences and hobbies of individual family members.

Family myths: A concept associated with family systems theory. Family myths refer to beliefs about family life that are not open for debate.

Family of origin: The family into which we are born.

Family portfolios: These are similar to classroom portfolios in that both are used to collect samples of children's work as documentation of their developmental and educational progress. In the case of family portfolios, children work with their parents rather than teachers to collect samples produced at home. The classroom and family portfolios can be shared during parent-teacher conferences.

Family resource centers: These empower families by providing them with their own space where they can read books, magazines, and other materials related to child development and childhood education. Family resource centers also contain educational materials and games that families can check out and work on at home with their children.

Family rituals: A concept associated with family systems theory. Family rituals include patterns of behavior and daily routines that give meaning to family life and interactions.

Family rules: A concept associated with family systems theory. Family rules refer to the standards of behavior that govern life within a family system.

Family stories: A concept associated with family systems theory. Family stories are used to transmit family values and rules between generations.

Family support groups: These allow parents who are in a similar stressful situation to share their experiences, receive comfort, and feel empowered.

Family survey: A device for gathering information about how best to communicate with families and for planning family involvement activities that are linked to families' interests.

Family systems theory: Theory in which the family is viewed as a social system that interacts with but is separate from other social systems, such as schools and religious institutions. Within the family are subsystems such as mother-child or siblings, each with its own interaction pattern. Family members are seen as interdependent, meaning that the behavior of one subsystem or family member has the potential to impact the entire family.

Family workshops: These empower families by providing them with opportunities to learn new information and develop new skills. There are at least three types of family workshops: informational, educational, and make-and-take.

Federal Children's Bureau: A forerunner of government-sponsored programs targeting children. Developed in 1912, the purpose of the bureau was to collect and disseminate information about children's development and education.

Fictive or **affiliated kin:** Individuals with no biological or legal relationship to a family but who are nevertheless viewed as part of the family and given family responsibilities. Fictive kin can include neighbors who care for children, godparents, youth workers, and teachers.

Food insecurity: This occurs when families lack the economic resources to access enough food for an active and healthy life.

Formal education: Education characterized by a planned learning environment dedicated to helping children master state educational standards.

Formal support: The types of support provided though community services.

Gay and lesbian families: Same-sex partners with or without children.

Generational poverty: Two of more generations of families who survive on limited family resources.

Goals 2000: Educate America Act: A document that set eight national goals for schools to meet by the year 2000. Federal grants were given to states to develop educational standards, assessments, and accountability systems. The act included a parent participation standard.

Grandparent caregiver: Grandparents who serve as their grandchild's primary caregiver or co-caregiver.

Group rewards: A collectivist teaching practice that focuses on rewarding group rather than individual behavior and accomplishments.

Head Start: A program created as part of President Johnson's war on poverty in 1965. The goal of Head Start is to promote school readiness among low-income preschool children. The program's focus on connecting classrooms, families, and communities reflects the family-school-community partnership model.

Health: A state of complete physical, mental, and social well-being and not merely the absence of disease or infirmity.

High-context cultures: Cultures that rely on more subtle forms of communication, such as nonverbal facial and hand gestures, than explicit verbalizations. For example, Asian cultures are perhaps best known for practicing a high-context style of communication. High-context cultures stand in contrast to **low-context cultures**.

Home-classroom dialogue journals: These are especially useful when parents and teachers must keep in close contact, such as when a doctor asks that a child's medical condition be closely monitored throughout the day.

Home visits: Visits made by teachers to children's homes before and/or during the school year. Home visits serve multiple purposes, including but not limited to developing a better understanding of children's home life and establishing rapport with families.

Homeless family: A family that lacks permanent housing.

Household: Everyone who occupies a housing unit.

Human capital: While businesses raise economic capital, families, teachers, and community professionals raise human capital in the form of knowledge and skills. It is our human capital that prepares us for life as productive workers and community citizens. The types of human capital valued by a society can change over time.

Human ecology: Urie Bronfenbrenner developed this theory. Human development is viewed as occurring within a network of social systems (microsystem, mesosystem, exosystem, macrosystem, and chronosystem). We are active participants in our human ecology, both adapting to and influencing the social interactions that take place around us.

IDEA: The Individual With Disabilities Education Act. IDEA is a federal law that specifies the rights of children with disabilities and the responsibilities of schools to ensure those rights.

IEP: The individualized education plan. The IEP contains goals and services to promote the development and education of children with disabilities who are three years of age and older.

IFSP: The individualized family service plan. The IFSP contains goals and services to promote the development and education of infants and toddlers (under age three) with disabilities.

Individualism: Emphasis on the priorities of individuals over those of the family.

Individualistic worldview: Worldview in which the rights, interests, and needs of the individual are important. Personal goals, independence, and self-fulfillment are valued. This worldview is associated with the dominant European American culture.

Informal education: The many informal ways that families support their children's learning experiences in the classroom, at home, and in the community.

Informal support: The types of social support provided by friends and family.

Informational workshops: These involve the delivery of factual information about topics related to childhood development and education, school policies, and health and safety issues.

Interactive bulletin boards: These actively engage viewers by requiring them to take some type of action.

Intergenerational (skipped) households: Households in which grandparents serve as the sole caregivers for their grandchildren.

Internalized behavior problems: These occur when children internalize their frustrations in unhealthy ways. Examples include withdrawal, somatic complaints, and anxiety.

Interpreting: Teachers make interpretations to help one child understand the verbal and nonverbal communication of another child.

Intervention approach to multicultural education: Teachers provide lessons on cultural respect only after observing children engaging in discriminatory behaviors.

Involved-vigilant parenting: A type of parenting in which African American parents (especially mothers) teach children (especially sons) how to protect themselves from possible acts of discrimination while also providing them with support and understanding.

Lanham Act: Developed in 1941, this act provided funding for child care programs for mothers who entered the workforce during World War II.

Learning environment: Any location in which children receive instruction and care. Learning environments commonly include public and private schools, nonprofit and private early learning centers, and Head Start programs. However, they can also include other locations.

Least restrictive environment: Educating and socializing children with disabilities within

regular classrooms to the extent that their educational needs allow.

Legal definition of family: According to the U.S. Census Bureau, "a family is a group of two people or more (one of whom is the householder) related by birth, marriage, or adoption and residing together." This definition is sometimes too narrow to encompass all the different family arrangements encountered by teachers.

Literally homeless: Families without homes who live in their cars, tents, emergency shelters, or other temporary locations.

Literature circles: An example of collaborative learning where children explore a book together.

Living wage: A wage that supports a reasonable standard of living in a given community.

Longitudinal studies: Research studies that focus on changes in behavior, attitudes, and scores over time.

Low-context cultures: Cultures that rely on more direct verbal communication than subtle forms of nonverbal communication. Individuals who practice this type of communication are most likely to come from the United States, Western Europe, and Australia. Low-context cultures stand in contract to **high-context cultures**.

Macrosystem: A concept associated with Bronfenbrenner's ecological theory. The macrosystem reflects the cultural values, beliefs, and customs that govern priorities and interactions in other social systems.

Mainstreaming: Integrating children with disabilities into classrooms with their typically developing peers.

Make-and-take workshops: Workshops in which parents make educational games and other instructional products for use at home.

Mastery experiences: The sense of self-efficacy we experience when we reflect on our mastery of even small successes. In short, "success builds success."

Material resources: The consumable supplies, door prizes, refreshments, rentals, and copying and printing charges that should be considered when planning family involvement activities.

Mesosystem: A concept associated with Bronfenbrenner's ecological theory. The mesosystem reflects the number and quality of linkages between children's microsystems. The family-school partnership is one example of a mesosystem.

Microsystem: A concept associated with Bronfenbrenners' ecological theory. The microsystem includes social systems closest to a child's daily life, such as the classroom and home.

Minimum wage: The lowest legal hourly wage, currently set at $7.25 by the federal government.

Minority: A fluid and relative social marker. At least some family scholars refuse to use the term in order to avoid confusion and negative stereotypes.

Misrepresentation: Characteristic of a multicultural festival approach to multicultural education, misrepresentation occurs when teachers use materials and information that misinform or fail to fully inform children about a particular culture.

Motivational development resources: Three personal resources influence parents' motivation to support their children's education: (a) their belief that they need to be involved in their children's education, (b) their sense that they can be effective in supporting their children's education, and (c) invitations from teachers to support their children's education.

Multicultural festival (tour and detour) approach to multicultural education: Teachers make use of isolated cultural celebrations to teach values and customs. For example, African American cultures are addressed only during Black History month.

Multigenerational households: Households that consist of three generations (child, parent, and grandparent) in which grandparents coparent with parents.

Multiple partner fertility: Refers to adults who have children with more than one partner. Multiple partner fertility may accompany serial monogamy.

Negative beliefs: Parents display negative beliefs when they ignore or downplay their child's ability to meet a learning challenge.

Neglect: The failure of a parent or caregiver to provide for the basic needs of a child.

Network (friendship) families: These families are formed when individuals who are not related join together to provide each other with emotional and/or financial support.

No Child Left Behind Act (NCLB): This is the major federal policy guiding American public education today. Included in NCLB are specific requirements for the involvement of families in their children's education.

Nonfamily household: A type of household in which a householder lives alone or with nonrelatives only.

Nonnormative stressors: Stressors that are extreme and outside a family's control, such as natural disasters, discrimination, or living in high-crime neighborhoods.

Normative stressors: Stressors that families experience during the family life cycle, such as the death of a family member or a child's entering school.

Normed families: Families that previously were viewed as atypical but are now considered a part of "normal" American society. Normed families include single-parent families, stepfamilies, and adoptive families.

Nuclear family: A traditional family consisting of a husband and wife and their children.

Offtime: An event is considered offtime in the life cycle when it occurs at a nonnormative age or life phase. Grandparent caregivers experience offtime when they are required to recycle their parenting role.

Parent: From a legal perspective, a biological or adoptive adult. This definition stands in contrast to a **professional definition of parenthood**.

Parent diaries: These are especially useful in facilitating communication within family support groups. The leader of the group assigns a topic for parents to write about between meetings. The entries are then used to structure group discussion.

Parenting: Child guidance practices used to socialize children.

Passive listening: This involves not speaking and only listening. This type of listening sends the message that we are focused on what the speaker is saying.

Peer mentoring: A collectivist teaching practice that encourages children to help each other.

Permissive parents: Parents who make few demands on their children and set few boundaries or rules.

Person-focused attitude: Parents exhibit a person-focused attitude toward their children's academic performance when they emphasize the importance of specific outcomes, such as receiving a certain grade or recognition.

Persona dolls and puppets: These take on personalities and have personal background stories, just like real people. They are used to facilitate children's discussion about and analysis of unfair acts, the feelings that resulted, and changes that can be made to create more respectful relationships.

Personal definitions of family: Our personal beliefs about how families should be structured and behave.

Photo newsletters: These contain photographs of children engaged in classroom activities and are especially useful following holidays and classroom celebrations when there are many photographs to share with families.

Physical abuse: The nonaccidental infliction of pain or injury.

Pickering/Connick balancing test: Disciplinary actions that school administrators can take against teachers for speaking out publicly against their school, when that speech is viewed as interfering with the efficient operations of the school.

Picture letter: A letter of welcome for young children who are just starting to read. Drawings and photographs are used to depict the children's new teacher and their new classroom.

Podcasts: A classroom audio or video feed that can be downloaded over the Internet or on a portable media player.

Policy briefing updates: These are used to inform families about early childhood polices. Policy updates can empower families to advocate their children's interests.

Positive beliefs: Parents display positive beliefs when they express confidence in their child's ability to overcome learning challenges.

Positive reappraisal: A problem-focused coping strategy that involves seeking out personal growth opportunities, rediscovering the important things in life, and engaging in inspirational and creative activities.

Positive reinforcement: Anything that is valued by an individual and once delivered results in more frequent displays of a target behavior.

Post-deployment and reintegration: The period of time following a military parent's return home.

Poverty spells: Short-term poverty experiences due to temporary changes in employment or a life crisis.

Precariously housed: Families who are precariously housed avoid becoming homeless by staying with friends and family members or by paying a high proportion of their income on rent.

Pre-deployment: The period leading up to a notice of deployment and ending when the military parent leaves home.

Process-focused attitude: Parents exhibit a process-focused attitude toward their children's academic performance when they emphasize the pleasure of educational pursuits and reinforce their children's efforts in accomplishing classroom tasks.

Professional definitions of family: Definitions of family provided by professional organizations. Professional definitions of family may not reflect legal definitions.

Professional definition of parenthood: This definition acknowledges the parenting role played by any adult who, regardless of his or her legal standing, cares and provides for a child. This professional definition often is at odds with legal definitions.

Professional knowledge: The knowledge teachers acquire through teacher training programs.

Professional study group: Teachers meeting to share their experiences in working with families, explore ways to address family involvement challenges, and discuss strategies for empowering family-teacher partnerships.

Prompting: Teachers' use of visual, verbal, and other cues to help children successfully complete tasks by themselves.

Protector role: In this family involvement role, parents help to ensure the physical and emotional safety of children.

Race: A socially constructed concept that categorizes individuals based on physical features.

Random acts of kindness awards: These recognize the contributions parents make to their children's well-being. Rather than being given for a specific contribution, as thank you notes are, these awards are randomly given throughout the year.

Reframing: Restating comments so they are more realistic and empowering.

Residence order: This hypothetical legal order would grant stepparents certain decision making rights related to the best interests of their stepchildren while not taking away the rights of nonresidential biological parents.

Rewards: A concept associated with social exchange theory. Rewards include any material, physical, social, and/or psychological experience that reinforces social relationships.

Role ambiguity: A concept associated with the theory of symbolic interactionism. Role ambiguity occurs when individuals are unsure of how to carry out an assigned or adopted role.

Role conflict: A concept associated with the theory of symbolic interactionism. Role conflict characterizes the stress we experience when we are unable to reconcile the different roles we are expected to perform.

Role overload: A concept associated with the theory of symbolic interactionism. Role overload occurs when we feel overwhelmed by our attempts to fulfill multiple role responsibilities.

Role strain: A concept associated with the theory of symbolic interactionism. Role strain occurs when we lack the resources needed to successfully carry out one or more roles. Role strain can result from role overload.

Same-sex marriage: A type of legal union between gay and lesbian partners. In a same-sex marriage, partners receive the same rights given to heterosexual couples. A few states recognize same-sex marriage, but no state is required to do so, according to the U.S. Defense of Marriage Act (DOMA).

Sanitizing: This involves not only the removal of soil and dirt (cleaning) but also the removal of some germs with additional chemical agents.

Schoolcentric perspective of family involvement: School policies, activities, and events defined by and primarily conducted for the benefit of teachers and school administrators reflect this perspective.

School development program model (SDP): Developed by James Comer, this model takes a comprehensive approach to school reform by mobilizing families, administrators, teachers, school support staff, and community professionals to support the developmental needs of the whole child.

School development program (SDP): Operations: The three SDP teams pursue three operations that, when taken together, create school changes that are supportive of the whole child: (a) a comprehensive school plan, (b) staff development, and (c) assessment and modification.

School development program (SDP): Parent team: One of three SDP teams. Members are responsible for planning family involvement strategies and activities at all levels of school life.

School development program (SDP): Processes: Three SDP processes are used to guide the social interactions of the three SDP teams: (a) no fault, (b) consensus, and (c) collaboration.

School development program (SDP): School planning and management team: One of three SDP teams. Members are responsible for overseeing the SDP comprehensive plan of action.

School development program (SDP): Student staff and support team: One of three SDP teams. Members are responsible for facilitating the well-being of staff and students.

School discourse: The language, materials, norms, expectations, and practices used by teachers and other school staff on a daily basis.

Schools as community centers: Also referred to as *full-service schools*, these centers provide comprehensive educational, welfare, health, and recreational services in one location.

Second-parent adoption (co-parent adoption): Allowed in some states, a second same-sex partner is allowed to adopt the first partner's biological or previously adopted child.

Selective acculturation: A mode of cultural adaptation in which immigrant families hold on to the values and behaviors of their home country while at the same time selectively incorporating the dominant American culture into their everyday lives.

Self-efficacy: A "Yes I can" attitude that is reflected in one's perseverance, even when challenges arise.

Serial monogamy: Describes the series of monogamous relationships individuals may experience over their lifetime.

Sexual abuse: The exploitation of children for sexual gratification.

Sharing circles: A collectivist teaching practice in which children meet in a group to share something important with their peers.

Skills development resources: The cognitive and academic skills children need to succeed in the classroom.

Social capacity: A community's social capacity is reflect in its ability to use formal and informal connections to provide for the physical, psychological, social, and material care of its neighborhoods.

Social capital: The time and energy families and communities devote to supporting the development of children and youth. Social capital can be used to support human capital.

Social exchange theory: Theory in which relationships are viewed as a series of social exchanges in which we attempt to maximize our rewards and minimize our costs.

Social mini-conferences: Informal discussions between parents and teachers that help to reinforce the parent-teacher partnership. Social mini-conferencing can occur during morning drop-off, afternoon pickup, home visits, and other social situations.

Social persuasion: A strategy for building a sense of self-efficacy in which our mentors persuade us that we have the ability to succeed. This is most effective when we are given honest but supportive feedback about our skills and behavior.

Sociological parents: Parents who assume the mother or father role even though they are not biologically related to a child. Examples include foster parents, adoptive parents, and stepparents.

Space resources: The classroom, school, or community space that is available to support family involvement activities.

Staff support resources: The types and degree of support needed from school secretaries, principals, and custodians before, during, and following family involvement activities.

Stepfamilies (blended families): These families contain stepchildren and their stepparents, half siblings, and stepsiblings.

Stereotypes: These occur when descriptions of a cultural, racial, or other group are applied to everyone in that group and individual differences are ignored.

Strengths report: Teachers may add this to a report card to inform parents about their child's positive social behaviors, unique interests, classroom contributions, and academic skills.

Strong (resilient) families: Families who respond positively to a life stressor and emerge feeling strengthened, more resourceful, and more confident than they did before the life stressor.

Student role: A family involvement role in which parents attend workshops or classes to advance their knowledge and skills.

Support role: A behind-the-scenes family involvement role in which parents help teachers prepare classroom lessons and activities.

Supportive scaffolding: Parents and teachers provide supportive scaffolding when they help children acquire new knowledge and skills at comfortable but increasingly challenging levels.

Symbolic interactionism: This theory is concerned with how we use symbols (e.g., language and roles) to guide our social interactions. The concepts of role ambiguity, role conflict, role overload, and role strain are part of this theory.

Task analysis: Breaking down a complex behavior into discrete parts, which are then reviewed and practiced by a child.

Teacher role: A family involvement role in which parents work directly with children to carry out activities in the classroom, at home, or in the community.

Teacher: Anyone who receives a professional license from his or her state to teach and care for children.

Thank you notes: These empower parents by acknowledging and honoring the contributions they make to their children's development and education.

Thrift economies: Thrift outlets, consignment and secondhand stores, and yard sales that allow families with limited incomes to stretch their budgets.

Time resources: The time commitments of families, community volunteers, and teachers themselves that should be considered when planning family involvement activities.

Tip sheets: These provide families with practical information about their children's education and general well-being.

Tokenism: Characteristic of a multicultural festival approach to multicultural education, tokenism occurs when one token item is used to represent an entire culture.

Traditional family: The family structure that is considered the norm in society at any given point in time.

Transformative approach to multicultural education: Approach in which teachers incorporate cultural diversity into children's daily learning experiences, introduce activities that help them personalize the cultural experiences of others, and explore with their students the similarities among cultures.

Transnational families: Families whose members are scattered across national borders.

Trivializing a culture: Characteristic of a multicultural festival approach to multicultural education, a culture is trivialized when its complex heritage is reduced to one event.

Vicarious experiences: Our sense of self-efficacy is reinforced when we have mentors who give us constructive criticism as we try out new skills. Role-playing different professional situations with our mentors is one example of a vicarious experience. Keeping a journal in which we document what we learn from our mentors is another type of vicarious experience.

Videotaped modeling: This involves videotaping one child as he or she performs a target behavior. The videotape is then used to teach another child with a disability the skills involved in carrying out that behavior.

Virtual family resource center: A Web-based center that provides links to educational tips, games, and other information to assist families in supporting their children's education.

Vulnerable families: Families who, because of their life circumstances, experience financial, emotional, and physical stress that can impair their functioning and well-being. **Homeless families** and **working-poor families** are two examples of vulnerable families.

Whole child perspective: Emphasis on the interplay among children's cognitive, psychological, language, social, ethical, and physical development.

Working-poor families: Families whose income remains below the poverty threshold despite family members' full-time employment.

Works Progress Administration (WPA): A government agency established in 1933 to provide jobs for the unemployed. One result was the establishment of nursery schools and the employment of teachers.

Worldview: A frame of reference for guiding our understanding of the world, our place in it, and our interpersonal relationships.

Zone of proximal distance: The distance between a child's actual developmental level (tasks completed independently) and his or her level of potential development (tasks completed with adult support or the support of more capable peers).

REFERENCES

Preface

Association for Childhood Education International. (2007). *Elementary education standards and supporting explanation.* Retrieved July 15, 2011, from http://acei.org/wp-content/uploads/ACEIElementaryStandardsSupportingExplanation.5.07.pdf

Duncan, A. (2010, March 15). *Reform, accountability, and leading from the local level: Secretary Arne Duncan's remarks to the National League of Cities'* *Congressional City Conference.* Retrieved April 20, 2010, from http://www2.ed.gov/news/speeches/2010/03/03152010.html

National Association for the Education of Young Children. (2009). *NAEYC standards for early childhood professional preparation programs.* Retrieved July 15, 2011, from www.naeyc.org/files/naeyc/file/positions/ProfPrepStandards09.pdf

Chapter 1

American Academy of Family Physicians. (2009). *Definition of family.* Retrieved December 18, 2010, from www.aafp.org/online/en/home/policy/policies/f/familydefinitionof.html. Reproduced with permission from definition of family from the 2009 issue of http://www.aafp/org/onlline/en/home/policy/policies/f/familydefinitionof.html. Copyright © 2009 American Academy of Family Physicians. All Rights Reserved.

American Association of Family and Consumer Sciences. (1997). *Public policy manual.* Alexandria, VA: Author.

Baumrind, D. (1989). Rearing competent children. In W. Damon (Ed.), *Child development today and tomorrow* (pp. 349–378). San Francisco, CA: Jossey-Bass.

Baumrind, D. (1991a). Effective parenting during the early adolescent transition. In P. A. Cowan & M. Hetherington (Eds.), *Family transitions* (pp. 111–163). Hillsdale, NJ: Lawrence Erlbaum.

Baumrind, D. (1991b). Parenting styles and adolescent development. In R. M. Lerner, A. C. Petersen, & J. Brooks-Gunn (Eds.), *Encyclopedia of adolescence* (pp. 746–758). New York, NY: Garland.

Bigner, J. J. (2006). *Parent-child relations: An introduction to parenting* (7th ed.). Upper Saddle River, NJ: Pearson.

Bowen, G. L., Richman, J. M., & Bowen, N. K. (2000). Families in the context of communities across time (pp. 117–128). In S. J. Price, P. C. McKenry, & M. J. Murphy (Eds.), *Families across time: A life course perspective.* Los Angeles, CA: Roxbury.

Cherlin, A. J. (2010). Demographic trends in the United States: A review of research in the 2000s. *Journal of Marriage and Family, 72*(3), 403–419.

Christian, L. G. (2006). Understanding families: Applying family systems theory to early childhood practice. *Young Children, 61*(1), 12–20.

Coleman, J. (1988). Human capital in the creation of human capital [Supplemental material]. *American Journal of Sociology, 94,* S95–S120.

Coleman, J. (1994). Social capital, human capital, and investment in youth. In A. C. Petersen & J. T. Mortimer

(Eds.), *Youth unemployment and society.* New York, NY: Cambridge University Press.

Crosbie-Burnett, M., & Lewis, E. A. (1993). Use of African-American family structures and functioning to address the challenges of European-American postdivorce families. *Family Relations, 42,* 243–248.

Davey, M., & Robbins, L. (2009, April 3). *Iowa court says gay marriage ban is unconstitutional. The New York Times.* Retrieved April 4, 2009, from www.nytimes.com

Goodnough, A., & O'Connor, A. (2009, April 8). Vermont legislature makes same-sex marriage legal. *The New York Times.* Retrieved April 8, 2009, from http://www.nytimes.com

Gramlich, J. (2011, February 11). Gay rights supporters cheer victories. *Stateline.org.* Retrieved October 13, 2011, from http://www.stateline.org/live/details/story?contentId=553330

Human Rights Campaign. (2006). *Rights and protections denied same-sex partners.* Retrieved June 14, 2007, from http://www.hrc.org/issues/5478.htm

Lamborn, S. D., Mounts, N. S., Steinberg, L., & Dornbusch, S. M. (1991). Patterns of competence and adjustment among adolescents from authoritative, authoritarian, indulgent, and neglectful families. *Child Development, 62*(5), 1049–1065.

Lewin, K. (1951). *Field theory in social science: Selected theoretical papers.* New York, NY: Harper & Row.

Muscott, H. S., Szczesiul, S., Berk, B., Staub, K., Hoover, J., & Perry-Chisholm, P. (2008). Positive behavior interventions and supports. *Teaching Exceptional Children, 40*(6), 6–14.

Parcel, T. L., Dufur, M. J., & Zito, R. C. (2010). Capital at home and at school: A review and synthesis. *Journal of Marriage and Family, 72*(4), 828–846.

Parke, R. (2004). Development in the family. *Annual Review of Psychology, 55,* 365–399.

Sampson, R. J., Morenoff, J. D., & Earls, F. (1999). Beyond social capital: Spatial dynamics of collective efficacy for children. *American Sociological Review, 64*(5), 633–660.

Sampson, R. J., Morenoff, J. D., & Gannon-Rowley, T. (2002). Assessing "neighborhood effects": Social processes and new directions in research. *Annual Review of Sociology, 28,* 443–478.

Sampson, R. J., Raudenbush, S. W., & Earls, F. (1997). Neighborhoods and violent crime: A multilevel study of collective efficacy. *Science, 277*(5328), 918–924.

Sapouna, M. (2010). Collective efficacy in the school context: Does it help explain victimization and bullying among Greek primary and secondary school students? *Journal of Interpersonal Violence, 25*(10), 1912–1927.

Scanzoni, J. (2000). *Designing families: The search for self and community in the information age.* Thousand Oaks, CA: Pine Forge Press.

Schutz, A. (2006). Home is a prison in the global city: The tragic failure of school-based community engagement strategies. *Review of Educational Research, 76*(4), 691–743.

Smith, S. R., Hamon, R. R., Ingoldsby, B. B., & Miller, J. E. (2009). *Exploring family theories* (2nd ed.). New York, NY: Oxford University Press.

Smock, P. J., & Greenland, F. R. (2010). Diversity in pathways to parenthood: Patterns, implications, and emerging research directions. *Journal of Marriage and Family, 72*(3), 576–593.

Tasker, F. (2005). Lesbian mothers, gay fathers, and their children: A review. *Developmental and Behavioral Pediatrics, 26*(3), 224–240.

Teti, D. M., & Candelaria, M. A. (2002). Parenting competence. In M. H. Bornstein (Ed.), *Handbook of parenting* (2nd ed., Vol. 4, pp. 149–180). Mahwah, NJ: Lawrence Erlbaum.

Thomas, R. M. (1996). *Comparing theories of child development* (4th ed.). Pacific Grove, CA: Brooks/Cole.

U.S. Census Bureau. (2007). *The living arrangement of children in 2005.* Retrieved May 23, 2007, from www.census.gov/population/pop-profile/dynamic/LivArrChildren.pdf

U.S. Census Bureau. (2010, May 10). *Current population survey (CPS)—Definitions and explanations.* Retrieved May 15, 2010, from http://www.census.gov/population/www/cps/cpsdef.html

Vega, W. A., Ang, A., Rodriguez, M. A., & Finch, B. K. (2011). Neighborhood protective effects on depression in Latinos. *American Journal of Community Psychology, 47*(1–2), 114–126.

White, J. M., & Klein, D. M. (2002). *Family theories* (2nd ed.). Thousand Oaks, CA: Sage.

Yonas, M. A., Lewis, T., Hussey, J. M., Thompson, R., Newton, R., English, D., & Dubowitz, H. (2010). Perceptions of neighborhood collective efficacy moderate the impact of maltreatment on aggression. *Child Maltreatment, 15*(1), 37–47.

Chapter 2

Association for Childhood Education International. (2007). *Elementary education standards and supporting explanation.* Retrieved July 15, 2011, from http://acei.org/wp-content/uploads/ACEIElementaryStandardsSupportingExplanation.5.07.pdf

Child Welfare League of America. (n.d.). *The history of White House conferences on children and youth.* Retrieved April 22, 2010, from http://www.cwla.org/advocacy/whitehouseconfhistory.pdf

Coleman, M., & Tymes, V. (2004). Family involvement: Connecting children's classroom and family environments. *ACEI Focus on Pre-K & K, 16*(3), 1–7.

Copple, C., & Bredekamp, S. (2009). *Developmentally appropriate practice in early childhood programs serving children from birth to age 8* (3rd ed.). Washington, DC: National Association for the Education of Young Children.

Dryfoos, J., & Maguire, S. (2002). *Inside full-service community schools.* Thousand Oaks, CA: Corwin.

Duncan, A. (2010, March 15). *Reform, accountability, and leading from the local level: Secretary Arne Duncan's remarks to the National League of Cities' Congressional City Conference.* Retrieved April 20, 2010, from http://www2.ed.gov/news/speeches/2010/03/03152010.html

Epstein, J. L. (2011). *School, family, and community partnerships: Preparing educators and improving schools* (2nd ed.). Boulder, CO: Westview Press.

Epstein, J. L., Sanders, M. G., Simon, B. S., Salinas, K. C., Johnson, N. R., & Van Voorhis, F. L. (2002). *School, family and community partnerships: Your handbook for action* (2nd ed.). Thousand Oaks, CA: Corwin.

Garwood, S. G., Phillips, D., Hartman, A., & Zigler, E. F. (1989). As the pendulum swings: Federal agency programs for children. *American Psychologist, 44*(2), 434–440.

Kaczmarek, L. A., Goldstein, H., Florey, J. D., Carter, A., & Cannon, S. (2004). Supporting families: A preschool model. *Topics in Early Childhood Special Education, 24*(4), 213–266.

Keyser, J. (2006). *From parents to partners: Building a family-centered early childhood program.* St. Paul, MN: Redleaf Press.

Kourofsky, C. E, & Cole, R. E. (2010). Young children can be key to fire-safe families. *Young Children, 65*(3), 84–87.

Lutton, A., & Ahmed, S. (2009). NAEYC revises standards for early childhood professional preparation programs. *Young Children, 64*(6), 88–89.

Markiewicz, D. (2008, August 9). In-school successes. *The Atlanta Journal-Constitution,* pp. D1, D6.

Moseman, C. C. (2003). Primary teachers' beliefs about family competence to influence classroom practices. *Early Education and Development, 14*(2), 125–153.

Muscott, H. S., Szczesiul, S., Berk, B., Staub, K., Hoover, J., & Perry-Chisholm, P. (2008). Positive behavior interventions and supports. *Teaching Exceptional Children, 40*(6), 6–14.

National Association for the Education of Young Children. (2005). *Code of ethical conduct and statement of commitment.* Retrieved May 21, 2011, from http://faculty.weber.edu/tlday/2610/code05.pdf

National Association for the Education of Young Children. (2007). *NAEYC early childhood program standards and accreditation criteria: The mark of quality in early childhood education.* Washington, DC: Author.

National Association for the Education of Young Children. (2009). *NAEYC standards for early childhood professional preparation programs.* Retrieved July 15, 2011, from http://www.naeyc.org/files/naeyc/file/positions/ProfPrepStandards09.pdf

National PTA. (2009). *PTA national standards for family-school partnerships: An implementation guide.* Retrieved July 15, 2011, from http://www.pta.org/Documents/National_Standards_Implementation_Guide_2009.pdf

No Child Left Behind Act of 2001, Pub. L. No. 107-110 (2002). Retrieved April 23, 2010, from http://ed.gov/policy/elsec/leg/esea02/107-110.pdf

Parke, R. D. (2004). Development in the Family. *Annual Review of Psychology, 55*(1), 365–399.

Parson, S. R. (2004). *Journey into community: Looking inside the community learning center.* Larchmont, NY: Eye on Education.

Perkins, F. (1937). *The children's bureau: Yesterday, today and tomorrow.* Retrieved April 22, 2010, from http://www.mchlibrary.info/history/chbu/20993.PDF

Pryor, J. (2004). Parenting in reconstituted and surrogate families. In M. Hoghughi & N. Long (Eds.), *Handbook of parenting: Theory and research for practice* (pp. 110–129). Thousand Oaks, CA: Sage.

Royea, A. J., & Appl, D. J. (2009). Every voice matters: The importance of advocacy. *Early Childhood Education Journal, 37*(2), 89–91.

Sheridan, S. M., Warnes, E. D., Cowan, R. J., Schemm, A. V., & Clarke, B. L. (2004). Family-centered positive psychology: Focusing on strengths to build student success. *Psychology in the Schools, 41*(1), 7–17.

Souto-Manning, M., & Swick, K. (2006). Teachers' beliefs about parent and family involvement: Rethinking our family involvement paradigm. *Early Childhood Education Journal, 34*(2), 187–193.

Spellings, M. (2007). *Building on results: A blueprint for strengthening the No Child Left Behind Act.* Retrieved April 23, 2010, from http://www2.ed.gov/policy/elsec/leg/nclb/buildingonresults.pdf

Superfine, B. M. (2005). The politics of accountability: The rise and fall of Goals 2000. *American Journal of Education, 112*(1), 10-43.

U.S. Department of Education. (2003). *Stronger accountability: Questions and answers on No Child Left Behind.* Retrieved June 23, 2010, from http://www2.ed.gov/nclb/accountability/schools/accountability.html

U.S. Department of Education. (2009). *A 25 year history of the IDEA.* Retrieved July 14, 2009, from http://www.ed.gov/policy/speced/leg/idea/history.html

U.S. Department of Education, National Commission on Excellence in Education. (1983). *A nation at risk.* Washington, DC: U.S. Government Printing Office.

U.S. Department of Education, National Goals Education Panel. (1997). *The national education goals report: Building a nation of learners, 1997.* Washington, DC: U.S. Government Printing Office.

Van Velsor, P., & Orozco, G. L. (2007). Involving low-income parents in the schools: Communitycentric strategies for school counselors. *Professional School Counseling, 11*(1), 17–24.

Vaughn, B. J., White, R., Johnston, S., & Dunlap, G. (2005). Positive behavior support as a family-centered endeavor. *Journal of Positive Behavior Interventions, 7*(1), 55–58.

Wallinga, C., Coleman, M., & Bales, D. (2007). Health and Safety: Involving Community Workers in the Early Childhood Classroom. *Dimensions of Early Childhood, 35*(2), 25–31.

White, S., & Coleman, M. (2000). *Early childhood education: Building a philosophy for teaching.* Columbus, OH: Merrill.

Chapter 3

Barnard, W. M. (2004). Parent involvement in elementary school and educational attainment. *Children and Youth Services Review, 26*(1), 39–62.

Bronfenbrenner, U. (1979). *The ecology of human development: Experiments by nature and design.* Cambridge, MA: Harvard University Press.

Bronfenbrenner, U. (1990). Discovering what families do. In *Rebuilding the nest: A new commitment to the American family.* Milwaukee, WI: Family Service Association of America.

Bronfenbrenner, U. (2005). *Making human beings human: Bioecological perspectives on human development.* Thousand Oaks, CA: Sage.

Darling, S., & Westberg, L. (2004). Parent involvement in children's acquisition of reading. *The Reading Teacher, 57*(8), 774–776.

Dearing, E., Kreider, H., Simpkins, S., & Weiss, H. B. (2006). Family involvement in school and low-income children's literacy: Longitudinal associations between and within families. *Journal of Educational Psychology, 98*(4), 653–664.

Dearing, E., McCartney, K., Weiss, H. B., Kreider, H., & Simpkins, S. (2004). The promotive effects of family educational involvement for low-income children's literacy. *Journal of School Psychology, 42*(6), 445–460.

Desimone, L. (1999). Linking parent involvement with student achievement: Do race and income matter? *Journal of Educational Research, 93*(1), 11–30.

Epstein, J. L., & Sheldon, S. B. (2002). Present and accounted for: Improving student attendance through family and community involvement. *Journal of Educational Research, 95*(5), 308–318.

Gonzalez-DeHass, A. R., Willems, P. P., & Holbein, M. F. D. (2005). Examining the relationship between parent involvement and student motivation. *Educational Psychology Review, 17*(2), 99–123.

Haskins, R., & Rouse, C. (2005). Closing achievement gaps. *The Future of Children, 15*(1), 1–7.

Henderson, A. T., & Mapp, K. L. (2002). *A new wave of evidence: The impact of school, family, and community connections on student achievement.* Austin, TX: National Center for Family & Community Connections with Schools, Southwest Educational Development Laboratory.

Hoover-Dempsey, K. V., Battiato, A. C., Walker, J. M. T., Reed, R. P., DeJong, J. M., & Jones, K. P. (2001). Parent involvement in homework. *Educational Psychologist, 36*(3), 195–209.

Izzo, C. V., Weissberg, R. P., Kasprow, W. J., & Fendrich, M. (1999). A longitudinal assessment of teacher perceptions of parent involvement in children's education and school performance. *American Journal of Community Psychology, 27*(6), 817–839.

Jeynes, W. H. (2005). A meta-analysis of the relation of parental involvement to urban elementary school student achievement. *Urban Education, 40*(3), 237–269.

Jimerson, S., Egeland, B., & Teo, A. (1999). A longitudinal study of achievement trajectories: Factors associated with change. *Journal of Educational Psychology, 91*(1), 116–126.

Kokoski, T. M., & Patton, M. M. (1997). Beyond homework: Science and mathematics backpacks. *Dimensions of Early Childhood, 25*(2), 11–16.

Luster, T., & McAdoo, H. (1996). Family and child influences on educational attainment: A secondary analysis of the High/Scope Perry preschool data. *Developmental Psychology, 32*(1), 26–39.

Miedel, W. T., & Reynolds, A. J. (1999). Parent involvement in early intervention for disadvantaged children: Does it matter? *Journal of School Psychology, 37*(4), 379–402.

Nye, C., Turner, H. M., & Schwartz, J. B. (2006a). Approaches to parent involvement for improving the academic performance of elementary school age children. *Campbell Systematic Reviews, 2006*(4). doi: 10.4073/csr.2006.4

Nye, C., Turner, H. M., & Schwartz, J. B. (2006b). *Approaches to parental involvement for improving the academic performance of elementary school children in grades K–6.* Retrieved May 13, 2010, from Harvard Graduate School of Education, Harvard Family Research Project website: http://www.hfrp.org/publications-resources/publications-series/family-involvement-research-digests

Patall, E. A., Cooper, H., & Robinson, J. C. (2008). Parent involvement in homework: A research synthesis. *Review of Educational Research, 78*(4), 1039–1101.

Reynolds, A. J., Temple, J. A., Robertson, D. L., & Mann, E. A. (2002). Age 21 cost-benefit analysis of the Title 1 Chicago child-parent centers. *Educational Evaluation and Policy Analysis, 24*(4), 267–303.

Schweinhart, L. J. (2005). *The High/Scope Perry preschool study through age 40.* Ypsilanti, MI: High/Scope Press.

Schweinhart, L. J., & Weikart, D. P. (1993). Success by empowerment: The High/Scope Perry preschool project study through age 27. *Young Children, 49*(1), 54–58.

Schweinhart, L. J., & Weikart, D. P. (1997). The High/Scope preschool curriculum comparison study through age 23. *Early Childhood Research Quarterly, 12*(2), 117–143.

Senechal, M., & LeFevre, J. A. (2002). Parental involvement in the development of children's reading skills: A five-year longitudinal study. *Child Development, 73*(2), 445–460.

Senechal, M., & Young, L. (2008). The effect of family literacy interventions on children's acquisition of reading from kindergarten to Grade 3: A meta-analytic review. *Review of Educational Research, 78*(4), 880–907.

Sheldon, S. B. & Epstein, J. L. (2002). Improving student behavior and school discipline with family and community involvement. *Education and Urban Society, 35*(1), 4–26.

Sheldon, S. B., & Epstein, J. L. (2005). Involvement counts: Family and community partnerships and mathematics achievement. *Journal of Educational Research, 98*(4), 196–206.

Small, D. (1985). *Imogene's antlers.* New York, NY: Random House.

Whipple, S. S., Evans, G. W., Barry, R. L., & Maxwell, L. E. (2010). An ecological perspective on cumulative school and neighborhood risk factors related to achievement. *Journal of Applied Developmental Psychology, 31*(6), 422–427.

Ziv, Y., Alva, S., & Zill, N. (2010). Understanding Head Start children's problem behaviors in the context of arrest or incarceration of household members. *Early Childhood Research Quarterly, 25*(3), 396–408.

Chapter 4

Bandura, A. (1977). Self-efficacy: Toward a unifying theory of behavioral change. *Psychological Review, 84*(2), 191–215.

Bandura, A. (1998). Self-efficacy. In H. S. Friedman (Ed.), *Encyclopedia of mental health* (pp. 421–432). San Diego, CA: Academic Press.

Barbarin, O. A., Downer, J., Odom, E., & Head, D. (2010). Home-school differences in beliefs, support, and control during public pre-kindergarten and their link to children's kindergarten readiness. *Early Childhood Research Quarterly, 25*(3), 358–372.

Bempechat, J. (1990). *The role of parent involvement in children's academic achievement: A review of the literature.* Retrieved from ERIC database. (ED322285)

Chrispeels, J., & Gonz, M. (2004). *Do educational programs increase parents' practices at home? Factors influencing Latino parent involvement.* Retrieved May 13, 2010, from Harvard Graduate School of Education, Harvard Family Research Project website: http://www.hfrp.org/publications-resources/publications-series/family-involvement-research-digests

Chrispeels, J. H., & Rivero, E. (2001). Engaging Latino families for student success: How parent education can reshape parents' sense of place in the education of their children. *Peabody Journal of Education, 76*(2), 119–169.

Clark, L. (2005). *SOS help for parents: A practical guide for handling common everyday behavior problems*

(3rd ed.). Bowling Green, KY: SOS Programs and Parents Press.

Copple, C., & Bredekamp, S. (2009). *Developmentally appropriate practice in early childhood programs* (3rd ed.). Washington, DC: National Association for the Education of Young Children.

Dearing, E., Kreider, H., & Weiss, H. B. (2008). Increased family involvement in school predicts improved child-teacher relationships and feelings about school for low-income children. *Marriage and Family Review, 43*(3/4), 226–254.

Dinkmeyer, D., McKay, G. D., & Dinkmeyer, D. (1997). *The parent's handbook: Systematic training for effective parenting.* Bowling Green, KY: STEP Publishers.

Fan, X., & Chen, M. (2001). Parental involvement and students' academic achievement: A meta-analysis. *Educational Psychology Review, 13*(1), 1–22.

Garcia, D. C. (2004). Exploring connections between the construct of teacher efficacy and family involvement practices. *Urban Education, 39*(3), 290–315.

Gordon, T. (2000). *Parent effectiveness training.* New York, NY: Three Rivers Press.

Han, H. S., & Thomas, S. (2010). No child misunderstood: Enhancing early childhood teachers' multicultural responsiveness in the social competence of diverse children. *Early Childhood Education Journal, 37*(6), 469–476.

Hoover-Dempsey, K. V., Bassler, O. C., & Brissie, J. S. (1992). Explorations in parent-school relations. *Journal of Educational Research, 85*(5), 287–294.

Hoover-Dempsey, K. V., & Sandler, H. M. (1995). Parental involvement in children's education: Why does it make a difference? *Teachers College Record, 97*(2), 310–331.

Hoover-Dempsey, K. V., & Sandler, H. M. (1997). Why do parents become involved in their children's education? *Review of Educational Research, 67*(1), 3–42.

Knopf, H. T., & Swick, K. J. (2008). Using our understanding of families to strengthen family involvement. *Early Childhood Education Journal, 35*(5), 419–427.

Moll, L. C., Amanti, C., Neff, D., & Gonzalez, N. (1992). Funds of knowledge for teaching: Using a qualitative approach to connect homes and classrooms. *Theory Into Practice, 31*(2), 132–141.

Moseman, C. (2003). Primary teachers' beliefs about family competence to influence classroom practices. *Early Education and Development, 14*(2), 125–153.

Patall, E. A., Cooper, H., & Robinson, J. C. (2008). Parent involvement in homework: A research synthesis. *Review of Educational Research, 78*(4), 1039–1101.

Pentimonti, J. M., & Justice, L. M. (2010). Teachers' use of scaffolding during read alouds in the preschool classroom. *Early Childhood Education Journal, 37*(4), 241–248.

Pomerantz, E. M., Moorman, E. A., & Litwack, S. D. (2007). The how, whom, and why of parents' involvement in children's academic lives: More is not always better. *Review of Educational Research, 77*(3), 373–410.

Senechal, M., & Young, L. (2008). The effect of family literacy interventions on children's acquisition of reading from kindergarten to Grade 3: A meta-analytic review. *Review of Educational Research, 78*(4), 880–907.

Skaalvik, E. M., & Skaalvik, S. (2010). Teacher self-efficacy and teacher burnout: A study of relations. *Teaching and Teacher Education, 26*(4), 1059–1069.

Small, S. A., Cooney, S. M., & O'Connor, C. (2009). Evidence-informed program improvement: Using principles of effectiveness to enhance the quality and impact of family-based prevention programs. *Family Relations, 58*(1), 1–13.

Vartuli, S. (2005). Beliefs: The heart of teaching. *Young Children, 60*(5), 76–85.

Vygotsky, L. S. (1978). *Mind in society: The development of higher psychological processes.* Cambridge, MA: Harvard University Press.

Chapter 5

Amato, P. R. (2000). Diversity within single-parent families. In D. H. Demo, K. R. Allex, & M. A. Fine (Eds.), *Handbook of family diversity.* New York, NY: Oxford University Press.

Amato, P. R. (2010a). Divorce and the well-being of adults and children. *National Council of Family Relations Report, 55*(3), F11–F13.

Amato, P. R. (2010b). Research on divorce: Continuing trends and new developments. *Journal of Marriage and Family, 72*(3), 650–666.

Azar, D., Naughton, G. A., & Joseph, C. W. (2009). Physical activity and social connectedness in single-parent families. *Leisure Studies, 28*(3), 349–358.

Bachman, H. J., & Chase-Lansdale, P. L. (2005). Custodial grandmothers' physical, mental, and economic well-being: Comparisons of primary caregivers from low-income neighborhoods. *Family Relations, 54*(4), 475–487.

Baker, L. A., & Mutchler, J. E. (2010). Poverty and material hardship in grandparent-headed households. *Journal of Marriage and Family, 72*(4), 947–962.

Bianchi, S. M., Subaiya, L., & Kahn, J. R. (1999). The gender gap in the economic well-being of nonresident fathers and custodial mothers. *Demography, 36*(2), 195–203.

Birkmayer, J., Cohen, J., Jensen, I. D., & Variano, D. A. (2005). Supporting grandparents who raise grandchildren. *Young Children, 60*(3), 100–104.

Blaisure, K. A., & Geasler, M. J. (2006). Educational interventions for separating and divorcing parents and their children. In M. Fine & J. Harvey (Eds.), *Handbook of divorce and relationship dissolution* (pp. 575–602). Hillsdale, NJ: Lawrence Erlbaum.

Braithwaite, D. O., Olson, L. N., Golish, T. D., Soukup, C., & Turman, P. (2001). Becoming a family: Developmental processes represented in blended family discourse. *Journal of Applied Communication Research, 29*(3), 221–247.

Cherlin, A. (2010). Demographic trends in the United States: A review of research in the 2000s. *Journal of Marriage and the Family, 72*(3), 403–419.

Coleman, M., Ganong, L., & Fine, M. (2001). Reinvestigating remarriage: Another decade of progress. In R. M. Milardo (Ed.), *Understanding families into the new millennium: A decade in review* (pp. 507–526). Minneapolis, MN: National Council on Family Relations.

Crosbie-Burnett, M., & Lewis, E. A. (1993). Use of African-American family structures and functioning to address the challenges of European-American postdivorce families. *Family Relations, 42,* 243–248.

Crosnoe, R., & Cavanagh, S. E. (2010). Families with children and adolescents: A review, critique, and future agenda. *Journal of Marriage and the Family, 72*(3), 594–611.

Davidson, S. R., & Boals-Gilbert, B. (2010). What age gap? Building intergenerational relationships. *Dimensions of Early Childhood, 38*(2), 23–28.

Dolbin-MacNab, M. L. (2006). Just like raising your own? Grandmothers' perceptions of parenting a second time around. *Family Relations, 55*(5), 564–575.

Emery, R. E., Sbarra, D. A., & Grover, T. (2005). Divorce mediation: Research and reflections. *Family Court Review, 43*(1), 22–37.

Entwisle, D. R., & Alexander, K. L. (2000). Diversity in family structure: Effects on schooling. In D. H. Demo, K. R. Allex, & M. A. Fine (Eds.), *Handbook of family diversity* (pp. 316–337). New York, NY: Oxford University Press.

Federal Interagency Forum on Child and Family Statistics. (2009). *America's children: Key national indicators of well-being 2009: Family structure and children's living arrangements.* Retrieved May 22, 2010, from http://www.childstats.gov/americaschildren/famsoc1.asp

Fuller, M. L., & Marxen, C. (2003). Families and their functions—past and present. In G. Olsen & M. L. Fuller (Eds.), *Home-school relations: Working successfully with parents and families.* Boston, MA: Pearson Education.

Ganong, L., Coleman, M., Fine, M., & Martin, P. (1999). Stepparents' affinity-seeking and affinity-maintaining strategies with stepchildren. *Journal of Family Issues, 20*(3), 299–327.

Ganong, L., Coleman, M., & Jamison, T. (2011). Patterns of stepchild-stepparent relationship development. *Journal of Marriage and Family, 73*(2), 396–413.

Ginther, D. K., & Pollak, R. A. (2004). Family structure and children's educational outcomes: Blended families, stylized facts, and descriptive regressions. *Demography, 41*(4), 671–696.

Goldscheider, F., & Kaufman, G. (2006). Single parenthood and the double standard. *Fathering, 4*(2), 191–208.

Greeff, A. P., & Fillis, A. J. (2009). Resiliency in poor single-parent families. *Families in Society, 90*(3), 279–285.

Grall, T. S. (2009, November). *Custodial mothers and fathers and their child support: 2007* (Current Population Report P60-237). Retrieved May 22, 2010, from http://www.census.gov/prod/2009pubs/p60-237.pdf

Hayslip, B., & Kaminski, P. L. (2005a). Grandparents raising their grandchildren. *Marriage and Family Review, 37*(1/2), 147–169.

Hayslip, B., & Kaminski, P. L. (2005b). Grandparents raising their grandchildren: A review of the literature and suggestions for practice. *The Gerontologist, 45*(2), 262–269.

Hetherington, E. M., & Kelly, J. (2002). *For better or for worse: Divorce reconsidered.* New York, NY: W. W. Norton.

Hetherington, E. M., & Stanley-Hagan, M. (2000). Diversity among stepfamilies. In D. H. Demo, K. R. Allex, & M. A. Fine (Eds.), *Handbook of family diversity* (pp. 173–196). New York, NY: Oxford University Press.

Heuveline, P., Yang, H., & Timberlake, J. M. (2010). It takes a village (perhaps a nation): Families, states, and educational achievement. *Journal of Marriage and Families, 72*(5), 1362–1376.

Hornberger, L. B., Zabriskie, R. B., & Freeman, P. (2010). Contributions of family leisure to family functioning among single-parent families. *Leisure Sciences, 32*(2), 143–161.

Hughes, M. E., & Waite, L. J. (2002). Health in household context: Living arrangements and health in late middle age. *Journal of Health and Social Behavior, 43*(1), 1–21.

Kennedy, S., & Bumpass, L. (2008). Cohabitation and children's living arrangements: New estimates from the United States. *Demographic Research, 19,* 1663–1692.

Knox, D., & Schacht, C. (2002). *Choices in relationships: An introduction to marriage and the family* (7th ed.). Belmont, CA: Wadsworth Thomson Learning.

Kreider, R. M. (2008). *Living arrangements of children: 2004* (Current Population Report P70-114). Retrieved May 23, 2010, from http://www.census.gov/prod/2008pubs/p70-114.pdf

Landry-Meyer, L., Gerard, J. M., & Guzell, J. R. (2005). Caregiver stress among grandparents raising grandchildren: The functional role of social support. *Marriage and Family Review, 37*(1/2), 171–190.

Landry-Meyer, L., & Newman, B. M. (2004). An exploration of the grandparent caregiver role. *Journal of Family Issues, 25*(8), 1005–1025.

Larkin, E., & Kaplan, M. S. (2010). Intergenerational relationships at the center: Finding shared meaning from programs in the U.S. and Japan. *Young Children, 65*(3), 88–94.

Lemanna, M. A., & Riedmann, A. (2000). *Marriages and families: Making choices in a diverse society* (7th ed). Belmont, CA: Wadsworth Thomson Learning.

Leon, K., & Angst, E. (2005). Portrayals of stepfamilies in film: Using media images in remarriage education. *Family Relations, 54*(5), 3–23.

Mahoney, M. M. (2006). Stepparents as third parties in relation to their schoolchildren. *Family Law Quarterly, 40*(1), 81–108.

Nord, C. W., & West, J. (2001). *Fathers' and mothers' involvement in their children's schools by family type and resident status* (NCES 2001-032). Retrieved May 23, 2010, from http://nces.ed.gov/pubs2001/2001032.pdf

Park, H. H. (2006). The economic well-being of households headed by a grandmother as caregiver. *Social Science Review, 80*(2), 264–295.

Pong, S. L., Dronkers, J., & Hampden-Thompson, G. (2003). Family policies and children's school achievement in single- versus two-parent families. *Journal of Marriage and Family, 65*(3), 681–699.

Potter, D. (2010). Psychosocial well-being and the relationship between divorce and children's academic achievement. *Journal of Marriage and Family, 72*(4), 933–946.

Pryor, J. (2004). Parenting in reconstituted and surrogate families. In M. Hoghughi & N. Long (Eds.), *Handbook of parenting: Theory and research for practice* (pp. 110–129). Thousand Oaks, CA: Sage.

Ricci, I. (2010). Divorce from the kids' point of view: From damage control to empowerment. *National Council on Family Relations Report, 55*(3), F20–F21.

Richards, L. N., & Schmiege, C. J. (1993). Problems and strengths of single-parent families: Implication for practice and policy. *Family Relations, 42*(3), 277–285.

Sands, R. G., & Goldberg-Glen, R. S. (2000). Factors associated with stress among grandparents raising their grandchildren. *Family Relations, 49*(1), 97–105.

Schmeeckle, M. (2007). Gender dynamics in stepfamilies: Adult stepchildren's views. *Journal of Marriage and Family, 69*(1), 174–189.

Schmeer, K. K. (2011). The child health disadvantage of parental cohabitation. *Journal of Marriage and Family, 73*(1), 181–193.

Shriner, M., Mullis, R. L., & Shriner, B. M. (2010). Variations in family structure and school-age children's academic achievement: A social and resource capital perspective. *Marriage and Family Review, 46*(6), 445–467.

Silverstein, M., & Giarrusso, R. (2010). Aging and family life: A decade review. *Journal of Marriage and Family, 72*(5), 1039–1058.

Smith, C. J., & Beltran, A. (2000). Grandparents raising grandchildren: Challenges faced by these growing numbers of families and effective policy solutions. *Journal of Aging and Social Policy, 12*(1), 7–17.

Smock, P. J., & Greenland, F. R. (2010). Diversity in pathways to parenthood: Patterns, implications, and emerging research directions. *Journal of Marriage and the Family, 72*(3), 576–593.

Stewart, S. D. (2010). Children with nonresident parents: Living arrangements, visitation, and child support. *Journal of Marriage and Family, 72*(5), 1078–1091.

Sweeney, M. M. (2010). Remarriage and stepfamilies: Strategic sites for family scholarship in the 21st century. *Journal of Marriage and Family, 72*(3), 667–684.

Tab, E. D. (2006). *Fifth grade: Findings from the fifth-grade follow-up of the early childhood longitudinal study, kindergarten class of 1998–99* (NCES 2006-038). Retrieved May 23, 2010, from http://nces.ed.gov/pubs2006/2006038.pdf

Tutwiler, S. W. W. (2005). *Teachers as collaborative partners: Working with diverse families and communities.* Mahwah, NJ: Lawrence Erlbaum.

Umberson, D., Pudrovska, T., & Reczek, C. (2010). Parenthood, childlessness, and well-being: A life course perspective. *Journal of Marriage and Family, 72*(3), 612–629.

U.S. Department of Health and Human Services. (2004, October). *The interaction of child support and TANF* [Research brief]. Retrieved May 23, 2010, from http://aspe.hhs.gov/hsp/CS-TANF-Int04/rb.pdf

U.S. Department of Labor. (2009, July). *Highlights of women's earnings in 2008* (Report No. 1017). Retrieved May 22, 2010, from http://www.bls.gov/cps/cpswom2008.pdf

Waldfogel, J., Craigie, T., & Brooks-Gunn, J. (2010). Fragile families and child wellbeing. *The Future of Children, 20*(2), 87–112.

West, J., Denton, K., & Germino-Hausken, E. (2000). America's kindergartners: Findings from the early childhood longitudinal study, kindergarten class of 1998–99: Fall 1998. *Education Statistics Quarterly, 2*(1). Retrieved May 23, 2010, from http://nces.ed.gov/programs/quarterly/vol_2/2_1/q2-1.asp

White, J. M., & Klein, D. M. (2002). *Family theories* (2nd ed.). Thousand Oaks, CA: Sage.

Whiting, J. B., Smith, D. R., Barnett, T., & Grafsky, E. L. (2007). Overcoming the Cinderella myth: A mixed methods study of successful stepmothers. *Journal of Divorce and Remarriage, 47*(1/2), 95–109. Reprinted by permission of the publisher (Taylor & Francis Group, http://www.informaworld.com)

Chapter 6

Alexander, K. L., Entwisle, D. R., & Olson, L. S. (2001). Schools, achievement, and inequality: A seasonal perspective. *Educational Evaluation and Policy Analysis, 23*(2), 171–191.

Biblarz, T. J., & Savci, E. (2010). Lesbian, gay, bisexual, and transgender families. *Journal of Marriage and Family, 72*(3), 480–497.

Brooks-Gunn, J., & Duncan, G. J. (1997). The effects of poverty on children. *The Future of Children, 7*(2), 55–71.

Brown, R. B., Goodsell, T. L., Stovall, J., & Flaherty, J. (2010). Adapting to hard times: Family participation patterns in local thrift economies. *Family Relations, 59*(4), 383–395.

Burt, T., Gelnaw, A., & Lesser, L. K. (2010). Creating welcoming and inclusive environments for lesbian, gay, bisexual, and transgender (LGBT) families in early childhood settings. *Young Children, 65*(1), 97–102

Child Trends. (2010). *Parental expectations for children's academic attainment.* Retrieved January 31, 2011, from http://www.childtrendsdatabank.org/alphalist?q=node/366

Children's Defense Fund. (2005, June). *Over 13 million children face food insecurity.* Washington, DC: Author. Retrieved August 20, 2010, from http://www.childrensdefense.org/child-research-data-publications/data/foodinsecurity2005.pdf

Conger, R. D., Conger, K. J., & Martin, A. M. J. (2010). Socioeconomic status, family processes, and individual development. *Journal of Marriage and Family, 72*(3), 685–704.

Crosnoe, R., & Cavanagh, S. E. (2010). Families with children and adolescents: A review, critique, and future agenda. *Journal of Marriage and Family, 72*(3), 594–611.

Cuthrell, K., Stapleton, J., & Ledford, C. (2010). Examining the culture of poverty: Promising practices. *Preventing School Failure, 54*(2), 104–110.

DeNavas-Walt, C., Proctor, B. D., & Smith, C. H. (2010). *Income, poverty, and health insurance coverage in the United States: 2009* (Current Population Report P60-238). Retrieved September 16, 2010, from http://www.census.gov/prod/2010pubs/p60-238.pdf

Dye, J. L., & Johnson, T. (2007, January). *A child's day: 2003* (Current Population Report P70-109). Retrieved May 24, 2010, from www.census.gov/prod/2007pubs/p70-109.pdf

Edin, K., & Kissane, R. J. (2010). Poverty and the American family: A decade in review. *Journal of Marriage and Family, 72*(3), 460–479.

Eisenberg, M. E., Neumark-Sztainer, D., Fulkerson, J. A., & Story, M. (2008). Family meals and substance use: Is there a long-term protective association? *Journal of Adolescent Health, 43*(2), 151–156.

Entwisle, D. R., & Alexander, K. L. (2000). Diversity in family structure: Effects on schooling. In D. H. Demo, K. R. Allex, & M. A. Fine (Eds.), *Handbook of family diversity* (pp. 316–337). New York, NY: Oxford University Press.

Fantuzzo, J., McWayne, C., Perry, M. A., & Childs, S. (2004). Multiple dimensions of family involvement and their relations to behavioral and learning competencies for urban, low-income children. *School Psychology Review, 33*(4), 467–480.

Fass, S. (2009, April). *Measuring poverty in the United States.* Retrieved May 24, 2010, from http://www.nccp.org/publications/pdf/text_876.pdf

Franko, D. L., Thompson, D., Affenito, S. G., Barton, B. A., & Striegel-Moore, R. H. (2008). What mediates the relationship between family meals and adolescent health issues? *Health Psychology, 27*(2), S109–S117.

Fuller, M. L. (2003). Poverty: The enemy of children and families. In G. Olsen & M. L. Fuller (Eds.), *Home-school relations: Working successfully with parents and families.* Boston, MA: Pearson Education.

Hart, B., & Risley, T. R. (2003). The early catastrophe: The 30 million word gap by age 3. *American Educator, 27*(1), 4–9.

Herek, G. M. (2006). Legal recognition of same-sex relationships in the United States: A social science perspective. *American Psychologist, 61*(6), 607–621.

Heymann, S. J., & Earle, A. (2000). Low-income parents: How do working conditions affect their opportunity to help school-age children at risk? *American Educational Research Journal, 37*(4), 833–848.

Human Rights Campaign. (2006). *Second-parent adoption.* Retrieved May 25, 2010, from http://www.hrc.org/issues/parenting/adoptions/2385.htm

Huston, A. C., & Bentley, A. C. (2010). Human development in societal context. *Annual Review of Psychology, 61,* 411–437.

Jarrett, R. L., & Jefferson, S. R. (2003). "A good mother got to fight for her kids": Maternal management strategies in a high-risk, African-American neighborhood. *Journal of Children and Poverty, 9*(1), 21–39.

Joint Center for Housing Studies of Harvard University. (2009). *The state of the nation's housing 2009.* Retrieved May 24, 2010, from http://www.jchs.harvard.edu/publications/markets/son2009son2009.pdf

Julien, D., Chartrand, E., & Begin, J. (1999). Social networks, structural interdependence, and conjugal adjustment in heterosexual, gay, and lesbian couples. *Journal of Marriage and Family, 61*(2), 516–530.

Lawson, M. A. (2003). School-family relations in context: Parent and teacher perceptions of parent involvement. *Urban Education, 38*(1), 77–133.

Lee, C. Y. S., Anderson, J. R., Horowitz, J. L., & August, G. J. (2009). Family income and parenting: The role of parental depression and social support. *Family Relations, 58*(4), 417–430.

Lee, J. S., & Bowen, N. K. (2006). Parent involvement, cultural capital, and the achievement gap among elementary school children. *American Educational Research Journal, 43*(2), 193–218.

Lugaila, T. A. (2003, August). *A child's day: 2000* (Current Population Report P70-89). Retrieved May 5, 2010, from http://www.census.gov/prod/2003pubs/p70-89.pdf

McBride, A. M., Sherraden, M. S., & Pritzker, S. (2006). Civic engagement among low-income and low-wealth families: In their words. *Family Relations, 55*(2), 152–162.

Meadan, H., & Jegatheesan, B. (2010). Classroom pets and young children: Supporting early development. *Young Children, 65*(3), 70–77.

Meezan, W., & Rauch, J. (2005). Gay marriage, same-sex parenting, and America's children. *Future of Children, 15*(2), 97–115.

Mercier, L. R., & Harold, R. D. (2003). At the interface: Lesbian-parent families and their children's schools. *Children and Schools, 25*(1), 35–47.

Meyer, D., Princiotta, D., & Lanahan, L. (2005). The summer after kindergarten: Children's activities and library use by household socioeconomic status. *Education Statistics Quarterly, 6*(3). Retrieved May 25, 2010, from http://nces.ed.gov/programs/quarterly/vol_6/6_3/3_1.asp

Moore, K. A., Chalk, R., Scarpa, J., & Vandivere, S. (2002, August). *Family strengths: Often overlooked, but real* [Research brief]. Retrieved May 26, 2010, from Child Trends website: http://www.childtrends.org/files/familystrengths.pdf

Moore, K. A., Glei, D. A., Driscoll, A. K., Zaslow, M. J., & Redd, Z. (2002). Poverty and welfare patterns: Implications for children. *Journal of Social Policy, 31*(2), 207–227.

Moore, K. A., Redd, Z., Burkhauser, M., Mbwana, K., & Collins, A. (2009, April). *Children in poverty: Trends, consequences, and policy options* [Research brief]. Retrieved October 20, 2011, from Child Trends website: http://www.childtrends.org/Files//Child_Trends-2009_04_07_RB_ChildreninPoverty.pdf

Murphy, C., de Cuba, S. E., Cook, J., Cooper, R., & Weill, J. D. (2008, November). *Reading, writing and hungry: The consequences of food insecurity on children, and on our national's economic success* (Issue Paper #6). Washington, DC: Partnership for America's Economic Success. Retrieved May 24, 2010, from Food, Research, and Action Center website: http://www.frac.org/pdf/reading_writing_hungry_report.pdf

National Center on Addiction and Substance Abuse at Columbia University. (2009, September). *The importance of family dinners V.* Retrieved on May 26, 2010, from http://www.casacolumbia.org/templates/publications_reports.aspx

National Institute of Child Health and Human Development, Early Child Care Research Network. (2005). Duration and developmental timing of poverty and children's cognitive and social development from birth through third grade. *Child Development, 76*(4), 795–810.

Nord, M., Andrews, M., & Carlson, S. (2008, November). *Household food security in the United States, 2008* (Economic Research Report No. 83). Retrieved May 24, 2010, from http://www.ers.usda.gov/Publications/ERR83/ERR83.pdf

Orthner, D. K., Jones-Sanpei, H., & Williamson, S. (2004). The resilience and strengths of low-income families. *Family Relations, 53*(2), 159–167.

Patterson, C. J. (2000). Family relationships of lesbians and gay men. *Journal of Marriage and the Family, 62*(4), 1052–1069.

Patterson, C. J. (2001). Family relationships of lesbians and gay men. In R. M. Milardo (Ed.), *Understanding families into the new millennium: A decade in review.* Minneapolis, MN: National Council on Family Relations.

Patterson, C. J. (2006). Children of lesbian and gay parents. *Current Directions in Psychological Science, 15*(5), 241–244.

Patterson, C. J., & Sutfin, E. L. (2004). Sexual orientation and parenting. In M. Hoghughi & N. Long (Eds.), *Handbook of parenting: Theory and research for practice* (pp. 130–145). Thousand Oaks, CA: Sage.

Peplau, L. A., & Beals, K. P. (2004). The family lives of lesbians and gay men. In A. L. Vangelisti (Ed.), *Handbook of family communication.* Mahwah, NJ: Lawrence Erlbaum.

Perrin, E. C. (2002). Technical report: Coparent or second-parent adoption by same-sex parents. *Pediatrics, 109*(2), 341–344.

Peterson, G. W., Bodman, D. A., Bush, K. R., & Madden-Derdich, D. (2000). Gender and parent-child relationships. In D. H. Demo, K. R. Allen, & M. A. Fine (Eds.), *Handbook of family diversity.* New York, NY: Oxford University Press.

Rank, M. R. (2000). Poverty and economic hardship in families. In D. H. Demo, K. R. Allex, & M. A. Fine (Eds.), *Handbook of family diversity* (pp. 293–315). New York, NY: Oxford University Press.

Roeters, A., van der Lippe, T., & Kluwer, E. S. (2010). Work characteristics and parent-child relationship quality: The mediating role of temporal involvement. *Journal of Marriage and Family, 72*(5), 1317–1328.

Romich, J. (2009). Trying to keep children out of trouble: Child characteristics, neighbourhood quality, and within-household resource allocation. *Children and Youth Services Review, 31*(3), 338–345.

Roy, K. M., Tubbs, C. Y., & Burton, L. M. (2004). Don't have no time: Daily rhythms and the organization of time for low-income families. *Family Relations, 53*(2), 168–178.

Savin-Williams, R. C., & Esterberg, K. G. (2000). Lesbian, gay, and bisexual families. In D. H. Demo, K. R. Allen, & M. A. Fine (Eds.), *Handbook of family diversity* (pp. 197–215). New York, NY: Oxford University Press.

Seccombe, K. (2001). Families in poverty in the 1990s: Trends, causes, consequences, and lessons learned. In R. M. Milardo (Ed.), *Understanding families into the new millennium: A decade in review.* Minneapolis, MN: National Council on Family Relations.

Seccombe, K. (2007). *Families in poverty.* New York, NY: Pearson.

Sen, B. (2010). The relationship between frequency of family dinner and adolescent problem behaviors after adjusting for other family characteristics. *Journal of Adolescence, 33*(1), 187–196.

Silvern, S. B. (1988). Continuity/discontinuity between home and early childhood education environments. *The Elementary School Journal, 89*(2), 146–159.

Smith, S. R., Hamon, R. R., Ingoldsby, B. B., & Miller, J. E. (2009). *Exploring family theories* (2nd ed.). New York, NY: Oxford University Press.

Swick, K. J. (2008a). Empowering the parent-child relationship in homeless and other high-risk parents and families. *Early Childhood Education Journal, 36*(2), 149–153.

Swick, K. J. (2008b). Exploring the dynamics of teacher perceptions of homeless children and families during the early years. *Early Childhood Education Journal, 36*(3), 241–245.

Swick K. J. (2009). Strengthening homeless parents with young children through meaningful parent education and support. *Early Childhood Education Journal, 36*(4), 327–332.

Swick, K. J., & Williams, R. (2010). The voices of single parent mothers who are homeless: Implications for early childhood professionals. *Early Childhood Education Journal, 38*(1), 49–55.

Tasker, F. (2005). Lesbian mothers, gay fathers, and their children: A review. *Developmental and Behavioral Pediatrics, 26*(3), 224–240.

Tutwiler, S. W. W. (2005). *Teachers as collaborative partners: Working with diverse families and communities.* Mahwah, NJ: Lawrence Erlbaum.

U.S. Department of Housing and Urban Development. (2007, February). *The annual homeless assessment report to Congress.* Retrieved May 24, 2010, from www.huduser.org/Publications/pdf/ahar.pdf

U.S. Department of Housing and Urban Development. (2010, May). *Affordable housing.* Retrieved May 24, 2010, from http://www.hud.gov/offices/cpd/affordablehousing/

U.S. Department of Labor. (2011, October). *Minimum wage.* Retrieved October 20, 2011, from www.dol.gov/dol/topic/wages/minimumwage.htm

Vaden-Kiernan, N., & McManus, J. (2005). Parent and family involvement in education: 2002–03. *Education Statistics Quarterly, 7*(1–2). Retrieved May 25, 2010, from http://nces.ed.gov/programs/quarterly/vol_7/1_2/4_9.asp

Valladares, S., & Moore, K. A. (2009, May). The strengths of poor families (Publication No. 2009-26) [Research brief]. Retrieved May 25, 2010, from Child Trends website: http://www.childtrends.org/Files/Child_Trends-2009_5_14_RB_poorfam-strengths.pdf

Van Velsor, P., & Orozco, G. L. (2007). Involving low-income parents in the schools: Communitycentric strategies for school counselors. *Professional School Counseling, 11*(1), 17–24.

Yeung, W. J., Linver, M. R., & Brooks-Gunn, J. (2002). How money matters for young children's development: Parental investment and family processes. *Child Development, 73*(6), 1861–1879.

Zill, N., & West, J. (2001). *Entering kindergarten: Findings from the Condition of Education 2000* (NCES 2001-035). Retrieved May 25, 2010, from http://nces.ed.gov/pubs2001/2001035.pdf

Chapter 7

Beckman, P. J. (2002). Providing family-centered services. In M. L. Batshaw (Ed.), *Children with disabilities* (5th ed., pp. 683–691). Baltimore, MD: Paul H. Brookes.

Bennett, K. S., & Hay, D. A. (2007). The role of family in the development of social skills in children with physical disabilities. *International Journal of Disabilities, Development and Education, 54*(4), 381–397.

Carothers, D. E., & Taylor, R. L. (2004). How teachers and parents can work together to teach daily living skills to children with autism. *Focus on Autism and Other Developmental Disabilities, 19*(2), 102–104.

Consortium for Appropriate Dispute Resolution in Special Education. (2009). *Facilitated IEP meetings: Am emerging practice.* Retrieved July 14, 2009, from http://www.directionservice.org/cadre/pdf/Facilitated%20IEP%20for%20CADRE%20English.pdf

Dempsey, I., & Dunst, C. J. (2004). Helpgiving styles and parent empowerment in families with a young child with a disability. *Journal of Intellectual and Developmental Disability, 29*(1), 40–51.

Dunlap, G., & Fox, L. (2007). Parent-professional partnerships: A valuable context for addressing challenging behaviors. *International Journal of Disability, Development and Education, 54*(9), 273–285.

Dunn, M. E., Burbine, T., Bowers, C. A., & Tantleff-Dunn, S. (2001). Moderators of stress in parents of children with autism. *Community Mental Health Journal, 37*(1), 39–52.

Dunst, C. J., & Dempsey, I. (2007). Family-professional partnerships and parenting competence, confidence, and enjoyment. *International Journal of Disability, Development and Education, 54*(3), 305–318.

Gallagher, S., Phillips, A. C., Oliver, C., & Carroll, D. (2008). Predictors of psychological morbidity in parents of children with intellectual disabilities. *Journal of Pediatric Psychology, 33*(10), 1129–1136.

Gargiulo, R. M. (2009). *Special education in contemporary society: An introduction to exceptionality* (3rd ed.). Thousand Oaks, CA: Sage.

Hastings, R. P., & Beck, A. (2004). Practitioner review: Stress intervention for parents of children with intellectual disabilities. *Journal of Child Psychology and Psychiatry, 45*(8), 1338–1349.

Head, L. S., & Abbeduto, L. (2007). Recognizing the role of parents in developmental outcomes: A systems approach to evaluating the child with developmental disabilities. *Mental Retardation and Developmental Disabilities, 13*(4), 293–301.

Individuals With Disabilities Education Improvement Act of 2004, Pub. L. No. 108-446 (2004). Retrieved July 6, 2009, from http://www.copyright.gov/legislation/pl108-446.pdf

Keen, D. (2007). Parents, families, and partnerships: Issues and considerations. *International Journal of Disability, Development and Education, 54*(3), 339–349.

Keilty, B. (2010). *The early intervention guidebook for families and professionals: Partnering for success.* New York, NY: Teachers College Press.

Mueller, T. G. (2009). IEP facilitation: A promising approach to resolving conflicts between families and schools. *Teaching Exceptional Children, 41*(3), 60–67.

Nachshen, J. S., & Minnes, P. (2005). Empowerment in parents of school-age children with and without developmental disabilities. *Journal of Intellectual Disability Research, 49*(12), 889–904.

Parish, S. L., Rose, R. A., Grinstein-Weiss, M., Richman, E. L., & Andrews, M. E. (2008). Material hardships in U.S. families raising children with disabilities. *Exceptional Children, 75*(1), 71–92.

Pottie, C. G., & Ingram, K. M. (2008). Daily stress, coping, and well-being in parents of children with autism: A multilevel modeling approach. *Journal of Family Psychology, 22*(6), 855–864.

Prezant, F. P., & Marshak, L. (2006). Helpful actions seen through the eyes of parents of children with disabilities. *Disability and Society, 21*(1), 31–45.

Ray, J. A., Pewitt-Kinder, J., & George, S. (2009). Partnering with families of children with special needs. *Young Children, 64*(5), 16–22.

Soresi, S., Nota, L., & Ferrari, L. (2007). Considerations on supports that can increase the quality of life of parents of children with disabilities. *Journal of Policy and Practice in Intellectual Disabilities, 4*(4), 248–251.

Summers, J. A., Marquis, J., Mannan, H., Turnbull, A. P., Fleming, K., Poston, D. J., … Kupzyk, K. (2007). Relationship of perceived adequacy of services, family-professional partnerships, and family quality of life in early childhood service

programmes. *International Journal of Disability, Development and Education, 54*(3), 319–338.

Taub, D. J. (2006). Understanding the concerns of parents of students with disabilities: Challenges and roles for school counselors. *Professional School Counseling, 10*(1), 52–57.

Umberson, D., Pudrovska, T., & Reczek, C. (2010). Parenthood, childlessness, and well-being: A life course perspective. *Journal of Marriage and Family, 72*(3), 612–629.

U.S. Department of Education. (2009). *A 25 year history of the IDEA.* Retrieved July 14, 2009, from http://www.ed.gov/policy/speced/leg/idea/history.html

U.S. Department of Labor, Bureau of Labor Statistics. (2010). *Occupational outlook handbook, 2010-11 edition/Teachers—Special education.* Retrieved October 15, 2010, from http://www.bls.gov/oco/ocos070.htm

Xu, Y., & Filler, J. (2008). Facilitating family involvement and support for inclusive education. *The School Community Journal, 18*(2), 53–71.

Chapter 8

American Academy of Child & Adolescent Psychiatry. (1999). Biracial children. *Facts for Families, No. 71.* Retrieved May 21, 2011, from http://www.aacap.org/galleries/FactsForFamilies/71_biracial_children.pdf

Bang, Y. S. (2009). Helping all families participate in school life. *Young Children, 64*(6), 97–99.

Baumrind, D. (1972). An exploratory study of socialization effects on black children: Some black-white comparisons. *Child Development, 43*(1), 261–267.

Bazron, B., Osher, D., & Fleischman, S. (2005). Creating culturally responsive schools. *Educational Leadership, 63*(1), 83–84.

Berkel, C., Murry, V. M., Hurt, T. R., Chen, Y., Brody, G. H., Simons, R. L., … Gibbons, F. X. (2009). It takes a village: Protecting rural African-American youth in the context of racism. *Journal of Youth and Adolescence, 38*(2), 175–188.

Bevin, T. (2001). Parenting in Cuban American families. In N. B. Webb (Ed.), *Culturally diverse parent-child and family relationships: A guide for social workers and other practitioners* (pp. 181–201). New York, NY: Columbia University Press.

Bigner, J. J. (2006). *Parent-child relations: An introduction to parents* (7th ed.). Upper Saddle, NJ: Pearson.

Bogenschneider, K. (2001). Has family policy come of age? A decade review of the state of U.S. family policy in the 1990s. In R. M. Milardo (Ed.), *Understanding families into the new millennium: A decade in review* (pp. 355–378).

Minneapolis, MN: National Council on Family Relations.

Brown, T. N., Tanner-Smith, E. E., Lesane-Brown, C. L., & Ezell, M. E. (2007). Child, parent, and situational correlates of familial ethnic/racial socialization. *Journal of Marriage and Family, 69*(1), 14–25.

Castagno, A. E., & Brayboy, B. M. J. (2008). Culturally responsive schooling for indigenous youth: A review of the literature. *Review of Educational Research, 78*(4), 941–993.

Chao, R., & Tseng, V. (2002). Parenting of Asians. In M. H. Bornstein (Ed.), *Handbook of parenting* (2nd ed., Vol. 4, pp. 59–93). Mahwah, NJ: Lawrence Erlbaum.

Cherlin, A. J. (2010). Demographic trends in the United States: A review of research in the 2000s. *Journal of Marriage and Family, 72*(3), 403–419.

Cheung, M., & Nguyen, M. H. (2001). Parent-child relationships in Vietnamese American families. In N. B. Webb (Ed.), *Culturally diverse parent-child and family relationships: A guide for social workers and other practitioners* (pp. 261–282). New York, NY: Columbia University Press.

Children's Defense Fund. (2011). *The state of black children and families: Black perspectives on what black children face and what the future holds.* Retrieved March 1, 2011, from http://www.childrensdefense.org/child-research-data-publications/data/the-state-of-black-children.html

Chun, C., Moos, R. H., & Cronkite, R. C. (2006). Culture: A fundamental context for the stress and coping paradigm. In P. T. P. Wong & L. C. J. Wong (Eds.), *Handbook of multicultural perspectives on stress and coping* (pp. 29–53). New York, NY: Springer.

Crosbie-Burnett, M., & Lewis, E. A. (1993). Use of African-American family structures and functioning to address the challenges of European-American postdivorce families. *Family Relations, 42*(3), 243–248.

Crosnoe, R., & Cavanagh, S. E. (2010). Families with children and adolescents: A review, critique, and future agenda. *Journal of Marriage and Family, 72*(3), 594–611.

Crosnoe, R., & Kalil, A. (2010). Educational progress and parenting among Mexican immigrant mothers of young children. *Journal of Marriage and Family, 72*(4), 976–990.

Crowley, J. E., & Curenton, S. (2011). Organizational social support and parenting challenges among mothers of color: The case of mocha moms. *Family Relations, 60*(1), 1–14.

Davis, J. (2010, May 27). Klan costumes at second school: Gwinnett students wore robes in re-enactment; officials investigating. *The Atlanta Journal-Constitution,* pp. B1, B5.

Diamond, J., Wang, L., & Gomez, K. (2006, May). *African-American and Chinese-American parent involvement: The importance of race, class, and culture.* Retrieved May 29, 2010, from Harvard Graduate School of Education, Harvard Family Research Project website: http://www.hfrp.org/publications-resources/publications-series/family-involvement-research-digests

Diller, J. V. (2004). *Cultural diversity: A primer for the human services* (2nd ed.). Belmont, CA: Brooks/Cole–Thomson Learning.

Dilworth-Anderson, P. & Marshall, S. (1996). Social support in its cultural context. In G. R. Pierce, B. R. Sarason, & I. G. Sarason (Eds.), *Handbook of social support and the family* (pp. 67–79). New York, NY: Plenum Press.

Espinosa, L. (2010). *Getting it right for young children from diverse backgrounds: Applying research to improve practice.* Boston, MA: Pearson Learning Solutions.

Glick, J. E. (2010). Connecting complex processes: A decade of research on immigrant families. *Journal of Marriage and Family, 72*(3), 498–515.

Glover, G. (2001). Parenting in Native American families. In N. B. Webb (Ed.), *Culturally diverse parent-child and family relationships: A guide for social workers and other practitioners* (pp. 205–231). New York, NY: Columbia University Press.

Harris, H. L. (2002). School counselors' perceptions of biracial children: A pilot study. *Professional School Counseling, 6*(2), 120–129.

Hernandez, D. J., Takanishi, R., & Marotz, K. G. (2009). Life circumstances and public policies for young children in immigrant families. *Early Childhood Research Quarterly, 24*(4), 487–501.

Hud-Aleem, R., & Countryman, J. (2008). Biracial identity development and recommendations in therapy. *Psychiatry, 5*(11), 37–44.

Huntsinger, C. S., & Jose, P. E. (2009). Parental involvement in children's schooling: Different meanings in different cultures. *Early Childhood Research Quarterly, 24*(4), 398–410.

Ishii-Kuntz, M. (2000a). Change and continuity in the Japanese family. *National Council on Family Relations Report, 45,* F16–F19.

Ishii-Kuntz, M. (2000b). Diversity within Asian American families. In D. H. Demo, K. R. Allen, & M. A. Fine (Eds.), *Handbook of family diversity* (pp. 274–292). New York, NY: Oxford University Press.

Joshi, A. (2005). Understanding Asian Indian families: Facilitating meaningful home-school relations. *Young Children, 60*(3), 75–78.

Kilson, M., & Ladd, F. (2009). *Is that your child? Mothers talk about rearing biracial children.* Lanham, MD: Lexington Books.

Landolt, P., & Da, W. W. (2005). The spatially ruptured practices of migrant families: A comparison of immigrants from El Salvador and the People's Republic of China. *Current Sociology, 53*(4), 625–653.

Lesane-Brown, C. L., Brown, T. N., Tanner-Smith, E. E., & Bruce, M. A. (2010). Negotiating boundaries and bonds: Frequency of young children's socialization to their ethnic/racial heritage. *Journal of Cross-Cultural Psychology, 41*(3), 457–464.

Lowinger, R. J., & Kwok, H. (2001). Parental overprotection in Asian American children: A psychodynamic clinical perspective. *Psychotherapy: Theory, Research, Practice, Training, 38*(3), 319–330.

Lundgren, D., & Morrison, J. W. (2003). Involving Spanish-speaking families in early education programs. *Young Children, 58*(3), 88–95.

McAdoo, H. P. (2001). Parent and child relationships in African American families. In N. B. Webb (Ed.), *Culturally diverse parent-child and family relationships: A guide for social workers and other practitioners* (pp. 89–105). New York, NY: Columbia University Press.

McLoyd, V. C., Cauce, A. M., Takeuchi, D., & Wilson, L. (2001). Marital processes and parental socialization in families of color: A decade review of research. In R. M. Milardo (Ed.), *Understanding families into the new millennium: A decade in review* (pp. 289–312). Minneapolis, MN: National Council on Family Relations.

Ng, F. F., Pomerantz, E. M., & Lam. S. (2007). European American and Chinese parents' responses to children's success and failure: Implications f or children's responses. *Developmental Psychology, 43*(5), 1239–1255.

Okagaki, L., & Diamond, D. E. (2000). Responding to cultural and linguistic differences in the beliefs and practices of families with young children. *Young Children, 55*(3), 74–80.

Oropesa, R. S., & Landale, N. S. (2004). The future of marriage and Hispanics. *Journal of Marriage and Family, 66*(4), 901–920.

Pachter, L. M., & Dumont-Mathieu, T. (2004). Parenting in culturally divergent settings. In J. Hoghughi & N. Long (Eds.), *Handbook of parenting: Theory and research for practice* (pp. 88–97). Thousand Oaks, CA: Sage.

Parke, R. D. (2004). Developing in the family. *Annual Review of Psychology, 55*, 365–399.

Patel, T. G. (2009). *Mixed-up kids? Race, identity and social order.* Dorset, England: Russell House.

Poston, W. S. C. (1990). The biracial identity development model: A needed addition. *Journal of Counseling Development, 69*(2), 152–155.

Pyke, K. (2005). Generational deserters and black sheep: Acculturative differences among siblings in Asian immigrant families. *Journal of Family Issues, 26*(4), 491–517.

Rockquemore, K. A., & Laszloffy, T. (2005). *Raising biracial children.* Lanham, MD: AltaMira Press.

Rothstein-Fisch, C., Trumbull, E., & Garcia, S. G. (2009). Making the implicit explicit: Supporting teachers to bridge cultures. *Early Childhood Research Quarterly, 24*(4), 474–486. Reprinted with permission from Elsevier.

Samuels, G. M. (2009). Being raised by white people: Navigating racial difference among adopted biracial adults. *Journal of Marriage and Family, 71*(1), 80–94.

Sanacore, J. (2004). Genuine caring and literacy learning for African American children. *The Reading Teacher, 57*(8), 744–753.

Sarkisian, N., Gerena, M., & Gerstel, N. (2007). Extended family integration among Euro and Mexican Americans: Ethnicity, gender, and class. *Journal of Marriage and Family, 69*(1), 40–54.

Shibusawa, T. (2001). Parenting in Japanese American families. In N. B. Webb (Ed.), *Culturally diverse parent-child and family relationships: A guide for social workers and other practitioners* (pp. 282–303). New York, NY: Columbia University Press.

Silverstein, M. (2000). The impact of acculturation on intergenerational relationships in Mexican American families. *National Council on Family Relations Report, 45,* F9–F10.

Smith, D. E. (1991). Understanding some behaviors of culturally different children. *International Education, 24*(1), 31–40.

Sohn, S., & Wang, X. C. (2006). Immigrant parents' involvement in American schools: Perspectives from Korean mothers. *Early Childhood Education Journal, 34*(2), 125–132. With the kind permission from Springer Science+Business Media.

Souto-Manning, M., & Swick, K. J. (2006). Teachers' beliefs about parent and family involvement: Rethinking our family involvement paradigm. *Early Childhood Education Journal, 34*(2), 187–193.

Stevens, G., & Ishizawa, H. (2007). Variation among siblings in the use of a non-English language. *Journal of Family Issues, 28*(8), 1008–1025.

Taylor, S. I. (2004). Let it be! Japanese preschoolers rule the classroom. *Young Children, 59*(5), 20–25.

Trumbull, E., Rothstein-Fisch, C., Greenfield, P. M., & Quiroz, B. (2001). *Bridging cultures between home and school: A guide for teachers.* Mahwah, NJ: Lawrence Erlbaum.

Tutwiler, S. J. W. (2005). *Teachers as collaborative partners: Working with diverse families and communities.* Mahwah, NJ: Lawrence Erlbaum.

Vesely, C. K., & Ginsberg, M. R. (2011). Strategies and practices for working with immigrant families in early education programs. *Young Children, 66*(1), 84–89.

Walker-Dalhouse, D., & Dalhouse, D. (2001). Parent-school relations: Communicating more effectively with African American parents. *Young Children, 56*(4), 75–80.

Watts, I. E., & Tutwiler, S. W. (2008). Diversity among families. In G. Olsen & M. L. Fuller (Eds.), *Home-school relations: Working successfully with parents and families* (3rd ed., pp. 41–65). Boston, MA: Allyn & Bacon.

Wilson, S. R., & Morgan, W. M. (2004). Persuasion and families. In A. L. Vagelisti (Ed.), *Handbook of family communication* (pp. 447–471). Mahwah, NY: Lawrence Erlbaum.

Wlodkowski, R. J., & Ginsberg, M. B. (1995). A framework for culturally responsive teaching. *Educational Leadership, 53*(1), 17–21.

Wu, S. J. (2001). Parenting in Chinese American families. In N. B. Webb (Ed.), *Culturally diverse parent-child and family relationships: A guide for social workers and other practitioners* (pp. 235–260). New York, NY: Columbia University Press.

Yeh, C. J., Arora, A. K., & Wu, K. A. (2006). A new theoretical model of collectivistic copies. In P. T. P. Wong & L. C. J. Wong (Eds.), *Handbook of multicultural perspectives on stress and coping* (pp. 55–72). New York, NY: Springer.

Zayas, L. H., Canino, I., & Suarez, Z. E. (2001). Parenting in mainland Puerto Rican families. In N. B. Webb (Ed.), *Culturally diverse parent-child and family relationships: A guide for social workers and other practitioners* (pp. 133–156). New York, NY: Columbia University Press.

Zinn, M. B., & Wells, B. (2000). Diversity within Latino families: New lessons for family social science. In D. H. Demo, K. R. Allen, & M. A. Fine (Eds.), *Handbook of family diversity* (pp. 252–273). New York, NY: Oxford University Press.

Chapter 9

Aldridge, J., Calhoun, C., & Aman, R. (2000). 15 misconceptions about multicultural education. *Focus on Elementary, 12*(3). Retrieved May 27, 2010, from http://www.udel.edu/bateman/acei/misconceptions.htm

American Anthropological Association. (1998, May 17). *American Anthropological Association statement of "race."* Retrieved, May 21, 2011, from www.aaanet.org/stmts/racepp.htm

Bevere, L. (2002). *Going home with Spanish.* Portage, MI: Spanish Steps.

Brittingham, A., & de la Cruz, G. P. (2004, June). *Ancestry: 2000* (C2KBR-35). Retrieved May 27, 2010, from www.census.gov/prod/2004pubs/c2kbr-35.pdf

Burton, L. M., Bonilla-Silva, E., Ray, V., Buckelew, R., & Freeman, E. H. (2010). Critical race theories, colorism, and the decade's research on families of color. *Journal of Marriage and Family, 72*(3), 440–459.

Cheatham, G. A., & Ro, Y. E. (2010). Young English learners' interlanguage as a context for language and early literacy development. *Young Children, 65*(4), 18–23.

Chun, C., Moos, R. H., & Cronkite, R. C. (2006). Culture: A fundamental context for the stress and coping paradigm. In P. T. P. Wong & L. C. J. Wong (Eds.), *Handbook of multicultural perspectives on stress and coping* (pp. 29–53). New York, NY: Springer.

Clark, L., DeWolf, S., & Clark, C. (1992). Teaching teachers to avoid having culturally assaultive classrooms. *Young Children, 47*(5), 4–9.

Cohen, L. E. (2009). Exploring cultural heritage in a kindergarten classroom. *Young Children, 64*(3), 72–77.

Copple, C., & Bredekamp, S. (2009). *Developmentally appropriate practice in early childhood programs serving children from birth through age 8.* Washington, DC: National Association for the Education of Young Children.

Council on Interracial Books for Children. (1980). *Guidelines for selecting bias-free textbooks and storybooks.* New York, NY: Author.

Daniel, J., & Friedman, S. (2005, November). Taking the next step: Preparing teachers to work with culturally and linguistically diverse children. *Young Children on the Web.* Retrieved May 8, 2010, from National Association for the Education of Young Children website: http://journal.naeyc.org/btj/200511/DanielFriedman BTJ1105.pdf

Derman-Sparks, L. (2004). Culturally relevant anti-bias education with young children. In W. G. Stephan, & W. P. Vogt (Eds.), *Education programs for improving intergroup relations: Theory, research, and practice.* New York, NY: Teachers College Press.

Derman-Sparks, L., & A.B.C. Task Force. (1989). *Anti-bias curriculum: Tools for empowering young children.* Washington, DC: National Association for the Education of Young Children.

Derman-Sparks, L., & Edwards, J. E. (2010). *Anti-bias education for young children and ourselves.* Washington, DC: National Association for the Education of Young Children.

Derman-Sparks, L., & Ramsey, P. G. (2005, November). What if all the children in my class are white: Historical and research background. *Young Children on the Web.* Retrieved May 8, 2010, from National Association for the Education of Young Children website: http://www.naeyc.org/files/yc/file/200511/DermanSparks BTJ1105.pdf

Diller, J. V. (2004). *Cultural diversity: A primer for the human services* (2nd ed.). Belmont, CA: Brooks/Cole-Thomson Learning.

Dilworth-Anderson, P., & Marshall, S. (1996). Social support in its cultural context. In G. R. Pierce, B. R. Sarason, & I. G. Sarason (Eds.), *Handbook of social support and the family* (pp. 67–79). New York, NY: Plenum Press.

Duarte, G., & Rafanello, D. (2001). The migrant child: A special place in the field. *Young Children, 56*(2), 26–34.

Dunn, M., Mutuku, M., & Wolfe, R. (2004). Developmentally and culturally appropriate practice in the global village:

The Kenya literacy project. *Young Children, 59*(5), 50–55.

Espinosa, L. (2010). *Getting it right for young children from diverse backgrounds: Applying research to improve practice.* Boston, MA: Pearson Learning Solutions.

Fine, M. A., Demo, D. H., & Allen, K. R. (2000). Family diversity in the 21st century: Implications for research, theory, and practice. In D. H. Demo, K. R. Allen, & M. A. Fine (Eds.), *Handbook of family diversity* (pp. 440–448). New York, NY: Oxford University Press.

Ford, D. Y., & Trotman, M. F. (2001). Teachers of gifted students: Suggested multicultural characteristics and competencies. *Roeper Review, 23*(4), 235–239.

Gadsden, V. L. (2004). Family literacy and culture. In B. H. Wasik (Ed.), *Handbook of family literacy* (pp. 401–423). Mahwah, NJ: Lawrence Erlbaum.

Gilliard, J. L., & Moore, R. A. (2007). An investigation of how culture shapes curriculum in early care and education programs on a Native American Indian reservation. *Early Childhood Education Journal, 34*(4), 251–258.

Han, H. S., & Thomas, M. S. (2010). No child misunderstood: Enhancing early childhood teachers' multicultural responsiveness to the social competence of diverse children. *Early Childhood Education Journal, 37*(6), 469–476.

Hernandez, D. J., Takanishi, R., & Marotz, K. G. (2009). Life circumstances and public policies for young children in immigrant families. *Early Childhood Research Quarterly, 24*(4), 487–501.

Humes, K. R., Jones, N. A., & Ramirez, R. R. (2011, March). *Overview of race and Hispanic origin: 2010.* Retrieved May 8, 2010, from http://www.census.gov/prod/cen2010/briefs/c2010br-02.pdf

Hyland, N. E. (2010). Social justice in early childhood classrooms: What the research tells us. *Young Children, 65*(1), 82–90.

Ladson-Billings, G. (1994). What we can learn from multicultural education research. *Educational Leadership, 51*(8), 22–26.

Lin, M., Lake, V. E., & Rice, D. (2008). Teaching anti-bias curriculum in teacher education programs: What and how. *Teacher Education Quarterly, 35*(2), 187–200.

Lopez, G. R., Scribner, J. D., & Mahitivanichcha, K. (2001). Redefining parental involvement: Lessons from high-performing migrant-impacted schools. *American Educational Research Journal, 38*(2), 253–288.

Luckenbill, J. (2011). Circle time puppets: Teaching social skills. *Teaching Young Children, 4*(4), 9–11.

McAdoo, H. P. (2000). Transference of values of African American families and children. *National Council on Family Relations Report, 45,* F5, F7–F8.

McGoldrick, M., Giordano, J., & Garcia-Preto, N. (2005). Overview: Ethnicity and family therapy. In M. McGoldrick, J. Giordano, & N. Garcia-Preto (Eds.), *Ethnicity and family therapy* (3rd ed., pp. 1–40). New York, NY: Guilford Press.

Morgan, H. (2009). Picture book biographies for young children: A way to teach multiple perspectives. *Early Childhood Education Journal, 37*(3), 219–227.

Okagaki, L., & Diamond, D. E. (2000). Responding to cultural and linguistic differences in the beliefs and practices of families with young children. *Young Children, 55*(3), 74–80.

Pierce, J., & Johnson, C. L. (2010). Problem solving with young children using persona dolls. *Young Children, 65*(6), 106–108.

Planty, M., Hussar, W., Snyder, T., Kena, G., KewalRamani, A., Kemp, J., . . . Dinkes, R. (2009). *The Condition of Education 2009* (NCES 2009-081). Retrieved May 8, 2010, from http://nces.ed.gov/pubs2009/2009081.pdf

Roberts, L., Dean, E., & Holland, M. (2005, November). Contemporary American Indian cultures in children's picture books. *Young Children on the Web.* Retrieved May 8, 2010, from National Association for the Education of Young Children website: http://www.naeyc.org/files/yc/file/200511/Roberts1105BTJ.pdf

Samuels, G. M. (2009). Being raised by white people: Navigating racial difference among adopted multiracial adults. *Journal of Marriage and Family, 71*(1), 80–94.

Shioshita, J. (1997). Beyond good intentions: Selecting multicultural literature. Retrieved May 7, 2010, from Children's Advocate website: http://www.4children.org/issues/1997/september_october/beyond_good_intentions_selecting_multicultural_literature/

Slonim, M. B. (1991). *Children, culture, and ethnicity: Evaluating and understanding the impact* (pp. 52, 61–81). New York, NY: Garland.

Sohn, S., & Wang, X. C. (2006). Immigrant parents' involvement in American schools: Perspectives from Korean mothers. *Early Childhood Education Journal, 34*(2), 125–132. With the kind permission from Springer Science+Business Media.

Tutwiler, S. J. W. (2005). *Teachers as collaborative partners: Working with diverse families and communities.* Mahwah, NJ: Lawrence Erlbaum.

U.S. Census Bureau. (2004). *U.S. interim projections by age, sex, race, and Hispanic origin: 2000–2050.* Retrieved May 8, 2010, from www.census.gov/ipc/www/usinterimproj/

U.S. Census Bureau. (2007). *Minority population tops 100 million.* Retrieved May 27, 2010, from http://www.census.gov/newsroom/releases/archives/population/cb07-70.html

U.S. Census Bureau. (2010). *The 2010 statistical abstract: Table 10: Resident population by race, Hispanic origin, and single years of age: 2008.* Retrieved July 29, 2010, from http://www.census.gov/compendia/statab/cats/population.html

U.S. Office of Management and Budget. (1997, October 30). *Revisions to the standards for the classification of federal data on race and ethnicity.* Retrieved May 27, 2010, from www.whitehouse.gov/omb/fedreg/1997standards.html

Webb, N. B. (2001). *Culturally diverse parent-child and family relationships: A guide for social workers and other practitioners.* New York, NY: Columbia University Press.

Williams K. M. (2007, May). *Racial statistics and race-conscious public policy* (PB-2007-2). Retrieved May 27, 2010, from Harvard Kennedy School for State and Local Government, Taubman Center website: http://www.hks.harvard.edu/taubmancenter/pdfs/williams_new.pdf

Chapter 10

Cellitti, A. (2010). Working effectively with interpreters. *Dimensions of Early Childhood, 38*(1), 31–37.

Chandra, A., Martin, L. T., Hawkins, S. A., & Richardson, A. (2010). The impact of parental deployment on child social and emotional functioning: Perspectives of school staff. *Journal of Adolescent Health, 46*(3), 218–223.

Clopton, K. L., & East, K. K. (2008a). Are there other kids like me? Children with a parent in prison. *Early Childhood Education Journal, 36*(2), 195–198.

Clopton, K. L., & East, K. K. (2008b). A list of books about a parent in prison. *Early Childhood Education Journal, 36*(2), 199–200.

Coffee, G. (2010, July 31). Teachers can get free supplies from Kroger. *The Atlanta Journal–Constitution,* p. B3.

Dallaire, D. H., Ciccone, A., & Wilson, L. C. (2010). Teachers' experiences with and expectations of children with incarcerated parents. *Journal of Applied Developmental Psychology, 31*(4), 281–290.

Flake, E. M., Davis, B. E., Johnson, P. L., & Middleton, L. S. (2009). The psychosocial effects of deployment on military children. *Journal of Developmental and Behavioral Pediatrics, 30*(4), 271–278.

Ginsberg, R., & Hermann-Ginsberg, L. (2005). *Accomplished teachers and their interactions with parents: A comparative analysis of strategies and techniques.* Retrieved May 13, 2010, from Harvard Graduate School of Education, Harvard Family Research Project website: http://www.hfrp.org/publications-resources/publications-series/family-involvement-research-digests

Glaze, L. E, & Maruschak, L. M. (2010). *Parents in prison and their minor children* (Report No. NCJ 222984) [Revision of 2008 report]. Retrieved April 3, 2011, from http://bjs.ojp.usdoj.gov/content/pub/pdf/pptmc.pdf

Goldfarth, K. P. (1999). Working together: Immigrant families and the schools. *National Council on Family Relations Report, 44*(2), 13.

Huebner, A. J., Mancini, J. A., Bowen, G. L., & Orthner, D. K. (2009). Shadowed by war: Building community capacity to support military families. *Family Relations, 58*(2), 216–228.

Interagency Policy Committee. (2011, January). *Strengthening our military families: Meeting America's commitment.* Retrieved May 27, 2011, from http://www.defense.gov/home/features/2011/0111_initiative/Strengthening_our_Military_January_2011.pdf

Kjellstrand, J. M., & Eddy, J. M. (2011). Parental incarceration during childhood, family context, and youth problem behavior across adolescence. *Journal of Offender Rehabilitation, 50*(1), 18–35.

Knopf, H. T., & Swick, K. J. (2008). Using our understanding of families to strengthen family involvement. *Early Childhood Education Journal, 35*(5), 419-427.

Laser, J. A., & Stephens, P. M. (2011). Working with military families through deployment and beyond. *Clinical Social Work Journal, 39*(1), 23–38.

Lester, P., Mogil, C., Saltzman, W., Woodward, K., Nash, W., Leskin, G., . . . Beardslee, W. (2011). Families overcoming under stress: Implementing family-centered prevention for military families facing wartime deployments and combat operational stress. *Military Medicine, 176*(1), 19–25.

Lester, P., Peterson, K., Reeves, J., Knauss, L., Glover, D., Mogil, C., . . . Beardslee, W. (2010). The long war and parental combat deployment: Effects on military children and at-home spouses. *Journal of the American Academy of Child and Adolescent Psychiatry, 49*(4), 310–320.

Lopez, C., & Bhat, C. S. (2007). Supporting students with incarcerated parents in schools: A group intervention. *The Journal for Specialists in Group Work, 32*(2), 139–153.

Mackintosh, V. H., Myers, B. J., & Kennon, S. S. (2006). Children of incarcerated mothers and their caregivers: Factors affecting the quality of their relationship. *Journal of Child and Family Studies, 15*(5), 581–596.

Murray, J., & Farrington, D. P. (2005). Parental imprisonment: Effects on boys' antisocial behavior and delinquency through the life-course. *Journal of Child Psychology and Psychiatry, 46*(12), 1269–1278.

Murray, J., Farrington, D., Sekol, I., & Olsen, R. F. (2009). Effects of parental imprisonment on child antisocial behavior and mental health: A systematic review. *Campbell Systematic Reviews.* Retrieved April 4, 2011, from http://www.eurochips.org/documents/1265621861.pdf

Pachter, L. M., & Dumont-Mathieu, T. (2004). Parenting in culturally divergent settings. In J. Hoghughi & N. Long (Eds.), *Handbook of parenting: Theory and research for practice* (pp. 88–97). Thousand Oaks, CA: Sage.

Phillips, L., & Evanshen, P. (2006). Family fun day: Make a difference in your community. *Dimensions of Early Childhood, 34*(2), 20–25.

Poehlmann, J. (2005). Children's family environment and intellectual outcomes during maternal incarceration. *Journal of Marriage and Family, 67*(5), 1275–1285.

U.S. Department of Defense. (2011, February). *Military deployment guide: Preparing you and your family for the road ahead.* Retrieved May 29, 2011, from http://cs.mhf.dod.mil/content/dav/mhf/QOL-Library/Project%20Documents/MilitaryHOMEFRONT/Service%20Providers/Deployment/2011_DeploymentGuide.pdf

Van Velsor, P., & Orozco, G. L. (2007). Involving low-income parents in the schools: Communitycentric strategies for school counselors. *Professional School Counseling, 11*(1), 17–24.

Chapter 11

Ableser, J. (2008). Literacy experiences to teach and support young children during stressful time. *Young Children, 63*(2), 74–79.

Bagdi, A., & Vacca, J. (2005). Supporting early childhood social-emotional well being: The building blocks for early learning and school success. *Early Childhood Education Journal, 33*(3), 145–150.

Bemak, R., & Cornely, L. (2002). The SAFI model as a critical link between marginalized families and schools: A literature review and strategies for school counselors. *Journal of Counseling and Development, 80*(3), 322–331.

Bentham, R. L. (2008). Rich environments for adult learners. *Young Children, 63*(3), 72–74.

Benzies, K., & Mychasiuk, R. (2009). Fostering family resiliency: A review of the key protective factors. *Child and Family Social Work, 14*(1), 103–114.

Christenson, S. L., & Sheridan, S. M. (2001). *Schools and families: Creating essential connections for learning.* New York, NY: Guilford Press.

Eckhoff, A. (2010). Using games to explore visual art with young children. *Young Children, 65*(1), 18–22.

Gilkerson, D., & Hanson, M. F. (2000). Family portfolios: Involvement families in portfolio documentation. *Early Childhood Education Journal, 27*(3), 197–201.

Harris, M. E. (2009). Implementing portfolio assessment. *Young Children, 63*(3), 82–85.

Lopez, G. R., Scribner, J. D., & Mahitivanichcha, K. (2001). Redefining parental involvement: Lessons from high-performing migrant-impacted schools. *American Educational Research Journal, 38*(2), 253–288.

Miller, S. (2010). Head, hands, heart, and hope: Helping to end global poverty. *Young Children, 65*(4), 64–69.

O'Nell, C., & Giannoni, L. (2010). Optimizing mothers' social networks: Information-sharing strategies. *Young Children, 65*(4), 38–44.

Patterson, J., & Kirkland, J. (2007). Sustaining resilient families for children in primary grades. *Childhood Education, 84*(1), 2–7.

Perkins, K. D., & Mackey, B. (2008). Supporting grieving children in early childhood programs. *Dimension of Early Childhood, 36*(3), 13–19.

Roberts, S. K., & Crawford, P. A. (2008). Real life calls for real books: Literature to help children cope with family stressors. *Young Children, 63*(5), 12–17.

Seitz, H. (2008). The power of documentation in the early childhood classroom. *Young Children, 63*(2), 88–93.

Sheridan, S. M., Clarke, B. L., Marti, D. C., Burt, J. D., & Rohik, A. M. (2005). *Conjoint behavioral consultation: A model to facilitate meaningful partnerships for families and schools.* Cambridge, MA: Harvard Family Research Project, Harvard Graduate School of Education.

Retrieved May 13, 2010, from http://www.hfrp.org/publications-resources/publications-series/family-involvement-research-digests/conjoint-behavioral-consultation-a-model-to-facilitate-meaningful-partner ships-for-families-and-schools

Simon, J. B., Murphy, J. J., & Smith, S. M. (2005). Understanding and fostering family resilience. *The Family Journal, 13*(4), 427–436.

Stinnett, N., & DeFrain, J. (1985). *Secrets of strong families.* Boston, MA: Little, Brown.

Swick, K. J. (1997). A family-school approach for nurturing caring in young children. *Early Childhood Education Journal, 25*(2), 151–154.

Swick, K. J. (2004). What parents seek in relations with early childhood family helpers. *Early Childhood Education Journal, 31*(3), 217–220.

Swick, K. J., & Graves, S. B. (1993). *Empowering at-risk families during the early childhood years.* Washington, DC: National Education Association.

Van Velsor, P., & Orozco, G. L. (2007). Involving low-income parents in the schools: Communitycentric strategies for school counselors. *Professional School Counseling, 11*(1), 17–24.

Walker-Dalhouse, D., & Dalhouse, D. (2001). Parent-school relations: Communicating more effectively with African-American parents. *Young Children, 56* (4), 75-80.

Weldin, D. J., & Tumarkin, S. R. (1998/1999). Parent involvement: More power in the portfolio process. *Childhood Education, 75*, 90–95.

Wilhelm, H. (1985). *I'll always love you.* New York, NY: Crown.

Wood, F. B. (2008). Grief: Helping young children cope. *Young Children, 63*(5), 28–31.

Chapter 12

Bouhebent, E. A. (2008). Providing the best for families: Developmental appropriate home visitation services. *Young Children, 63*(2), 82–87.

DeSteno, N. (2000). Parent involvement in the classroom: The fine line. *Young Children, 55*(3), 13–17.

Inger, M. (1992). *Increasing the school involvement of Hispanic parents.* Retrieved May 8, 2010 from ERIC database. (ED350380)

Lopez, G. R., Scribner, J. D., & Mahitivanichcha, K. (2001). Redefining parental involvement: Lessons from high-performing migrant-impacted schools. *American Educational Research Journal, 38*(2), 253–288.

Mayer, E., Ferede, M. K., & Hou, E. D. (2006). The family involvement storybook: A new way to build connections with families. *Young Children, 61*(6), 94–97.

Meyer, J. A., & Mann, M. B. (2006). Teachers' perceptions of the benefits of home visits for early elementary children. *Early Childhood Education Journal, 34*(1), 93–97.

Steen, B. F. (2011). Promoting health transitions from preschool to kindergarten. *Young Children, 66*(2), 90–95.

Szente, J., Hoot, J., & Taylor, D. (2006). Responding to the special needs of refugee children: Practical ideas for teachers. *Early Childhood Education Journal, 34*(1), 15–20.

Chapter 13

American Federation of Teachers. (2010). *Classroom tips: Appropriate uses of modern technology.* Retrieved July 9, 2011 from, www.aft.org/pdfs/tools4teachers/CT-Technology0409.pdf

Barrett, L. (2007). Not just "your space": Educators urged to be careful on the Internet. *Education Digest, 73*(2), 9–11.

Carter, H. L., Foulger, T. S., & Ewbank, A. D. (2008). Have you Googled your teacher lately? Teachers' use of social networking sites. *Phi Delta Kappan, 89*(9), 681–685.

Coleman, M. (1991). Planning for the changing nature of family life in schools for young children. *Young Children, 46*(4), 15–20

Davis, M. R. (2010). Social networking goes to school. *Education Digest, 76*(3), 14–19.

Gordon, T. (2000). *Parent effectiveness training.* New York, NY: Three Rivers Press.

Greenhow, C. (2009). Tapping the wealth of social networks for professional development. *Learning and Leading With Technology, 36*(8), 10–11.

Lucina, J. (2008). Learning English with iPods. *Childhood Education, 84*(4), 247–249.

McEwan, E. K. (2005). *How to deal with parents who are angry, troubled, afraid, or just plain crazy* (2nd ed.). Thousand Oaks, CA: Corwin.

Mitchell, S., Foulger, T. S., & Wetzel, K. (2009). Ten tips for involving families through Internet-based communication. *Young Children, 64*(5), 46–49.

Olson, M., & Hyson, M. (2003). Supporting teachers, strengthening families: A new NAEYC initiative. *Young Children, 58*(3), 74–75.

Olson, M., & Hyson, M. (2005). NAEYC explores parental perspectives on early childhood education. *Young Children, 60*(3), 66–68.

Ray, J. A., & Shelton, D. (2004). Connecting with families through technology. *Young Children, 59*(3), 30–32.

Seplocha, H. (2004). Partnerships for learning: Conferencing with families. *Young Children, 59*(5), 96–99.

Sohn, S., & Wang, C. (2006). Immigrant parents' involvement in American schools: Perspectives from Korean mothers. *Early Childhood Education Journal, 34*(2), 125–132. With the kind permission from Springer Science+ Business Media.

Szente, J., Hoot, J., & Taylor, D. (2006). Responding to the special needs of refugee children: Practical ideas for teachers. *Early Childhood Education Journal, 34*(1), 15–20.

Wanat, C. L. (2010). Challenges balancing collaboration and independence in home-school relationships: Analysis of parents' perceptions in one district. *The School Community Journal, 20*(1), 159–186.

Chapter 14

Coleman, M. (2007). A family bill of rights. *Democracy and Education, 16*(4), 6–14.

Coleman, M, & Wallinga, C. (2000). Connecting families and classroom using family involvement webs. *Childhood Education, 76*(4), 209–214.

Comer, J. P., Haynes, N. M., & Joyner, E. T. (1996). The school development program. In J. P. Comer, N. M. Haynes, E. T. Joyner, & M. Ben-Avie (Eds.), *Rallying the whole village: The Comer process for reforming education* (pp. 1–26). New York, NY: Teachers College Press.

Comer, J. P., Joyner, E. T., & Ben-Avie, M. (2004). *Six pathways to healthy child development and academic success: The field guide to Comer schools in action.* Thousand Oaks, CA: Corwin.

Desteno, N. (2000). Parent involvement in the classroom: The fine line. *Young Children, 55*(3), 13–17.

Emmons, C. L., Comer, S. P., & Haynes, N. M. (1996). Translating theory into practice: Comer's theory of school reform. In J. P. Comer, N. M. Haynes, E. T. Joyner, & M. Ben-Avie (Eds.), *Rallying the whole village: The Comer process for reforming education* (pp. 27–41). New York, NY: Teachers College Press.

Haynes, N. M., Ben-Avie, M., Squires, D. A., Howley, J. P., Negron, E. N., & Corbin, J. N. (1966). It takes a whole village: The SDP school. In J. P. Comer, N. M. Haynes, E. T. Joyner, & M. Ben-Avie (Eds.), *Rallying the whole village: The Comer process for reforming education* (pp. 42–71). New York, NY: Teachers College Press.

Hu, W. (2007, February 23). PTAs go way beyond cookies. *The New York Times.* Retrieved December 16, 2010, from http://www.nytimes.com/2007/02/23/education/23pta.html?pagewanted=1&_r=1&sq=PTAs%20go%20way%20beyond%20cookies&st=nyt&scp=1

Jackson, S., Martin, N., & Stocklinski, J. (2004). Families as partners: Parent teams and parent/family involvement. In E. T. Joyner, M. Ben-Avie, & J. P. Comer (Eds.), *Transforming school leadership and management to support student learning and development.* Thousand Oaks, CA: Corwin.

Lopez, G. R., Scribner, J. D., & Mahitivanichcha, K. (2001). Redefining parental involvement: Lessons from high-performing migrant-impacted schools. *American Educational Research Journal, 38*(2), 253–288.

Staples, G. B. (2009, August 14). Dads take charge at local schools. *The Atlanta Journal-Constitution*, pp. A1, A10.

Chapter 15

American Academy of Pediatrics. (2001). Committee on public education: Children, adolescents, and television. *Pediatrics, 107*(2), 423–426.

American Academy of Pediatrics. (2010). *When to keep your child home from school.* Retrieved June 6, 2010, from http://www.healthychildren.org/English/ages-stages/gradeschool/school/Pages/When-to-Keep-Your-Child-Home-from-School.aspx

American Diabetes Association. (2011). *Diabetes basics: Overweight.* Retrieved November 11, 2011, from http://www.diabetes.org/diabetes-basics/prevention/checkup-america/overweight.html

Anderson, P. M., & Butcher, K. F. (2006). Childhood obesity: Trends and potential causes. *The Future of Children, 16*(1), 19–45.

Anthonysamy, A., & Zimmer-Gembeck, M. J. (2007). Peer status and behaviors of maltreated children and their classmates in the early years of school. *Child Abuse and Neglect, 31*(9), 971–991.

Aronson, S. S. (2002). *Model child care health policies.* Rosemont, PA: Healthy Child Care Pennsylvania.

Aronson, S. S., & Shope, T. R. (2005). *Managing infectious diseases in child care and schools: A quick reference guide.* Elk Grove Village, IL: American Academy of Pediatrics.

Aronson, S. S., & Spahr, P. M. (2002). *Healthy young children: A manual for programs.* Washington, DC: National Association for the Education of Young Children.

Baker, L., & Cunningham, A. (2009). Inter-parental violence: The pre-schooler's perspective and the educator's role. *Early Childhood Education Journal, 37*(3), 199–207.

Barros, R. M., Silver, E. J., & Stein, R. E. K. (2009). School recess and group classroom behavior. *Pediatrics, 123*(2), 431–436.

Birch, L. L., & Fisher, J. O. (1998). Development of eating behaviors among children and adolescents. *Pediatrics, 101*(3 Pt. 2), 539–549.

Byrne, D., & Taylor, B. (2007). Children at risk from domestic violence and their educational attainment: Perspectives of education welfare officers, social workers and teachers. *Child Care in Practice, 13*(3), 185–201.

Byrne, S. M., & Puma, M. L. (2007). Psychosocial aspects of childhood obesity. In A. P. Hills, N. A. King, & N. M. Byrne (Eds.), *Children, obesity and exercise: Prevention, treatment and management of childhood and adolescent obesity* (pp. 80–91). London, England: Routledge.

Cardon, G., Van Cauwenberghe, E., Labarque, V., Haerens, L., & De Bourdeaudhuij, I. (2008). The contribution of preschool playground factors in explaining children's physical activity during recess. *International Journal of Behavioral Nutrition and Physical Activity, 5,* 1-6.

Cawley, J. (2006). Markets and childhood obesity policy. *The Future of Children: Childhood Obesity, 16*(1), 69–88.

Coleman, M., Wallinga, C., & Bales, D. (2010). Engaging families in the fight against the overweight epidemic among children. *Childhood Education, 86*(3), 150–156.

Cook-Cottone, C., Casey, C. M., & Feeley, T. H. (2009). A meta-analytic review of obesity prevention in the schools: 1997–2008. *Psychology in the Schools, 46*(8), 695–719.

Council on Sports Medicine and Fitness and Council on School Health. (2006). Active healthy living: Prevention of childhood obesity through increased physical activity. *Pediatrics, 117*(5), 1834–1842.

Crosson-Tower, C. (2003). *The role of educators in preventing and responding to child abuse and neglect.* Washington, DC: U.S. Department of Health and Human Services, Office of Child Abuse and Neglect.

Daniels, S. R. (2006). The consequences of childhood overweight and obesity. *The Future of Children, 16*(1), 47–67.

Davis, M. M., Gance-Cleveland, B., Hassink, S., Johnson, R., Paradis, G., & Resnicow, K. (2007). Recommendations for prevention of childhood obesity. *Pediatrics, 120*(Suppl. 4), S229–S253.

Denney-Wilson, E., & Baur, L. A. (2007). Clinical correlates of overweight and obesity. In A. P. Hills, N. A. King, & N. M. Bryne (Eds.), *Children, obesity and exercise: Prevention, treatment and management of childhood and adolescent obesity* (pp. 25–36). London, England: Routledge.

Dowda, M., Brown, W. H., McIver, K. L., Pfeiffer, K. A., O'Neill, J. R., Addy, C. L., & Pate, R. R. (2009). Policies and characteristics of the preschool environment and physical activity of young children. *Pediatrics, 123*(2), 261–266.

Dwyer, G. M., Higgs, J., Hardy, L. L., & Baur, L. A. (2008). What do parents and preschool staff tell us about young children's physical activity: A qualitative study. *International Journal of Behavioral Nutrition and Physical Activity, 5,* 66–76.

Eliassen, E. K. (2011). The impact of teachers and families on young children's eating behaviors. *Young Children, 66*(2), 84–89.

Fallin, K., Wallinga, C., & Coleman, M. (2001). Helping children cope with stress in the classroom setting. *Childhood Education, 78*(1), 17–24.

Federal Trade Commission. (2010). *FTC staff weighs in on food labels and obesity.* Retrieved June 5, 2010, from http://www.ftc.gov/opa/2003/12/fdaobesity.shtm

Fierro, M. P. (2002). *The obesity epidemic—how states can trim the fat* [Issue brief]. Retrieved June 4, 2010, from National Governor' Association Center for Best Practices website: http://www.nga.org/cda/files/obesityib.pdf

Francis, L. A., & Susman, E. J. (2009). Self-regulation and rapid weight gain in children from age 3 to 12 years. *Archives of Pediatric and Adolescent Medicine, 163*(4), 297–302.

Freedman, D. S., Dietz, W. H., Srinivasan, S. R., & Berenson, G. S. (1999). The relation of overweight to cardiovascular risk factors among children and adolescents: The Bogalusa heart study. *Pediatrics, 103*(6), 1175–1181.

Georgia Department of Education. (2008). *Georgia performance standards for physical education.* Atlanta, GA: Author.

Gimpel, G. A., & Holland, M. L. (2003). *Emotional and behavioral problems of young children: Effective interventions in the preschool and kindergarten years.* New York, NY: Guilford Press.

Hinkelman, L., & Bruno, M. (2008). Identification and reporting of child sexual abuse: The role of elementary school professionals. *The Elementary School Journal, 108*(5), 376–391.

Jaffee, S. R., Caspi, A., Moffitt, T. E., & Taylor, A. (2004). Physical maltreatment victim to antisocial child: Evidence of an environmentally mediated process. *Journal of Abnormal Psychology, 113*(1), 44–55.

Johnson, S. L. (2000). Improving preschoolers' self-regulation of energy intake. *Pediatrics, 106*(6), 1429–1435.

Kenny, M. C. (2004). Teachers' attitudes toward and knowledge of child maltreatment. *Child Abuse and Neglect, 28*(12), 1311–1319.

Kitzmann, K. M., Dalton, W. T., & Buscemi, J. (2008). Beyond parenting practices: Family context and the treatment of pediatric obesity. *Family Relations, 57*(1), 13–23.

Kitzmann, K. M., Gaylord, N. K., Holt, A. R., & Kenny, E. D. (2003). Child witness to domestic violence: A meta-analytic review. *Journal of Consulting and Clinical Psychology, 71*(2), 239–352.

Lennell, A., Kuhlmann-Berenzon, S., Geli, P., Hedin, K., Peterson, C., Cars, O., . . . Study Group. (2008). Alcohol-based hand-disinfection reduced children's absence from Swedish day care centers. *Acta Paediatrica, 97*(12), 1672–1680.

Lindsay, A. C., Sussner, K. M., Kim, J., & Gortmaker, S. (2006). The role of parents in preventing childhood obesity. *The Future of Children, 16*(1), 169–186.

Mayo Clinic. (2010). *Hand washing: Do's and don'ts.* Retrieved June 5, 2010, from http://mayoclinic.com/health/hand-washing/HQ00407

Nammi, S., Koka, S., Chinnala, K. M., & Boini, K. M. (2004). Obesity: An overview of its current perspectives and treatment options. *Nutrition Journal, 3*(3), 1475–2891.

National Association for Sport and Physical Education. (2010a). *Active start: A statement of physical activity guidelines for children from birth to age 5* (2nd ed.). Retrieved June 5, 2010, from http://www.aahperd.org/naspe/standards/nationalGuidelines/ActiveStart.cfm

National Association for Sport and Physical Education. (2010b). *Physical activity for children: A statement of guidelines for children ages 5–12* (2nd ed.). Retrieved June 5, 2010, from http://www.aahperd.org/naspe/standards/nationalGuidelines/PA-Children-5-12.cfm

National Association for the Education of Young Children. (2004). *Where we stand on child abuse prevention.* Retrieved June 4, 2010, from http://www.naeyc.org/files/naeyc/file/positions/ChildAbuse Stand.pdf

National Health and Medical Research Council. (2005). *Staying healthy in child care: Preventing infectious diseases in child care* (4th ed.). Retrieved June 5, 2010, from http://www.nhmrc.gov.au/_files_nhmrc/file/publications/synopses/ch43.pdf

National Resource Center for Health and Safety in Child Care and Early Education. (2007). *Cleaning and sanitizing.* Retrieved June 5, 2010, from http://healthykids.us/chapters/cleaning_main.htm

Olshansky, S. J., Passaro, D. J., Hershow, R. C., Layden, J., Carnes, B. A., Brody, J., . . . Ludwig, D. S. (2005). A potential decline in life expectancy in the United States in the 21st century. *New England Journal of Medicine, 253*(11), 1138–1145.

Pica, R. (2006). Physical fitness and the early childhood curriculum. *Young Children, 61*(3), 12–19.

Pierce, J., & Johnson, C. L. (2010). Problem solving with young children using persona dolls. *Young Children, 65*(6), 106–108.

Pollack, M. B. (1994). *School health instruction: The elementary and middle school years* (3rd ed.). St. Louis, MO: Mosby.

Prader-Willi Association. (2010). *What is Prader-Willi syndrome?* Retrieved June 5, 2010, from http://www.pwsausa.org/syndrome/index.htm

Prelip, M., Slusser, W. M., Lange, L., Vecchiarielli, S., & Neumann, C. (2010). Participatory prevention research model promotes environmental change for healthier schools. *Health Promotion Practice, 11*(1), 54–61.

Satter, E. M. (1996). Internal regulation and the evolution of normal growth as the basis for prevention of obesity in children. *Journal of the American Dietetic Association 96*(9), 860–864.

Savage, J. S., Fisher, J. O., & Birch, L. L. (2007). Parental influence on eating behavior: Conception to adolescence. *Journal of Law, Medicine and Ethics, 35*(1), 22–34.

Schumacher, D., & Queen, J. A. (2007). *Overcoming obesity in childhood and adolescence: A guide for school leaders.* Thousand Oaks, CA: Corwin.

Sedlak, A. J., Mettenburg, J., Basena, M., Petta, I., McPherson, K., Greene, A., and Li, S. (2010). *Fourth National Incidence Study of Child Abuse and Neglect (NIS–4): Report to Congress.* Retrieved June 5, 2010, from http://www.acf.hhs.gov/programs/opre/abuse_neglect/natl_incid/nis4_report_congress_full_pdf_jan2010.pdf

Sothern, M. S., & Gordon, S. T. (2003). Prevention of obesity in young children: A critical challenge for medical professionals. *Clinical Pediatrics, 42*(2), 101–111.

Stien, P. T., & Kendall, J. C. (2004). *Psychological trauma and the developing brain: Neurologically based interventions for troubled children.* New York, NY: Haworth Maltreatment and Trauma Press.

Tousman, S., Arnold, D., Helland, W., Roth, R., Heshelman, N., Castaneda, O., . . . Bileto, S. (2007). Evaluation of a hand washing program for 2nd graders. *The Journal of School Nursing, 23*(6), 342–348.

U.S. Department of Health and Human Services, Centers for Disease Control and Prevention. (n.d.). *Stopping the spread of germs at home, work & school.* Retrieved November 9, 2011, from http://www.cdc.gov/flu/protect/stopgerms.htm.

U.S. Department of Health and Human Services, Administration for Children and Families, Administration on Children, Youth and Families, Children's Bureau. (2010). *Child Maltreatment 2009.* Retrieved April 3, 2011, from http://www.acf.hhs.gov/programs/cb/stats_research/index.htm#can

U.S. Department of Health and Human Services, Centers for Disease Control and Prevention (2008, September 24). *Healthy youth! Coordinated school health.* Retrieved June 6, 2010, from http://www.cdc.gov/healthyYouth/CSHP/

U.S. Department of Health and Human Services, Centers for Disease Control and Prevention. (2009a, April 20). *Child maltreatment: Definitions.* Retrieved June 5, 2010, from http://www.cdc.gov/ViolencePrevention/child-maltreatment/definitions.html

U.S. Department of Health and Human Services, Centers for Disease Control and Prevention. (2009b, October 20). *Defining childhood overweight and obesity.* Retrieved June 5, 2010, from http://www.cdc.gov/obesity/childhood/defining.html

Vessey, J. A., Sherwood, J. J., Warner, D., & Clark, D. (2007). Comparing hand washing to hand sanitizers in reducing elementary school students' absenteeism. *Pediatric Nursing, 33*(4), 368–372.

Wechsler, H., McKenna, M. L., Lee, S. M., & Dietz, W. H. (2004, December). *The role of schools in preventing childhood obesity.* Retrieved June 5, 2010, from http://www.cdc.gov/HealthyYouth/physicalactivity/pdf/roleofschools_obesity.pdf

World Health Organization. (2006). *Constitution of the World Health Organization* (45th ed.). Retrieved June 5, 2010, from http://www.who.int/governance/eb/who_constitution_en.pdf

Yetter, G. (2009). Exercise-based school obesity prevention programs: An overview. *Psychology in the Schools, 46*(8), 739–747.

Young, L. R., & Nestle, M. (2002). The contribution of expanding portion sizes to the U.S. obesity epidemic. *American Journal of Public Health, 92*(2), 246–249.

PHOTO CREDITS

INDEX

ABOUT THE AUTHOR

Mick Coleman, PhD, is a Professor of Child and Family Development at the University of Georgia (UGA). He developed and has taught for over a decade a course on Families, Schools, and Communities in the undergraduate and graduate interdisciplinary teacher training programs at UGA. During this same time period, he has also supervised undergraduate and master's level student teachers in the public schools. Other courses taught by Dr. Coleman have included Classroom Behavior Management, Family Development, Family Policy, Parent Education and Child Guidance, Introduction to Child Development, and Marriage and Family Problems. In addition, Dr. Coleman has served as the coordinator of the human service internship program in his department for two decades. He also served as coordinator of the legislative internship program in his college for almost a decade.

In addition to his published scholarly work and grant-funded projects related to family involvement, Dr. Coleman has made state, national, and international presentations on the same topic. These included a 2001 keynote address before the Association for Early Childhood Educators in the Republic of Singapore. Teaching recognitions have included Teacher of the Year from his college in 1997 and Educator of the Year from the Georgia Association on Young Children in 2004.

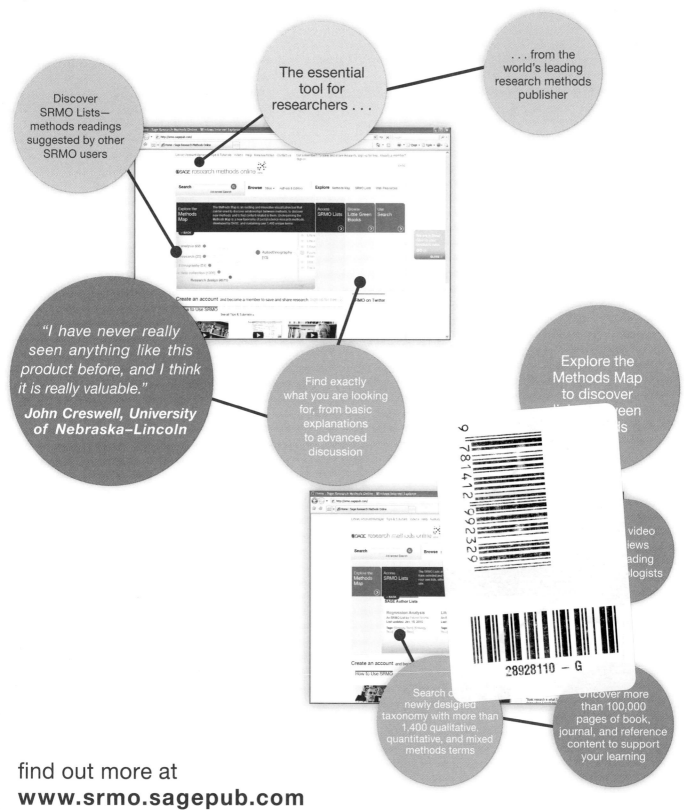